RICHARD NIXON
and the Quest for
a New Majority

ROBERT MASON

RICHARD NIXON
and the Quest for
a New Majority

The University of North Carolina Press

Chapel Hill and London

Designed by Heidi Perov

Set in Minion and Franklin Gothic

by Keystone Typesetting, Inc.

✶

Library of Congress Cataloging-in-Publication Data

Mason, Robert, 1970–

Richard Nixon and the quest for a new majority / Robert Mason.

p. cm.

Includes bibliographical references and index.

ISBN 0-8078-2905-6 (cloth : alk. paper)

1. United States—Politics and government—1969–1974.

2. Nixon, Richard M. (Richard Milhous), 1913—Political and social views.

3. Conservatism—United States—History—20th century.

4. Republican Party (U.S.: 1854–)—History—20th century. I. Title.

E855.M375 2004

973.924′092—dc22

2004008918

08 07 06 05 04   5 4 3 2 1

THIS BOOK WAS DIGITALLY PRINTED.

To my father
and the memory of my mother

⋆ CONTENTS ⋆

Acknowledgments *ix*

Introduction *1*

⋆

ONE. THE FORGOTTEN AMERICANS
The Republican Quest for a Majority in the 1960s *5*

⋆

TWO. MIDDLE AMERICA AND THE SILENT MAJORITY
Issues, 1969–1970 *37*

⋆

THREE. THERE'S A REALIGNMENT GOING ON
The Redefinition of the Republican Party, 1970 *77*

⋆

FOUR. THE NEW AMERICAN REVOLUTION
Issues, 1970–1972 *113*

⋆

FIVE. PRESIDENT NIXON FOR PRESIDENT
The Rejection of the Republican Party, 1972 *161*

⋆

SIX. FROM NIXON TO REAGAN
The End of the Quest for a New Majority,
1972–1976 *192*

Conclusion *235*

Notes *241*

Bibliography *267*

Index *281*

★ ACKNOWLEDGMENTS ★

In completing this book, I am particularly happy to have an opportunity to express my thanks to those who have so generously helped me in my work on it. I owe an enormous debt of gratitude to Byron Shafer, whose excellence as an adviser and mentor I cannot overstate. Tony Badger, Nigel Bowles, Gareth Davies, Nelson Polsby, Sukhdev Sandhu, and Marc Stears all read the entire manuscript, and their comments were immensely beneficial, as were those of the anonymous reviewers. I have also been very lucky to receive advice, assistance, and encouragement from many others, including Sybill Bidwell, Richard Fenno, Anupam Gupta, Paul Martin, John Mason, Sarah Mason, David Mayhew, Bent Nielsen, Richard O'Leary, Jacqui Pearse, Tom Perrett, Allen Pitt, John Rowett, Petra Schleiter, Rebecca Short, and Robert Singh. Of great benefit to my research was the guidance of librarians and archivists at Rhodes House Library in Oxford, the Nixon Presidential Materials Project at the National Archives, the Gerald R. Ford Library, and the Manuscripts Division at the Library of Congress. I am most fortunate to work among a supportive and generous group of historians at Edinburgh, and my fellow Americanists—Frank Cogliano, Alan Day, Owen Dudley Edwards, and Rhodri Jeffreys-Jones—have been especially dependable and valuable sources of advice and help. At Edinburgh I have learned much, too, about this topic from my students. For their financial support, I am grateful to the British Academy; Nuffield College, Oxford; the University of Edinburgh; the Gerald R. Ford Foundation; and the Eisenhower World Affairs Institute. The staff at the University of North Carolina Press, notably Charles Grench, Amanda McMillan, Paula Wald, and, until his departure, Lewis Bateman, have guided this book toward publication in an encouraging as well as expert way, and the contribution of copyeditor Ellen Goldlust-Gingrich was valuable. To all those who have provided in countless ways help and support—absolutely essential during this project—I am deeply grateful.

RICHARD NIXON
and the Quest for
a New Majority

★ INTRODUCTION ★

Richard Nixon and the Quest for a New Majority is the study of an effort to shift the mass politics of the United States at a potentially crucial moment in recent history. The late 1960s and early 1970s represented a period of upheaval in American society, when opportunities for political change seemed more substantial than at any time since the Great Depression. This is the story of bold political ambition in response to the perception of a great political possibility.

For a generation, Democrats had dominated national politics. This era of Democratic dominance began with the economic crisis that took hold under Herbert Hoover, a crisis that discredited the Republican Party in the eyes of many Americans. Franklin Roosevelt then mobilized an electoral majority for the Democratic Party in support of his administration's New Deal. This majority included many of America's less privileged people, and the Roosevelt coalition had remarkable endurance. In the years that followed, Republicans won no more than passing success in elections for the presidency and for Congress. Their moments of triumph were few and brief. In both 1946 and 1952, they took control of Congress, but in each case for two years only; Dwight Eisenhower won the two presidential elections of the 1950s but did so because of his public standing as a great leader rather than because of his Republican identity. As a political entity designed to win elections, the Republican Party was a disaster. More Americans consistently preferred the Democratic Party. Following Hoover came a generation that rarely offered Republicans anything but frustration.

Decades after Roosevelt's defeat of Hoover in 1932, prospects at last looked brighter for the Republican Party. At the end of the 1960s and the beginning of the 1970s, many people believed that this record of disappointment was about to change, that the country stood on the verge of a conservative realignment that would completely transform American politics. A new generation of Republican success might replace the generation of Democratic dominance.

Richard Nixon and the Quest for a New Majority looks at the reasons why these beliefs became widespread, investigating how a Republican administration responded to this perception of a truly significant political opportunity.

Richard Nixon, the figure at the center of this work, became president at this time of opportunity and developed a plan to exploit it. Because of his achievements and his failings, Nixon was one of the most important politicians of his century. Achieving national prominence not long after his election to the House of Representatives in 1946, he remained on the political stage for the rest of his life and played a key role in many of the principal events and developments of post–World War II American history. When Nixon died in 1994, Senator Robert J. Dole, a Republican from Kansas, exaggerated perhaps only slightly when he commented that "the second half of the twentieth century [would] be known as the age of Nixon."[1]

Nixon's idiosyncrasies as a politician would influence his handling of what he saw as a historic opportunity for Republicans. Some of these quirks equipped him well for the task, which was to disrupt the Democratic coalition by reaching out to a larger constituency. Although as a Republican he represented the party of privilege, he harbored a sense of exclusion from privilege and instead felt a sense of identity with ordinary Americans. This identity was absolutely at odds with the dominant image of his party and represented an asset in seeking to improve its fortunes. Ray Price, a longtime aide and Nixon sympathizer, later observed to journalist Tom Wicker that "Nixon's pretense was to be *less* than he was—less thoughtful, less introverted, less skeptical and analytical, less cerebral—to present himself deliberately as an Average American: patriotic, conventionally religious and responsible, gregarious, sports-loving, hardworking and hard-nosed." According to Wicker, this pretense often succeeded, investing Nixon with a "remarkable appeal to American voters." But there was a darker edge to this connection between politician and people, Wicker noted; it was clouded by a "condescending and contemptuous attitude toward the commonality of the American people." Nixon did not believe that the high ground was the place to succeed in politics. Among the more ubiquitous politicians of his generation, he was unarguably the most controversial. To his opponents, he was "Tricky Dick" almost from the start.[2]

Nixon rarely strayed far from the campaign trail, where he learned lessons that he remembered when president. He started to master electoral politics when campaigning for the House in 1946 and then for the Senate in 1950. In these races, he learned the value of aggressive partisan attacks, identifying his popular opponents with damagingly unpopular policies. Nixon's anticommunism defeated first Jerry Voorhis and then Helen Gahagan Douglas. In achieving these victories, Nixon also learned the importance of reaching out to Democratic and independent voters, an essential tactic in his home state of California, where, as in the nation as a whole at the time, Republican supporters constituted a minority within the electorate. Both of these lessons proved important when Nixon looked for a new majority as president.

Throughout the 1950s and 1960s, Nixon was a standard-bearer for Republican candidates, further amassing political skills and frequently attracting criticism for his hard-line partisan aggression. Still, Nixon could not manage to secure election in his own right either for the presidency in 1960 or for the governorship of California in 1962. Those defeats provided a reminder of still another lesson, rather obvious to politicians, that their aim is electoral victory. In Nixon's case, his urgent desire to secure a huge majority when facing reelection in 1972 would have two paradoxically counterproductive implications. First, to some extent, this personal goal distracted his attention from the greater partisan goal of a new majority. Second, his interest in popularity encouraged him to countenance illegality during the campaign; crimes committed in pursuit of victory eventually brought the greatest defeat of all, resignation from the presidency.

In seeking a new majority, Nixon attempted to foster an electoral realignment that would benefit conservative politics. The paradigm of realignment was widespread among scholars of this period, originating in the 1950s as an effort among political scientists to explain electoral patterns across time. Its innovator was V. O. Key Jr., and a team of researchers at the University of Michigan subsequently further developed the theory. These writers investigated and documented the remarkable stability of U.S. electoral behavior. Throughout the history of the two-party system, in any particular period, one of the two parties enjoyed a continuing advantage in winning elections and in maintaining the support of a majority within the electorate. Individuals possessed astonishing levels of loyalty to their favored parties. Once a Democrat or a Republican, people tended to retain this party identification. But from time to time, this stability was disrupted. Larger numbers of Americans suddenly reassessed their party loyalty; people changed their minds about politics. Others, previously apathetic about politics, started to vote on one side or another. What precipitated this upheaval was the arrival of some great crisis that caused two significant problems for incumbent politicians: first, they could not convince voters that they had the right answer to deal with this crisis; second, they often could not agree with each other about how to do so, bringing party disunity. A third-party or protest candidate sometimes appeared at such a moment of political instability to articulate concerns that mainstream politicians seemed to be addressing inadequately. The result was decline for the dominant party and resurgence for the minority party. This electoral transition, driven by significant new issues that divided politicians and voters alike, was a realignment.[3]

The most recent of these turning points took place during the 1930s. The Republicans' fall from grace at that time was part of a realignment driven by the Great Depression. The key question facing the United States was the federal government's level of involvement in regulating the economy and in offering the people welfare protections. A majority preferred the Democratic answer that the government should play such a role to the dominant Republican position that although some activism was necessary, it should take place on a smaller scale.

During the 1960s, arguments based on the concept of an electoral realignment edged into discussions about current electoral politics.[4] This achievement was remarkable for an idea driven by theory and by academic investigation. The achievement resulted from the persuasiveness of the way in which the idea captured the essence of continuity and change in American politics. Still, toward the end of the Johnson administration, it was not at all necessary to read political science to understand that apparently insurmountable problems plagued the nation and caused disarray among the incumbent Democrats. The Democrats' travails created an opportunity for the Republicans to seek the support of "forgotten Americans." *Richard Nixon and the Quest for a New Majority* begins by looking for the origins of this potential turning point in American politics within the changes of the 1960s. The period was one of upheaval so great that Democratic discontent had many roots, including frustration (both hawkish and dovish) with the progress of the war in Vietnam, alarm (both sympathetic and hostile) at the continuing problems of race, and dissatisfaction (both conservative and radical) with the Great Society's socioeconomic goals.

ONE

THE FORGOTTEN AMERICANS

The Republican Quest for a Majority in the 1960s

The 1960s began, as it would end, with appeals by a leading Republican for the support of forgotten Americans. In January 1961, Barry Goldwater, a senator from Arizona and an influential conservative, issued "A Statement of Proposed Republican Principles, Programs and Objectives," speaking to the "forgotten" and "silent" Americans "who quietly go about the business of paying and praying, working and saving." Goldwater identified them as the voters who could restore the Republican Party to majority status.[1]

As Goldwater saw it, the Republican Party should seek new support by campaigning vigorously in opposition to the dominant strand of American liberalism. While mainstream liberals did not question the basic structures of the capitalist system, they saw two significant roles for government to fulfill. First, the government should ease human problems created by the capitalist economy, primarily through programs of social insurance that helped the needy poor. Second, the government should undertake limited intervention in the economy to promote its continuing buoyancy. Democrats were the more enthusiastic advocates of government activism, but many Republicans supported a paler version of similar policies, prompted by pragmatism if not by principle.

Goldwater offered a devastating criticism of these ideas. This government activism, he insisted, dangerously attacked traditional virtues of individual enterprise and self-reliance. Such policies pandered to the demands of interest groups and did not respond to individuals' needs. The growth of government, he maintained, fundamentally threatened freedom. Goldwater was sure that a majority of Americans agreed with him. If the Republican Party dedicated itself to the defense of individual liberty by scaling back the role of government, then the party could overwhelm the powerful Democratic coalition, which had dominated electoral politics since the time of Franklin Roosevelt.[2]

Goldwater spoke of potential Republican supporters as "forgotten" because neither party demonstrated a commitment to their laissez-faire, antigovernment conservatism; they were the key to electoral victory. Many activists within the party liked this message and gave him their enthusiastic support. In 1964 Goldwater, as the Republican nominee for the presidency, had a chance to test his ideas. He suffered a resounding defeat. His belief in a possible majority of forgotten Americans was, it seemed, an illusion.

At the end of the decade, however, Richard Nixon engaged in a similar effort to mobilize forgotten Americans in support of his presidency and the Republican Party. Most famously, in a November 1969 speech, he called them "the silent majority." Elected president in the three-way 1968 race with 43.4 percent of the vote, Nixon needed to find new support to secure reelection. But Nixon had a larger goal. Like his predecessor Goldwater, Nixon believed that the Republicans could piece together an enduring majority that would take the place of the Democratic coalition.

Yet the substance of this effort differed greatly from Goldwater's even as the rhetoric remained familiar. While Nixon continued to sound a theme of opposition to big government, he did not seek to challenge the existing emphasis on government activism. He limited his criticisms to the argument that the implementation of most programs depended too much on an unresponsive bureaucracy and that the new programs of the 1960s helped small numbers of Americans while ignoring the problems of others. Not only did Nixon leave unchanged most of the programs developed by Democrats between the 1930s and the 1960s, but he was even ready to propose new programs and to increase federal spending further. He was no Goldwaterite.

Instead, Nixon's vision for the Republican Party rested on the assumption that in the aftermath of the great victory over Goldwater in 1964, the Johnson administration had alienated many Americans, who, by extension, were now ready to rethink their previous support for the Democrats. In short, Nixon's idea of the forgotten American represented a reaction to the tumult of the 1960s. Under the Johnson administration, the nation faced an almost unbearable array of problems—an intractable overseas war that caused social conflict at home, a growing exasperation with the measures liberals used to pursue egalitarian goals, serious racial unrest at a moment of significant racial progress, and a widespread malaise within a society seen as plagued by increasing lawlessness and by challenges to traditional notions of morality. Nixon promised to solve these problems and saw this promise as a route to revitalizing his party's fortunes on a more permanent basis.

When Goldwater and Nixon referred to forgotten Americans, the phrase had historical resonance. In 1932, Franklin Roosevelt had pledged to help "the forgotten man at the bottom of the economic pyramid," a reference to people who were enduring immense hardship because of the Great Depression.[3] When he became president, Roosevelt launched the New Deal, intending to rescue the economy from its crisis and to ameliorate some of the forgotten Americans' suffering. These people then formed the basis of the electoral coalition that Roosevelt mobilized, leading in time to the generation of Democratic dominance of national politics. Both Goldwater and Nixon argued that important sections of the Democratic coalition had once again been forgotten. These groups of Americans were not at the bottom of the pyramid. They were overlooked for different reasons. In Goldwater's eyes, most politicians had forgotten the individualistic conservatism of the American populace. By contrast, in Nixon's view, what had been forgotten was people's anxiety about the upheaval of the latter half of the 1960s.

GOLDWATER'S SEARCH FOR A MAJORITY

In the early 1960s, Goldwater's vision for a Republican future won powerful support within the party. Goldwater won the party's nomination for the presidency thanks to a remarkable surge of grassroots enthusiasm and organization for the conservative cause, further aided by the relative weakness of the opposing candidates he faced. This activity reflected many conservatives' agreement with Goldwater's identification of forgotten Americans whose needs were unanswered by government. "To gain public support," wrote historian Mary Brennan, "many on the right believed that all they had to do was deliver their message to the American people." Among them was a former Hollywood actor who had become a spokesman for General Electric. During Nixon's unsuccessful 1960 campaign against John Kennedy, Ronald Reagan—"convinced that America is economically conservative"—wrote to the Republican candidate with some advice about how to mobilize support: "I don't pose as an infallible pundit, but I have a strong feeling that the twenty million *non voters* in this country just might be conservatives who have cynically concluded the two parties offer no choice between them where fiscal stability is concerned." But Nixon in 1960 failed to take the advice of conservatives, a decision about which he had no regrets. In a postelection meeting at the White House, he argued that the conservative approach was disastrously wrongheaded. "The Vice President commented," noted Bryce Harlow, an aide to Eisenhower and later to Nixon, "that anyone within the Party who is a cold-blooded analyst would have to say that the Goldwater view, had it been adopted in the campaign, would have lost by seven or eight million votes."[4]

After 1960, moderation lost to Goldwaterite conservatism. Goldwater's message mobilized a constituency that counted in the contest for the Republican nomination. "The explanation for Goldwater's convention strength," observed sociologist Seymour Martin Lipset, "is to be found in the fact that the Republican Party is run largely by men who are active because of a very conservative ideology and who can afford the time for politics." Outnumbering within activist ranks the urban professionals and executives who often preferred a more moderate form of Republicanism, these conservatives had a special commitment to laissez-faire economics—car dealers, real estate agents, lawyers in small or medium-sized practices, and owners of small businesses. As Nixon noted in 1960, the pursuit of conservative conviction indeed had dangers. Faith in the existence of a conservative majority seemed to be based on illusive instinct rather than political calculation. Even rank-and-file Republicans had serious doubts about the way forward offered by Goldwater. Shortly before the convention that nominated Goldwater, a survey found that 60 percent of Republican voters supported William Scranton, the moderate governor of Pennsylvania and presidential aspirant, and only 34 percent preferred the Arizonan.[5] Such figures were hardly encouraging. To succeed, a Republican presidential candidate needed not only to secure the votes of most Americans who identified with his party but also to reach out to a sizable number of Democratic supporters and to many "independents," or loyal supporters of neither party. If, having tapped the enthusiasm of many activists, Goldwater could not even secure enthusiastic support among voters who usually supported Republicans, his ability to find a majority came into question.

Nevertheless, Goldwater and his supporters remained convinced of the existence of a hidden majority in favor of conservatism. The way to find it, they thought, was twofold. First, as Reagan suggested to Nixon in 1960, Republicans should articulate with absolute clarity a commitment to conservative principles rather than blurring differences with the Democrats. The argument assumed that voters stayed home because "me-tooist" Republicans running for the presidency failed to enthuse and mobilize potential supporters. The conservative strategy intended to offer the electorate "a choice, not an echo," according to the phrase popularized by Phyllis Schlafly in her book explaining the approach. Second, Goldwaterites thought that the South offered an especially promising source of votes. The South's solid support for the Democratic Party represented an ideological aberration. Despite widespread conservatism in the region, hostility to Republicans remained the legacy of the Civil War and Reconstruction. The conservatives sought to persuade white southerners at last to overcome this hostility; national Democrats' increasing commitment to the cause of civil rights created a propitious moment in which Republicans could make their case. They calculated that the addition of the South to existing areas of party strength would create a sound majority within the Electoral College.[6]

Despite his confidence in the fundamental conservatism of the American people, Goldwater sensed that 1964 was not a promising time to mobilize this majority. The nation was prosperous and the president popular; Goldwater doubted that Americans wanted a further change of leader in the aftermath of John Kennedy's assassination.[7] Nevertheless, Goldwater did not compromise his conservative mission. His acceptance speech emphasized his rejection of compromise: "I would remind you that extremism in the defense of liberty is no vice." During the campaign, Goldwater's conservative mission included four distinctive components. First, he attacked activist government and advocated fiscal conservatism. As his book *The Conscience of a Conservative* indicated, this was the most important element of his politics. Second, within the contemporary context of the struggle for civil rights, his stress on states' rights had the important implication that, under Goldwater, the federal government would not challenge practices of racial inequality. Third, his foreign policy emphasized strident anticommunism and an urgent requirement for a strong defense to protect all American interests. Fourth, he raised a set of concerns about ills within American society, most notably crime and what became known as "permissiveness."

The contrast with Lyndon Johnson was sharp. At the center of his new administration, Johnson placed his goal of a "Great Society," announced at the

University of Michigan in May 1964. "We stand at the edge of the greatest era in the life of any nation," he said in Detroit the following month. "For the first time in world history, we have the abundance and the ability to free every man from hopeless want." By the fall, as the elections approached, a set of task forces was hard at work creating the legislation necessary to achieve this breathtakingly ambitious goal. Moreover, significant action as well as rhetoric was already occurring. First, in response to the campaign for legal equality for African Americans, Johnson worked strenuously to persuade Congress to pass the 1964 Civil Rights Act. Second, Johnson requested and Congress delivered the Economic Opportunity Act, a multifaceted initiative that created ten anti-poverty programs.[8]

Goldwater's rejection of activist government constituted a serious mis-understanding of the contemporary mood. While many Americans in fact possessed a conservative impulse, it often coexisted with liberal beliefs. Ac-cording to a fall 1964 survey of public opinion, a majority of the American electorate was indeed "ideologically" conservative. The majority of Americans favored the principles of limited government and individual self-reliance. But at the same time, most people were "operationally" liberal, strongly support-ing specific examples of governmental programmatic activism. For example, more than three-quarters of respondents agreed with the abstract statement that the poor were at least partly to blame for their predicament, but many respondents also agreed with the specific statement that the government had a role in trying to reduce unemployment and poverty. Traditional beliefs regard-ing individualism remained strong, while support for government activism, in place since the Great Depression, had also gained force. On the one hand, the strength of ideological conservatism explains the confidence of Goldwater and his supporters that they could win the allegiance of many voters. In some senses, many Americans were indeed conservative. On the other hand, the strength of operational liberalism exposes the misguided nature of that con-fidence. "As long as Goldwater could talk ideology alone, he was able to ride high, wide, and handsome," wrote public opinion analysts Lloyd Free and Hadley Cantril. "But the moment he was forced to discuss issues and pro-grams, he was finished."[9]

Race was not an important element of the Goldwater philosophy, but issues of civil rights formed a vital part of the American scene at the time of his candidacy. Treating them in the same way as other examples of federal govern-ment activism, Goldwater applied his antigovernment philosophy in response to civil rights issues. Although he did not hold racist beliefs, he did not believe that the federal government should have a significant role in race relations. Because of his dedication to the concept of states' rights, he voted against the Civil Rights Act of 1964. After rioting occurred in a number of cities later that summer, Goldwater met with Johnson and offered to mute discussion of their differences on this inflammatory topic; Johnson readily agreed.[10]

Even though there was little direct debate about civil rights, the disagreement between the candidates was clear. The Republican platform supported the Civil Rights Act, but the party's overall approach to civil rights was lukewarm. The party endorsed the ideal of equality without making a commitment to use governmental powers in its pursuit. The contrast between this approach and that of the Democratic Party—a dedication to use the federal government to eradicate formal inequalities—was stark. The development of this partisan difference was new. Just four years earlier, in 1960, there had been barely any difference between the parties' civil rights positions as revealed by their platforms. According to political scientists Edward Carmines and James Stimson, the presidential election of 1964 "marked the decisive turning point in the political evolution of racial issues." The Democratic Party was becoming the party of racial liberalism, while the Republican Party was becoming the party of opposition to racial liberalism.[11]

On the Cold War, Goldwater developed a distinctive line, characterized by ardent anticommunism, in contrast with Johnson's more conciliatory approach. "If Communism intends to bury us," Goldwater said during the campaign, "let us tell the Communists loud and clear we're not going to hand them the shovel." In retrospect, the most important matter of foreign policy was America's growing commitment to protect the South Vietnamese government against communism. This commitment, affirmed in the August 1964 Gulf of Tonkin resolution, enjoyed support of a nature so consensual that it was an issue of little controversy. As with civil rights, Goldwater privately offered to withhold any criticism of Johnson's Vietnam policy. In fact, the candidates raised the issue from time to time, but it played a minor role in the campaign.[12]

More significant was the general impact of Goldwater's campaign against Johnson's foreign policy "of drift, deception and defeat." Goldwater's uncompromising and sometimes careless rhetoric created an image of a "trigger-happy candidate"—sanguine, even, about the prospect of using nuclear weaponry. The Johnson campaign encouraged this perception, most notably in a controversial set of television commercials. Public opinion polls during this period often revealed that although Democrats enjoyed a better reputation as custodians of the economy, Republicans were considered somewhat more successful at running the nation's foreign policy. But the Goldwater candidacy seriously damaged this reputation as the party of peace.[13]

Goldwater's appeal to the electorate did not include only a hawkish approach to the Cold War and a conservative critique of the New Deal tradition of government activism. He also discussed a new set of issues relating to personal morality and its public manifestations. Goldwater had only recently started to speak about this subject: until the early 1960s, he had barely strayed from his anticommunist, antigovernment, and economically traditionalist message. Responding to a climate in which numerous changes were occurring and in which those changes were prompting anxieties—perhaps, for the moment, concentrated within the conservative constituency—Goldwater added a new dimension to this message. In 1963, for example, he cosponsored a constitutional amendment that would end the Supreme Court's ban on prayer in public schools.[14]

When he received the Republican nomination, Goldwater spoke out about the "moral decline and drift" in the United States. On opening his campaign, he cited "the sick joke, the slick slogan, the off-color drama, and the pornographic book" as evidence of this crisis. He also emphasized the problem of rising crime; women did not feel safe in the streets, he said. During the fall, because of the apparent ineffectiveness of his rhetoric about foreign policy and the economy, Goldwater tended increasingly to stress these issues. In the candidate's view, the problems were the product of a failure of leadership; concretely, he sought to remind voters of Lyndon Johnson's accumulation of a private fortune while in public service and of ethical lapses among the president's close associates.[15]

References to the ethics of Johnson and his circle were included in a campaign film that intended to make the Republican case on the subject of moral decline. Sponsored by Mothers for a Moral America and originally to be introduced by John Wayne, who was famous for his good-guy roles in Western movies, Choice linked ethical questions with other crises of morality. The film depicted urban unrest, drug abuse, crime, and pornography and suggested that all would plague America under the Democrats. Together with his campaign team, however, Goldwater decided that that the film would generate an unfavorable reaction, and the piece was not broadcast.[16] The incident vividly demonstrates the ways in which the Goldwater campaign was attempting to develop different themes to reach American voters as well as the existence of a certain caution about the wisdom of engaging in this politics of morality.

Altogether, Goldwater failed as a national candidate. He secured only 38.5 percent of the popular vote, and Johnson secured one of the greatest landslide victories in American history. Goldwater did, however, succeed as a candidate in the Deep South, largely as a result of the Democratic Party's commitment to civil rights. Soon after signing the Civil Rights Act of 1964, Johnson had remarked to an aide, "I think we delivered the South to the Republican Party for your lifetime and mine." An organizer of the racist Citizens' Council movement later made a similar point: "We took four states for Goldwater in 1964, and hell, we didn't even like him. He voted against the Civil Rights Act, and we just showed our appreciation."[17]

In the short run, the partisan polarization over civil rights had a great impact. The only states won by Goldwater—in addition to his home state of Arizona—were five in the Deep South; all had been dependably anti-Republican since Reconstruction. Across the South as a whole, Goldwater secured 55 percent of the white vote. Overall, black Americans voted decisively for Johnson; rather less than 10 percent voted for Goldwater, while about a third had chosen Nixon just four years previously. The losses suffered by the Democratic Party within the nation's white majority were smaller than Johnson had feared, however. During the primary season, George Wallace, the segregationist governor of Alabama, had found a surprising amount of support in Wisconsin, Indiana, and Maryland, especially in ethnic neighborhoods there. But this support for Wallace among northern Democrats did not become support for Goldwater in the general election.[18]

In the longer run, the results of 1964 did not necessarily determine that the parties would remain polarized in this way. The Republican Party might remember its heritage as "the party of Lincoln" and renew its commitment to racial equality. Such a development had become less likely, however. While the activists and officeholders of the Democratic Party increasingly supported governmental action on racial matters, their Republican counterparts were increasingly characterized by skepticism about such policies.[19]

Reasons other than the content of Goldwater's message may account for the scale of his defeat. Goldwater often clumsily explained his proposals, and he made mistakes in the conduct of his campaign against Johnson. Moreover, from the start Goldwater faced a difficult task in challenging a popular and successful incumbent.[20] Nevertheless, the basic reason for Goldwater's defeat is more simple. The forgotten Americans did not exist in numbers nearly great enough to bring victory. The political ideas that Goldwater espoused were the choice of a minority, not a majority.

The landslide defeat left the Republicans in some disarray, and an immediate effort to rebuild the party followed. Dean Burch, Goldwater's appointee as national chairman, lost the post. Burch's successor, Ray Bliss, began work on plans to improve the party's organization, downplaying ideology and emphasizing the reconciliation of differences among Republicans. Leading Republicans met as the Republican Coordinating Committee to heal the damage caused by Goldwater's disastrous candidacy. While the party's electoral problems in 1964 caused reassessments of policy, strategy, and party organization at the elite level, they did not shake the conservatives' grassroots influence. In many areas, the lower levels of the party remained dominated by the activists who had been most enthusiastic about Goldwater and his brand of conservatism. Future presidential aspirants would need to recognize these people's importance and to cultivate their support.[21]

CHANGE

The Goldwater candidacy deepened the Republican disadvantage within the electorate. In place since the New Deal, the disadvantage had grown since World War II and grew still more in response to the Democratic buoyancy linked with the Johnson landslide. According to Gallup polls, the number of American voters who identified themselves as Republicans declined by 5 points to 25 percent between 1960 and 1964, while in the same period Democratic identifiers increased by 6 points to 53 percent; the remaining slice of the electorate was independent of partisan identification. These discouraging statistics concealed one small advantage for the Republican Party: its supporters were more likely to turn out to vote than Democratic supporters were. Nevertheless, in a "normal" election, the Republicans could expect to receive only a minority of the vote, and the party's minority status was gradually becoming more rather than less pronounced. "[T]he GOP," wrote political scientist Walter Dean Burnham in early 1965, "is becoming less and less relevant to the central issues and concerns of American politics in the last half of the century."[22]

But even as the Democratic Party achieved the pinnacle of success, its easy dominance of American politics was about to face new challenges and its strong base of support was about to experience erosion and fragmentation. Following the Johnson landslide, the sources of change were many. First, civil rights achievements followed by further urban riots intensified America's racial agonies. Second, the war in Vietnam was a disaster for Johnson's reputation as president and tore apart a Cold War consensus about the appropriate U.S. role in global affairs. Third, the New Deal tradition of programmatic liberalism reached fresh heights of achievement within the Great Society, but in so doing, liberalism became more controversial. Fourth, the nation faced new manifestations of the "moral decline" about which Goldwater had spoken during the 1964 campaign.

Indeed, a shock to the American political system took place very soon after Johnson's inauguration. Support for the parties declined suddenly as many Americans became less willing to embrace either the Republicans or the Democrats, preferring instead to remain partisan independents. Although both parties suffered from the decline, its impact was a little greater on the Democratic Party, which had recently enjoyed a new boost of support. An analysis of survey data by Philip Converse offered a precise timing of the change: it took place between June and October 1965. During that time, there was a noticeably sharp break in the national support for the Democratic Party. The break is not explained by public reactions to the Vietnam War, because, although this was the period when the administration escalated the war, most Americans remained supportive of the policy. The greater cause of the change, Converse argued, is probably race. From the troubled voting-rights demonstrations in Selma, Alabama, to the rioting at Watts in Los Angeles, the period featured rapidly declining faith in the possibility for progress in race relations.[23]

A matter of days after Johnson signed the Voting Rights Act, which deepened further the federal government's commitment to ensuring legal equality for African Americans, rioting broke out in Watts. This example of urban unrest offered a sharp reminder that economic and social inequalities persisted and existed outside as well as within the South. After the achievement of legal equality, public enthusiasm for the cause of civil rights declined. When Johnson became president in 1963, according to polls, only 31 percent of Americans believed that the federal government was pushing racial integration "too fast." By 1968, however, that figure exceeded a half. At the same time, new splits emerged between liberals and radicals within African American movements. Black nationalists won prominence, and their high-profile activities under the "black power" slogan further alienated many in the white American mainstream.[24]

The Johnson administration became increasingly dominated by the U.S. involvement in the Vietnam War. In 1964, Goldwater's bellicose rhetoric had harmed the Republican reputation as the "party of peace," but the events of that campaign were soon forgotten. Much more important were the administration's military and diplomatic efforts to ensure a secure future for the South Vietnamese government in its struggle against the rebels of the National Front for the Liberation of Vietnam (popularly known as the Vietcong) and against their North Vietnamese supporters. These efforts experienced little success and were costly. While there were 23,000 American troops in Vietnam at the start of 1965, that number had risen to 184,000 within a year. The nation's troop commitment grew to 385,000 by the end of 1966 and reached 535,000 by early 1968.[25]

As the scale of America's commitment to South Vietnam increased, so too did the level of controversy created by that commitment. In Congress, support was almost unanimous when Johnson requested the passage of the Gulf of Tonkin resolution in August 1964. While congressional Democrats continued to support the administration, albeit sometimes with misgivings, the unanimity disappeared; by 1968, more than thirty Democratic senators and representatives opposed Johnson's policies. A key turning point took place in early 1966 when Senator J. William Fulbright of Arkansas, chair of the Senate Foreign Relations Committee, held hearings on American involvement in Vietnam. Fulbright had become a critic of that involvement, claiming that the United States was guilty of an "arrogance of power." He questioned not only the wisdom of the Vietnam policy but also the nation's general approach to the Cold War.[26]

The questioning of America's role in the world took place much more acutely outside Congress. Antiwar protest began on a rather small scale in 1965 but by 1968 had become pervasive. Protest was particularly noticeable on the nation's major college and university campuses, where the threat of the draft sharpened discontent about the war and its aims. The antiwar movement included a variety of views about the country's involvement in Vietnam. Within the movement, a majority was liberal, believing that the Vietnam policy transgressed a cherished tradition of positive American involvement in the world. But a small minority was radical, believing that the policy was the product of a corrupt regime; these radicals supported victory for the Vietcong and revolutionary change at home. Radical protest was often particularly noisy, attracting disproportionate attention.[27]

Among the public at large, opinion about the war, while complex and diverse, became steadily more critical. As tracked by polls, unease about the nation's role in Vietnam had become noticeable by the middle of 1966 and was clear by 1967. At first, this unease led to wider support for more vigorous prosecution of the war; in the words of political scientists William Lunch and Peter Sperlich, 1967 was "the year of the hawk," when polls briefly reported a majority in favor of escalation. But it was also the year when a majority of Americans came to believe that the nation's involvement in the war had been a mistake. Nevertheless, while opposition to the war grew, most Americans did not support withdrawal as the way in which to secure the conflict's end. Moreover, even many doves opposed the noisier examples of antiwar protest. A poll in 1968, for example, reported that 53 percent of those who saw the war as a mistake viewed the protesters in a negative light; nearly three-quarters of all Americans saw protesters in this way.[28]

The war caused a questioning not only of Vietnam policy but also of the larger U.S. world mission. Since the relatively early years of the Cold War, a more or less national consensus had emerged in favor of internationalism. The presence of Soviet communism apparently demanded that the United States take an active role in global affairs and be ready to stand up to any communist challenge. Because of the war in Vietnam, the number of Americans who argued against this idea increased. Again, polls offer some insight into this change. In 1964, just 18 percent of respondents agreed with the anti-internationalist position that the country "should mind its own business internationally and let other countries get along as best they can on their own." By 1968, 27 percent agreed with the statement. While two-thirds of Americans remained internationalists, a small but significant uptick in isolationism had occurred.[29]

War and riots had a terribly destructive impact on American liberalism, creating new divisions among its advocates and alienating some of its supporters. At the same time, war and rioting undermined Johnson's efforts to consolidate the Great Society. In 1965 and 1966, Johnson introduced 200 legislative proposals designed to tackle a vast array of social ills. Especially important were the civil rights measures, together with further antipoverty initiatives and new federal funding for health and education. Congress, more liberal in complexion following Republican defeats in 1964, approved 181 of the proposals.

Despite Goldwater's insistence that government activism threatened individual freedom, advocates of the Great Society justified many of its measures as removing barriers to opportunity, reducing the obstacles that disadvantage posed to individual advancement.[30] American liberalism had reached a high point of programmatic achievement. But its victory was short-lived.

Opponents soon found it easy to label the Great Society a failure. They called attention to the gaps between lofty rhetoric and the more mundane reality, to examples of waste and abuse. Because of the prominence assigned to the "War on Poverty," the Great Society gained a reputation as an effort to help the few rather than the many. In reality, some of its programs offered significant benefits to middle-class Americans, including support for higher education, Medicare's health funding for the elderly, and protections of consumer rights. Nevertheless, new forgotten Americans now often decided that they still had pressing social and economic needs, which Democrats under Johnson were neglecting in favor of focusing on the problems of marginal groups, especially racial minorities. A Democratic congressman from the West observed in 1968 that new forgotten Americans were "being ignored in favor of people who live in the 'ghettos'—the poor and the indolent."[31]

Some short-term grounds existed for economic grievances. Inflation in 1966 ran at 3.4 percent, the highest figure since 1951, while the unemployment rate remained just under the "full-employment" level of 4 percent. Johnson avoided any increase in income tax until toward the end of his administration, although taxes in the states and localities were often rising. But Robert C. Wood, undersecretary of housing and urban development, identified some more fundamental problems faced by "working Americans," a category involving as many as 23 million families. Wood's "working American" was a white male with a steady job, but "the frontiers of his career expectations [had] been fixed since he reached the age of thirty-five, when he found that he had too many obligations, too much family, and too few skills to match opportunities with aspirations."[32]

The pursuit of the Great Society also damaged American liberalism in a more subtle way, causing frustration among leading Democrats about the attempt's outcomes. What principally informed the programs of the Great Society was a faith in an individualistic ideal; they set out to help the disadvantaged to compete on a more equal footing within society—because of improved access to education or because of job training, for example. To some supporters, the experience of the War on Poverty revealed the limits of policies based on a belief in individualism. Poverty manifestly remained, and people began to think that the meaningful way to tackle it shrugged off an insistence on individualistic methods and accepted the need for direct cash payments that ensured an adequate standard of living. The Great Society therefore set in motion a redefinition of the liberalism that had enjoyed long-running popularity. "Many liberals," according to historian Gareth Davies, "who had endorsed the self-help ethos of President Johnson's War on Poverty in 1964 came, by 1972, to embrace a very different approach, one that emphasized entitlement rather than opportunity." In Davies's view, liberals were taking a dangerous turn. While Americans were often receptive to political arguments based on the extension of opportunity, Americans also had a widespread tendency to be unsympathetic to the notion that the poor were entitled to governmental financial support independent of their efforts to help themselves.[33]

Liberalism's agonies had other causes during the 1960s. As Goldwater pointed out in 1964, crime was on the increase. As he recognized, it was becoming important for politicians to address the resulting public concern. Johnson's response differed from Goldwater's. Instead of emphasizing decaying morality, Johnson linked the problem of crime with social and economic deprivation. "Effective law enforcement and social justice must be pursued together," he commented in 1966, "as the foundation of our efforts against crime."[34]

Different understandings of the problem represented by crime led to conflicts over policy. Despite Johnson's emphasis on socioeconomic factors, many in Congress—particularly Republicans and southern Democrats—cast the problem as one of law enforcement and as one made more acute by court protections of defendants' rights. Shortly before the midterm elections of 1966, an anticrime bill arrived at the White House for Johnson's signature. The work mostly of conservatives, it included a reduction in the scope of defendants' rights and new measures to control pornography. Despite the sensitivity of the political moment, Johnson vetoed the bill.

In 1967, Johnson proposed his own anticrime bill after receiving the report of a presidential commission on the subject. The Commission on Law Enforcement and the Administration of Justice—the formation of which had been prompted by the crime concerns of the 1964 campaign—supported his emphasis on socioeconomic problems in tackling crime, underpinned by a confidence in finding governmental solutions to many of the problems. The proposals became the subject of a long-standing controversy within Congress that presented new testimony about political differences on crime. Nevertheless, the commission's two major recommendations won implementation. The Omnibus Crime Control and Safe Streets Act of 1968 created the Law Enforcement Assistance Administration, which for the first time fed substantial amounts of federal money to local policing authorities. Furthermore, the report lent its weight to the trend, already in place, toward efforts to rehabilitate criminals, often in community-based schemes. Parole and probation, rather than prison, were in favor.[35]

But attitudes about crime were becoming more conservative. Public opinion about the death penalty offers one example. A 1966 poll showed the culmination of a decade-long trend toward opposition to the death penalty for murderers; more Americans opposed than favored the death penalty. Within a year, however, the trend had been reversed, and a growing majority again supported capital punishment. Another example involves attitudes toward the courts' treatment of convicted criminals. In 1965, just under a half of those interviewed said that the courts were not harsh enough; by the start of 1969, the proportion had risen to three-quarters. This conservatism was the product of deepening concerns about crime. Worries were running high. By the summer of 1968, according to the Harris organization, 81 percent of people surveyed even believed that the system of law and order had broken down. These worries were not limited to the nation's big cities, which were most affected by crime. A reporter for the *New York Times* made the surprising discovery that street crime was the most urgent concern in the small, peaceful community of Webster City, Iowa. Its citizens were especially anxious about lawless demonstrations, even though their actual experience with crime had been limited to misdemeanors such as underage drinking and the occasional breaking of a window.[36]

In addition to detecting a growing problem of crime, Americans noticed that their society was becoming more "permissive." In films, television, art, and novels, previously unacceptable content was increasingly common; pornography was becoming more widespread. Speaking in 1967, a lawyer estimated that two-thirds of currently released films would have been banned according to the censorship regulations of 1950. At the same time, there were challenges to traditional attitudes concerning sexual mores—premarital sex, contraception, and sex education, for example. In the fall of 1967, *Newsweek* reported that such areas had "changed more dramatically in the past year than in the preceding 50."[37]

The strongest attacks on prevailing customs and values originated with the "counterculture" of people who repudiated American norms to pursue an alternative lifestyle. Numerically, members of the counterculture were an unimportant group, but, thanks to the attention their activities received, their influence was disproportionate. Despite these challenges created by the tide of permissiveness, majority sentiment in the United States remained traditionalist in terms of its sexual mores. Another dimension of permissiveness—seen within a wider youth culture as well as the counterculture—was the growing use of illegal drugs after a long period during which narcotics had been very uncommon in the United States. Although the number of people using drugs remained a minority, state-level arrests for marijuana possession rose from 18,000 in 1965 to 188,000 in 1970 while the number of heroin users rose from around 50,000 in 1960 to approximately 500,000 in 1970. "Many people," wrote Mary Brennan, "shocked by scenes from Haight Ashbury and college campuses, began to reassess the traditionalist values of Goldwater that they had found old-fashioned only a few years earlier."[38]

The Supreme Court under Earl Warren acted as a significant force for liberalism in the 1960s. Critics then charged the Court with some responsibility for the nation's problems of permissiveness and crime. Decisions handed down during that decade gave constitutional protection to films and literature with sexually explicit content provided that they had some "redeeming social value." In 1965, the landmark decision in the case of *Griswold v. Connecticut*, which voided a state law against contraception, affirmed that individuals had a constitutionally protected right to privacy. These controversial decisions with respect to freedom of speech and individual rights were accompanied by controversial decisions about the rights of defendants, particularly the 1966 *Miranda v. Arizona* decision. Warren's majority opinion confirmed that those accused of crimes must be informed of the right to counsel and the right to remain silent. "What the court has done," Michael Murphy, a former New York police commissioner, later commented, "is to make one boxer fight to the Marquis of Queensbury [*sic*] rules while permitting the other to butt, gouge, and bite."[39]

Many people found this relentless change within American society to be disturbing. One journalist noted the dislocating impacts of change in the small town of Millersburg, Pennsylvania. Like Webster City, Millersburg was largely remote from crime, racial conflict, radical protest, and permissiveness but was nevertheless profoundly affected by the turbulence of the late 1960s. "Everything seems so prosperous and secure now," commented one woman, "but I have never felt more insecure in my life." Another Millersburg resident articulated some of the reasons for the sense of insecurity: "Crime, the streets being unsafe, strikes, the trouble with the colored, all this dope-taking, people leaving the churches. It is sort of a breakdown of our standards, the American way of life." A favored remedy in Millersburg to deal with this breakdown was uncompromising treatment of those involved. Criticizing protesters in general as well as a radical black activist in particular, a factory foreman explained, "These punk kids, draft-card burners, all those Rap Browns think we are afraid of them. If we would crack down hard a few times, they would straighten out in a hurry."[40]

Inescapably, the White House recognized these problems. During preparations for the 1968 State of the Union address, Joseph Califano, a senior aide to Johnson, wrote to the president that the nation's problems were cumulatively "so immense our society seems to be coming apart at the seams." Outside the White House, an academic and former official in the Kennedy and Johnson administrations was even more alarmed. For Daniel Patrick Moynihan, America in 1968 more and more "exhibits the qualities of an individual going through a nervous breakdown." It seemed appropriate to quote W. B. Yeats: "The centre cannot hold." Moynihan explained, "The sheer effort to hold things together has become the central issue of politics in a nation that began the decade intent on building a society touched with moral grandeur. Increasingly men of the center watch with dismay." Moynihan was disturbed that significant questioning of the American purpose at home and abroad originated with a privileged, professional, and educated elite. They "do not hesitate to conclude . . . that American society is doomed, and make no effort to conceal their great pleasure at this prospect."[41]

The fortunes of Johnson and the Democrats swiftly changed. The 1966 midterm elections offered the first electoral testimony to the problems faced by the president and his party. Just two years after his landslide, Johnson suffered an unusually and unexpectedly sharp rebuke from voters. The Republicans gained forty-seven seats in the House of Representatives and three seats in the Senate as well as other advances in state contests. Republicans from across the party's ideological spectrum benefited. Winning conservatives included new governors in Nevada and Arizona, Paul Laxalt and John Williams, in addition to some southern congressmen. But a larger number of victories went to Republicans of a more moderate stripe, including Governors John Chafee of Rhode Island, John Volpe of Massachusetts, and Raymond Shafer of Pennsylvania and Senators Edward Brooke of Massachusetts, Mark Hatfield of Oregon, and Charles Percy of Illinois. Even the Republican Right's new hero, California Governor Ronald Reagan, who was admired for his ability to sound conservative concerns in an attractive manner, offered an analysis that explained his victory through success in winning moderate votes. Still another winner was Richard Nixon, who earned the party's gratitude for his energetic campaigning in support of its candidates.[42] The 1966 midterm elections thus signaled popular dissatisfaction with the Johnson administration; by 1968, this dissatisfaction had deepened still further.

THE REEMERGENCE OF RICHARD NIXON

The upheaval within American society in the late 1960s caused some observers, among them political writer James Reichley, to contemplate the possibility of electoral change to the long-term advantage of the Republican Party. "There is solid reason to believe," Reichley wrote in the summer of 1967, "that an entirely new cycle in American political history may well be beginning—a political change as profound as those initiated by the Democrats under Jackson, the Republicans under Lincoln, and the Democrats again under Franklin Roosevelt."[43] Given the Democratic Party's accumulating difficulties in the years after Johnson's overwhelming victory over Goldwater, the idea of an incipient realignment made sense.

The profound disruptions within American society provided a good opportunity for a candidate in opposition to Johnson and a party in opposition to the Democrats. But it was by no means clear how that opportunity could be exploited. A climate of political flux does not dictate any one uniform response but instead produces a debate. Republicans reacted in different ways to the emerging Democratic disarray. Different groups had different visions for the party's future and disagreed sharply about the detail and even underlying philosophy of a majority-seeking strategy.

Democrats, too, responded to the changing context of politics. Some people believed—despite the evidence of conservative discontent in the face of social change—that the overall, longer-term trend within America was toward fresh liberalization. Combined with the conviction that additional far-reaching reforms were necessary, this belief fueled a powerful movement within the Democratic Party to revitalize and deepen its egalitarian commitments. Many within this "New Politics" movement combined these egalitarian commitments with an adamant opposition to the Vietnam War as unjust and as disruptive to social progress at home.[44]

In the eyes of some observers, the significant American demographic trend was the growth of an educated, professional, and often young middle class. This group was expanding thanks to the post–World War II baby boom, the greater availability of higher education, and the decline of the industrial and agricultural sectors in relation to managerial and technical professions. To some Democrats of the New Politics, this new middle class offered a foundation for a revitalized liberalism in coalition with America's underprivileged— the poor and minorities. These party leaders were often frustrated by working-class Democratic supporters who favored the war and viewed with alarm the prospect of further racial progress.[45]

Liberal Republicans identified the same demographic trends as politically important but interpreted them as promising to their cause. The Ripon Society was the most prominent among a number of liberal Republican organizations created in response to the proliferation of conservative groups in the 1960s. The Ripon Society also became the most successful at developing proposals for ideologically coherent policy and strategy. A group of young and intellectually minded activists, the society argued that party leaders should embrace imaginative and liberally inclined policies to present a reasonable response to the demands of the 1960s. The party would thus uncover the support of "New Americans," whether new members of the suburban middle classes, new college graduates and professionals, or "New South" moderates.[46] The Ripon supporters' vision for the party and for the American future therefore differed considerably from that of more conservative Republicans.

George Wallace, the segregationist Democrat from Alabama who appeared on the national scene during his party's 1964 primaries, provided still another vision for America's future. Wallace appealed aggressively to those who experienced alienation and frustration in response to the convulsive social changes of the decade. "George Wallace," wrote one contemporary journalist, "is the Cicero of the cab driver." This alienation and frustration frequently focused particularly on racist intolerance of progress toward civil rights for African Americans. By this point in his career, Wallace's racism was often subtle; journalist Jules Witcover noted Wallace's "considerable talent for wrapping racism in rationalizations that permit many voters to go along without much nagging from their consciences." Wallace rarely mentioned desegregation but instead spoke of federal interference in education, housing, and business. His audience understood. Although racial conservatism constituted the heart of Wallace's appeal, he combined this conservatism with economic activism and an assertive nationalism. The common strand running through his positions was a populist attack on an out-of-touch elite.[47]

As politicians of greatly differing views continued to debate, the identity of the next Republican candidate for president was important. This candidate would have an especially significant opportunity to shape the way in which the party collectively responded to the upheaval of the 1960s and to understand how he and his party could benefit from this tumult and improve their fortunes. The face of the Republican future was a face from the past. A deeply controversial career behind him, Richard Nixon was now a Manhattan lawyer who had apparently given up his active political ambitions. His defeat in the 1962 California gubernatorial contest followed his defeat at the hands of John Kennedy in the 1960 presidential election. But Nixon would soon emerge from premature political retirement to fight for his party's presidential nomination. In this effort, his good relationship with the activist wing of the Republican Party was helpful. This relationship was the product of a career characterized by party loyalty. As Eisenhower's vice president, Nixon had played a particularly important role in Republican campaigning, and he subsequently continued to do so. "Dick knows almost everything there is to know about the party's inner workings and geography," observed Charles McWhorter, an aide to Nixon, during the 1968 primary campaigns.[48]

Despite liberals' and moderates' efforts to regain some momentum, the essential insight about the party's inner workings during this period was the impact of the Goldwater movement. Nixon, whose 1964 campaigning had earned an early foundation of conservative support (including that of Goldwater), was aware of this influence. Aspiring once more to the party's nomination, Nixon wooed the Right. Writer Andrew Kopkind saw these efforts as early as September 1966. "The newest of the new Nixons," Kopkind noted, "seems to be materializing in the Goldwater image." Although Nixon's cultivation of conservatives did not necessarily mean that he had "gone all the way to the right," it nevertheless did "indicate that he [knew] the way to the nomination [lay] in that direction."[49]

In seeking conservative support, Nixon benefited from party activists' taste for pragmatism, gained following the flirtation with ideological purity in 1964.

Nixon was not, in general, the conservatives' ideal candidate, even if he was more acceptable than most of his rivals. Instead, many conservatives preferred Reagan, though pragmatic calculation tempered this preference; they were concerned about Reagan's chances of winning the presidential election, and this concern made it difficult for sentiment in his favor to build. "A lot of us regard Ronnie as a soul brother," commented a Georgia Republican in the summer of 1967, "but we also think he needs some seasoning."[50]

Nixon did not intend to repeat Goldwater's mistakes and did not rely solely on the support of conservatives. Nixon ensured that his team represented a wide spectrum of political thinking. Exemplifying this variety were two of the more important recruits to the campaign, Leonard Garment and Patrick Buchanan. Garment, a member of Nixon's law firm, was a liberal Democrat; Buchanan, a journalist, was a conservative Republican. Nixon's closest political confidants disagreed strongly about the right way to fashion a political response to the upheaval of the 1960s. Robert Finch and John Mitchell were especially close to Nixon during the long search for the presidency. On the one hand, Finch, a longtime friend of Nixon's and lieutenant governor of California, was convinced that the Republican future was rather liberal. "This is the last election," Finch is said to have commented to reporters during the 1968 campaign, "that will be won by the un-black, the un-poor and the un-young." To secure long-term success, the party had to find ways to appeal to more liberal groups within society. Mitchell, on the other hand, a senior member of Nixon's law firm, was devoted to a much more conservative view of politics. As he saw the future, "the un-black, the un-poor, and the un-young" remained a solid foundation for electoral success. In doing so, he agreed with the originator of the phrase, political analyst Richard Scammon.[51] Judging by the opinions of those in whom Nixon confided, there remained an openness about the way in which Nixon would guide the Republican Party.

As an aspirant for the presidency, Nixon paid special attention to the problems of Vietnam and to the political possibilities that those problems created. As a result of his experience as vice president, he alone among the Republican presidential hopefuls could legitimately claim expertise in the realm of foreign affairs, and he sought to publicize this experience and to emphasize its potential value to the nation's war efforts. Nixon wanted to fight the war and to win: he supported the administration's aims in Vietnam but opposed the manner in which the Johnson administration had conducted the war. In general, Nixon tended to argue for a more vigorous level of intervention. By contrast, while

Nixon endeavored to position himself as the politician best able to solve the Vietnam War, the electoral chances of his principal rival, George Romney, the governor of Michigan, were irrevocably damaged by ill-considered comments relating to the conflict. When Romney said that he underwent "the greatest brainwashing that anybody can get" when generals and diplomats briefed him on the situation in Vietnam, his candidacy was effectively over.[52]

NEW ALIGNMENT

In 1968, aides to presidential aspirant Nixon enthusiastically embraced the idea that the United States stood on the threshold of significant political change. "There was much talk among them," reported Garry Wills, "all through 1968, of 'new coalitions,' of 'the passing of the New Deal'—the meeting of their man with a great historic hinge and moment of reversal." The optimism was unsurprising in view of the idea's enormous promise. Within the Nixon team, Kevin P. Phillips was most identified with these beliefs. Phillips had won his job at campaign headquarters by catching Garment's attention with a manuscript on the subject of electoral change.[53] Phillips analyzed evolving patterns of voting and argued that the Democratic coalition was crumbling. In 1969, the manuscript was published as *The Emerging Republican Majority*, a book that foresaw a new conservative era in American politics. For the moment, however, Phillips's theories were reserved for private consumption.

A debate about the cultivation of a new majority would become central when Nixon won the presidential election and entered the White House. But Nixon was already pondering the matter. On one occasion during his campaign for the Republican nomination, he publicly joined this debate about the possibility for long-range political change. In a May 16, 1968, radio speech, he called his vision for a putative Republican constituency "a new alignment for American unity." Nixon claimed that the basic theme uniting groups within the new alignment was the reassertion of individualism against the growth of government bureaucracy. He therefore contrasted his vision of an electoral majority with his characterization of the Democratic Party's coalition as groups united by selfish economic interests: "The new majority is not a grouping of power blocs, but an alliance of ideas. . . . Many of these men and women belong to the same blocs that formed the old coalitions. But now, thinking independently, they have all reached a new conclusion about the direction of our nation. . . . People come first, and government is their servant. The best government is closest to the people, and most involved with people's lives. Government is formed to protect the individual's life, property, and rights, and to help the helpless—not to dominate a person's life or rob him of his self-respect." As described by Nixon, the groups that constituted the majority interest in the new alignment built on the base of traditional Republicans, who emphasized the importance of free enterprise, to include sections of the population whose needs and expectations differed superficially from the Republican core of support, such as "new liberals," who emphasized participatory democracy; the "new South," interested in "interpreting the old doctrine of states' rights in new ways"; most surprisingly, black militants, rejecting welfarism in favor of self-help; plus the "silent center."[54]

The "silent center" was the numerically most important segment of the new alignment, according to Nixon. He described this group as "the millions of people in the middle of the American political spectrum who do not demonstrate, who do not picket or protest loudly." Nixon claimed that their opposition to government was based on a belief that federal authority should not apply to areas such as prayer in schools and local obscenity laws. As Wills pointed out, the groups making up the new alignment did not come together in pursuit of a positive goal but to register their discontent against government. TRB in the *New Republic* offered a more skeptical reaction: "To us this is just silly. When the South and black militants get into the same boat we want to watch—from another boat."[55]

The speech, "like all of those trying to probe for a realignment of voters[,] was in part realistic and in part unrealistic," Nixon later admitted. After all, as a campaign speech, its primary purpose was to convince Americans of Nixon's qualifications to be president rather than to make a carefully argued case about his interpretation of political change. "Perhaps the most significant line in the speech was the one that dealt with the 'silent Americans.' "[56] At one level, the speech suggested how much America had changed during the 1960s. In speaking of "participatory democracy," of black militants, and of a postsegregation South, Nixon was referring to novel trends of the decade. At another level, the speech indicated that Republican aspirations had barely changed in the face of those new developments. The "silent Americans" were the same group that Goldwater had identified in 1961 as the party's target for expanding its electoral base. Moreover, the antigovernment message remained, though in a different cast and framework from that of 1964.

It was first necessary for Nixon to secure his party's nomination, a task for which he needed very different skills from those required to win the general election. Nixon performed well throughout the nomination season, while his main rivals, Romney and Nelson Rockefeller, campaigned poorly and were unable to challenge Nixon's impressive delegate count. But when Republicans met at their convention at Miami Beach, Florida, in August, Nixon faced a serious challenge from Ronald Reagan, who became an active candidate only at that time. Reagan worked with Rockefeller in an effort to break Nixon's support on two flanks, both conservative and liberal. What followed was an impressive groundswell of convention support for Reagan, a reminder that Nixon was no better than the second choice of many activists representing the party's new conservatism.

The enthusiasm for Reagan meant that Nixon had to work hard at Miami Beach to keep the nomination. The key to resisting the Reagan challenge was Strom Thurmond, the senator from South Carolina with special influence among the southern conservatives who were the heart of the effort to deny Nixon the nomination. To retain the support of these southerners, Nixon insisted that he sympathized with their concerns. In particular, he assured them that he would be no liberal on questions of civil rights. While Nixon secured the nomination, the pro-Reagan bubble vividly demonstrated the conservatives' muscle. They were willing to bide their time. "All in all, I would say that the Reagan effort was well worth the trouble," wrote William Rusher, the *National Review* publisher, to a fellow conservative, Congressman John Ashbrook of Ohio, "and that the troops are in good shape for the future."[57]

In his acceptance speech at the convention, Nixon laid claim to the allegiance of the "forgotten Americans" by reminding them of the troubles facing the nation:

As we look at America, we see cities enveloped in smoke and flame. We hear sirens in the night. We see Americans dying on distant battlefields abroad. We see Americans hating each other, fighting each other, killing each other at home. And as we see and hear these things, millions of Americans cry out in anguish: Did we come all this way for this? Did American boys die in Normandy and Korea and in Valley Forge for this?

Listen to the answers to those questions. It is another voice, it is a quiet voice in the tumult of the shouting. It is the voice of the great majority of Americans, the forgotten Americans, the non-shouters, the non-demonstrators. . . . They give drive to the spirit of America. They give lift to the American dream. They give steel to the backbone of America. They're good people. They're decent people; they work and they save and they pay their taxes and they care.

The nation, Nixon said, needed "new leadership," because the problems resulted from failed leadership. "And what America needs are leaders to match the greatness of her people."[58]

Nominated as Nixon's running mate was Spiro Agnew, the rather obscure governor of Maryland. Agnew possessed certain moderate credentials. He had won the 1966 Maryland gubernatorial election against a racially bigoted Democratic candidate and was an early supporter of Rockefeller for the 1968 Republican nomination. Agnew's record in Maryland was relatively progressive. But he also had notably conservative credentials. He was a sharp critic of civil disorder, and when riots erupted in Baltimore, as elsewhere, following the assassination of Martin Luther King Jr., Agnew reacted with unsympathetic hostility. Agnew was acceptable to the party's conservatives. Informed journalistic reaction immediately interpreted the nomination of Agnew as confirming the importance of the Republican Right within the party. Pundits also pronounced him a competent vice presidential figurehead but deemed him unsuited to the demands of the presidency. On the campaign trail, Agnew swiftly became a politician of some controversy, partly as a result of gaffes but partly also as a result of his rather strident rhetoric about issues.[59]

THE FALL CAMPAIGN

The politics of nomination proceeded smoothly among the Republicans. The contrast with the Democrats was great; 1968 was an especially agonizing year for the Johnson administration and the Democratic Party. Johnson first faced a primary challenge from an antiwar candidate, Senator Eugene McCarthy, whose case was strengthened in February when the Tet Offensive demonstrated vividly the intractability of the war in Vietnam. The challenge became serious, and McCarthy almost managed to rob Johnson of victory in the New Hampshire primary. Disunity within the Democratic Party then deepened when Robert F. Kennedy, a senator from New York and a leading exponent of the New Politics, announced his candidacy. At the end of March, Johnson withdrew from the effort to win another term so that he could concentrate on Vietnam instead of campaign politics. His vice president, Hubert Humphrey, became a candidate instead.

When Kennedy was assassinated in June following his victory in the California primary, Humphrey became the favorite to win the Democratic nomination. Humphrey won no primaries but was the choice of the party establishment, which enjoyed significant influence over the nomination process. George Wallace was among the unsuccessful contenders for the Democratic nomination, but he continued to campaign as a third-party candidate.

At Chicago in August, the Democratic convention exposed the party's bitter divisions stemming from opposition to Johnson's war policy and from unhappiness with Humphrey's candidacy. Discontent did not remain solely in the convention halls but played out dramatically in the city streets. Protesters met with a harsh response from the police. Altogether, the events of the convention offered the sharpest of reminders that the Democrats were in disarray and that the nation faced serious problems for which Americans could not agree on answers. It was unquestionably a favorable moment to stage a challenge to the incumbent party. "In 1968 any sensible Republican candidate," wrote historian David Burner, "had a good chance to win."[60]

Three main issues remained under debate. The first was the Vietnam War. Relatively few Americans wanted an immediate withdrawal without the achievement of war aims, but many felt that the administration had handled the war badly. The second was the continuing struggle for racial equality. Public opinion on desegregation was becoming more liberal, but many whites, including liberals, were uneasy about the tense state of race relations. The third was "law and order." "[V]iolence was the background condition of American life," noted journalist Theodore White. The concern was frequently linked with opposition to antiwar protest and, still more controversially, to racial unrest. This connection allowed politicians to promise action on crime, knowing that some voters heard this promise as a coded language for racial conservatism. Nixon's private remarks showed that he understood the connection. Yet the concern about disorder and crime had grown, too. Rising levels of crime meant that some Americans questioned the success of the law enforcement system quite apart from any connection with radical protest or racism.[61]

Following the convention, Nixon ran a very safe campaign. His lead was comfortable, and he intended to do nothing that might endanger it. According to Gallup, in early September Nixon was supported by 43 percent of voters against Humphrey's 31 percent and Wallace's 19 percent. During September, Nixon's performance in polls remained solid, while Wallace gained some ground at Humphrey's expense. In campaign appearances, Nixon repeated his convention rhetoric about the forgotten Americans—"those who did not indulge in violence, those who did not break the law, people who pay their taxes and go to work, people who send their children to school, who go to their churches, people who are not haters, people who love this country, and because they love this country are angry about what has happened to America."[62] He promised to bring calm after the storms of the 1960s that had resulted, he claimed, from liberalism's excesses.

Nixon pledged to deal with the matters that concerned these Americans, including a return to "law and order," peace in Vietnam, a sounder economy, and "more people on payrolls" rather than "more people on welfare rolls." As elsewhere, a Denver audience reacted favorably: "The suggestion that they were hard done by seemed to touch a chord in the audience," observed a team of British reporters, "although the people so addressed . . . looked prosperous and well clad, rather than forgotten." As journalist James Reston noted, the campaign was squarely targeted at "a new and larger middle class, which resents the racial turmoil, the demonstrations in the cities and all the permissiveness of contemporary American life." Despite Nixon's references on the stump to tackling inflation—which, in large part because of spending on Vietnam, had reached 4.2 percent—the state of the economy did not play an important part in the campaign. Price rises were more than matched by wage increases, and, for most Americans, inflationary pressures had yet to erode general prosperity.[63]

Wallace sought to benefit from resentments within American society, especially those linked with race. He continued to talk about race without mentioning it, speaking instead of an out-of-touch elite's interference in the lives of ordinary people. "I think there's a backlash against the theoreticians and the bureaucrats in national government," Wallace said during a 1967 television interview, for example. "There isn't any backlash among the mass of American people against anybody because of color. There's a backlash against big government in this country." His hard-line rhetoric won widespread success not only in the South, where his support numbered a third of the total population, but also outside the region, where polls suggested that at least a tenth of Americans preferred Wallace to Nixon or Humphrey. Indeed, during the campaign, there was serious speculation that Wallace might perform strongly enough to deny either Humphrey or Nixon a majority in the electoral college.[64]

Humphrey agreed with the thesis of the forgotten American. His party's traditional supporters, he thought, now believed that Democratic leaders were neglecting the coalition's needs in favor of those of racial minorities and of society's poorest. "It isn't that [the blue-collar worker] is against the black or the poor," he wrote privately. "In fact, he would like to help. But he just feels that everybody in government has forgotten him. Yet he pays the taxes and his kids fight the war." Humphrey's response to the thesis differed from Nixon's or Wallace's. The Democratic candidate wanted to convince these voters that his party's liberalism remained in their best interests as well as those of the wider society.[65]

Humphrey began by seeking to neutralize two of his opponents' most significant issues against him. First, he distanced himself somewhat from the Johnson administration's Vietnam policy. At the end of September, Humphrey announced that he would halt the bombing of North Vietnam if this action promised to bring peace talks. Second, the candidate emphasized his concerns about crime and unveiled ambitious proposals, to cost almost a billion dollars a year, to tackle the problem. Nevertheless, unlike Nixon and Wallace, he continued to speak of rising crime as a problem of social deprivation as well as one of law enforcement. Humphrey then spoke of the ways in which his party worked for ordinary Americans. "Now, our Republican friends have fought every piece of social legislation that has benefited this country, they have fought against social security, they have been against all forms of Federal aid to education, they have been against Medicare for our senior citizens," he said in Las Vegas toward the end of the campaign. "The Democrats have been responsible for every piece of constructive legislation that has passed in these last thirty-five years." Humphrey ridiculed Nixon's claim to the support of the forgotten Americans. "[I]f he is a friend of the workingman, Scrooge is Santa Claus," Humphrey said. In the North, organized labor, many leaders of which viewed with alarm Wallace's success among their supporters, provided Humphrey with energetic help. Humphrey took his case to the South as well. "I don't recall any Republicans that have ever done anything for Georgia except Sherman," he told one interviewer there, "and you know what he did to it."[66]

At this point, Nixon's safe campaign became imperiled. Even as different issues emerged to the Democrats' disadvantage, the traditional Democratic advantage, in place since the Great Depression, remained. One working-class voter summarized the differences between Republicans and Democrats in a way that reflected its persistence: "One side has plenty of money and the other side doesn't," he said. "I'd have to say the Democrats are better for us cause they're supposed to be more for the working people." Nixon feared the power of this perception and warned his speechwriters about it. "If there's war, people will vote for me to end it," he told them. "If there's peace, they'll vote their pocketbooks—Democratic prosperity." Lloyd Free and Hadley Cantril's *The Political Beliefs of Americans*, which discussed the distinction between the "ideological conservatism" and the "operational liberalism" of most voters and which attributed Goldwater's defeat to his failure to understand this distinction, reportedly received "considerable attention" from members of Nixon's team.[67]

At the end of the campaign, the war in Vietnam returned to the forefront of debate. In terms of approach, little separated Nixon and Humphrey; Humphrey's position was only marginally more dovish. Humphrey could not, however, fully escape association with the administration's unpopular conduct of the war, while Nixon criticized its mistakes and promised "new leadership." Suddenly, the possibility arose that voters might revise their negative evaluation of Johnson's policy. On October 31, Johnson announced a bombing halt because negotiators had overcome an obstacle to peace talks. But the breakthrough was brief. Within days, Nguyen Van Thieu, the president of South Vietnam, refused to participate in talks, unhappy with the terms. Anxious about the possible impact of the breakthrough on his electoral prospects, Nixon's campaign used private channels to advise South Vietnamese leaders that they could expect more favorable terms if its candidate won election and that they should therefore wait.[68]

THE LESSONS OF 1968

Despite the failure of Johnson's peace initiative, Humphrey enjoyed a late surge of support. The story of the campaign was the gradual loss of Nixon's lead to the very edge of defeat. Nixon won, but his margin of victory was extremely thin. The election results testified to the continuing vitality of the Democratic coalition even in the face of the torturous events and developments that had built between 1964 and the especially painful year of 1968. The new president was the choice of a minority of Americans. Winning only a half million more votes than Humphrey, Nixon secured 43.4 percent of the popular vote, compared with Humphrey's 42.7 percent and Wallace's 13.5 percent. In the South, Nixon's victory over Wallace was more narrow still: the new president took 34.7 percent of the vote in the eleven states of the former Confederacy, while Wallace's share was 34.3 percent. Wallace won his own state of Alabama together with Arkansas, Georgia, Louisiana, and Mississippi.

Nixon was the choice of a minority, and his party was the congressional minority. Democrats easily retained control of both houses of Congress. After the Republicans gained 4 seats, the partisan division in the House was 248 to 187 in favor of the Democrats. Republicans gained 5 seats in the Senate to narrow the Democrats' advantage to 58 to 42. A larger picture of party fortunes provided further evidence of the Republicans' minority status. Of all seats in state legislatures, 57.5 percent were Democratic, and 55 percent of Americans felt at least some degree of party identification with the Democrats compared to just 34 percent for the Republicans.

The racial division was deep. Despite their higher-than-average opposition to the Vietnam War, 97 percent of African American voters chose Humphrey, as did less than 35 percent of whites. By contrast, many whites who voted in the presidential elections of both 1964 and 1968 changed party. One-fifth of Goldwater's voters chose Humphrey or more frequently Wallace instead of Nixon, while as much as 40 percent of the Nixon vote was provided by people who had supported Johnson in 1964.[69]

Nixon's advisers were talking about the end of a political era dominated by the Democratic Party. But the realistic basis for this speculation remained open to question. Nixon's campaign benefited from an anti-incumbent discontent that took many forms, including displeasure with the administration's failure to win the Vietnam War, unease about crime and about permissiveness, anxiety about racial tensions and even resentment because of moves toward racial equality, and concern that programmatic innovations benefited the few and not the many. Nixon's minority share of the electorate did not represent a coherent vote of confidence in a Republican future.[70]

While contemporaries could not deny the current turbulence of American society, they did not unanimously share the conclusions of Phillips and others that majority identification with the Democratic Party was about to be replaced by majority identification with the Republicans. "I don't think that we have anything today like the Depression, which was the real watershed that led to the overturn in 1932," commented political scientist Howard R. Penniman. "You may see some slight movement towards the Republican Party, but until there is a crisis of greater magnitude than we now see, I don't think you can talk about it in terms of a major shift."[71] The election results could easily be read as demonstrating Democratic strength, remarkably persistent at a time of such difficulty.

The challenge facing Nixon was to transform this vote against the Democrats into a vote in favor of the Republicans, and he had to do so with no assurances that the crisis within the Democratic Party would persist beyond 1968. The problems of opponents formed a fragile basis for political success. As president, Nixon needed to find better reasons why forgotten Americans should offer him their support.

TWO

MIDDLE AMERICA AND THE SILENT MAJORITY

Issues, 1969–1970

On the morning after Election Day 1968, President-elect Richard Nixon spoke of a sign he had seen held by a teenager in Deshler, Ohio, during the campaign: "Bring us together." "And that will be the great objective of this administration at the outset," Nixon said, "to bring the American people together." The answer to the turbulence of the 1960s, Nixon suggested, was the reconciliation of differences. If indeed Nixon placed this goal as the priority of his administration, its initiatives might differ strikingly from those expected on the basis of his political reputation. Some of his senior aides had already told a journalist about Nixon's interest in reaching out to Americans beyond his "great 'silent majority'" after the election. "In short, this line of Nixon talk implies," wrote journalist John Osborne in October, "Richard Nixon in the White House may turn out to be more liberal, more humane, more attuned to the world about us than Nixon the candidate appears to be or than President Hubert Humphrey could even try to be."[1]

But "this line of Nixon talk" was based on an incorrect assumption. Nixon had not yet won over any majority; he owed his election to the votes of a minority rallied in opposition to the mistakes of the Democrats rather than in support of his promise. About to begin was a long and hard struggle to identify a majority and to win its loyalty. Although the task was formidable, Nixon believed that the times offered great potential for such a struggle. He became sure that a realignment to the advantage of conservative politicians was possible.

Yet Nixon was not as sure how to encourage this realignment. As the early

months of his administration slipped by, outside observers noted the continuing promise of a coalition based on the new forgotten Americans but often
overestimated the coherence of the administration's strategy to cultivate such a
coalition. Eventually, almost exactly a year after his election to the presidency,
Nixon caught unmistakable sight of his electoral opportunity. He did so when
he appealed to America's "silent majority" for support of his increasingly
controversial Vietnam policy. In time, when seeking to consolidate this support, he would sacrifice any dream to "bring us together" by accepting the
utility of division and polarization in search of creating an electoral majority.

THE STRATEGISTS

When the administration embarked on its quest for a new majority, the central
figure behind this effort—primarily responsible for most of its achievements
and shortcomings—was the president, who turned to several aides for support
for his administration's political endeavors. Some members of his administration played key roles in the creation of electoral strategy by discussing ideas
with Nixon, by preparing for him interpretations of current political developments, and by implementing the president's instructions about how to mobilize support.

The most significant member of Nixon's circle was chief of staff H. R.
Haldeman, a former advertising executive from Los Angeles. Another aide
estimated that Nixon spent almost three-quarters of his staff time with Haldeman, who acted as a sounding board for the president.[2] Haldeman was then
responsible for overseeing the implementation of presidential directives. Second in significance on many matters was a friend of Haldeman's, John Ehrlichman, a Seattle lawyer. Ehrlichman began work in the White House as counsel
to the president, a relatively obscure position, but soon rose to become Nixon's
main domestic policy adviser.

The concept of a continuing national political majority was overtly partisan.
It was underpinned by the belief that broader Republican successes could
follow Nixon's victory. But Nixon's strategic team had conspicuously few links
with the Republican Party across America. Instead, the political careers of
Haldeman and Ehrlichman depended straightforwardly on their involvement
in the various Nixon campaigns. "Their loyalty is to God, to country, and to
Nixon," remarked a junior White House staffer. "In reverse order."[3]

Unlike Haldeman and Ehrlichman, Charles Colson, who joined the White House in the fall of 1969, had wider Republican experience, having worked as an aide to Leverett Saltonstall, a senator from Massachusetts. Charged with responsibility for liaison with outside groups, Colson staged an impressively swift climb to prominence within the Nixon circle, emerging as a leading adviser on political strategy between 1970 and 1972. Despite Colson's background within the party, his job oriented him to the identification of potential support beyond traditional Republican sympathizers. He owed this rise to his effectiveness in articulating an electoral opportunity for the administration among lower-middle-class and ethnic Americans. Furthermore, Nixon found useful Colson's "instinct for the political jugular and ability to get things done."[4]

No one in 1968 foresaw the centrality of Haldeman, Ehrlichman, and Colson to the Nixon White House. Instead, it was widely expected that Robert Finch and John Mitchell, both Nixon friends as well as political associates, would play significant roles as political advisers. But their importance was soon eclipsed. Finch first concentrated his attention on his duties as secretary of the Department of Health, Education, and Welfare (HEW), but his tenure in the department was unsuccessful and short-lived, and he did not regain his influence when he moved to the White House in 1970 with an advisory role. Mitchell, by contrast, continued to enjoy some influence with Nixon. Appointed attorney general, he still talked politics with the president, but these conversations became more occasional than regular. Haldeman, Ehrlichman, and Colson became closer to the president, and Nixon developed many of his ideas about political strategy in consultation with those three men.

The administration included a much wider array of officeholders who offered political advice to Nixon. Prominent among these was Patrick Buchanan, who wrote speeches for Nixon and for a long time was responsible for the preparation of the president's daily news summary. Buchanan had a burning interest in the identification of a new majority and regularly wrote political analyses for Nixon with speculation about how to win this electoral goal. Buchanan viewed it as demanding an approach more conservative than most of his fellow aides did. For example, he sometimes called Colson a "Massachusetts liberal."[5]

Seeking a new majority led to an important debate about its achievement in which many people—from junior aides to members of the cabinet—wished to participate. For example, at different times, domestic adviser Daniel Patrick

Moynihan, cabinet officer George Shultz, and Department of Labor official Jerome Rosow all made especially crucial contributions to this debate. Nevertheless, the number of people with whom Nixon spoke regularly on this topic was relatively small, and his ideas about politics developed among a select group of aides.

CONGRESS, THE PUBLIC, AND THE WHITE HOUSE

The institutional context of the Nixon administration was historically exceptional. No president since Zachary Taylor in 1849 had arrived in the White House with both houses of Congress in opposition hands. Achieving many policy goals would therefore require a special sensitivity to congressional relations. The appointment of Bryce Harlow as congressional-relations chief seemed to demonstrate Nixon's desire to develop this sensitivity: Harlow, a veteran of the Eisenhower administration, was famed for his skill in cultivating political support on Capitol Hill.[6]

But the symbolism of Harlow's appointment was misleading. The congressional-relations operation was truly successful under neither Harlow nor his successors, Clark MacGregor and William Timmons. Although this failure was partly linked with the Democratic majorities' hostility to Nixon, the totality of the failure was more significantly linked with Nixon's personal shortcomings. Political scientist Nigel Bowles noted that Nixon showed little interest in the work of his congressional staff and that his general attitude toward Congress was one of "disdain." Nixon did not, moreover, enjoy the tasks of asking for votes and of cultivating political intimacies. Strangely, Nixon's career had left him without a detailed knowledge of legislative politicking. His tenure in Congress had been relatively brief; then, as later, he showed little interest in matters congressional. Nixon was, in the words of Michael Genovese, a scholar of the presidency, "never a congressional insider" and "never a legislative tactician."[7] Especially at a time of divided government, these shortcomings had very significant implications.

The administration included few experienced legislative politicians in key positions, and Nixon's closest aides were notably dismissive of Congress. Haldeman told one writer that the nation's constitutional design did not call for cooperation between the legislative and executive branches. "I don't think Congress is supposed to work with the White House—it is a different organization and under the Constitution I don't think we should expect agreement," he said. Ehrlichman was no more enthusiastic about cooperation. According to two Washington journalists of the era, he expressed his "ignorance" of Capitol Hill and his "arrogant disdain" toward it by dismissing its importance. "The President *is* the government," he used to say. Many congressional Republicans viewed these attitudes with dismay.[8]

Nixon combined his dislike of Washington's ways with a keen interest in the nation's views. Even among successful politicians, his attention to the wider political scene was notable. According to Harlow, Nixon skillfully thought about "visceral behavior down at the precinct level clear across America." Similarly, Herbert Stein, a member of Nixon's Council of Economic Advisers, observed that Nixon was "a close student of what the 'country'—meaning the electorate—wanted."[9] Correspondingly, while his White House was not excessively engaged by the problem of maximizing votes on Capitol Hill, it was, by contrast, consistently interested in effective communication with the public at large.

Nixon sometimes attached more importance to the communication of policy than to policy itself. In his first week in the White House, he wrote that he did not need "reams of advice as to what he should say in his speeches, what bills he should introduce and what appearances he should make," because—rather astonishingly—"[t]his [was] the easiest part of our job." Instead, public relations should be a priority. "Our success or failure," he wrote, "will depend on how everyone around RN is able to take whatever he says and does and make the very most out of it." Nixon's personal interest in matters of public relations extended beyond the substance of policy to include more trivial issues of presidential image. He wanted the public to know, for example, that he was hardworking and had impressive leadership abilities and, furthermore, that he was a witty man and kind to his staff.[10]

The concern with public relations was constant. Ehrlichman later estimated that Nixon spent as much as "half his working time on the nonsubstantive aspects of the Presidency." As a key media aide, Herbert Klein was keenly aware that Nixon was very sensitive about his portrayal in the press. "From the President on down," he wrote, "an amazingly excessive amount of time was spent worrying about plans to conjure up better and more favorable coverage."[11]

The obsession with electoral implications did not necessarily weaken the policy-making process, but it certainly risked the counterproductive image of a public-relations-obsessed administration. It might also have engendered a short-termism unhelpful to grander political goals. In early 1971, Haldeman studied the way in which presidents' ratings tended to decline during their tenures. He discovered that presidents won surges in support because of either crises or successes in international affairs but experienced slumps in popularity because of domestic crises or "gradual deterioration"—a long period of war, a succession of economic difficulties, or racial turmoil. "This would indicate a domestic course of making every effort to keep things on an even keel, but no effort to take strong decisive action or to intervene in any way in either a positive or negative direction," decided Haldeman. "On the other hand, it would indicate the strong desirability of major action in the international area, *but looking to short-term effects rather than long-term* . . . If he is successful he will get short term strong approval for the success. If on the other hand he is not successful and a major crisis ensues, he will experience a rallying of support during the period of the crisis."[12]

Thanks to technical advances, the Nixon administration used polls to track public opinion with some sophistication and detail. Nixon eagerly pursued this opportunity to assess the response to his presidency. If American politics really were undergoing a realignment, then tools were available to observe the contours of opinion change. But poll data, however sophisticated, are never a substitute for political skill. The utility of polls depends on the effective design and interpretation of information. More seriously, Nixon's attention to the cultivation of public opinion threatened to divert too frequently his focus on policy questions. Buchanan certainly feared that the president might be guilty of losing the appropriate balance between the formation of policy and its presentation. "In my heretical view," he wrote in September 1971, "we are *never, never* going to [break out of our minority base] with public relations. . . . We need to do it with issues and budget dollars, and we are not."[13]

The administration thus seemed especially ready to take advantage of any political opportunity because there was so much interest in electoral politics. In October 1970, Elizabeth Drew reported that in the Nixon administration, "more than in any other within memory, policy and politics intermix." "Members of Congress," she wrote, "say that a briefing by Mr. Nixon on some subject is invariably followed by a presidential expatiation which begins: 'Now let me talk about the politics of this thing; how it will turn out in October and November; how it will translate into votes.' "[14] In principle, an acute political sensitivity was an asset in the search for a new majority. In practice, it was not necessarily so helpful. First, Nixon could be wrong about the electoral implications of policies. Second, as Buchanan noted, this focus—even if insightful—might be unproductive if it distracted the administration's attention from the production of effective policy. Votes could be won on the basis of a successful record.

MIDDLE AMERICA

National attention to the problems of the forgotten Americans did not disappear after 1968. Indeed, it grew. In the words of historian Herbert Parmet, these problems constituted "the social story preoccupying America." They demanded attention. One journalist wrote, "I find the bitterness of these whites so deep, so widespread that I whistle in relief that they are not organized for action." No longer forgotten, the members of this group were described as the "troubled Americans" in a special issue of *Newsweek* devoted to the topic. But they became most familiar as the "middle Americans." One indication of their prominence was *Time* magazine's announcement at the end of 1969 that middle Americans were the "man and woman of the year," a decision that annoyed Nixon, despite his interest in middle America. He thought that he deserved *Time*'s honor.[15]

The definition of "middle America" usually lacked precision. According to political scientist William Hixson, it was "an aggregate which at its widest included all those whites who were neither affluent nor poor: its center appeared to lie somewhere between the upper ranks of blue-collar workers and the lower ranks of white-collar workers and the self-employed."[16] The concept therefore represented a large and diverse group. Over time, the Nixon administration identified different (usually overlapping) pieces of middle America with different specific concerns, including Catholics, Americans of ethnic minorities (especially such groups as Italian, Irish, and Polish Americans), blue-collar workers, labor families, and the white South. These groups shared a long-standing adherence to the Democratic Party. From an electoral perspective, the debate about middle America presented an especially intriguing prospect for Republicans. Since Franklin Roosevelt, the group had been at the heart of the Democratic coalition. If Democrats lost much of middle America without developing large new sections of support, they would lose their national majority.

The debate about middle America was fraught with complexity. Observers disagreed about the nature of its concerns. Some analysts identified the problem as essentially economic: while these Americans were not poor, their share of the nation's affluence was small. At a time when the median family income was $7,974 each year, the Labor Department estimated that a city-dwelling family needed $9,076 each year for a "moderate" standard of living. Moreover, wages for workers did not always rise in line with usual expectations. For example, the average weekly wage for factory hands and clerks actually fell slightly in real terms between 1965 and 1970. Not poverty, then, but a lack of affluence fueled discontent. Exacerbating this economic discontent in many cases was an array of workplace concerns, including the mundane nature of many blue-collar and lower-white-collar jobs and the limited prospects for promotion within many sectors.[17]

Not all analysts of middle America agreed with this diagnosis, pointing out that the nation remained prosperous and was even becoming increasingly so and that this group shared in this prosperity. Arguably of greater relevance was a racial dimension of economic change. During the 1960s, African Americans made significant economic gains, even if their prosperity still did not match that of whites overall. Between 1963 and 1969, the median income of African Americans rose by 30 percent, twice the rate of increase for whites. By the end of the 1960s, the income of working African American women reached 90 percent of that of white women. Nevertheless, African American unemployment remained twice that of whites.[18] According to this perspective, the economic unease was not absolute but relative, generated by the sense that African Americans were advancing faster than whites were.

A related argument emphasized middle-American dissatisfaction with the forms of government activism during the 1960s. A widespread impression persisted that the federal government was paying too much attention to the problems of minorities and too little to those of middle Americans. This average American was "mad as hell," according to Saul Alinsky, a working-class activist. "He is almost out of his mind with frustration—call it hate," Alinsky said. "He sees his Government, with programs for blacks and for the indigent and with programs for everyone except him, and he figures, 'Goddamit, I'm paying for this out of my pocket.'"[19]

Other analysts saw a more raw form of racial prejudice, not necessarily connected with economic insecurity, as important in understanding the tensions of middle America. The tide of desegregation meant that, according to one journalist, "[t]o greater or lesser degree, the black man turns up threat-eningly in the private nightmares of white Middle Americans . . . competing for jobs, taking over neighborhoods, and schools[,] and adding to tax bur-dens." George Wallace's 1968 success outside as well as within the South sup-ported this emphasis on race. By contrast, academic Robert Coles, who was undertaking an extensive study of middle America, found a remarkable ab-sence of racism per se: "The longer I do my work, the less convinced I am that prejudice—as a psychological phenomenon—is the decisive issue confronting our cities," he commented.[20]

In the eyes of still others, the woes of middle America were both greater and less tangible, an accumulation of malaise at the end of a perplexing decade. Bill Moyers, a former aide to Lyndon Johnson, traveled around the country in 1970 to assess the national mood. "People are more anxious and bewildered than alarmed," he concluded. "They don't know what to make of it all: of long hair and endless war, of their children deserting the country, of congestion on their highways and overflowing crowds in the national parks; of art that does not uplift and movies that do not reach conclusions; of politicians who come and go while problems plague and persist; of being lonely surrounded by people, and bored with so many possessions; of the failure of organizations to keep their air breathable, the water drinkable, and man peaceable; of being poor." Anxieties, if vague overall, took on specific forms. If people did not know what to make of change within American society, they nevertheless often wanted politicians to tackle particular problems, such as rising crime, the growing use of illegal drugs, and "permissive" content within contemporary examples of arts and entertainment.[21]

The problem of middle America was thus open to many different interpre-tations. In his capacity as president, Nixon's evaluation of middle-American needs was especially relevant and would become the key to expanding his constituency and hence to a realignment. But despite the attention devoted to forgotten Americans in the election year of 1968, in 1969 the attention paid to the idea at the White House was at first lackluster. A magazine article kindled the debate within the administration. Written by journalist Pete Hamill and published in *New York* magazine, the piece offered one of the most impas-sioned descriptions of middle-American problems and also one of the most alarming. Blue-collar New Yorkers, Hamill wrote, were "on the edge of open, sustained and possibly violent revolt." Financially, they were not poor enough to benefit from the welfare system, but they were not wealthy enough to enjoy a comfortable existence. According to Hamill, they felt neglected by politicians. These people were accumulating large grievances toward the black community, the needs of which politicians apparently addressed. The sharp edge of this putative revolt was racial conflict, but its substance encompassed other economic and social problems. "The working-class white man," wrote Hamill, "is actually in revolt against taxes, joyless work, the double standards and short memories of professional politicians, hypocrisy and what he considers the debasement of the American dream."[22]

Some five months after the inauguration, Hamill's article powerfully reminded the president of middle America's problems. Nixon circulated the article widely within the administration, asking for comments. His request uncovered an array of opinion, mirroring the disagreements within the wider debate about middle America. Despite disagreements, most respondents, like Hamill, explained the phenomenon through some formula of economic needs combined with racial resentments.[23]

The purview of the Labor Department, where George Shultz was secretary, gave it a special role in Nixon's desire to investigate middle America. Shultz had expertise in the field, having conducted academic work on blue-collar issues. When Shultz received a copy of Hamill's article and a request for comments, such matters were already the object of analysis within the department, the responsibility of Jerome Rosow, assistant secretary for policy, evaluation, and research. Shultz identified the crisis as an interaction of economic and racial factors. The income of less affluent whites did not match that of their aspirations; he agreed that this sense of relative deprivation lay behind some racial animosity. "The other side of the coin," he wrote, "is the emotional and social hostility of working class whites towards minorities, and especially the blacks."[24]

As Rosow pointed out, these resentments concealed the existence of much common ground between poorer whites and many blacks. While the average black family remained poorer than its white counterpart, about a third of black families fell into the economic category (an annual income of between $5,000 and $10,000) that was Rosow's definition of troubled Americans. According to analysis by the Department of Labor, they shared not only similar socioeconomic problems but also similar concerns about attacks on traditional values and about rising crime.[25]

When he received a copy of Hamill's article and read about the discontents of blue-collar New Yorkers, Winton Blount, the postmaster general, thought of his fellow Alabamian, George Wallace. The economic, social, and racial resentments cataloged by Hamill were food for Wallaceite success. While spokespeople for the administration should not emulate Wallace's politics, Blount wrote, the administration needed to find ways to undermine the causes of resentment. Tom Charles Huston, a conservative member of the White House speechwriting staff, noted similarly that Republicans should "develop a rhetoric which communicates concern for the legitimate claims of this class, yet avoids any incitement to the baser instincts of man afraid."[26]

Nixon did not need to be reminded of the potential threat posed by Wallace. Vague about his future intentions, Wallace declared them contingent on the administration's performance, especially with respect to the South. The continuation of his political ambitions was made clear by the ongoing publication of the Wallace newsletter from a campaign headquarters with the postal address P.O. Box 1972. In response to the Nixon administration's early activity, Wallace espoused policies not substantially different from his campaign rhetoric of 1968. He spoke about an array of issues, including the need for tax reform, demands for tough law-and-order policies, and the restoration of local authority over local matters.[27] Race remained the often unspoken but always essential theme of his politics.

THE EMERGING REPUBLICAN MAJORITY

While administration aides tackled the problem of middle America in private, one of them was about to launch a public investigation of the same question. His argument was controversial. As speechwriter William Safire warned Ehrlichman in July 1969, a "most dangerous" book was about to be published: *The Emerging Republican Majority* by Kevin P. Phillips, who was a special assistant to Mitchell. It was a revision of the manuscript that had won Phillips his job as an aide during the presidential campaign. Safire was concerned that the book's thesis would alienate moderate support for the administration because Phillips insisted that the administration must appeal to conservative and southern constituencies.[28] At stake, according to Phillips, was an electoral majority for a generation.

For Phillips, the crucial voters for the Republican Party were those who had supported Wallace in 1968. Phillips shared Mitchell's idea that the Wallace vote was a "way station" for voters who would become Republicans. In this view, the new majority consisted of all the voters who had not voted for Hubert Humphrey in 1968. The mobilization of the majority depended on fashioning an appeal to convert the Wallace supporters without losing any significant piece of the existing Republican base. Phillips described the target constituency on another occasion as "the great, ordinary, Lawrence Welkish mass of Americans from Maine to Hawaii."[29] Republicans needed neither the votes of black Americans nor those of liberal northeasterners.

To support his argument, Phillips offered a demographic analysis across history, using an encyclopedic collection of statistics about electoral trends. Ethnicity offered important insights into the voting behavior of Americans, he believed. He suggested that the "emerging majority" was a conservative and populist movement, firmly established in suburbia, in the South, and in what he called the Sun Belt area of the Southwest. According to Phillips, convulsive shocks to the political status quo dependably originated in the South and West on the basis of frustrations with the exclusive politics of an eastern elite. Unlike previous eras of upheaval, however, the new momentum for change was finding its vehicle in the traditional party of economic conservatism—indeed, in that of the economic elite—the Republicans. Phillips saw the political revolt in the late 1960s and early 1970s as directed against the values of a liberal establishment, which he described as "a toryhood of change, people who make their money out of plans, ideas, communication, social upheaval, happenings, excitement." To take advantage of their opportunity, the Republican Party needed to overcome its economic elitism as well as speak out against this new liberal elitism.[30]

The concept of electoral realignment, developed within political science, informed Phillips's work. The book securely placed the idea into popular debate about politics. As interpreted by Phillips, the occurrence of realigning elections and the progression of electoral cycles was precise and rather mechanical. In American political history, he saw a pattern of electoral eras lasting between thirty-two and thirty-six years, during which time one party dominated the presidency with usually one interruption. The last era had been Democratic, beginning with the election of Franklin Roosevelt in 1932 and interrupted by the electoral success of Dwight Eisenhower. By 1968, change was due. "The Nixon administration," he wrote, "seems destined by precedent to be the beginning of a new Republican era."[31]

Because Phillips was a member of the administration, his book generally overlooked the theory's implications for policy making. But he made it clear

enough that he thought the Great Society was the product of a liberal Democratic elite and that, among other developments of the 1960s, some of its
elements had alienated many Democrats who were now potential converts to
the Republicans. "The emerging Republican majority spoke clearly in 1968," he
wrote, "for a shift away from the sociological jurisprudence, moral permissiveness, experimental residential, welfare and educational programming and
massive federal spending by which the Liberal (mostly Democratic) Establishment sought to propagate liberal institutions and ideology—and all the while
reap growing economic benefits."[32]

Less clear were the limits to the conservatism of the "emerging majority." In
fact, Phillips's vision for the Republican Party demanded acceptance of some
important Democratic achievements. His opposition to 1960s liberalism was
selective, as he noted after reading a review of his book that understandably
had missed the point. "For 'Great Society,' read social engineering, *not* medicare, social security or aid to education," he wrote in the margin of the article.
What the administration needed, he thought was "[j]ust populist economics,"
he thought. He made the point more clear when he wrote the preface for
the paperback edition of the book. Phillips emphasized that the areas of the
"emerging majority" were not "reactionary" but had "been the seat of every
popular, progressive upheaval in American politics—Jefferson, Jackson, Bryant
[*sic*], Roosevelt."[33]

Race was a significant part of the theory. Phillips believed in the electoral
strength of "ethnic polarization," where group differences motivated political
conflict. In this period, the greatest example of this polarization was the white
response to African American civil rights advances. He felt that essential to the
mobilization of the Republican majority was the Democratic association with
the concerns of black Americans.[34]

The idea that Nixon should use racial conflict as the route to electoral
victory was profoundly disturbing. This dimension of the argument overwhelmed others, such as the need for the Republican Party to embrace "populism" and to shed its reputation for economic elitism. Rogers Morton, the
party's national chair, identified the book as a "southern strategy" and then
dismissed its importance as the work of a "clerk" whose ideas could not
possibly change the nation's political profile. William F. McLaughlin, the chair
of the Michigan state party, responded with alarm, connecting the Phillips
thesis with administration policy. "I can't believe we are going the route of the
Southern strategy," he wrote in an impassioned letter to Elly Peterson, assistant

chair of the Republican National Committee. "It killed us in 1964. It will ruin us in 1970. It will destroy us in 1972." In the words of William Saxbe, a senator from Ohio, the thesis was "a ticket on the Titanic." By contrast, William Rusher, the *National Review* publisher, enthusiastically supported Phillips. The book, Rusher wrote, "will do for conservative Republicanism what 'Uncle Tom's Cabin' did for the cause of abolitionism."[35]

The controversial nature of the book ensured that Nixon denied publicly that he had read it, as did Mitchell. To some aides, such denials were not enough; Safire and Peter Flanigan objected to Phillips's presence in the administration. But for the moment, Phillips remained in the Justice Department. Nixon was very interested in Phillips's interpretation of Republican fortunes in different parts of the country and in his ideas about the Republican future, although his was just one voice within a much larger internal debate.[36]

VIETNAM, CRIME, AND RACE

Phillips's book further fostered the debate about the political implications of middle-American problems. Regardless of that debate, it was clear to Nixon that he should move quickly to tackle the issues at the center of national debate during 1968—the problems of war, law and order, and racial desegregation. At the top of the agenda was the war. The guiding theme was Nixon's often-declared devotion to "peace with honor." He aimed to end the war but to do so without a communist victory and without damage to the global reputation of America's strength. Nixon remained intrigued by the possibility that the United States might yet deploy its massive military capability unequivocally to defeat the North Vietnamese, but his policy emphasized "Vietnamization," a concept inherited from the Johnson administration. Its design was a carefully planned American withdrawal, leaving a South Vietnamese army able to defend the Thieu regime from southern insurgents and from the north. In public, Nixon maintained this policy through draft-reform proposals, through reductions in the numbers of U.S. troops committed to the conflict, and through appeals for popular support of "peace with honor." In private, complicated and difficult peace negotiations continued.[37]

By ending the war, Nixon would encourage the return of domestic tranquillity. But the nation's preoccupation with law and order extended far beyond the relatively few examples of violent unrest associated with antiwar protest. In his campaign for the presidency, Nixon had promised to tackle crime and now needed to do so. In the early months of the administration, the political analyst Richard Scammon even suggested that a victory for Wallace was possible in 1972 if Nixon failed to address adequately the national concerns about law and order.[38] Scammon probably exaggerated the threat, but action was clearly necessary.

There was thus a determination to reduce crime. Attorney General Mitchell ushered in a new philosophy about law and order, rejecting his Democratic predecessors' emphasis on the social context of crime. He remarked that the Justice Department was "a law-enforcement agency [and] not a place to carry on a program aimed at curing the ills of society." The problem was how to implement this approach, particularly because crime was a matter under local and state rather than federal authority. Law enforcement in the District of Columbia, for which the federal government did have responsibility, offered one opportunity to make good on campaign pledges. Egil "Bud" Krogh Jr., who ran the administration's liaison with the district, later told of an early presidential meeting. "Alright, Bud, I'd like you to stop crime in the District of Columbia," said Nixon. Krogh agreed to do so and then called Walter Washington, the district's mayor, with the same instruction.[39]

More substantial measures followed. In July, Mitchell proposed a package of measures for the District of Columbia, including provisions for "no knock" searches and, most controversially, preventative detention—allowing the imprisonment of suspects for sixty days without bail if a court determined that they were likely to commit other crimes. Krogh later straightforwardly described these measures as "political," designed to display "a tough law and order demeanor by the Administration" despite their limited practical impact. Beyond the rhetoric, Mitchell's measures for the rest of the nation included the announcement of the increased use of wiretapping and the launch of a concerted campaign against organized crime.[40]

Nixon's arrival in the White House took place at a crucial moment in race relations. After years of widespread southern resistance to school desegregation, as required by the 1954 *Brown v. Board of Education* decision, the Supreme Court had grown impatient with tactics of delay. In 1968, the decision in the case *Green v. County School Board of New Kent County* signaled this impatience. "The burden on a school board today," the decision read, "is to come forward with a plan that promises realistically to work, and promises realistically to work *now*." It was, moreover, a promising time for the implementation of desegregation, because increasing numbers of southerners were ready to accept it, even if they remained wary of affirmative methods such as busing.[41]

The administration could not resist the momentum of desegregation, but Nixon chose an approach of minimal compliance with court orders.[42] As far as possible, the administration disassociated itself from their implementation, hoping to defuse the political salience of the issue. Much of the responsibility for executive enforcement of judicially required desegregation moved from HEW's Civil Rights Office to the Justice Department. Officials at HEW had sought desegregation by threatening to cut off federal funds to recalcitrant school districts, a practice that often created animosity in the South.

An emphasis on judicial means for demanding compliance was intended to identify the courts and not the White House as responsible for the policy. The administration found an opportunity to demonstrate its new emphasis by supporting an appeal in 1969 by a number of Mississippi school districts for still more time to implement desegregation. It was the first occasion on which the federal government took the opposite side from the National Association for the Advancement of Colored People's Legal Defense and Educational Fund in such a suit. In *Alexander v. Holmes County Board of Education*, the federal executive and the Mississippi districts lost; the force of the courts was now firmly behind immediate desegregation, over the Nixon administration's objections. Harry Dent, who had worked for Strom Thurmond before joining the White House as an aide with special responsibility for the cultivation of the South, later noted that in the aftermath of *Alexander*, the "southern reaction was one of placing the blame on the court and recognizing that Nixon had tried to be helpful."[43]

Furthermore, Nixon established a cabinet subcommittee on desegregation under Shultz (but nominally chaired by the vice president) with a mission to ensure the peaceful implementation of desegregation policies through cooperation with affected localities. The low-key approach to desegregation proved an effective route to compliance with court orders that avoided much race-related disturbance. But critics argued that this success came at the cost of a larger failure. Leon Panetta, the first head of HEW's Civil Rights Office under Nixon who was fired for disagreeing with the policy, charged that the administration's concern with electoral considerations led it to allow a loss of momentum in pursuit of equal education. While the policy could not satisfy segregationist Democrats, it offered a clear message: white southerners who viewed the onward progress of integration with alarm could see that this administration, unlike its predecessor, was ready to slow down that progress. As a demonstration of the policy's success, in January 1970 Dent sent to Nixon the results of a poll, conducted in a North Carolina congressional district, according to which 80 percent of respondents believed that desegregation was moving too fast but 81 percent approved of Nixon's performance as president.[44]

Few observers doubted that a desire to win votes in the South helped to shape the school desegregation policy, but in other areas of policy, the administration maintained the momentum of racial reform. Nixon's administration was responsible for implementing the first federal affirmative-action program based on quotas, the Philadelphia Plan. Although in his memoirs, Nixon claimed responsibility for the plan, it was developed and promoted by Shultz, the secretary of labor, building on a program initiated by the Johnson administration. The plan sought to promote integration in the construction industry's hiring practices by imposing quotas for minority workers employed by companies with federal contracts, an impressive civil rights innovation. To escape the 1964 Civil Rights Act's ban on racial quotas, the plan demanded that contractors choose targets for minority employment within a suggested range and explicitly did not give any one figure at which minority employment was required.[45]

Shultz promoted the plan for a wealth of reasons, but Nixon's acceptance of the Philadelphia Plan may have depended partly on a manipulative political calculation. Shultz pointed out that its implementation could encourage conflict between two groups essential to the Democratic coalition—African Americans and organized labor. Conflict among Democrats benefited the Republican cause. Many labor leaders were indeed dismayed at the administration's initiative and opposed its introduction. However, historian Dean Kotlowski has argued that policy considerations rather than electoral expediency explain Nixon's support for the plan. Regardless of his motivation, Nixon's commitment to this innovation of affirmative action was limited. In his study of the administration's policies on civil rights, Hugh Davis Graham found no evidence that Nixon paid close attention to the plan after December 1969. In January 1970, after reading an attack on the plan by George Meany, the leader of the American Federation of Labor and Congress of Industrial Organizations (AFL-CIO), Nixon signaled this lack of commitment. "[T]his hurts us," he thought, according to aide John Brown. "With our constituency we gained little on the play." Nevertheless, at the same time he endorsed the expansion of the plan to cover all employment generated by government contracts worth $50,000 or more.[46]

The Philadelphia Plan was not the sole administration initiative in the realm of racial policy. In 1969 the administration created the Office of Minority Business Enterprise to encourage small businesses run by African Americans and by members of other minorities, a program that would enjoy modest success. While these policies were important advances, most civil rights activists placed greater priority on a proposal with wider implications for equality in employment overall, the granting of stronger enforcement powers to the Equal Employment Opportunities Commission (EEOC). Although the administration favored increased EEOC authority, most congressional Democrats preferred a formula of much more sweeping powers. The resulting conflict within Congress between the two visions for expansion of the EEOC meant that no change occurred until 1972 and that the eventual increase in its powers was limited.[47]

In the longer term, the most consequential piece of Nixon's racial policy was the nomination of justices to the Supreme Court. Because of the Court's activism under Earl Warren, nominations were important to a host of sensitive policy areas, such as the rights of defendants, an individual's right to sexual privacy, and the separation between church and state. The Court's changing membership would determine whether these and other constitutional protections would be consolidated and even expanded. Nixon criticized many elements of the new judicial activism, and he was determined to replace outgoing justices with lawyers who had conservative interpretations of the Constitution.

Nixon was soon able to begin the reshaping of the Court, receiving two opportunities to nominate new members within his first year in office. Because of Warren's retirement, one vacant seat was that of the chief justice. Nixon looked for conservatives. To replace Warren, he successfully nominated Warren E. Burger, who met the philosophical requirement and who was young enough to serve for at least a decade. For his next nomination, Nixon wanted a conservative southerner and chose Clement Haynsworth. It was a controversial nomination and led to a confirmation battle of many months. Haynsworth's conservative views drew opposition among labor and civil rights groups and among congressional liberals, but his chances were fatally undermined by convincing allegations of a conflict of interest in his work as a judge.[48]

But the Senate's November 1969 defeat of the nomination did not deal much of a blow to the strategic achievement that the administration wanted. The hostile vote actually provided grounds for emphasizing White House support of the southern cause, in spite of "establishment" opposition. Haldeman noted that the administration "politically, probably came out ahead" and that the defeat made "all the points with the South." At a press briefing, Bryce Harlow described the Haynsworth defeat as "the majorest [*sic*] repulse the President had" but smiled while saying the words.[49] Nixon sometimes enjoyed making a point as much as changing policy.

Nixon wanted to emphasize the point still more. He said that he wanted to find "a good federal judge further south and further to the right."[50] G. Harrold Carswell filled the latter two criteria but not the first. A series of damaging revelations undermined his candidacy. As an aspiring local politician in Georgia during the 1940s, Carswell had spoken of his support for segregation and the notion of white supremacy. Carswell had not sufficiently distanced himself from this racist past; he belonged to a segregated country club in Florida and in 1966 had sold a plot of land under a racially restrictive covenant. Moreover, his judicial record was undistinguished. Senator Roman Hruska of Nebraska sought to answer this criticism but did so in way that strengthened the case of Carswell's opponents. "Even if he were mediocre, there are a lot of mediocre judges and people and lawyers," he said. "They are entitled to a little representation, aren't they, and a little chance?" With friends like Hruska, Carswell's cause was doomed.

The nomination was defeated in April 1970. Again, Nixon looked for a victory in defeat. He claimed that the reasons for the rejection of both Haynsworth and Carswell were their conservative judicial views and their southern origins. Otherwise, the "vicious assaults" on them amounted to "hypocrisy," he said.[51] After Carswell, Nixon successfully nominated Harry Blackmun, whose record would reveal the limitations of presidential influence on the Court. Seen as Burger's ideological as well as geographical "twin" (both were Minnesotans), Blackmun instead played an important role as a liberal justice through the 1970s and 1980s.

By emphasizing symbolism over substance, Nixon endeavored to salvage victory from defeat. The politics of symbolism constituted more generally a significant strand of the administration's effort to find a majority. Nixon tried to demonstrate that he felt an affinity with middle Americans and with white southerners. Aides devoted some energy and imagination to creating such an image for the administration, shedding the Republican reputation for out-of-touch elitism. One example is an initiative by Charles Colson shortly after he joined the White House in the fall of 1969. Colson suggested the release of photographs showing Nixon in the bowling alleys of the Executive Office Building. "President Nixon has done for bowling what President Eisenhower did for golf," he wrote. The White House publicized Nixon's enthusiasm for sports, particularly football, in the belief that it appealed to middle America. When the president attended a University of Texas–University of Arkansas football game, Dent wryly observed that commentators would describe the event as an element of "southern strategy."[52] In fact, Nixon's presence was exactly that—the soft side of a strategy to cultivate the South as well as middle America more generally.

REFORM

With few exceptions, Nixon ran his policies on Vietnam, civil rights, and crimes in ways that met contemporary expectations of a Republican president. But he also initiated a range of domestic policies that, rather like the Phila-delphia Plan, confounded those expectations. "I was determined to be an activist President in domestic affairs," he wrote in his memoirs. That determi-nation reflected Nixon's understanding of electoral realities. Throughout his career, a majority of American voters generally preferred the Democratic ap-proach to the domestic problems of the day rather than that of the Republi-cans, an approach that embraced rather than questioned the need for govern-ment activism. Nixon arrived in the White House at a time when mainstream political debate remained dominated by activist and not conservative pro-posals. The zenith of liberal impetus—enshrined in the Great Society—had passed, and, as the 1968 election demonstrated, the Democratic coalition was subject to severe tensions. But many Americans still had activist expectations of their government. As Leonard Garment would note in 1971, in spite of their "conservative philosophy," Americans wanted " 'liberal' benefits—complete health care, more social security, etc."[53]

Nixon reacted to the public desire for government activism in an idiosyn-cratic way. His inaugural address signaled his search for a new approach in place of Great Society liberalism. On the one hand, he endorsed the goals of liberals: "In pursuing the goals of full employment, better housing, excellence in education; in rebuilding our cities and improving our rural areas; in pro-tecting our environment, enhancing the quality of life—in all these and more, we will and must press urgently forward," he said. On the other hand, he sounded a traditionally Republican note of distrust toward the role of government: "[W]e are approaching the limits of what government alone can do," he warned. The speech did not resolve the tension between these domestic priorities except by referring to a rather vague formula of increased reliance on individual voluntarism in tackling problems.[54]

But a return to voluntarism was not a practical response to the need for the reform of government structures while meeting varied expectations of government activism. "Early in the Administration," Daniel Patrick Moynihan later confirmed, "there was considerable talk about 'voluntarism,' but little real belief." It took time for the administration to create a program of Nixonian reform. After extensive internal debate, Nixon announced his first major proposals in August 1969. They were the Family Assistance Plan (FAP), which was an initiative of welfare reform, and revenue sharing, which aimed to move control over spending in certain areas from the federal government to state and local governments. Together, these plans represented the "New Federalism." According to the *New York Times*, they constituted "a baffling blend of Republicanism and radicalism."[55]

The New Federalism synthesized Nixon's desire for activism and his antigovernment impulse, seeking to discover the right level of government at which responsibility for policy implementation should be placed. Thanks to revenue sharing, most changes would cut away the role of the federal government; FAP, however, would centralize welfare policy under federal jurisdiction. "In a word," noted historian Joan Hoff, "under his New Federalism Nixon addressed national problems by spending more and by redistributing power away from Congress and the federal bureaucracy, toward local, state, and presidential centers of control."[56]

In the short run, FAP took priority over revenue sharing as the pioneering piece of the New Federalism. The plan was designed to reform the welfare system and thereby eliminate the "welfare crisis" about which Nixon had talked in 1968. In effect, FAP offered an annual guaranteed income of $1,600 to a family of four, creating national standards for welfare. FAP would thereby spend more money, not less, than existing programs, adding an estimated $4.4 billion to the welfare budget for fiscal year 1971.

In successfully championing FAP, Moynihan overcame conservative objections within the administration. He did so by persuading Nixon of the plan's attractions, including its imposition of work requirements on welfare recipients, its financial aid to the working poor, and its hostility to the existing welfare bureaucracy. Moynihan also responded to Nixon's desire for domestic activism by presenting FAP as possessing a compelling potential to establish his reputation as a bold reformer. Moynihan drew a parallel with nineteenth-century British prime minister Benjamin Disraeli, a conservative politician responsible for lasting liberal achievement. Nixon could become the American Disraeli.[57]

As an American Disraeli, Nixon could unlock the support of a majority within the electorate, Moynihan argued. In answer to Hamill's *New York* article, Moynihan suggested that welfare reform, revenue sharing, and other initiatives would meaningfully address the concerns of these lower-middle-class whites. "Taken together," Moynihan argued, "these measures have the making of a social revolution which preserves the fabric of American society, rather than tearing it to shreds. At long last the people-in-between would begin benefitting from the efforts of the government to redress the long standing and fully documented grievances of the people at the bottom." Moynihan made the point still more explicit in June 1969 after a meeting with a group of businesspeople discussing a forerunner to FAP, the Family Security System. He notified Nixon that Arjay Miller of the Ford Motor Company had responded to the idea of welfare reform by saying, "[I]f you can (1) get out of Vietnam, and (2) put through a Family Security System, the Republicans will become the majority party in the United States."[58]

FAP possessed great promise and appeal and met with an overwhelmingly positive reaction when Nixon announced the plan: polls reported that almost two-thirds of the public responded favorably. But FAP, in common with later reform initiatives, faced a series of threats. Nixon lacked the necessary political skills to ensure that he was bold in domestic deed as well as word. The first problem was his relative lack of interest in the area. Nixon enjoyed the formulation of foreign policy but not, in general, that of domestic policy. Joseph Sisco, a State Department official, for example, noticed the president's "monumental disinterest in domestic policies." Nevertheless, there was an important exception, as Ehrlichman later pointed out. If Nixon decided that a particular piece of domestic policy possessed some special electoral importance, he escalated his attention. Nixon was often disinterested in domestic policy but was usually fascinated by the idea of a new majority.[59] If he became convinced of FAP's electoral as well as substantive importance, the chances of welfare reform were greater.

But still more obstacles lay in the way of the achievement of any ambition for reform. Contrary to the president's expectations, little money was available for new programs. As the nation scaled back its military presence in Vietnam, the demands of the defense budget declined. At the same time, however, the cost of other government commitments was rising. "I'm afraid the peace dividend tends to become evanescent," remarked Moynihan in August 1969 at the president's Western White House in California, "like the morning clouds around San Clemente." In fact, far from encountering an opportunity to increase domestic spending to any significant extent, Nixon was increasingly forced to contemplate ways to control its rise so that spending did not outstrip revenues.[60] He was willing to see more money spent on welfare, but he could not countenance much more generosity even in pursuit of a reputation for reform.

Just as seriously, it was by no means clear that Congress contained a majority in favor of Nixonian reforms. His natural supporters there—congressional Republicans—were among the least likely to vote in favor of new social initiatives. The bloc of liberal and moderate Republicans was relatively weak. In any case, Nixon's party was in the minority. It was essential to enlist the support of congressional Democrats, but they owed no partisan loyalty to Nixon and usually did not share the conviction that liberal commitment should be tempered by conservative caution. Moreover, other, more conservative elements of Nixon's policies—including those on race and on foreign policy—were even less attractive to mainstream Democrats and had alienated many liberal Republicans.[61] A talent for careful congressional liaison was therefore essential to achieve the goal of welfare reform. As a whole, however, the administration lacked this talent.

Despite Moynihan's enterprising advocacy of FAP as appealing to a new majority, the argument was not robust, and Moynihan knew it.[62] At best, FAP tackled problems of concern but not of direct relevance to potential Nixon voters. The area of that concern was the perceived welfare crisis and an impatience with the apparently undeserving welfare recipients described by Hamill and others. The direct beneficiaries of FAP were the poor, most unlikely to support Nixon.

A further political problem of FAP was its impact on the South. Although the administration assiduously cultivated whites in the South through the Court nominations and the school desegregation policy, southern politicians were natural opponents of FAP. The impact of national levels of welfare payment, to be imposed by the program, would be greatest on the South, where payments were currently the lowest. Southerners expressed concern that FAP would disrupt the region's low-wage economy, on which agriculture and key industries depended.[63] Altogether, reformism therefore stood on shaky foundations from the start.

More generally, some of Nixon's critics have cast doubt on his responsibility, as opposed to that of Congress, for reform initiatives. For example, historian Arthur M. Schlesinger Jr. later pointed out that "the liberal tide was still running strong" when Nixon became president. "Not a man of profound convictions," Schlesinger observed, Nixon "rolled with the punches and went along with a reform-minded Congress." Such criticism fails to recognize the thirst for creative innovation represented by the New Federalism. But this criticism does come close to capturing the nature of the administration's reformism in some areas. One example is environmental policy. Nixon viewed it with a notable lack of enthusiasm but also with a sense of its growing importance to the electorate. Much of the impetus for new legislation lay with members of Congress, notably Senators Henry "Scoop" Jackson of Washington and Edmund Muskie of Maine. Nevertheless, the White House's contribution was significant even if reactive. The administration's concern with the creation of effective governmental structures led to the 1970 establishment of the Environmental Protection Agency, with overall responsibility for the area.[64]

In formulating economic policy, Nixon was anxious to avoid sacrificing political advantage for adherence to Republican notions of fiscal conservatism. He often blamed his defeat in the 1960 presidential election on an economic downturn and on the Eisenhower administration's conservative response to the difficulties. Nixon was determined not to make a similar mistake. In the early months of his administration, he emphasized the point to White House visitors—he was concerned about the threat of recession and hence unemployment as much as about the threat of inflation. He even reportedly commented on one occasion "that if he were to allow a serious recession it would be the end of the Republican party."[65]

The trouble was how to translate this electoral concern into economic policy. Nixon began his term as president with little confidence in his command of economics, leaving him, as historian Allen Matusow noted, "a nervous spectator" in policy making. Haldeman suspected that Nixon never fully gained this confidence.[66] Inflation, which had run at 4 percent in 1968, was the principal problem, while unemployment remained low. The administration developed a policy of "gradualism" to cut inflation while avoiding Nixon's bugbear of a recession or of politically painful levels of unemployment. Unlike its Democratic predecessors, the Nixon administration adopted a greater emphasis on monetary policy—involving the control of money supply—while continuing to view fiscal policy as significant.

Questions of taxation demonstrated Nixon's desire to cultivate a new constituency and his willingness in so doing to downplay the demands of more traditional Republican supporters. The issue of tax reform arrived unexpectedly in January 1969, when, in congressional testimony, Joseph Barr, the outgoing secretary of the treasury, predicted "a taxpayer revolt" among middle-income Americans on the grounds of the system's unfairness. Thanks to loopholes, those with high incomes often paid relatively little tax. Liberals in Congress took up the issue.[67]

Nixon needed to respond to the concern to secure congressional support for a tax package. He had already sponsored the repeal of an investment tax credit, despite its attractiveness to his business constituency, in search of votes as well as of revenues for programmatic innovation. By contrast, he was not ready to contemplate reducing tax relief on mortgage payments. Despite personal skepticism about the effectiveness of such moves, he then endorsed measures to close some of the loopholes. Nixon also proposed a low-income allowance that would exempt 5 million poor families and individuals from paying any tax. Congress completely transformed the bill; to Nixon's concern, it offered new breaks from taxation that used up the revenues created by the bill's extension of a tax surcharge. In reviewing its contents in December 1969, Nixon particularly sought benefits for middle Americans, but the bill lacked any help for those "in the middle." "We have to do something for *them*," he told his economic advisers. "I'm for helping the poor but we must be political—must speak to our constituency." He signed the bill only with reluctance.[68]

THE SILENT MAJORITY

During 1969, the lines of the administration's approach to policy making became more clear. The Nixon White House was adopting a blend of conservatism and reform-minded activism, an apparently paradoxical mixture that nevertheless seemed to make sense in light of a desire to mobilize a new majority. This was the finding of journalist Robert Semple, for example, when he investigated differences between White House advocates of conservatism and reformism. "They liken themselves—and the President—to the motorist who may zig from left to right but stays on the same road," Semple wrote. "In their view, this is the road of 'pragmatic' and 'flexible' moderation, leading, they hope, toward a new Republican majority." Another journalist observed that some people in Washington saw the administration's "highest priority" as being to nurture "this historic realignment of forces."[69]

But if the administration's approach to politics was sophisticated, wise, and sensitive to electoral trends, these qualities sometimes escaped Nixon. When in the fall of 1969 he saw the special issue of *Newsweek* devoted to troubled Americans, Nixon was worried. He thought that the administration was failing to tackle their concerns and complained to aides that it was neglecting this American majority.[70] In fact, he was about to uncover a strong manifestation of support for his policies, and this event would help him to identify in detail a majority that he could then consolidate. The reason for this discovery was his anxiety to retain adequate public backing for his Vietnam policy.

Public opinion was a cause for concern because it had become increasingly impatient with Vietnamization. Dissent found voice in Congress. Antiwar sentiment grew there not only among Democrats, who no longer owed partisan loyalty to the commander in chief, but also among some Republicans. In September 1969, Charles Goodell, the junior Republican senator from New York, announced his intention to introduce a disengagement bill that threatened to cut off congressional funding for the war unless Nixon brought all troops home. Other senators followed Goodell's lead in articulating disillusionment with the war.[71]

Vietnamization only briefly mollified the antiwar movement. Once it was clear that Nixon's policy involved a gradual approach to ending the war, the movement regrouped and sought to broaden its base of support. In an attempt to illustrate the growing war-weariness of ordinary Americans, antiwar organizer Sam Brown devised the "moratorium" demonstrations, moving protest from campuses to the nation's communities and emphasizing peaceful, mainstream demands for peace rather than the violent outrage of fringe groups. A national demonstration would take place each month until the war's end. The first took place on October 15 and won widespread observance. In the words of historian Charles DeBenedetti, the demonstration achieved "a diversity, pervasiveness, and dignity unprecedented in the history of popular protest."[72]

Nixon needed to check the growth of antiwar sentiment, which he believed jeopardized his Vietnam policy because threats to unleash new offensives against the enemy lacked credibility if domestic public opinion became a powerful obstacle to escalation. If Nixon failed to conduct the war in a manner acceptable to most Americans, his political future came into severe doubt. In seeking support for his Vietnam policy, Nixon confronted a paradox in the way many Americans viewed the war. On the one hand, there was no question that most saw the war as a mistake. By the fall of 1969, only 32 percent of respondents told pollsters that the United States had not made a mistake in sending soldiers to Vietnam. On the other hand, a majority remained unwilling to countenance an American withdrawal without the achievement of war aims; immediate withdrawal had the support of 36 percent, according to a September 1969 poll. A commander of an American Legion post in Richmond, Indiana, explained in 1970 to a journalist the paradox of his own view about the war. "We have this undesirable thing in Vietnam. Should never have been there in the first place," he said. "But if only the force of arms can stop Communism, we have to use force of arms. You can't back down or they'll take more and more."[73]

On seven occasions between 1969 and 1971, Nixon appeared on television in attempts to maintain support for his policy. The most significant took place on November 3, 1969, when he delivered a patriotic appeal to the American people, "To the Great Silent Majority," in which the president argued forcefully in favor of his policy of gradualism in Southeast Asia, attempting to undercut congressional opposition and to diminish the moratorium movement's popularity. Nixon linked the appeal with that of the 1968 "New Alignment" speech. "You will note that I picked up this theme [of the 'silent Americans'] and used it in my November 3rd speech—the silent majority," he wrote to Haldeman.[74]

The idea of the silent majority proved to have a powerful impact. Nixon's speech helped to sap the effectiveness of the moratorium movement, reducing the extent of its support and ensuring the quick demise of its plans for monthly demonstrations against the war. The speech also briefly took away the antiwar bloc's momentum within Congress. Most significantly, the speech isolated a group of Americans potentially sympathetic to the Nixon administration and did so vividly and inescapably. This was how Nixon fully woke up to the electoral promise of middle America: he would not forget this show of support. In conversation just over three years later, Nixon and Buchanan agreed "that November 3, 1969[,] was probably the critical turning point in the election of 1972—and Nixon Presidency."[75]

The patriotic emphasis of Nixon's internationalism, stated with such clarity in this speech, represented a strong rallying point. In a sociological study of an ethnic community in Brooklyn, Jonathan Rieder discovered the importance of a patriotic justification for foreign policy among Italian American workers—key members of middle America—especially in opposition to demonstrators. "We're Americans, and if being in Vietnam is what we were supposed to do, then you should do it and support the country," one told Rieder. "Those protesters shouldn't have been allowed to do what they were doing." Vietnam was a war in which a disproportionate number of American soldiers had blue-collar backgrounds. Although workers were, in fact, somewhat more dovish overall than middle-class Americans, their opposition to protesters was stronger.[76]

The "silent majority" speech both managed to provide Nixon with an extension of general public support for his foreign policy and seemed to isolate a coherent group that sympathized with the administration's politics. In the long as well as short term, public reaction to the speech was positive. White House polls revealed repeatedly that many Americans considered themselves members of the silent majority, who mostly supported Nixon's policies. Three-quarters of voters identified with the silent majority, and about 70 percent of that number generally supported the administration. These figures remained more or less constant in the twelve months between the speech and the midterm elections.[77]

Nixon was anxious to consolidate his apparently high levels of support among the silent majority. Polls suggested that majorities among all ethnic, regional, and age groups identified with the silent majority. According to an administration plan, the president wanted to encourage this silent majority to remain supportive of his Vietnam policy and increasingly "to orient the Silent Majority toward issues other than foreign policy (e.g.: inflation, crime, law and order, etc.) and then to increase public support for the President's foreign and domestic proposals."[78] The midterm campaign would offer Nixon the first major opportunity to reap electoral benefit from this support.

The loyalty of the silent majority did not depend only on Nixon's insistence on the patriotic nature of his policies in Vietnam. Nixon also needed to demonstrate that he was making progress toward ending the war. He continued to withdraw American troops, announcing in December 1969 the return of 50,000 soldiers by the following spring. In addition, in November Congress approved an administration proposal to replace the existing draft system with a lottery system as an interim measure before Nixon could fulfill his 1968 campaign promise to create an all-volunteer force.[79]

AGNEW

In seeking to consolidate and deepen the silent majority's support for his administration, Nixon turned to his vice president, Spiro Agnew. Agnew articulated grievances of the silent majority beyond opposition to the antiwar movement and identified the administration with a host of issues of interest to these voters. He had already embarked on a series of prominent speeches that attacked a dissident minority for causing chaotic national disunity and for contributing to the emergence of a corrosive mood of permissiveness in the nation. His targets included student protesters and sympathetic university administrators, along with dovish liberal politicians. For example, in reaction to the first moratorium day, he commented, "A spirit of national masochism prevails, encouraged by an effete corps of impudent snobs who characterize themselves as intellectuals." In his public statements, the vice president articulated positions on a wide array of concerns that emerged in the mid- to late 1960s. He talked about drug use, changing sexual mores, student unrest, and rising rates of violent crime.[80]

These efforts merged overtly with the mobilization of the silent majority when Buchanan proposed a speech that aimed to add broadcast journalists to Agnew's list of middle America's enemies. Like other members of the administration, Buchanan was angry about what he saw as television commentators' unenthusiastic reaction to Nixon's November 3, 1969, speech. Although Agnew had already started to acquire a reputation as the administration's hatchet man, he did not like Buchanan's proposed speech, considering it "abrasive." The vice president nevertheless delivered it a few weeks later in Des Moines, Iowa, condemning the "establishment" bias of network television news and its excessively "eastern" identity. As a consequence, Agnew became a focus of national debate.[81]

These high-profile speeches developed Agnew's political identity. Before his vice presidential nomination, he had been largely unknown outside Maryland; to secure an independent political future as well as fulfill expectations of loyalty to Nixon, Agnew needed to become indispensable to the ticket in 1972 and beyond. Once Agnew realized that his aggressive speechmaking had increased his newsworthiness and popularity, he became eager to continue. At the same time, Nixon was relaxed about the controversial nature of Agnew's political role. A few hours before the Des Moines speech, the president remarked that Agnew's reputation posed "a real dilemma for an assassin."[82]

Nixon programmed the overall course of Agnew's contribution to the national debate but did not always do so in detail. The vice president could speak in a more harshly partisan manner than the president could and, if Agnew overstepped any widely perceived line of political acceptability, the Oval Office could repudiate his position. Until he crossed that line, however, upsetting the sensibilities of some people could prove politically productive. As a result, Agnew became very popular at party fund-raising dinners.[83]

In these ways, Nixon sought to identify his administration as antipermissive, which he saw as a winning position. He encouraged attacks on people associated with trends of the 1960s that he believed the silent majority found alarming. Nixon personally viewed with distaste the emergence of permissiveness: for example, the style as well as the views of student dissidents offended him. In a memorandum to Buchanan, Nixon noted his desire for a return to more conservative fashions. "Make it 'out' to wear long hair, smoke pot and go on the needle," he wrote. "Make it 'in' to indulge in the lesser vices, smoking (cigars preferably—non-Castro!) and alcohol in reasonable quantities on the right occasions." Nixon did not explain how Buchanan might achieve such a transformation of youth culture; the memo merely advocated the development of a new conservative youth organization.[84]

In fact, antipermissiveness was generally rhetorical rather than substantive. A few exceptions included the administration's new approach to law and order and increased attention to the trade in illegal drugs. Otherwise, it was difficult for legislation to influence the cultural trends that concerned Nixon and Agnew. One journalist noted that this "overture to the silent majority" depended not on lawmaking but on "a psychological appeal to the instincts of those who are less concerned about, say, welfare reform than they are about drugs, rebellious youth and other activities that Mr. Agnew and millions of others regard as a threat to the 'American way.' "[85]

THE LESSONS OF 1969

Belief in the electoral promise of the blue-collar vote as well as of the southern vote received a strong boost from the results of the 1969 elections, when Republicans won the governorship in New Jersey as well as Virginia. As interpreted by Kevin Phillips at the White House, the lessons of these victories rested on the successful championing of silent-majority needs. These successes delighted Nixon, who read with fascination Phillips's analysis of their implications.[86]

In New Jersey, William T. Cahill, a Republican congressman, won the governorship with 61 percent of the vote and a half million majority over his Democratic opponent, Robert B. Meyner. Administration analysis of the victory attributed Republican success to the personal intervention of Nixon, who visited the state to campaign and thus supposedly turned a close, nonideological contest into a landslide victory. But most pointedly, Phillips asserted, the triumph was "forged in Middle America," combining the 1968 votes of Nixon, Wallace, and the "alienated Middle American Democratic" supporters. In a series of advertisements in the final weeks of campaigning, Cahill had emphasized his support for family values and state aid to religious schools and his tough approach to law enforcement and pornography. In making this appeal, the Republicans surely benefited from the fact that the state of the economy was not a significant concern to voters.

The largest Republican gains were registered, Phillips wrote, in the areas of Wallace strength in 1969. They were "the unfashionable 80 to 85 per cent of New Jersey of blue collars, tract houses, VFW halls, dilapidated commuter trains, neighborhood bars, suburban shopping centers and parochial schools—so-called Middle America." In New Jersey, the most heavily suburbanized state after California, blue-collar areas and the lower-middle- and middle-class suburbs cast almost 60 percent of the total vote. The Republican success there provided support for those in the administration who advocated a more aggressive blue-collar strategy in the industrial Northeast based on the silent majority.[87]

While Cahill was victorious in New Jersey, voters in Virginia elected their first Republican governor since Reconstruction. Linwood Holton, a moderate with progressive views on desegregation, said that his victory signaled "a ground swell toward two-party democracy." Holton owed his victory to a division between moderates and conservatives within the Democratic Party as the power of the state's Byrd machine faltered.[88] The dynamic resembled that in the national party, which had produced presidential candidates for whom many southern Democrats did not want to vote. It remained to be seen whether other state parties in the South would experience similar divisions. In any case, the White House paid more attention to the New Jersey case, which seemed to offer new promise at the presidential level.

In analyzing the 1969 elections, Phillips omitted one point that some observers had raised: that Republican efforts had been boosted by Nixon's "silent majority" speech, delivered on the eve of the elections. But other analysis supported Phillips. On the New Jersey vote itself, national chair Rogers Morton received advice that the speech had little impact on the outcome, which was instead decided by the campaign and statewide issues.[89]

The citywide elections of 1969 offered still more lessons about political change. They seemed to confirm the significance of middle America. In Minneapolis, Charles Stenvig, a policeman, became mayor after a campaign of tough talk about the promotion of law and order. Running as an independent, he beat the Democratic-Farmer-Labor candidate. In Los Angeles, Sam Yorty won the mayorship on a similarly tough law-and-order platform. In New York, Mario Procaccino failed to defeat liberal Republican John Lindsay, the incumbent mayor, but the impressive reach of Procaccino's aggressive appeal to ethnic voters surprised observers. Yorty, Stenvig, and Procaccino were "making Alabama speeches with a Los Angeles, Minneapolis, and New York accent," said George Wallace. "The only thing they omitted was the drawl." Two Democratic political analysts, Richard Scammon and Ben Wattenberg, were among those who thought that these campaigns were significant. One year later, Scammon and Wattenberg would present in book form their analysis of American political change, using the 1969 elections, among others, as examples. The appearance of *The Real Majority* would ensure that many politicians as well as members of a wider public listened closely to the lessons of 1969.[90]

One year after Nixon's victory in the presidential election, more and more signs indicated that American politics was changing, that the electoral upheaval of 1968 was no isolated incident, and that conservative concerns were taking deeper hold. Altogether, the prospect of long-term electoral change was becoming a topic of interest for many politically minded Americans. "The search for [a] new majority," wrote journalist David Broder in 1971, "has become almost a national sport in the past three years," played out in books, newspaper columns, and "innumerable Washington cocktail party conversations."[91]

In 1969, many voters across the country who usually chose Democrats looked for alternatives, whether Republicans or Wallace-like Democrats. The prospect of political change therefore inspired special optimism among Republicans. By early 1970, they seemed near euphoria as they contemplated their party's prospects, as reports from Washington demonstrated. Many Republicans became convinced that the political tide was turning to the party's advantage for the first time in almost forty years. Opinion polls indicated that the percentage of Republican identifiers had increased, albeit by only a few points, since Nixon's 1968 victory. Better yet, a smaller proportion of Americans called themselves Democrats than at any other time since the New Deal. On February 17, 1970, the Harris poll organization announced that Democratic identifiers represented less than a majority—but still easily a plurality—of the electorate for the first time in the modern political era.[92] In fact, such statistics were grounds for encouragement but hardly for euphoria. After all, they revealed that most Americans remained unwilling to consider themselves natural supporters of the Republican Party.

At the start of 1970, Nixon fully believed in his ability to use the silent majority as the foundation of a new majority coalition. But he increasingly doubted his party's ability to maximize the potential for partisan change in its favor. Instead, his view of the party was often overshadowed by frustrations. Nixon enjoyed more popularity than did the party at large. During discussions about the success of the "silent majority" tag, Haldeman suggested a change of the party's name "as a start on [a] new realignment." The president "very seriously took me up on it," Haldeman wrote in his diary.[93]

POLARIZATION

Toward the end of 1969, mobilization of support for the administration's Vietnam policy offered Nixon an indication of who constituted his coalition. The foreign policy connection with the identification of Nixon's base of support was strengthened in the spring of 1970, when Nixon's Vietnam policy became more divisive. Foreign policy consequently became more effective in identifying Nixon supporters and opponents. On April 30, Nixon informed his television audience that to abbreviate the war, military involvement would have to be escalated, although he did not express the action in these terms, speaking instead of an "incursion." He explained that he had ordered U.S. troops into Cambodia to cut off Vietcong supply routes.

Nixon sought to justify his action by explaining the military situation, but the justification was framed in terms of his belief that the stakes of the domestic debate about the war were high. Speaking of "an age of anarchy both abroad and at home," he condemned "mindless attacks on all the great institutions which have been created by free civilizations in the last 500 years." He asked, "Does the richest and strongest nation in the history of the world have the character to meet a direct challenge by a group which rejects every effort to win a just peace, ignores our warning, tramples on solemn agreements, violates the neutrality of unarmed people and uses our prisoners as hostages?" Nixon said that he recognized that differences existed about whether the nation should have become involved militarily in Vietnam and how the war should have been pursued. However, his decision, which concerned the lives of American soldiers, transcended such differences, he claimed.[94] Once more, Nixon chose a rationale for his foreign policy that emphasized its patriotism.

Public opinion was more favorable when Nixon asked for national patience as he deescalated the war than when he explained that further military involvement was necessary to secure deescalation. But however low the public's estimation of the Nixon record as a whole might fall, support nevertheless remained reasonably consistent and fairly high for the Nixon approach to foreign policy. In July, for example, the White House received a private poll showing popular approval for Nixon's Vietnam policy while revealing disapproval of his performance in all other policy areas.[95]

Nixon's announcement of the expansion of the war into Cambodia sparked renewed antiwar protest. At Kent State University, national guardsmen killed four students participating in a demonstration. At first, Nixon was "very disturbed"—especially because the demonstration had occurred in reaction to his speech—and he wanted to encourage calm on the nation's campuses. But within a few days his thoughts had turned to the possible political opportunity. He sensed that "college demonstrators [had] overplayed their hands" and that he could mobilize blue-collar discontent against them. When polls reached him indicating that most Americans did indeed disapprove of the student demonstrations and that support for the Cambodian incursion was potentially strong, Nixon wanted an "all-out offensive" to reap the political advantage. Nixon was not the only Republican politician to welcome the prospect of mobilizing voters against protesters. James Whetmore, a state senator from Orange County, California, observed, "Every time they burn another building, Republican registration goes up."[96]

Nixon's claim to transcend differences among Americans actually exacerbated domestic divisions, and protest returned to an extent almost as great as before the "silent majority" speech. Only days after a demonstration in Washington against the administration's Cambodian action, a New York demonstration added a remarkable twist to the history of counterculture dissent. A crowd mostly of construction workers marched on Wall Street to show their opposition to young activists. The participants included a homemaker from Bay Ridge who some months previously had named her baby son Richard Nixon. The march was not unique, and it inspired similar rallies in Buffalo, San Diego, and Pittsburgh.[97]

The Wall Street protest offered vivid and real evidence of a (not-so) silent majority, the support of which might be available to Nixon. The White House reacted with excitement. Staffer Stephen Bull wrote that "this display of emotional activity from the 'hard hats' provides an opportunity, if under the proper leadership, to forge a new alliance and perhaps result in the emergence of a 'new right.'" The alliance would "cut completely across racial and economic lines," and the "emphasis would be upon some of these supposedly trite mid-America values that the liberal press likes to snicker about: love of country, respect for people as individuals, the Golden Rule, etc." Tom Charles Huston, a fellow aide, argued similarly, urging that the administration "quit talking about the great Silent Majority and start talking to it." Nixon did so. He was delighted with his hard-hat support and soon thereafter invited a group of construction workers to the White House.[98]

This demonstration of support for Nixon contrasted sharply with widespread congressional dismay about the war's escalation. The Senate passed an amendment sponsored by John Sherman Cooper, a Republican from Kentucky, and Frank Church, a Democrat from Idaho, to withdraw funds from the Cambodian operation after the end of June; the Senate also repealed the Gulf of Tonkin resolution. The Cooper-Church amendment met defeat in the House, but the extent of congressional opposition, concentrated in the Senate, was clear. Nixon announced that he would independently end military activities in Cambodia on June 30, claiming their success. American forces had indeed inflicted major losses on the enemy but had not, in truth, wiped out the sources of enemy supplies that had been the target.[99] The electoral challenge for Nixon would be to mobilize his silent majority against congressional politicians who opposed his policies.

The hard-hat incident convinced Nixon that he should cultivate the electoral support of elements within organized labor. Organized labor offered one way to reach the elusive middle Americans, even if—according to the Labor Department's categorization of this group—a minority of such heads of household belonged to unions. Given the centrality of labor to the Democratic coalition since the time of Franklin Roosevelt, unions' potential support represented a considerable prize. It was not a trouble-free prize, however. Even if unionists endorsed the administration's patriotic internationalism, they were much less likely to be enthusiasts about other pieces of Nixon's record. The attitude of AFL-CIO President George Meany demonstrated this division of political sentiment. Little more than two months after Nixon took office, Meany said that he was "sympathetic toward and in agreement with [Nixon's] policy" in various foreign and defense matters. Meany offered to speak strongly on behalf of the AFL-CIO in support of the administration's Vietnam policy and its then-controversial funding of an antiballistic missile program. The AFL-CIO executive continued to announce positions friendly to the administration's foreign policy. But Meany found much else to criticize. For example, he not only condemned such conservative initiatives as the Haynsworth and Carswell nominations but in private opposed FAP.[100]

Nevertheless, the prize of organized labor seemed within reach. The foundation of patriotic internationalism was sturdy enough to construct a better relationship between Republicans and unionists. Jay Lovestone, a key aide to Meany, told Colson that the AFL-CIO president's endorsement of Nixon in 1972 was possible. Of yet more direct electoral significance, Lovestone volunteered to visit some states in the fall for "discussion meetings," designed to undermine dovish Democratic Senators Frank Moss of Utah and Albert Gore of Tennessee. The availability of labor support for Nixon reflected dissatisfaction with the Democrats as well as approval of the administration. Meany and Lovestone "no longer believe the Democratic party is a viable political institution; they believe it has no responsible political leadership and that, in fact, it is being taken over by extremist elements," wrote Colson.[101]

THE ROSOW REPORT

By this time, the Nixon administration had devised a serious blueprint for dealing with middle Americans' substantive problems. If Nixon wanted to pursue policies to win over members of this group more broadly than on the basis of patriotic internationalism, he had a raft of possible proposals. The Rosow Report was ready. It was an analysis of work-related problems experienced by an economic slice of the American population between the poor and the affluent, including many blue-collar but also some white-collar workers. The report investigated the situation of about 20 million families—in 1969, 37 percent of nonwhite and 34 percent of white families—with incomes between $5,000 and $10,000, placing them "above the poverty line but below what is required to meet moderate family budget needs."

Rosow concluded that the economic plight of these troubled Americans was a matter of special concern. Their wages were not keeping pace with their increased budget needs, and they had few opportunities for career advancement—even across generations, as access to college education was closely linked to a family's economic status. Poor workplace conditions and poor benefits contributed to many people's more general sense of job dissatisfaction, but their concerns extended beyond narrowly economic issues. Their neighborhoods often suffered from severe decay and were plagued by increasing crime. Despite these problems, the experience of the 1960s apparently indicated that government help for the poor came at the expense of lower-middle-income workers; Rosow saw the resulting resentment as sometimes "unrealistic" but "understandable." Despite a racial component to such government help—Rosow mentioned college aid to black students and special subsidies to "ghetto schools"—this category of troubled citizens included many African Americans.[102]

According to the report, the administration's program of reform activism would help lower-middle-income Americans. But Rosow also advocated an additional series of federal, state, and local government programs as well as employer and union initiatives. His suggestions for government action included the enlargement of access to education, the provision of funds to child-care facilities, reforms of tax policy, regulation of workplace conditions, and attention to the government's status as a "model employer." Rosow also advocated action to restore the status of blue-collar work. "These frustrated individuals, caught in a situation from which they see no escape, are likely to vent their feelings in actions harmful to both themselves and society," he wrote. "Beyond that, our system of values signals that something is very wrong when conscientious, able, and hardworking people cannot make it."[103]

Rosow identified the problems of lower-middle-class workers as an area for administration attention and for potential Republican gains. On that basis, a government panel, including Haldeman, Moynihan, Ehrlichman, Dent, and Harlow, advocated the implementation of the report. But its implementation faced obstacles, the first of which was its enormous scope. Although the "much-discussed" report was "closely" studied within the administration, offering new financial benefits to such a large group of Americans would prove enormously expensive.[104]

The report demanded that the balance of the administration's domestic policy should be firmly on the side of reformism rather than on that of an antigovernment impulse. For more conservative Republicans, the formula was unacceptable. Tom Huston, a member of a group that met to discuss middle America, was horrified by the results of the work elsewhere in the administration on the same problem. "The Rosow Report is a blue-print for an expanded welfare state," he wrote. "It envisions a program which we cannot afford politically or budgetarily." By contrast, Herbert Stein of the Council of Economic Advisers thought that the administration could easily afford at least some of Rosow's recommendations but did not believe that an economic crisis existed among middle Americans.[105]

For the moment, the report remained unimplemented. Shultz, an enthusiast for the Rosow Report, left the Labor Department in July 1970 to become the first director of the Office of Management and Budget. His successor as labor secretary, James D. Hodgson, shared Shultz's enthusiasm. The new secretary wrote to Nixon and urged him to pay close attention to the report and its recommendations. "Active initiatives by President Nixon in pushing for these goals," Hodgson argued, "would reflect his sensitivity and concern for the needs of low-income workers." Indeed, it was a historic opportunity. The Republican Party had rarely offered a welcome to American workers, but now it could. According to Hodgson, White House interest in that opportunity alarmed the Democrats.[106]

THE RECORD

On August 12, 1970, as the campaign season approached, Hodgson spoke publicly about the chance of a new Republican constituency within middle America. "I find these working people are squarely behind the Administration on two really big things—first, scaling down the war, and second, taking a firm approach to crime and unrest at home," he told a meeting of the Republican

Governors Conference. "[O]nly one big issue" remained to the Republicans' disadvantage, he said. This was the economy.[107]

But that issue was important enough to eclipse the administration's achievements that otherwise apparently won blue-collar Americans' approval. The state of key economic indicators was unimpressive. Moreover, the agenda of reformism had seen little progress. In July, Nixon had decided that revenue sharing would not assume legislative priority until it was made a significant aspect of his next budget. In Congress, FAP was debated, but without much effect. The plan secured the support of Wilbur Mills of Arkansas, the skeptical chair of the House Ways and Means Committee, but was defeated by the Senate Finance Committee under Russell Long of Louisiana. A revised version of FAP, presented in July, addressed the question of potential work disincentives by lowering proposed welfare payments, but the changes did not impress Long. At the same time, several more generous schemes were floated, including one by Minnesota Senator Eugene McCarthy, who planned hearings in November to highlight the views of welfare-rights activists. FAP's fortunes were hindered by what Robert Novak described as the administration's "inept and lackadaisical approach" to the management of the bill in Congress.[108]

The dreams of reform did not define the public image of the administration. As time passed, the more controversial elements of the administration's activity tended to transcend its reformist impulse—the shrillness of Agnew's antipermissive rhetoric, the uncompromising nature of the Supreme Court nominations, and the harsh response to antiwar protest. "No longer was there any pretense that the Nixon White House might serve as a forum of conciliation, a temple of togetherness," observed journalists Dan Rather and Gary Paul Gates.[109]

The desire to cultivate middle America faced some formidable obstacles. One was the Republican Party itself. Active concern for blue-collar Americans was new to the Republican Party and was out of step with its experience in recent decades. It was by no means obvious that an administration could impose a fresh vision for the party's future, supported by programmatic innovation, without the support of the party at large. The Phillips thesis demanded that the old Republican elite lose its influence in the party, making way for a new set of activists interested in the mixture of "conservatism," "progressivism," and "populism" of which he wrote. "I wish we could drop into the Potomac all those obsolescent conservatives who are still preoccupied with Alger Hiss and General MacArthur, and who keep trotting out *laissez faire* economics and other dead horses," Phillips told a reporter. "They make the Republican party look musty to millions of ignored working-class people who are looking for a party that relates to their needs."[110]

Even with the infusion of new activists, some observers believed that it might well not be possible to persuade the party to join any such effort for a majority. "The Republican party *is* a middle-class party, and it will never be anything else," wrote James Reichley. For Andrew Hacker, Republican dinners in "American Legion halls rather than at the local Sheraton Inn" were impossible to imagine. "Phillips seems willing to have the catering done by Kentucky Fried Chicken," he wrote, "but I am not sure how many other Republicans have an appetite for paper cups and plastic plates."[111]

THREE'S A REALIGNMENT GOING ON

The Redefinition of the Republican Party, 1970

In 1970 Richard Nixon waged a midterm campaign with very few parallels in American history. He intervened extensively in congressional contests, particularly those for the Senate, both behind the scenes and on the stump. This large-scale intervention had an ambitious goal. Nixon wanted to revitalize his party and even to redefine the lines of difference between the nation's parties. Presidents have only rarely seen their parties gain congressional seats at the midpoint of their administration, and personal involvement in a prominent effort to defy this historical norm was a gamble for Nixon.[1]

The effort was especially risky because current economic conditions were inauspicious for the party in office. But Nixon believed that he could mobilize members of the "silent majority" by sidestepping any debate about the economy and instead focusing attention on a different set of issues. His reformism, however, could not provide an alternative focus because the administration had achieved so few of these goals. Instead, Nixon wanted to emphasize the patriotic internationalism of his foreign policy and the conservative traditionalism of his fight against permissiveness. In July, Nixon discussed with Kevin Phillips the electoral potential of social conservatism as strong enough even to overcome the electoral damage of economic difficulties. H. R. Haldeman recorded the surprising conclusion that "patriotic themes to counter economic depression will get response from unemployed." On this basis, Nixon hoped to pick up three or four seats in the Senate, which he was convinced was a realistic goal, to begin the consolidation of a conservative majority.[2]

This activity, therefore, aimed at increasing the Republican Party's strength. Self-interest underpinned the effort. Nixon wanted to strengthen his administration by securing a Congress more supportive of his policies. Legislative acceptance of his foreign policy was an especially consequential consideration. The campaign was thus a challenge to the growing antiwar bloc in Congress, just as the "silent majority" speech had challenged antiwar sympathies within the wider public. There was still another merit in the intervention, this one deeply personal. Nixon intended the campaign to level damaging accusations of permissive sympathies against three Democrats who were promising contenders for their party's 1972 presidential nomination. In this way, he would make an early start to his campaign against Maine Senator Edmund Muskie, Massachusetts Senator Edward Kennedy, and former Vice President Hubert Humphrey, seeking to brand them as leftists rather than moderates. Finally, Nixon wanted Republican candidates to ensure that their campaigns included sufficient praise of Nixon and his administration, thus building up his personal political strength.[3]

Nixon's efforts on behalf of the Republican Party were not straightforwardly partisan in a conventional sense. Polls provided Nixon with an urgent reminder of the "enormous weakness" of the Republican Party. He did not intend to invest political capital in an unpromising cause. Instead, the theme for the campaign, he decided, was the need for a new Congress, supportive of the president, while the term "Republican" should be avoided. Seeking to reduce the level of normal partisanship, Nixon was anxious that the campaign should offer praise to some "good Dem[ocrat]s." Support for his foreign policy was the key test of legislators' sympathy to the administration. On this basis, Nixon not only could potentially justify a failure to endorse a Republican's challenge to an incumbent Democrat but could also read Republicans out of his party. Nixon chose one senator for this treatment. The first victim of this policy, Nixon decided, was Charles Goodell of New York, prominent for his antiwar views; Nixon preferred Goodell's challenger from the state's Conservative Party, James Buckley.[4]

In the longer term, Nixon remained interested in the possibility of engineering a wholesale upheaval of the Republican Party. The president "[k]eeps trying to figure out how to implement his idea of changing [the] name of [the] Republican Party to [the] Conservative Party," Haldeman noted in his diary in July. "Based on polls, there are twice as many conservatives as Republicans."

Such discussions were not restricted to the highest levels in the White House. Jeb Magruder, a second-level aide, remembered that the possibility of a name change was "sometimes kicked around" and that the "title that most attracted us was Conservative Party." Shortly before the campaign started, Nixon noted that during the 1960s the number of Americans calling themselves "liberal" declined from 49 to 33 percent, while the corresponding number of "conservatives" rose from 46 to 51 percent. Although such figures supported his speculations about renaming the Republican Party, there was a "[t]ough legal and technical problem."[5] The federal, decentralized nature of an American political party made this problem particularly acute.

Still, the behavior of Congress as well as the results of opinion polls offered some support to Nixon's interest in seeking a conservative party. There were signs of decay within the cohesiveness of the Democratic Party, as its conservatives increasingly disagreed with the liberals and moderates. The policies of the Nixon administration created a minor surge of significance for the "conservative coalition" of Republicans and southern Democrats, a surge that had started under Johnson. In both houses of Congress, the coalition appeared in about a third of contested roll calls, including many of particular interest to the White House on racial policy, national defense, and foreign policy. According to analysis conducted by Barbara Sinclair, the area of particular incoherence among congressional Democrats was in votes about the shape of foreign policy after Vietnam. On such questions, southern Democrats disagreed with their northern counterparts overall; their opinion instead resembled that of many congressional Republicans.[6] This support was significant to Nixon as he worked for an adequate level of congressional acceptance of his Vietnam policy while rallying the silent majority within the country behind it.

But Republicans and southern Democrats did not always see eye to eye. On issues concerning the role of the federal government in economic matters, the two groups had less in common. Southern Democrats were more conservative than their fellow party members but still offered more support to such measures than Republicans did. In this regard, the southern Democratic opinion balanced liberalism and conservatism.[7] In principle, the Nixon approach, involving some reform-oriented expansions while stressing their antibureaucratic implications, seemed to match the concerns of southern Democrats, probably with even more success than it matched those of his fellow Republicans in Congress. In practice, it did not. The way in which the administration combined reformism with conservatism did not find a stable foundation of congressional support. The Nixon administration's impulse for reform proved too liberal for many Democrats from the South. In particular, senior figures within the southern contingent, many of whom were influential on congressional committees, were often skeptical of reformist ideas.

The major plank so far of this reformism was the Family Assistance Plan (FAP), which potentially threatened the South's low-wage economy and was therefore peculiarly effective in unlocking southern Democrats' domestic conservatism. In search of Democratic votes in favor of White House proposals, Bryce Harlow, Nixon's first chief of congressional liaison, had devised a "floating-coalition" strategy, looking to the conservatives on some issues but to the liberals on others.[8] FAP was one occasion on which he could not depend on the conservatives. FAP passed the House as a result of the support of liberal Democrats; southern opposition loomed as a threat to the plan's enactment. The state of congressional politics therefore suggested that there was no easy route to a conservative party. Conservative sentiment there was real, but as a voting bloc it was incoherent. Nixon could often find common ground between Republicans and conservative Democrats on questions of foreign policy—the issues about which the president most cared. The politics of race and antipermissiveness were usually sources of unity, too. But conservative Democrats did not offer the same support to Nixon's reformist domestic policy.

NIXONOMICS

While FAP faltered, Nixon found it necessary to oppose the Democratic Congress's spending plans. He began a campaign against "big spending" in January 1970 with the first televised veto of a bill. The bill in question concerned Labor–Health, Education, and Welfare appropriations and added $1.1 billion to the sum recommended by Nixon. An electoral calculation influenced the decision to veto. He expected high inflation but not unemployment in the fall and consequently looked for opportunities to depict the Democrats as fiscally reckless and thus responsible for rising prices. At some cost to relations with both Democrats and Republicans on Capitol Hill, he later vetoed a hospital construction bill and, as the campaign approached, further appropriations bills for education and housing, though Congress sustained only two of the vetoes.[9]

More than electoral factors had motivated his vetoes. Nixon was no avid budget cutter, but he remained convinced that he needed to control increases in federal spending to keep down inflation; that concern was genuine. Moreover, if Democrats spent money on their projects, he could not spend money on his own. Nixon had not yet gained the initiative. Having attempted to initiate legislation of bold reformism, he was now on the defensive and preaching caution instead of adventure.

In foreseeing inflation as the principal economic problem, Nixon had misread the future. His policy of gradualism had not yet managed to stabilize the economy, in part because the Federal Reserve Board was having little success in implementing the monetarist goals that were one feature of the policy. From an electoral perspective, the result was unfortunate. Inflation did not fall, but unemployment increased. With a certain glee, Lawrence F. O'Brien, the Democratic national chair, correctly identified the economy as his party's strongest issue in 1970. He used a memorable tag, "Nixonomics," to associate the nation's ills closely with the president.[10]

In the fall, unemployment reached nearly 6 percent, the same level as inflation. It was an unappealing combination. The economic situation was exacerbated by a serious and seemingly intractable strike at General Motors; 400,000 GM workers were participating in the strike, which was estimated to cost the economy $1 billion a week. Across the economy, strike action was at a level nearly unmatched in the post–World War II period. Lower-middle-class Americans—the middle Americans apparently open to Nixon's cultivation—were especially susceptible to these economic woes. A Harris poll reported that 58 percent of Americans felt that the economy was in a recession and that a speedy recovery was not likely. Supporting the long-term promise of Nixon's policies, an administration economist was reported nevertheless to remark, "I sure as hell wouldn't want to run on the economy now."[11]

Still confident that his policies would produce prosperity by 1972, Nixon decided that even an attempt to neutralize the economic issue in 1970 was risky. He certainly wanted "to stay off of economic conservatism" during the campaign, as he told Haldeman. Indeed, the president wished to avoid discussion of the economy altogether. Instead, his campaign would place other issues before the electorate. Remarkably, despite the economic downturn, he did not place on hold his desire to mobilize the silent majority at the polls, even deciding that the fall of 1970 was a good time to implement the plan.[12]

THE REAL MAJORITY

Shortly before the 1970 campaigns began, a new book appeared with an interpretation of current U.S. political developments, offering strategic advice to both parties. The book immediately gained a wide audience, not least in the White House itself. Although it was even reported that *The Real Majority* forced Nixon to reassess his strategy for the midterms, the book's impact was not quite so great.[13] In fact, Nixon had already decided to appeal for the votes of the silent majority through themes of patriotism and antipermissiveness, and he saw the book's argument as supporting this decision. As he perceived the situation, the book did something else as well. Nixon felt that its appearance raised the stakes, thus encouraging him to stress these themes with yet more force.

The authors of *The Real Majority* were Richard Scammon and Ben Wattenberg, both Democrats. Scammon had served as census director under Lyndon Johnson, while Wattenberg was a Democratic speechwriter who had worked for Johnson, among others. Like Kevin Phillips in *The Emerging Republican Majority*, Scammon and Wattenberg argued that the country was undergoing change that would have wide-ranging and long-term effects. But their mode of analysis and their conclusions differed substantially from Phillips's. Where Phillips investigated demography and its impact on electoral history, Scammon and Wattenberg devoted more attention to issues and how politicians addressed them. Change in American politics was linked to the emergence of a new issue area, which they called the "Social Issue." In doing so, they provided a convenient phrase to describe the complicated cluster of issues relating to problems of permissiveness.

As Scammon and Wattenberg described it, the Social Issue originated in the mid-1960s with concerns about law and order. It then broadened in scope when disorder became increasingly associated with racial tensions, activism, and college radicalism in the later part of the decade. In turn, the opposition of many young people to the war in Vietnam was complicated and deepened by their more general support of a lifestyle different from that of the American mainstream and their liberal attitudes on subjects such as drug use and sexual behavior.[14] The electorate—"unyoung, unpoor, and unblack"—did not share this kind of liberalism, Scammon and Wattenberg emphasized. Their median voter was the forty-seven-year-old wife of a machinist in Dayton,

Ohio. In short, the book offered another thesis about the significance of middle America.

While the arguments of both *The Emerging Republican Majority* and *The Real Majority* addressed the changing political attitudes of middle Americans, the two theses were underpinned by different partisan concerns. Phillips was enthusiastic about the prospect that the Democrats might lose their majority; Scammon and Wattenberg were alarmed by the same prospect. Indeed, they sought to alert Democratic politicians that their party was in danger of losing the allegiance of many voters and of losing its majority status if it failed to address appropriately the Social Issue.[15] The authors noticed a tendency among many Democrats to assume a rather liberal position with respect to the problems of permissiveness and of law and order. This tendency was potentially disastrous, Scammon and Wattenberg thought.

Crucial to the argument was the statement that the Social Issue did not replace but merely joined older concerns about the economy and the welfare state, the "Economic Issue." While the "real" majority was, in terms of the Social Issue, rather conservative, it was also more liberal in terms of the Economic Issue: a majority of Americans still favored activist government. On the basis of this insight, Scammon and Wattenberg offered some advice to their Republican opponents as well as to fellow Democrats. "There can be no question," the authors noted, "that a good deal of Republican gardening will be done on the Social Issue." But this was not enough, they argued: "Just as Democrats must move on the Social Issue to keep in tune with the center, so Republicans must move on the Economic Issue to capture the center. A Republican Party perceived of as go-slow on the problems of unemployment or the cities or transportation or pollution or against Medicare or Social Security will be vulnerable. America has problems; Americans of the center are aware that America has problems; Americans of the center in the seventies will want an activist problem-solving government. Republicans must offer up such an image or face trouble; they cannot keep the image of the party of the small-town banker. There aren't enough small-town bankers to elect a President."[16]

Although Nixon had already decided to place antipermissiveness and his foreign policy at the heart of the campaign, *The Real Majority* was important to the evolution of his drive to mobilize his silent majority in two ways. First, he welcomed the book as a useful and insightful interpretation of current political change, and he speedily encouraged Republicans to read it. Second, and more importantly, he saw the book as effective in realizing its authors' aim of convincing Democrats that they were losing sight of the social conservatism of many Americans. He thought the book had created a climate in which Democrats were freshly alert to a need to articulate conservative positions with respect to the Social Issue. The resulting diminution of difference between Republicans and Democrats posed a major threat to Nixon's desire to reap electoral benefit from his stance against permissiveness. Nixon became very anxious not to lose this advantage, and this anxiety drove his strategy for the midterms. In reacting like this, Nixon probably exaggerated the impact of *The Real Majority* on Democrats; the book was observational as well as analytical, and some Democrats already wanted to check any trend toward Social Issue liberalism within their own party.

Central to the White House understanding of the Scammon-Wattenberg thesis was an analysis of *The Real Majority* written by Patrick Buchanan, who noted that the Republicans' target constituency in 1970 essentially consisted of "law and order Democrats, conservatives on the 'Social Issue,' but 'progressive' on domestic issues":

> We should win these Democrats to the Presidential banner by contending that RN is a progressive on domestic policy blocked by "obstructionists" in the left-wing leadership of the Democratic Party; that RN is a hard-liner on crime, drugs and pornography, whose legislation is blocked by "ultra-liberals" in the Senate . . . ; that the President is a man trying with veto after veto to hold down the cost of living but is being thwarted by radicals and wild spenders . . . ; that the President is a man in foreign policy who is moving toward peace with honor but whose efforts are being attacked and undercut by unilateral disarmers and isolationists who think peace lies in an abject retreat from the world and the dismantling of the Army, Navy and Air Force. This is said strong—but these would be the ways we could best appeal to the patriotic, hard-line pro-medicare Democrats who are the missing element in the Grand New Party.

At the core of Scammon and Wattenberg's influence in the White House was this interpretive summary, a step away from their argument itself. Nixon instructed that this analysis should be circulated widely within the administration and among Republican candidates. He wanted his campaign team to follow Buchanan's recommendations about how the White House should respond to *The Real Majority*.[17]

Buchanan's analysis underscores the lack of any inconsistency between Nixon's reformism on welfare issues and his conservatism on social issues. In the minds of many American voters who held such views, such positions were not contradictory. When Nixon read in Buchanan's memo that a fundamental observation of Scammon and Wattenberg—the heart of their "wake-up" call to the Democratic Party—was that the "attitudional [*sic*] center of American politics" involved "progressivism on economic issues and toughness on the Social Issue," he scribbled in the memorandum's margin, "of course." But once observed by Buchanan and Nixon, the recognition that "economic progressivism" was important immediately disappeared from the campaign debate. Both "Nixonomics" and the travails of the reform agenda ensured the idea's disappearance.

The analysis also offers a reminder of the limits of the administration's interest in reformism. It existed together with an antigovernment instinct that included an active desire to keep careful control of government spending. Within those limits and operating in an institutional context demanding legislative-executive cooperation, administration initiatives were easily overshadowed. While Buchanan boasted of the administration's "progressivism," he pointed out that reformist policies were facing defeat in the Democratic Congress. He also showed special concern about the inflationary implications of policies supported by Democratic "radicals" and "wild spenders."[18] In reality, this was not a promising way in which to challenge the Republican Party's electoral weakness, as identified by Scammon and Wattenberg, as "the party of the small-town banker."

If Nixon listened carefully to the message of *The Real Majority*, wider dissemination of the book's arguments in the White House was less successful. It took time to produce a judiciously expressed précis of the book, and this became a matter of concern. By mid-September Haldeman's assistant, Larry Higby, complained that rather more staffers were reading Scammon and Wattenberg than were understanding their arguments. One of the staffers, Magruder, found himself expected to embrace the thesis of *The Real Majority*. He struggled to do so, and his efforts to explain the strategy of the campaign in terms of the thesis were greeted by criticism and even ridicule from Haldeman and Higby. As far as they were concerned, Magruder did not understand that campaign debate must be straightforward, stark, and at times aggressive. In fact, at the top of the administration there remained the sense that true understanding of the new majority was a rare commodity. Even during the reelection campaign two years later, Nixon would complain that high-level officials did not share his insight into what motivated crucial swing voters to support him. In 1970 more general dissemination of the message was slower still. Only at the end of September did leading Republicans receive from the Republican National Committee (RNC) a letter drawing attention to *The Real Majority* along with a summary of its primary findings. Even then, at least one White House staffer involved with the campaign, Charles Colson, had not yet read the book. He asked his secretary immediately to obtain a copy for his weekend reading.[19]

By contrast, Nixon was impressed by the book's instant impact on liberal politicians. Shortly after publication, he called Haldeman's attention to attacks by Senator George McGovern of South Dakota on radicals, which Nixon saw as clearly influenced by Scammon and Wattenberg. The president's reaction was not to downplay these issues. Instead, by stressing his own conservatism on the Social Issue, he hoped to expose the shallowness and hollowness of the Democrats' commitment to this position. The administration, he told Haldeman, should not allow the Democrats to "soft-pedal the issue." Nixon wanted "to really ram home [the thinking of *The Real Majority*] and make all decisions based on it." He wanted "to hit pornography, dope, [and] bad kids," noted Haldeman.[20]

PARTY REDEFINITION

Scammon and Wattenberg were describing a change in the issue context of American politics. In the 1970 campaign, Richard Nixon ambitiously attempted to respond to this change by reshaping the contours of political debate. By doing so, he hoped to consolidate his coalition of support within the nation and to see this reflected in a supportive coalition within Congress. In the campaign, membership in Nixon's party of Congress was redefined to stress not partisan loyalty but ideological loyalty to the president on issues he identified as especially salient. There was thus little incompatibility between the aims of winning support for Nixon personally (with an eye on his reelection prospects for 1972) and of winning support for other Republicans (with an eye on the more immediate prospects for 1970).

During the ideological redefinition, the Republican label was deemphasized, supplanted by support for the Nixon administration. "It's important that you stress more strongly than you have in speeches that you are preparing for other people, the point of supporting the President, praising the President, building up the President, etc.," Haldeman wrote to Buchanan in July. "This is the principle [sic] political asset we have according to all the available poll data and it should be played strongly by all of our top level speakers. The higher level the speaker is, the more important this point is." Haldeman explained the point to speechwriter James Keogh, who was preparing a basic campaign speech for congressional candidates. Haldeman recommended that the theme should "be either elect a new Congress or elect a Conservative Congress, depending on the district, and there should be a major emphasis on supporting the President." Again, Haldeman pointed out that candidates' prospects were improved by presidential rather than Republican identification. Nixon remained concerned that the campaign build up his image of leadership.[21] A unity of interests existed between the personalized presidency and the larger party in its redefined form.

The strategy of redefinition focused on the Senate. In terms of priorities, state legislatures—with control over impending reapportionment—were of more interest than the House, according to Haldeman. "It is felt," he wrote, "that the House elections will go basically 'with the swing' and that other than a few special circumstances, no major effort should be extended there." In 1972 there would be "a more realistic chance of making major gains or gaining control of the House."[22] By implication, Senate elections somehow might go against the swing. History bolstered the hope. The senators standing for reelection had won their seats in 1964, the year of the Goldwater candidacy, which marked a record low for Republican fortunes. It therefore did not seem unreasonable now to contemplate Republican success in winning back some seats.

Gains in the Senate were attractive for another reason. It was more hostile to Nixon than was the House, where, among other advantages, the southern Democrats were more cooperative. The Senate was both more liberal and more dovish, and its responsibilities for foreign policy and approving executive nominations had led to a series of bitter conflicts.[23] Formal control of the Senate was unlikely because Republicans needed at least seven seats to achieve this goal. But a less troublesome Senate seemed entirely within reach. And a more supportive Senate would be an important asset for the administration, leaving Nixon better able to implement his agenda, especially on foreign policy, about which he cared most.

In addition to his specific interest in the Senate, Nixon had a more general interest in his party's candidates. He asked his political staff to watch closely districts with elderly incumbents. Even a district that seemed to be strongly Democratic could be open to a Republican advance on the incumbent's retirement, he observed. Correspondingly, older Republican incumbents should be encouraged to retire at an appropriate time. "Effective party leadership," he told Haldeman, "requires that we examine all of these cases and be ready for a contingency plan to deal with them in the future."[24]

THE CAMPAIGN OF REDEFINITION

Concretely, Nixon pursued his aim of redefining the shape of partisan difference in two broad ways. First, he chose the issues. Second, he chose the candidates, most running as Republicans, although some were not. He supported these moves with massive administration intervention in the campaign. The White House funded candidates and provided them with advice. Spiro Agnew led a national campaign for the benefit of local candidates. Nixon took part to convince the electorate that the issues dividing his supporters and opponents were important and that voters should endorse the administration's policies through the means of the congressional elections.

Nixon's chosen candidates included a number of promising House Republicans who gave up their seats to run for the Senate, among them Texas's George H. W. Bush, who intended to run against Ralph Yarborough, a liberal. Yarborough, however, lost his party's primary to the more conservative Lloyd Bentsen. Another House Republican who surrendered his seat was Richard Roudebush, who ran against Vance Hartke in Indiana. Hartke was a leading dove, while Roudebush caught Nixon's eye for activity in the House that included a requirement that only the U.S. flag could be planted on the moon and a bill making a flag patch part of the District of Columbia police uniform. Others were William Brock in Tennessee, Lowell P. Weicker Jr. in Connecticut, J. Glenn Beall in Maryland, Thomas Kleppe in North Dakota, William V. Roth Jr. in Delaware, Clark MacGregor in Minnesota, Robert Taft Jr. in Ohio, Lawrence J. Burton in Utah, and John Wold in Wyoming. It was an impressive list, but Nixon's recruitment drive did not always succeed. Some leading Republicans lacked Nixon's enthusiasm for the possibilities of 1970, and a number of his choices refused to stand for the Senate, including Rogers Morton, the Republican national chair, and Paul Laxalt, the governor of Nevada.[25]

At the same time, Nixon discouraged one interested candidate from standing—Arthur Fletcher, assistant secretary of labor, who contemplated a candidacy against Henry "Scoop" Jackson, a Democratic senator from Washington. When informed of Fletcher's idea, Nixon noted that it would be "a great mistake" because it would appear that he was encouraging a candidate from within his administration to challenge a senator who had been friendly on crucial foreign policy issues.[26]

Nixon's candidate in Florida was congressman William Cramer. But Claude Kirk, the state's governor, helped to persuade G. Harrold Carswell, Nixon's unsuccessful nominee for the Supreme Court, to enter the primary. Nixon then had second thoughts about Cramer: "The election of Carswell," he wrote in April, "of course, would be enormously effective in justifying my position in appointing him in the first place." He instructed his friend, Bebe Rebozo, to encourage the organization of a committee of Democrats for Carswell and to raise money nationally for the cause. Nixon envisioned a target of a million dollars. Rebozo made a start. Nixon noted that likely contributors were "offbeat people who would probably contribute minimally if at all to regular committees but who would love to get in a battle like this." In addition to Nixon's covert support, Carswell benefited from the fund-raising skills of Richard Viguerie, who would emerge later in the decade as a leading figure of the "New Right." Despite this array of advantages, Carswell did not win Florida's primary election, losing to Nixon's official choice, Cramer, who rather surprisingly attacked Carswell as a racial liberal for his work as a judge in implementing Supreme Court decisions on desegregation. The bitter intraparty conflict left the Republicans less able to fight the Democrats in the fall.[27]

Money was also the object of administration direction. At the end of 1969, Nixon instructed Haldeman to ensure that major contributors channeled their donations to the 1970 campaigns through the White House, sending only token donations directly to congressional candidates' campaign committees. Nixon justified the instruction on the grounds that it would avoid waste and corruption, but, more importantly, he wanted to know that the money was going to "the right people." A surreptitious finance committee was established to raise and distribute the money, acting under White House orders. In total, the large donors gave $3 million, which was divided among Republican campaigns in twenty states. For example, MacGregor received $110,000 from the fund, Brock $203,000, Bush $106,000, and Beall $230,800. The key campaigns were therefore richly funded, while many Democratic campaigns lacked sufficient money.[28]

For the strategy of redefinition to be credible, it was necessary to believe that, despite the inevitable variety of individual contests, a midterm campaign could have a strong national dimension. Indeed, when discussing the campaign with Phillips in July, Nixon had intended to encourage candidates to stress local issues favorable to them and even to distance themselves from unpopular Republican policies at the national level, provided that the candidates stressed their loyalty to Nixon's leadership. By the fall and the emergence of the strong Social Issue emphasis, Nixon believed that this theme could contribute to the success of local candidates through national as well as local promotion.

The election strategy centered on issues and pointed to implications for coalitions in Congress as well as for the campaign at hand. Rather than campaigning against Democrats, the administration campaigned against "radical liberals." The definition of that label was designed to identify members of Congress unfriendly to Nixon's political goals. The action of defining ideological criteria in such a way was an attempt to assert control of the political agenda and the terms of debate about it—to the advantage, of course, of Nixon and his supporters.

Quite apart from the need to crowd out economic issues, the Nixon camp strongly believed in the intrinsic power of antipermissiveness as a political issue. Nixon had a very clear impression of the political attitudes of the group to whom he sought to appeal. He read a newspaper column in which James Reston, attempting to summarize the president's political thinking, had written that the White House "must get with the mood of the country which is fed up with the liberals." Nixon felt that the article had succeeded well, and he distributed its text widely among his staff. The piece included references to economic issues but emphasized aspects of antipermissiveness:

> [D]espite the passionate political minorities on the right and left, the majority of people in the West between the Alleghenies and the Rockies believe most of the following: the Vietnam war is a mess we never should have gotten into—"but after all, it is coming to an end." The rebellious kids are both wrong and a menace. More cops and tougher penalties are needed to stop crime—not slum clearance. The Supreme Court has assumed too much "legislative" power. "Taxes are too damn high." The poor are poor, mainly though not entirely because they don't work and have too many kids. Education is in trouble because "they" teach everything but what

counts, i.e., reading and writing. The Communists are still a menace and at the very least cutting the defense budget is dangerous. Negroes have rights but forced integration will leave everyone worse off. One of the our main national problems is permissive parents.

"It is very late—but we still have time to move away from the line of our well-intentioned liberals on our staff," Nixon thought, as indicated in a memo written by staff secretary John Brown. "We must get turned around on this before it is too late—emphasize anti-crime, anti-demonstrations, anti-drugs, anti-obscenity."[29] Because it reflected these concerns, the strategy was not a defensive one but was indeed extremely aggressive and therefore unusual for a party in power.

On the day after Brown wrote this memo, Nixon briefed his leading campaign operatives. Reading the meeting's agenda, prepared by midterm campaign coordinator Bryce Harlow, Nixon wrote in the margin, "Hang the Radical Left tag on the Dem Candidates." Harlow had an extensive list of issues to tackle in the campaign, including the achievements in racial policy and the reformist aims in domestic policy. For Nixon, this plan was too diffuse.[30] Nixon knew which issues he wanted to stress. He thought that the stakes were high. "There's a realignment going on," Nixon said, as recorded by William Safire:

> [W]e are not out for a Republican Senate. We are out to get rid of the radicals. The point is that the only Republican coming up who is a radical is Goodell. . . . The President's usual rule of endorsing all Republican candidates is being revoked in this case.
>
> Have you all read the Scammon-Wattenberg book? All the Democrats are reading it. . . . All Democrats are trying to blur their image; they are petrified about permissiveness being hung on them—toward crime, toward students. . . .
>
> The Administration thrust is centrist. But now even a way-out type like McGovern is racing toward the center. We have to force them to repudiate the left, which loses them votes, or else take the left—which gives us the center.
>
> That's the way this campaign has to be fought. The Democrats are trying to move over to the center, keeping us on the defensive on the economic issue. On inflation: don't go into the drawn-out business about the trade-off between price stability and unemployment. Just say this is what happens

when you go from war to peace. We should hit them hard on the Vietnam issue. But on the left-right business, get them on the defensive: "I don't question his sincerity—he deeply believes this radical philosophy." . . . Permissiveness is the key theme.[31]

To identify Nixon's enemies, aides drew up the "radical-liberal" index, which focused on how legislators had voted on the issues that mattered to Nixon, including his Vietnam policy as well as national defense more generally, and his Supreme Court nominations of Clement Haynsworth and G. Harrold Carswell. Initiatives for domestic reform did not appear, and economic issues appeared on the index only in the context of "big spending" measures. But when in mid-September some votes on crime bills were added to the index, it was discovered that "our radi-libs let us down on the crime issue."[32]

THE POLITICS OF THE SOCIAL ISSUE

Even at its moment of construction, the ideas behind the radical-liberal strategy revealed weakness. Many Democrats resisted such easy categorization. The radical liberals let down the White House by voting for Nixon's anticrime initiatives. As the campaign season approached, the emphasis of political debate and the focus of congressional attention shifted away from reformism and toward the politics of antipermissiveness. Legislators about to face elections tackled anticrime proposals in preference to other major policy proposals—most notably FAP but also reform of the Electoral College, food-stamp reform, and consumer protection measures. Nixon expected an opportunity to describe Democrats as soft on law and order because Congress had at first paid little attention to his proposals on crime and in some cases reacted with hostility.[33]

As members of Congress became wise to Nixon's strategy, the mood on Capitol Hill changed. The result was the enactment of four major anticrime bills, which received very little meaningful opposition. Most controversial was a package for Washington, D.C., that Nixon had signed into law in July, with provisions including the possibility of preventive detention before trial and "no knock" search warrants. The act was controversial because of serious doubts about its constitutionality. Senator Sam J. Ervin Jr., a Democrat from North Carolina, called the administration bill "a garbage pail of some of the most repressive, nearsighted, intolerant, unfair and vindictive legislation that the Senate has ever been presented." It represented "an affront to the constitutional principles and to the intelligence of the people of the United States." Even so, the conference report on the bill received only thirty-three dissenting votes in the Senate and sixty-four in the House. The district was the only part of the nation over which the federal government had any direct responsibility for routine matters of law enforcement, so the measure's impact was limited, but Attorney General Mitchell held up the act as a model for other parts of the country.

Similar constitutional questions were raised during the debate over the Organized Crime Control Act, but it passed with little opposition shortly before the election recess. Both houses of Congress also passed versions of an Omnibus Crime Control Act that authorized more than $3.5 billion in federal aid to states and localities over three years. Two representatives voted against the House version; no senators voted against their version of the bill. The final version of the act would be passed in December. Again with barely any opposition, Congress passed in October the Comprehensive Drug Abuse Prevention and Control Act of 1970, both strengthening penalties for drug offenses and extending programs against drug abuse.[34]

Indeed, members of Congress joined the administration in proposing anti-crime legislation, including a bill to provide for the imprisonment of anyone who urged "the desirability or necessity of urban terrorism" or belonged to an organization that did; another measure sought to make the murder of a policeman, fireman, or judge a federal crime when the victim was singled out as "a symbol of the Establishment." The White House hit back with a hastily instituted a "Law Officers Appreciation Week" during the fall campaign.[35]

Pornography, a further element of the Social Issue, became newsworthy as the campaign approached, and the administration eagerly sought political benefit in the issue. Before he left the White House, Lyndon Johnson had established a National Commission on Obscenity and Pornography; it was now preparing to publish its report. Based on its findings, the commission favored the liberalization of antipornography laws, an outcome that dissatisfied the Nixon White House. Instead, administration staffers found private funds for a minority report that disagreed with that conclusion and sought publicity for this alternative to the majority report.[36]

In private, concerns about pornography as a political issue tended to eclipse any concerns relating to the wisdom of public debate and policy wherever any trace arose of a conflict between the two areas. When it appeared that commission members might moderate some of their recommendations because of the adverse publicity that their work was attracting, Haldeman was alarmed. "Obviously we don't want to let them do this—we want to develop the issue and we need to move hard to be sure that this is done," he wrote to Buchanan. Nixon wanted controversy to emphasize his antipermissive credentials. The White House should therefore disagree publicly with the commission's recommendations. Colson's outside-liaison operation worked hard to publicize that disagreement. What mattered to Nixon was the rhetoric; his administration did not look for policies to substantiate this concern.[37]

Nixon avoided one emerging element of the Social Issue, women's right to abortions. New York's legalization of abortion in July 1970 despite significant Catholic opposition was a turning point that made the question one of national salience. In this case, Nixon was wary of social conservatism. During his campaign planning, he determined that the issue should remain a concern of the states and courts and not of the executive, although he manifestly failed to apply a similar argument about federalism to questions of law enforcement.[38]

GOODELL AND BYRD

The impact of the radical-liberal strategy was seen most acutely in the career of Charles Goodell. In 1968, New York Governor Nelson Rockefeller had appointed Goodell, then in the House, to fill the Senate seat of the assassinated Robert Kennedy. Goodell's record, reasonably conservative in the House, became noticeably more liberal, largely because he saw the needs and demands of his statewide constituency as different from those in his district. Nevertheless, despite the high rating that his voting attracted from Americans for Democratic Action, Goodell supported the administration line more consistently than did Barry Goldwater, and Goodell's senior New York colleague, Jacob Javits, received a much higher rating from the group in 1969.[39] What particularly irritated Nixon was Goodell's opposition to the war.

Nixon found the idea of opposing Goodell appealing not only because his defeat would remove a dove from the Senate but also because failing to support Goodell might diminish Republican opposition to Nixon in the next congressional session. The activity against Goodell also made the radical-liberal strategy seem less aggressively partisan. There was a pragmatic calculation, too.

Goodell's showing in opinion polls was poor, while his Conservative opponent, James Buckley, not a Republican but supportive of Nixon on many issues, seemed to have a good chance at election. Moreover, Buckley emphasized conservatism on the Social Issue. By contrast, Nixon was prepared even to offer active support to Winston L. Prouty, a Vermont senator whose record was more liberal overall than Goodell's; unlike Goodell, however, Prouty had not challenged Nixon's foreign policy.[40]

Harry Byrd, a conservative Democrat from Virginia, benefited from the radical-liberal strategy when Nixon decided not to offer White House support to the Republican senatorial candidate in Virginia, Ray L. Garland, whom the local organization considered a model "new southern" Republican politician. Important Virginia Republicans were not happy about this decision.[41] For a time, the administration had hoped that Byrd would decide to run as a Republican or at least vote for Republican organization of the Senate. As in Goodell's case, political practicality was particularly important, and Byrd's eventual decision to run for reelection in 1970 as an independent was chiefly influenced by political practicality. He would almost certainly win in a three-way contest, but his chances would diminish if he ran as a Republican against a Democratic candidate.

The transfer of Byrd's allegiance would have represented a major achievement for the Republican Party with respect to its southern ambitions and would have increased the odds of Republican control of the Senate. But Byrd was not motivated to change his allegiance out of any special affinity for the Republican Party; instead, he severed his connection with the Democrats because it seemed unlikely that he would be renominated despite his family's historical dominance of the Virginia party.

The success of the radical-liberal strategy in Virginia was limited. Byrd's failure to fulfill Nixon's hopes indicated that undermining the conservative southern Democratic tradition remained a formidable task and that perhaps the White House should seek ideological rather than partisan control as a more realistic goal. Byrd was unwilling to contribute to the erosion of southern conservative power by depriving his political allies of their influential positions as committee chairs. He ran and won as an independent candidate and voted for Democratic organization when the Ninety-second Congress convened.[42]

After discouraging Arthur Fletcher from standing, the White House did nothing to encourage the Republican campaign against Scoop Jackson in

Washington. Nixon was also unenthusiastic about opposing Mike Mansfield, a Montana Democrat who supported Nixon on Vietnam; moreover, if Mansfield lost his seat, his likely successor as Senate majority leader would be Edward Kennedy, and Nixon did not wish to see this presidential aspirant in a position of such prominence.[43]

MIDDLE AMERICA

Most contributors to the 1969–70 debate about middle America emphasized, at least in part, economic needs and the importance of tackling them. In the absence of substantive achievement in this regard, the White House fashioned a special appeal to segments of middle America in addition to the general strategy against radical liberalism.

Most notable among these groups was labor. Important qualifications to the possible extent of labor's support had already appeared, and these qualifications became yet more apparent in the fall. At the start of the congressional campaign, American Federation of Labor and Congress of Industrial Organizations (AFL-CIO) leader George Meany publicly described his group's relationship with the administration as "fairly good." But the news for the Republican Party was not entirely encouraging, it seemed. He said that the situation was "not so much that our people are looking to the Republicans, but they are looking less to the Democrats because, actually, the Democratic party has disintegrated." His members were more conservatively oriented than in previous years, thanks to their increased prosperity, he said, and more interested in issues such as rising crime rates. The labor movement remained preeminently concerned with pocketbook issues, and the leadership's commitment to a hawkish position on the war was in no way compromised by the growing number of leading Democrats who argued for immediate disengagement. In response, there was some caution at the White House. "Don't be totally taken in by this—What he's trying to do is force the Dems back to the right—*not* to help us," wrote Haldeman.[44]

Meany's expression of qualified support for the administration did not represent endorsement either of Nixon or, less likely still, of Republican congressional candidates. The AFL-CIO's Committee on Political Education (COPE) decided to support particular candidates exclusively on the grounds of their service to labor. Despite Jay Lovestone's private offer to work covertly against

Albert Gore, the Tennessee senator benefited from COPE donations averaging $10,000, as did his colleagues Vance Hartke and Gale McGee of Wyoming, who supported the war as well as labor. COPE lent its most strenuous support, both organizational and financial, to the candidacy of New Jersey Democratic Senator Harrison W. Williams. From the administration's perspective, Williams was a hopeless radical-liberal. But COPE found irrelevant his views on the war and on crime; instead, organized labor valued Williams's chairmanship of the Senate Labor Subcommittee.

Nixon nevertheless enthusiastically cultivated labor. On Labor Day, he hosted a high-profile dinner for unionists, described as "a real coup" by Haldeman. Meany gave a toast in which he referred to Nixon's reputation as "Tricky Dick" but pointed out that Franklin Roosevelt was "just as tricky, and Lyndon [Johnson was] no slouch either." Democratic National Chair Lawrence F. O'Brien insisted as often as he could that organized labor's natural political home was with his party, but individuals were now questioning that traditionally automatic allegiance.[45] In view of labor's recent history of hostility to the Republican Party, these developments, however limited in extent, were remarkable.

Nixon knew that endorsements by union leaders remained most unlikely, although he could neutralize their hostility on issues other than the economy and cultivate their personal friendship. In the absence of endorsements from the leadership, greater support from union members became more feasible. Unionists were alert to the potential threat to Democratic loyalties. According to Bill Dodds, legislative director of the liberal United Auto Workers, liberal candidates could challenge the rightward shift among rank-and-file unionists by emphasizing workplace issues. "If they get all swept up in something emotional like a lot of student bombings," Dodds admitted, "workers are going to work against their economic interest. But there is no reason why we cannot articulate that interest."[46]

Charles Colson urged Nixon to work harder in search of labor support, arguing that the administration should undertake a thoroughgoing and multi-faceted effort to convert unionists' sympathy for Nixon into a long-term alliance between labor and the Republican Party. Essential to this effort was the identification of policies that appealed to labor. The Rosow Report was a good starting point. "We need to identify with labor on a major substantive issue other than national security," wrote Colson. Nixon commended the ideas as "[e]xcellent" and instructed their implementation under Colson's supervision.

The president asked John Ehrlichman to assign one of his domestic-policy staffers to the task of finding "some area in which we can clearly pre-empt the field with a pro-labor cause."[47]

With no time for substantive achievement before the elections, Nixon pressed for other demonstrations of the administration's affinity with American workers. He told budget director George Shultz to "proceed with some initial implementation of the Rosow blue collar report even if it is only symbolic." Political aides Harry Dent and Murray Chotiner received instructions to ensure that "all of our Republican candidates address themselves to the subject of the 'working man' and the 'build America' theme on a regular basis." Harry Flemming, responsible for patronage in the administration, was told to "insure that representatives of organized labor are appointed to virtually every Commission that we announce." Nixon told press aide Herbert Klein to work with Colson on publicizing "how this Administration is pro-workingman, not anti-labor as other Republican Administrations have appeared to be."[48]

In search of middle America, Nixon was interested in fashioning a special appeal—again, symbolic rather than substantive—to ethnic groups as well as to labor families, traditionally Democratic groups estimated to number around 40 million people and concentrated in major cities of the Midwest and Northeast. While the administration made little immediate progress toward this goal, the Republican Party had rather more success in some areas. Indeed, lists of Republican candidates for 1970 in areas such as northwest Chicago were for the first time sprinkled with ethnic names. Local party leaders observed that ethnic voters in the cities were more responsive to Republican appeals, thanks to concerns such as rising crime. Illinois Governor Richard B. Ogilvie regularly used the ethnic press to chronicle his appointments of Polish, Italian, and Hungarian Americans.[49]

The RNC also paid attention to the promise of the ethnic vote. At the start of the Nixon administration, a nationalities committee was established with the intention of strengthening ties between ethnic Americans and the Republican Party, in partial replacement of the minorities division. But the White House usually ignored the many ethnic game plans of the committee's chair, Laszlo Pasztor, a Hungarian immigrant who was forced instead to concentrate on mobilizing RNC resources to implement his proposals. In July 1970, Chotiner, for many years a political aide to Nixon, attempted to move the ethnic operation into the White House, assuming that its target constituency would be more susceptible to appeals connected with the president than with the Republican Party. For the moment, however, the ethnic committee remained at the national committee, receiving little support within the administration.[50]

Some Americans were the target not of cultivation but of demonization. The radical-liberal strategy depended on the identification of enemies of the administration's project. Young antiwar protesters fell into this category. The first speech that Nixon contributed to the campaign was an attack on student radicalism, given as the Alf Landon Lecture at Kansas State University. Nixon believed in the political value of such attacks, but dangers also existed. In response to Agnew's even stronger rhetoric on the same subject, a Minnesota Republican explained its possible impact on "straight kids" earlier in the year: "Even though they don't approve of the antics of the 'weirdos' and 'hippies,' they resent [attacks] and stick up for their own generation," he said. "This language risks alienating kids who are with us." Nixon seemed ready to run the risk. In September, a presidential commission on campus unrest, convened in the aftermath of the deaths at Kent State, issued a report. The commission, chaired by William Scranton, the former governor of Pennsylvania, criticized most parties involved, including Nixon. Nixon dismissed the report; Agnew said that it was "more pablum for the permissivists."[51]

AGNEW, PHILLIPS, AND WATTENBERG

Spiro Agnew's pugnacious rhetoric dominated the early campaign, which began with his announcement that the White House wanted "to represent the workingmen of this country, the Forgotten Man of American politics; white collar and blue collar." To do so, the vice president unveiled the idea of "radical liberalism" as the enemy of Nixon's plan, distinguishing it from older Democratic thinking. "Today's radical-liberal posturing in the Senate," he said at the opening of the campaign in Springfield, Illinois, "is about as closely related to a Harry Truman, as is a chihuahua to a timber wolf." The offenses of radical liberalism included "a whimpering isolationism in foreign policy, a mulish obstructionism in domestic policy, and a pusillanimous pussyfooting on the critical issue of law and order." As the campaign proceeded, Agnew paid relatively little attention to this "mulish obstructionism" or to the offense of "big spending," focusing instead on criticisms of the administration's Vietnam policy and antipermissiveness stance. Indeed, his speeches added up to an introductory course on permissiveness and its ills. Agnew condemned pornographic content in movies, drug references in music, and Dr. Benjamin Spock's ideas about child rearing.[52]

Observing the early weeks of the campaign, Kevin Phillips thought that Agnew's rhetoric effectively reached out to an emerging Republican majority, blue-collar and northern, in addition to new southern converts to the party. But Phillips, now working as a newspaper columnist, did not think that the administration's record matched its rhetoric:

> The fulcrum of Republican appeal is more or less the "social issue." . . . As Scammon and Wattenberg suggest, the "social issue" may be on a par with the cyclical realignment issues of 1896 and 1932. By moving towards a me-too position, the Democrats are probably giving way to history. . . .
>
> However, the pre-September Republican record is one of ineptness and ambiguity. Exertions on behalf of expanded welfare, the Philadelphia Plan, and suburban integration, as well as the activities of the Presidential Commission on Campus Unrest have all detracted from the Nixon administration's ability to use the "social issue," and lessened pro-Republican realignment. . . .
>
> The administration cannot build a lasting new GOP coalition until it can articulate a positive philosophy and program to replace liberalism's failure to meet the needs of Middle America.[53]

Nixon was still a careful reader of Phillips, and his words caused the president to question the direction of his administration. His reaction mirrored his response to the Reston column just a few weeks earlier—doubt again about the place of liberalism or reformism within the administration. This time, the consequences were dramatic. Ehrlichman, by now Nixon's chief domestic policy adviser, later wrote that as a result of the article, he was frozen out of Nixon's inner circle for several weeks. The president refused to see Ehrlichman, and his memoranda went unanswered. "Domestic-policy work came to a halt," Ehrlichman recalled.[54]

Nixon told Ehrlichman that Phillips's column represented a "correct view" and that Ehrlichman should "take action to correct" the problems identified by Phillips. In response, Ehrlichman defended his work on welfare and the Philadelphia Plan. After all, Scammon and Wattenberg had insisted that the White House should take an activist approach to problems within society. "Young Kevin's column," wrote Ehrlichman, "either shows he misunderstands or misuses the concept to impeach some non-conservative initiatives deliberately designed to furnish some zigs to go with our conservative zags." Ehrlichman regained the initiative, at least for the moment. Nixon noted his agreement with much of Ehrlichman's argument, and soon thereafter Haldeman allegedly informed John Mitchell that, in Nixon's opinion, Phillips had "flipped."[55]

Another observer of middle America had a yet more direct role in the campaign. Ben Wattenberg was working as an adviser to Hubert Humphrey, who was seeking to return to the Senate from Minnesota. Though Wattenberg admitted that he found "it difficult to work up all those partisan juices against Nixon," Wattenberg's approval of the president was decidedly limited. "On inspiration he bats zero," Wattenberg said. Wattenberg's candidate had good prospects. At the end of September, a poll conducted for the *Minneapolis Tribune* indicated that Humphrey stood 17 points ahead of his Republican opponent, Clark MacGregor, one of Nixon's handpicked candidates. Still, confidence in the radical-liberal strategy reached a stage where a White House analysis gave MacGregor "at least a fighting chance."[56]

The White House lavished considerable attention on MacGregor's fortunes and particularly on the tactics that his campaign team was deploying against Humphrey. Even as confidence in MacGregor's prospects started to decline, the administration continued to hope that the campaign would damage Humphrey's national prospects. "The key here," wrote Haldeman, "is that [MacGregor] should be working hard to drive Humphrey to the left and he should be pushing Humphrey hard."[57]

Humphrey's campaign resisted these efforts. Wattenberg tried to ensure that his candidate could not be depicted as soft on crime, as he had in 1968. For example, in a speech written by Wattenberg, Humphrey told the American Bar Association that liberals "must let the hardhats, Mr. and Mrs. Middle America, know that they understand what is bugging them, that they too condemn crime and riots and violence and extreme turbulence, that they scorn extremists of the left as well as extremists of the right." Humphrey not only ensured that his stance on the Social Issue was appropriate but campaigned hard against MacGregor, discussing other issues—particularly bread-and-butter issues—as Election Day approached.[58]

In fact, MacGregor's campaign also resisted White House urgings to stress the charges of radical liberalism. MacGregor largely ignored the theme of the Social Issue in a campaign considered old-fashioned by administration strategists. In late September, Haldeman wrote of his frustration to Chotiner, who was responsible for White House liaison with the MacGregor campaign: "He should be using Hubert's horrible quotes and not let him get back into the side of law and order and tough on students, etc., that he so adeptly is doing right now, while MacGregor just stands and watches," wrote Haldeman.[59]

Despite MacGregor's lack of enthusiasm, the strategy formulated in the White House won support among many other Republicans nationwide. Activists uttered some words of caution about the dramatic nature of the campaign rhetoric but frequently greeted Agnew's intervention with enthusiasm. In Nevada, for example, the campaign manager for senatorial candidate William Raggio was delighted: "He's tremendously popular here," said Alan Abner of Agnew. "Not just with Republicans but with Democrats, too—the hard hats, if you want to put it that way. A guy like Agnew really speaks their language."[60]

Some Republican candidates tried to follow suit, as Nixon wanted. In Tennessee, William Brock used aggressive rhetoric against incumbent radical-liberal Albert Gore, who questioned Nixon's Vietnam policy and had opposed the nominations of Haynsworth and Carswell. Gore sought to challenge accusations that he had failed to support his nation's cause overseas by appearing in campaign commercials with his son, Albert Gore Jr., who was serving in the U.S. Army and was awaiting deployment to Vietnam. The Gore family was sure that the White House had intervened to delay the assignment of the senator's son to Vietnam until after the election in an effort to undermine the strength of this symbolism. While Gore tried to insulate himself from attacks on his patriotism, he spoke of his endeavors during his congressional career to secure economic development for his state. Brock responded by escalating his charges of radical liberalism against Gore, alleging that he favored busing and opposed school prayer.[61]

In Ohio, Robert Taft Jr. accused his opponent, Howard Metzenbaum, of similar radical-liberal offenses. Taft called Metzenbaum an "ultraliberal Democrat" who advocated a "bug-out position" on Vietnam and declined to take tough positions on campus unrest and crime. The Ohio campaign was a rarity in that it also featured a Wallaceite candidate, Richard B. Kay of the American Independent Party. Kay's position in the race was marginal, but his rhetoric sometimes made Agnew's and Taft's sound mild. Kay opened his remarks during a television debate by observing, "Satan is loose in America." While denying Taft's charges, Metzenbaum emphasized the poor state of the economy, saying, "I believe unemployment is un-American."

Taft accused Metzenbaum of insincerity in denying the charges of radical liberalism and claimed that Metzenbaum had read *The Real Majority*. "[M]y opponent has been following literally the advice of two Democrat authors who have urged liberal Democrats to pretend to modify their election views on problems of social unrest to get elected," Taft said. "It won't work, I don't believe. The people won't be fooled."[62]

Democrats commonly cast aside the charges of radical liberalism, as the congressional politics of an anticrime consensus indicated. Ben Wattenberg later observed that the party's average candidate "went out of his way to show he was as tough as the guy in the barroom and no one was going to call him soft on law and order." In the Illinois campaign for the Senate, Ralph Smith, the incumbent, accused his challenger, Adlai Stevenson III, of radical liberalism. "When I see Adlai," Smith commented, "I see red." Stevenson refused to allow such accusations to stand. He wore a flag pin in his lapel and made it clear that he was no radical. Having earlier criticized the actions of the Chicago police at the 1968 Democratic National Convention, he emphasized his condemnation of violence whether "by Black Panthers, white students or state troopers." When William Cramer pressed the same strategy into action in Florida, it simply lacked credibility from the start to suggest that his opponent, Lawton Chiles, was a radical. Similar problems of credibility arose in efforts to conduct radical-liberal campaigns in other states, including Utah, Wyoming, and Texas.[63]

No Democrats were willing and inactive victims of the radical-liberal campaign. In response, the Nixon campaign charged its opponents with lying. Radical liberals were "trying to pull the fastest switcheroo in American politics," according to Agnew. "The new election-time patriot is still our old undependable friend, the radical-liberal," he said. "The overnight hard-liner on crime is still that old bleeding heart, not worried about his heart but his seat." Nixon was confident that the key to success in making this charge was archival investigation. Haldeman told Colson to take charge. "The point here . . . is to get those quotes, going back as far as is necessary, from each of these individuals on which we can hang the guy," Haldeman wrote. "We should specifically zero in on the areas of permissiveness, law and order, students, the moratoriums, Black Panthers, and all the other so-called social issues that Scammon and Wattenberg have pointed out so clearly to us are the key issues of our time." As a result, the campaign against radical liberalism would short-circuit Democrats' efforts to moderate their positions. "If we get the right phrase we can kill each one of these guys with one phrase," Haldeman asserted.[64]

RACE

In general, Nixon did not directly address questions of race during the fall of 1970. He had decided that race was unlikely to be important to the campaign, although racial integration would be "hot for '72." The late summer of 1970 was, however, a period of great significance to racial policy, with a successful wave of school desegregation across the South. Two million African American pupils out of a total of 3 million in southern schools attended desegregated institutions for the first time. Closely monitored by Nixon, the process unfolded peacefully in the vast majority of localities. Its success was arguably a tribute to the administration's accomplishments in implementing court-ordered desegregation through a conciliatory and low-profile approach to the problem.[65] But Nixon did not try to make the argument in his favor.

Race played an important part in a number of states. As Brock's campaign in Tennessee demonstrated, the politics of race focused on busing, a method of desegregation employed to overcome residential patterns of racial separation. The issue was seen as hugely important wherever it was a pressing policy option. One Democratic congressman who was experiencing difficulty in his campaign to secure reelection in a conservative suburb told a journalist, "All I would have to do is campaign against busing, and all my other stands would be lived with." When Nixon visited such areas, he was ready to address racial issues and to do so in a conservative manner. In Tallahassee, Florida, for example, he told voters about his opposition to busing, giving a surprising reason to justify it. "[I]f you put children on a bus for an hour," he explained, whether black or white, "they are going to be fighting."[66]

Historian Dan T. Carter has argued that race was more important to Nixon's strategy than the relatively few references to busing suggest. Racist ideas underpinned the politics of antipermissiveness that Nixon had stressed in his campaign against radical liberalism. Attempts to separate social issues from racial concerns were possible only in theory. "In reality," according to Carter, "fears of blackness and fears of disorder were the warp and woof of the new social agenda, bound together by the subconscious connection many white Americans made between blackness and criminality, blackness and poverty, blackness and cultural degradation."[67] For Nixon, the Social Issue partly reinforced his attempt to mobilize support behind his Vietnam policy through criticisms of antiwar protesters. But at the same time, crime remained a very prominent concern, and the connection made by Carter has powerful force in this arena.

NIXON

When Nixon discussed the strategy for the midterms with Kevin Phillips in July, the two men noted that the announcement of a foreign policy success during the fall campaign could improve Republican fortunes. Given the centrality of domestic issues at the state and local levels, it is a superficially surprising judgment. But it becomes more understandable in light of a number of factors. Most significantly, the Vietnam War was an overwhelmingly important issue facing the nation. The way in which Nixon conducted the campaign stressed his need for congressional supporters of his foreign policy, together with his contempt for antiwar protesters. Moreover, public opinion about Nixon was usually most favorable with respect to his foreign policy; the way he was waging the Vietnam War was winning him support. Nixon drew a parallel with the campaign of 1962, dominated by the Cuban Missile Crisis. The handling of the missile crisis benefited the Democrats, dealing the final blow, he thought, to his campaign against Edmund "Pat" Brown for the governorship of California.[68]

Nixon demonstrated his foreign policy ability in mid-September when he successfully contained a confrontation between Jordan and Syrian-supported Palestinian forces. In the same month, he departed to visit six European countries, having handed out careful instructions about how to fight the campaign. He intended to offer reassuring images of the president demonstrating his national-leadership qualities. Newspapers in the United States at this time were therefore dominated by reports of Nixon's visits to fellow world leaders along with the vice president's latest condemnations of domestic permissiveness.[69]

The Vietnam War remained the president's most significant test. By the early fall of 1970, some elements of the administration's diplomacy were beginning to show fresh promise. On Nixon's return to Washington, developments at the Paris peace talks allowed him to propose a peace conference and the unconditional release of prisoners of war on both sides. A key American condition remained that the Thieu regime retain power until free elections could be held. The important concession offered by the October 7 proposal was a call for a cease-fire, during which American troops would continue their withdrawal. At a subsequent news conference, however, Nixon said that the withdrawal should be mutual, a point that limited the significance of what he claimed as a breakthrough. Following the initial statement, the immediate reaction from press and politicians was overwhelmingly favorable.[70] But Hanoi quickly rejected the proposals, and the way in which Nixon had hastily revised and repackaged them left many people believing that electoral considerations had dictated the timing of his announcement.

Even in the shorter term, Nixon did not think that the announcement had boosted public support for him, though he did not understand why. He was quietly satisfied with the appeasement of some administration foes but was puzzled by the response of the American people at large. He was "[c]oncerned that this still doesn't seem to get across the leadership image" and raised the "[q]uestion of what we are doing wrong, or whether we could ever get through the media regardless of what we do," wrote Haldeman. When Nixon confirmed that troop withdrawals would continue, it was clear that voters supported such moves, but this support did not translate into better ratings for Republican politicians. Taft's campaign in Ohio offered one clue to solving the puzzle. During his campaign, Taft spoke of his support for Nixon's policies on Vietnam and contrasted it with the skepticism of his Democratic opponent. But Taft remained unsure about the importance of foreign policy to his candidacy, because "foreign policy issues could be removed to some extent as issues" in light of the importance of "domestic and particularly economic issues."[71]

Another puzzle for Nixon was the discovery that the Agnew-led campaign to summon the silent majority to the ballot box was, at best, hardly proving an unequivocal success. When the tour of Europe reached Ireland, Haldeman noted that Nixon was "really intrigued with the campaign" and could not understand the poor showing by the administration's favored candidates in Republican polls.[72] On his return to Washington in October, Nixon reassessed the campaign, reaching the inescapable conclusion that the strategy was not working.

The main thrust of the campaign—the condemnation of so-called radical-liberals as the basis of a redefinition of the Republican Party—was failing. According to administration pollster David R. Derge, reaction to the label "radical-liberal" was partisan. Voters' approval of the term and their agreement with it depended on their general support for Nixon and the Republican Party. In short, this aspect of Agnew's campaign was ineffective in winning over new voters, and potential "swing" voters were ambivalent rather than enthusiastic about such a characterization of certain senators. Only about half of the respondents to the poll was aware of the "radical-liberal" label. In response to this unwelcome news, Nixon decided that it might be wise to tone down the rhetoric, a decision that caused some misgivings within the White

House. Buchanan, Haldeman, and Safire were all rather enthusiastic about the vice president's campaign and about the defensiveness they thought it engendered in Democratic candidates.[73]

In fact, there was no reason for such misgivings. Nixon entered the fray with rhetoric that was far from restrained. In his basic campaign address he asked for the election of candidates who supported him on the major issues of the day, and he mentioned the progress achieved in foreign policy, especially with regard to Vietnam. Reviewing the administration's record and its goals and omitting only race, he talked about his reform agenda as well as antipermissiveness. His presentation of these arguments quickly shed its quiet moderation, reflecting Nixon's conviction that America faced an unusual moment of political upheaval. "[T]his is not a traditional election," he said, because "today, in America, there are two separate and distinct political and social philosophies competing for the right to determine the destiny of this nation. . . . These elections are another phase of the political and philosophical conflict of 1968—a conflict between the dogmas of the old elite that dominated America in the sixties and, on the other side, a new leadership that represents the values and beliefs of a new emergent majority in American politics."

In place of Agnew's characterization of many Democratic senators as radical liberals, Nixon borrowed from a speech of Woodrow Wilson to refer to a "little group of willful men." In describing this willfulness, Nixon's message sometimes became strident. On foreign policy, he attacked the "officeholders and candidates who try to demean their country and who counsel defeat and humiliation for America"; on crime, he said that those politicians had "all but forgotten the right of innocent people to enjoy freedom from fear"; on New Federalism, he said that "the controlling clique in Congress refused to change."[74]

Lawrence O'Brien of the Democrats claimed that the radical-liberal campaign relied on the "politics of fear," drawing a parallel with McCarthyism. Many observers were dismayed that Nixon sought electoral benefit from polarization instead of trying to heal the nation's divisions. The many critics included journalist James Reston, who identified "a sense of loneliness in the country, even of helplessness and doubt about the fidelity of our institutions." This malaise was "something to be approached with sympathy and a reconciling spirit," he wrote, "rather than trifled with and twisted into a party argument for a few Congressional seats."[75] Reston therefore suggested that Nixon was guilty of neglecting his presidential responsibility for national leadership.

The claim did not bother Nixon. On the stump, his perception of a rare opportunity for political gain further overwhelmed any possible desire to moderate the campaign. To begin his first tour of the campaign, he traveled to Burlington, Vermont. As he climbed off his airplane, a protester threw a small piece of concrete toward the president. Nixon immediately seized the incident as a chance to dramatize his conservative position on the Social Issue and added some new lines to his previously prepared speech. He attacked "a small group in this country, . . . that shouts obscenities . . . , that throws rocks . . . ; a group of people that always tear America down; a group of people that hate this country, actually, in terms of what it presently stands for; who see nothing right with America." As he would in any other campaign, at each stop Nixon talked about local issues and concerns, but the Social Issue remained at the heart of this campaign. Protesters were his foil, an essential presence to illustrate his point and to convince voters that radical liberalism posed a real danger. In search of controversial confrontation, he therefore instructed advance aides to admit protesters to his campaign appearances.[76]

The publication of the obscenity and pornography commission's report provided Nixon with an opportunity to relate his rhetoric to a set of substantive proposals. In rejecting that substance—the commission's "morally bankrupt conclusions and major recommendations"—his rhetoric was dramatic. Commenting that "American morality is not to be trifled with," he emphasized, "[s]o long as I am in the White House, there will be no relaxation of the national effort to control and eliminate smut from our national life."[77]

At the end of October, Nixon took the campaign to his home state. As he left a rally in San Jose, protesters attacked the president's motorcade, living up to Nixon's characterization by shouting obscenities and throwing rocks. It was a particularly disturbing example of violent demonstration, but many observers thought that Nixon had provoked the incident. On seeing the angry crowds waiting for his departure from the auditorium, he jumped onto his car to wave his Nixon salute at them. Strategists were delighted at what they immediately perceived as an excellent opportunity to dramatize the Social Issue for their middle-American audience. Nixon's advisers were nearly euphoric; the campaign team was convinced that the president had unquestionably managed, with the help of Agnew, to define the salient election issues as those that favored the administration. From the White House, Murray Chotiner sent an excited note to Haldeman. "The only thing left for the Demos to do now—is to withdraw their candidates," wrote Chotiner. "They can't win if we can keep on the heat." Nixon was no less pleased. "All through the day he delighted in giving the V to the peaceniks," Haldeman noted. The campaign team's enthusiasm for the political possibilities of the incident was not affected by the eagerness of prominent Democrats to describe how they, too, deplored the attack on the president while they questioned some of his campaign tactics.[78]

A few days after the San Jose incident, Nixon gave a speech at Sky Harbor Airport in Phoenix, Arizona, where he denounced violent protesters with the greatest force yet. "The time has come to draw the line," he said. "The time has come for the great silent majority of Americans, of all ages and of every political persuasion, to stand up and be counted against the appeasement of the rock throwers and obscenity shouters. . . . The new approach to violence requires men in Congress who will work and fight for laws that will put the terrorists where they belong—not roaming around civil society, but behind bars. . . . If we do not act now to protect our freedom, we shall lose our freedom."[79]

The Republican campaign ended on this note. The party used Nixon's Sky Harbor speech as an election-eve broadcast. The rhetoric was dramatic and even harsh; the quality of the film was poor. For the Democratic broadcast that immediately followed Nixon's, Edmund Muskie delivered a calm, reassuring message. "The contrast was devastating," Jeb Magruder would later recall. "It was like watching Grandma Moses debate the Boston Strangler." Still, Nixon thought that the campaign had gone well. He agreed with the observations of his daughter, Tricia, that his intervention had brought excitement to the campaign. If he were running, moreover, he would win by ten million votes.[80]

RESULTS

A Dayton newspaper, in conjunction with the local machinists' union, identified Scammon and Wattenberg's typical American voter as most closely resembling Bette Lowrey. Lowrey, who lived in the suburb of Fairborn, was deeply concerned about the Social Issue but was unsure whether the Agnew line provided the appropriate answer. The press attention that she attracted gave her no time to study the candidates and issues in depth, she said, and she voted Democratic. "When in doubt, stick to your party," she explained. Another reporter identified the average voter as a teamster in Akron whose economic concerns transcended his hostility to antiwar protesters. Like Lowrey, Mike Mango resisted Taft's appeal and voted for Metzenbaum.[81]

Despite Lowrey's and Mango's disinclination to support the Republican Party, Robert Taft Jr. won in Ohio. In the Senate overall, Republicans gained two seats, leaving them five short of the number needed for control. In the House, Republicans suffered a net loss of nine to the Democrats. The picture was particularly disappointing across the nation's governorships; forty-five states held gubernatorial elections, and Republicans lost control in eleven, reducing their total to twenty-one compared to the Democrats' twenty-nine. The administration quickly attributed this setback to local issues.

Nixon's campaign thus failed to meet its goals. Of the thirty-six candidates in twenty-one states for whom Nixon personally stumped, two-thirds lost. Of the ten House members recruited by Nixon for senatorial races, seven lost. There was some good news for the "radical-liberal" campaign, as three targeted senators went down to defeat—Brock defeated Gore in Tennessee, Buckley defeated Goodell, and Glenn Beall defeated Joseph Tydings in Maryland. But at best only some movement away from liberalism and toward conservatism occurred in the Senate, while a number of hawks lost their seats to candidates less supportive of the administration's Vietnam policy—Connecticut Republican Lowell Weicker, Adlai Stevenson III, and California Democrat John Tunney. In the House, Nixon lost ten supporters of his Vietnam policy, while some antiwar politicians gained seats.[82]

The results represented a reasonable showing by the party in power because the contemporary midterm expectation was a loss of thirty-eight seats in the House, though some Democrats questioned the comparison because of the relative weakness in 1968 of Nixon's coattails in marginal districts. But the results were unquestionably disappointing when contrasted with Nixon's real expectations, as opposed to his publicized expectations, which had of course been intentionally low. On the day after the election, Haldeman noted that the president seemed to have hoped for "at least several more" new Republican senators. Moreover, the losses among Republican governors far exceeded the four Nixon had expected. Nixon's political sense had been rather sharper about a week earlier when he predicted to Haldeman a loss of between twelve and fifteen House seats and a gain of either two or three seats in the Senate.[83]

The evidence suggested that the strategy had failed. In 1970, appeals based on the Social Issue were not effective enough to secure a majority in support of

Nixon for two reasons. Economic troubles were pressing, and many Democrats defeated attempts to characterize them as "radical liberals." Nevertheless, Nixon publicly tried to claim victory. "We have increased our majority now," he said some days after the election. "I hope that all the American people realize that now the majority has spoken, the real majority in this country."[84]

Privately, Nixon was disappointed. He explained the failure of the strategy not because of its inadequacies but because of the shortcomings of the Republican Party. He complained about the party's candidates. They were "so poor," he said, and failed to inspire excitement among the electorate. Perhaps, he thought, the White House had worked too hard on their behalf, causing candidates to forget that they, too, had to work hard for victory. In public, Nixon played down the extent of White House involvement as a means of promoting the idea that the failure had been the party's, not the administration's.[85]

Nixon's partisan effort had ended not in success but in disillusionment with his party. This outcome did not surprise some observers. According to contemporary political science, a defining characteristic of American politics was a long-term trend toward the declining electoral salience of parties. In landmark work published in 1970, Walter Dean Burnham wrote that the trend, in place throughout the twentieth century with the sole interruption of the New Deal, coexisted with emerging indicators of an electoral realignment. Having observed such developments as the growth of split-ticket voting and the increasing self-identification of voters as independents, Burnham concluded, "The political parties are progressively losing their hold upon the electorate."[86]

This insight was largely absent from the popular applications of realignment theory produced by Kevin Phillips and Richard Scammon and Ben Wattenberg.[87] Instead, these authors argued that the problem of voter disaffection was smaller; appropriately modified strategies would enable the parties to capture cohesive sections of the public. Nixon's strategy in 1970 was animated by exactly this belief. His self-assigned task—breathtaking in its ambition—was to redefine the lines of partisan conflict in American politics and to place his party on the side of the majority. Where Burnham contemplated the increasingly apartisan nature of electoral politics, Nixon fought a partisan campaign. In doing so, he undertook his presidential responsibilities as party leader with an aggressiveness that very few of his predecessors matched.

While most observers argued about who had won the partisan advantage at this partisan moment, some thought that its apartisan dimension was more compelling. In an article that Nixon considered "[v]ery perceptive," Alan L.

Otten of the *Wall Street Journal* argued that the impact of personality in determining the outcome of the 1970 elections was significant. His examples included Buckley and Brock, whose victories the White House preferred to see as indicating the success of its strategy. "Time and again," Otten wrote, "the voters—perhaps confused about the issues, perhaps indifferent to them—seem to have picked the man 'they could trust' as against one they weren't quite so sure about." Another journalist, James M. Perry, reached a similar conclusion, leading him fundamentally to question the Nixon project. "Perhaps it's nonsense to talk these days of an 'emerging Republican majority' or a 'Democratic coalition,'" Perry wrote. "People are picking and choosing, regardless of party."[88]

FOUR

THE NEW AMERICAN REVOLUTION
Issues, 1970–1972

Many in the White House were dismayed about the conduct of the 1970 campaign. Most of Richard Nixon's advisers told him that the rhetoric against the "radical liberals" had damaged his reputation. As speechwriter Raymond Price put it, "Essential . . . is a return to lowered voices, reason, bring-us-together; and identifying ourselves not so much with angers and frustrations as with the desperate popular yearning for an end to bombast," he wrote. But Nixon did not decide to emphasize the ideal of "bring-us-together." Instead, he was convinced that division was the key to the mobilization of an electoral majority. "Get the word out," he told William Safire in December 1970, "we're not afraid of controversy. . . . [A]ll the people aren't going to come together, old and young, black and white, rich and poor—not on the bread and butter issues where interests are different. We can't pretend to want to unify everybody, we've got to build our majority."[1]

The prospects for that majority were reaching their lowest ebb. The early months of 1971 were gloomy for Nixon, who faced serious problems that threatened his electoral future. There were even rumors that he would not seek a second term as president because of the first major problem, the continuing war in Vietnam. Although Nixon had reduced the extent of America's military commitment there, "peace with honor" was apparently no closer. In search of this goal, the U.S. government again escalated the war. In February, South Vietnamese forces, with American support, invaded Laos, leading to what historian Robert Schulzinger described as "six weeks of the bloodiest fighting of the war." The offensive failed both abroad and at home, where it received a hostile reaction. Despite Vietnamization, the Thieu regime obviously could not fight alone.[2]

The second major problem was the state of the economy, which had harmed Nixon's midterm campaigning. Conditions remained sluggish, and it was unclear whether the policy of gradualism could produce an electorally attractive combination of strong growth and low unemployment by the following fall. Altogether, despite Nixon's aspirations to mobilize his silent majority, the mood was much less optimistic than that of the previous winter. "[H]is popular support is a mile wide and an eighth of an inch thick," one pollster reportedly observed.[3]

At the same time, leading Democrats were preparing to frustrate Nixon's efforts to win a majority. The election-eve television addresses of the 1970 midterms had offered a sharp reminder of the potential effectiveness of Democratic opposition. In the judgment of most observers, even including those in the administration, Edmund Muskie was more persuasive than Nixon in that forum. Muskie became the leading contender for the Democratic nomination, potentially a formidable opponent. Indeed, by April, a Gallup poll suggested that Nixon would win only 39 percent of the vote in a presidential election against Muskie, whose support stood at 47 percent.[4]

On balance, Nixon preferred to run against a less attractive candidate than Muskie. The president clearly could not control the identity of his opponent, but he closely followed developments in the Democratic Party and was ready to encourage political "dirty tricks" to create problems for his opponents.[5] Moreover, although he had failed to identify Democratic presidential hopefuls as "radical liberals" in 1970, Nixon looked for public policies that would characterize his opponents as unacceptably liberal to the silent majority and that could encourage divisions within the Democratic Party. The ideas animating the radical-liberal strategy thus remained.

Most important was the need for Nixon to establish a record that made the electorate unwilling to choose an alternative. Indulging in his political passion for the bold and the unexpected, Nixon would unveil new policy initiatives to create that record. In the realm of foreign policy, Nixon would make his mark. In the realm of domestic policy, Nixon offered some equally bold proposals, but he failed in his efforts to convince the public that he was the American Disraeli.

A NEW ESTABLISHMENT

Nixon saw himself and his administration as "in a deadly battle with the establishment." The "establishment" was a significant political constraint, he thought, to the realization of his goals. In his view, influential voices in American society were usually those of liberals, frequently Democrats, and almost invariably opponents. This hostile establishment extended through the mass media, the bureaucracy, and the universities. Nixon denounced this influence, as did Agnew in still more colorful terms. It is therefore possible, as historian Michael Kazin has demonstrated, to claim that the effort to rally the silent majority, unusually for the Republican Party, represented the populist tendency of American politics, involving the mobilization of voters against an out-of-touch and remote elite.[6]

One aim of the new majority project acknowledged "the need of building our establishment." First and most important, a powerful motivation for the antigovernment strand of Nixon's public policy was to undermine the influence of the federal bureaucracy, which Nixon saw as often determined to thwart his goals. Second, even as he relied heavily on figures from the nation's existing academic elite—Henry Kissinger, George Shultz, and Daniel Patrick Moynihan are three especially prominent examples—Nixon sought to use appointments to find a new elite. Third, he wanted to challenge the "liberal establishment" among journalists. Nixon became closely involved in one plan designed to embarrass leading Washington reporters into covering the administration more favorably. He personally drafted letters to Dan Rather of CBS and John Osborne of the *New Republic*, purportedly from Nixon opponents, with glowing praise for what the letters described as ardently negative coverage of the administration. The point was to convince these journalists that they were guilty of anti-Nixon bias. Presidential aides were convinced that Osborne, at least, rethought his approach to covering the White House after receiving the letter. There were yet grander ideas. One was that a group of sympathetic investors might launch a takeover bid for one of the broadcasting networks or even establish a new network.[7]

Nixon's sense that he inhabited a hostile world was to some extent justified as far as the realm of ideas was concerned. Despite the birth of a modern movement of conservative thought in the 1950s and its growth in the 1960s, conservative ideas remained relatively marginal to intellectual and wider public debate. Moreover, many members of this conservative movement were not unequivocally pledged to the cause of the new majority. Their approach to politics often emphasized an anticommunist foreign policy and a laissez-faire domestic policy. Nixon shared neither guiding principle, so his relationship with movement conservatives was at best uneasy.[8]

"The silent majority is silent," observed Moynihan shortly after the midterms, "because it has nothing to say." Moynihan shared many of the concerns that led Nixon to pursue his politics of antipermissiveness. Indeed, Moynihan offered much less criticism of the radical-liberal campaign than did many of his colleagues in the White House. Moynihan explained to Nixon that the main problem facing American society was a decline in traditional authority; most Americans were troubled by this development but felt powerless to fight back. The silent majority remained silent because no spirited advocacy of this form of conservatism had followed the arrival of a Republican in the White House. The United States was indeed experiencing nothing less than a Kulturkampf, according to Moynihan, but supporters of traditional values had failed to articulate coherent and convincing arguments on behalf of their position.

Moynihan, about to leave the White House, was unimpressed by the administration's ability to frame a response to this climate of social upheaval. There were, he wrote, too many "fourth rate minds" on the presidential staff, but the problem was not ineffective recruitment. "It is a matter of odds: the odds are against you in the cultural struggle of this period," he wrote to Nixon, who was impressed by this diagnosis of an intellectual crisis within the administration. In fact, the White House was already seeking to address the problem. A year earlier, Lyn Nofziger, a conservative aide responsible for political affairs, advocated the creation of a right-wing think tank, independent but supportive of the administration. Instead, the administration looked for ways to foster the growth of an existing organization, the American Enterprise Institute, which was relatively small at that time.[9]

Tom Charles Huston, an aide to H. R. Haldeman, suggested a different remedy for the intellectual deficiency within the administration. "All the demographic, social, and political indicators suggest that we are on the verge of a potentially significant political realignment," he wrote. "We ought to be studying these indicators and relating them to concrete political actions. There is a surprising amount of politically applicable work being done in the political science community and in the academic world generally." During his first two years as president, Nixon was interested in the work of both Kevin Phillips and Richard Scammon and Ben Wattenberg, who offered popular analyses of politics informed by electoral realignment theories from political science. Nixon's instinctive distrust of academics made it unlikely that he would choose to follow Huston's idea of paying closer attention to this political science. Still, one way to do so remained a step away from academia. Phillips would be a useful source of advice, Huston suggested. But Phillips was by now unwilling to undertake private work for the administration: the administration could access his thoughts only through his public work.[10]

REFORMISM

When Nixon spoke of his urgent commitment to build his majority, he listed a set of reform measures that would help this project. They included the reorganization of the cabinet, the implementation of revenue sharing, and the reintroduction of welfare reform. Nixon recognized that the administration had achieved very few reform-oriented goals. "We haven't gotten across the whole area of reform," he wrote to Haldeman, mentioning postal reform—the replacement of the Post Office Department with the Postal Service, a public corporation—as a lonely example of achievement. Nixon continued, "We obviously aren't getting any credit on the environmental initiatives we have undertaken."[11]

The theoretician of "the emerging Republican majority" fully agreed that Nixon needed to establish an identity for reform. Unimpressed by the midterm campaign, Phillips told a meeting of Republican governors that his prescription for the administration was bolder policy making. Republicans were making gains only where Democratic candidates were too leftist, he claimed, not where "success depended on more positive programs or putting forward a more positive image." Such proposals were essential to win over voters who usually supported the Democratic Party. These potential converts were "socially conservative," but social conservatism was inadequate as the basis for new support. More was necessary. Phillips offered some policy ideas, including national health insurance, welfare reform underpinned by strong work incentives, and aid to needy agricultural and redundant industrial areas and to small towns. Despite the disappointments of the campaign, Phillips insisted that "the desire of the country for realignment" remained.[12]

To strengthen his record in the aftermath of the 1970 elections, Nixon tried to create an image for his presidency that confounded normal expectations of the Republican Party. He intended to initiate a renewed burst of activism in domestic policy. This activism was not directly grounded in the recommendations of the Rosow Report. Indeed, one of Nixon's first actions in 1971 was to veto as too expensive and inflationary a bill establishing a system linking pay for blue-collar federal employees with private-sector wages for comparable work, though Rosow had suggested that the federal government should develop a reputation as a model employer of blue-collar workers. Nevertheless, the administration remained attentive to middle America's concerns. One indication came in December 1970 when Nixon signed the Occupational Safety and Health Act, which created a set of worker rights and the mechanisms to enforce them. It was, according to Nixon, "probably one of the most important pieces of legislation, from the standpoint of the 55 million people who will be covered by it, ever passed by the Congress of the United States." Presidential support recognized a momentum for reform, the responsibility of liberal Democrats, that was almost irrepressible. But it was also informed by a desire to be responsive to blue-collar workers, even if the result disturbed traditional Republican allies in the business world.[13]

Now on the administration's agenda was still more reform. Nixon announced a series of bold initiatives in his 1971 State of the Union address. Together, he said, his measures represented a "new American revolution," encompassing "six great goals." The "most important" goal, he said, was welfare reform. (In November, the Senate Finance Committee had rejected a yearlong trial of the Family Assistance Plan [FAP].) The other goals were prosperity, fostered by an expansionary budget; improvements in the environment; better health care; revenue sharing; and reform of the federal government. This new American revolution was the product of the domestic council under John Ehrlichman. Following the publication of the Rosow Report, Ehrlichman established a subcommittee on blue-collar matters under James Hodgson. Committee members offered advice on dealing with the problems of workers. The spirit, if not always the substance, of the Rosow debate remained. Journalists were told that the proposals unveiled in the State of the Union represented "a strong pitch for the blue-collar vote." One wrote that the new emphasis on domestic issues was "plainly dictated by the political calendar." Another noted that Nixon's "program is tailored especially to the constituency the President has sought to identify, since 1968, as 'Forgotten Americans,' the silent tax-payers, neither rich nor poor[,] for whom government has seemed to represent more and more either another tax break for the haves or another handout for the have-nots."[14]

The culmination of Nixon's search for bold domestic policy, the proposals of the new American revolution combined reformism with an antigovernment impulse. Nixon articulated that impulse bluntly in his address. "Most Americans today," he asserted, "are simply fed up with government at all levels." As his proposals in the realm of health and welfare revealed, he was ready to urge the expansion of federal responsibilities. But a key strand of the new American revolution was a challenge to the centralization of governmental activities at the federal level. By instead emphasizing the revitalization of the role of states and localities, Nixon claimed to advocate a "historic shift" that would bring "a new burst of creative energy throughout America."[15]

It was impossible to be confident about Republican support for reformism, even in this Republican form. To achieve the new American revolution, Nixon needed the effective support of congressional Republicans. Although congressional Republicans alone could not pass the program of reform, it would be impossible in most cases without party members' votes—and in many cases, without congressional Republicans' active support. But they often viewed such policies with caution or even hostility. Nixon could not be sure of this necessary support. His first chief of congressional liaison, Bryce Harlow, often complained about the negativism of Republicans on Capitol Hill. "The Republicans have been out of power so long they act by instinct," he observed to colleagues. "If they see a political critter moving, they instinctively snap at it."[16]

Soon after the State of the Union address, Nixon invited Republican members of Congress to breakfasts at which he spoke about his proposals and urged the legislators to embrace a new approach to politics. He said that long years in opposition had made the Republican Party comfortable with negativism, but it now had an important opportunity to become "the party of change . . . of imagination, of innovation." In this forum, he couched this spirit of innovation in conservative terms by reminding his fellow Republicans of the antigovernment impulse that informed his proposals. Nixon attacked the role of an out-of-touch "bureaucratic elite" in the guidance of federal activity. "Now the Democrats—many of them—want to keep things as they are," Nixon said. "Or they want to pour more money into the old programs. We can *never*

compete with them in dollar terms." Instead, the Republican Party now com-
peted on the basis of ideas. Nevertheless, he pointed out that partisanship had
to be tempered to win congressional Democrats' votes.[17]

With absolute clarity, Nixon had identified his cause of reformism, shaped
by his antigovernment impulse. He was right to fear his party's reaction. This
reformism was at odds with dominant trend among grassroots Republicans.
The conservative tide within the party, so clearly obvious in the 1960s, had not
ebbed. Harry Dent later commented that when traveling the country, the
"degree of conservatism" of rank-and-file Republicans, even outside his native
South, "amazed" him. "I found that the more conservative I talked and the
more I turned up my southern accent, the louder was the applause," he wrote.
"Being introduced as a former Thurmond sidekick was a plus."[18]

To what extent would the Republican Party offer enthusiastic support for
the new American revolution? This question had already attracted debate
when Nixon unveiled for staffers the content of his reform package. A few
weeks before the State of the Union address, Patrick Buchanan posed this
question to describe the likely alarm of conservative activists in response to the
"revolutionary" new initiatives. "Can one seriously imagine," he asked, "in
1972 those little old ladies in tennis shoes ringing doorbells in Muncie for 'FAP,'
'FHIP' [Family Health Insurance Plan] and the 'full employment budget'?" In
Buchanan's mind, the neglect of the Right was a mistake with much larger consequences than the alienation and loss of activists. By embracing reformism,
Nixon was in danger of squandering his larger political opportunity, Buchanan
warned, "the opportunity to become the political pivot on which America
turned away from liberalism, away from the welfare state—the founder of a
new 'Establishment.' " Buchanan argued that moderation was the wrong response to the 1970 result, that a Wallace candidacy in 1972 would provide a
compelling alternative to those alienated by Nixon's reformism, and that the
Republican Party's largely conservative activist base might find a more palata-
ble presidential hopeful than Nixon. Nixon, Buchanan wrote, had won by
promising to reduce government and to balance the budget, but the president
was "no longer a credible custodian of the conservative political tradition of
the GOP."[19]

At the other end of the ideological spectrum within the White House was
Leonard Garment, who responded to Buchanan's criticism of the proposed
new American revolution with a sturdy defense: "The President's natural—and
strongest position—is not on the Right but in the middle—and the middle is

exactly where he is," Garment wrote. But Garment was clearly concerned about the reform agenda's security within the administration. "The important thing now . . . is to hold our course consistently enough and long enough so that it's clear we're not wobbling and being buffeted or panicked by the kind of reaction [Buchanan's] carefully thought-through polemic represents."[20]

But Nixon was susceptible to wobbling, even in advance of his announcement of his proposed revolution. Despite his confident reassertion of the reform agenda, Nixon was to some extent receptive to Buchanan's criticisms. "I think the point is getting through to the P[resident] that our movement is somewhat to the left, and he doesn't want to get too far off of his natural base," wrote Haldeman. "The Buchanan theory, of course, is to go all conservative, which would be equally bad; but, we do seem to be moving too far leftward at this point."[21]

Other members of Nixon's inner circle shared Buchanan's doubts about the wisdom of reformism. Charles Colson, the aide with special responsibility for cultivation of the new majority, argued, "To propose vast environmental programs, new schemes to help the poor, expanded aid to the cities gets us absolutely nothing politically. Whatever political benefit is in it, the Democrats will take away from us by showing that they can do more in the Congress than we have proposed." But Nixon remained unconvinced.[22] Congressional Democrats almost certainly would react to administration proposals with more sweeping counterproposals. But the new majority might respond positively to the more modest version of reformism, in combination with the administration's other policies.

"GREAT GOALS"

In view of the political events of the fall of 1970, the electoral importance of the economy's performance was inescapable. To capture the "emerging Republican majority," Kevin Phillips recommended "the type of expansive economics which would put the needs of middle America ahead perhaps of the needs of the board room." Such a policy would favor dealing with unemployment as opposed to "keeping stability in terms of inflation or noninflation." On this question, Nixon did not need advice from Phillips. Suspicious of big business and acutely aware of the electoral necessity of low unemployment, he wanted prosperity in time for the next presidential election. "[T]he economy must *boom* beginning July 1972," he remarked shortly after the midterms. To help this effort, in December 1970 he replaced Secretary of the Treasury David Kennedy with John Connally, a former governor of Texas and a leading Democrat. Connally had no special expertise in economics, and political considerations dominated his approach to economic questions.[23]

Milton Friedman, the monetarist economist—"a great mind," Nixon told a meeting of congressional Republicans—assured the president that the policy of gradualism would bring prosperity and solid economic growth.[24] The mild recession of 1970 was likely to lead to a noninflationary recovery, but it would be slow. Some of Nixon's economic advisers disagreed and advocated stronger economic medicine. But thanks to the influence of budget director George Shultz, still confident in the policy, gradualism remained in place. Critical to the future of economic policy was the extent to which Nixon could emulate Shultz and Friedman in waiting patiently for the promised recovery.

While the administration's approach to the economy largely stayed the course, Nixon packaged it in a way that demonstrated his desire to be seen as a new kind of Republican, more concerned about unemployment than inflation. He told journalist Howard K. Smith that he was "now a Keynesian in economics" as evidenced by his embrace of the "full-employment budget." His budget for fiscal year 1972 included large spending increases, intended to stimulate the economy; it projected a deficit of $11.6 billion and could be balanced only with the assumption of full employment. "By spending as if we were *at* full employment," he said in his State of the Union address, "we will help to *bring about* full employment." Herbert Stein has noted that the policy was "both innovative and conservative—conservative in that it incorporated a rule which set a limit to fine-tuning and expansionism." At the same time, under administration pressure, the Federal Reserve Board was seeking to increase the supply of money at a rate intended to stimulate the economy.[25]

Even while liberals viewed them as inadequate, the spending increases marked Nixon as a Republican not wedded to fiscal orthodoxy. But with its deep roots, the party's reputation was difficult to shrug off. As Haldeman later noted at a dinner meeting, "We're never strong against [unemployment] (like we are against inflation)." In the spring of 1971, Colson wrote that even if the economy improved as projected, "the Democrats [would] argue that it was another Hoover-type Administration, that unemployment soared under the Republicans, that we vetoed 'job' bills but gave tax breaks to business, and that it will happen again; they will try to create the unemployment scare even if we have gotten it under control."[26]

Another "great goal" was revenue sharing. Its aim, Nixon said, was to "reverse the flow of power and resources from the States and communities to Washington." The initiative consisted of two distinct proposals. Under general revenue sharing, the federal government would transfer $5 billion to the states and localities to spend however they saw appropriate. Under special revenue sharing, the government would replace a series of categorical programs—a total of 129, representing one-third of all federal programs—with $11 billion in block grants. The states and localities could then decide the most pressing needs within six areas—education, transportation, urban community development, workforce training, rural community development, and law enforcement. In principle a revenue-neutral initiative, revenue sharing was not so in practice, as a result of a billion-dollar sweetener. In time, general revenue sharing added to overall federal spending rather than simply changing the manner of its delivery.[27]

Despite its centrality to Nixon's new American revolution, revenue sharing did not find an enthusiastic reception. An important reason was institutional. The measure undercut Congress's influence in determining how federal money should be spent, reducing the representatives' and senators' role in winning funds for their districts or states. In the case of special revenue sharing, the proposals also often elicited the hostility of interest groups and of legislative experts in the various fields. Consequently, two of the six received no serious consideration by Congress at all, and a further two won that consideration but were rejected. Only in the areas of job training and urban community development did the proposals win enactment, but they did not do so until 1973 and 1974, respectively, and were in greatly modified forms. What distinguished these proposals was the desire of those affected—primarily officials of local governments—to find a replacement for the current system of grants. Their support, not the administration's efforts, accounted for these successes.[28]

While special revenue sharing sped toward failure, the fortunes of general revenue sharing at first seemed little more promising. Again, Congress offered widespread opposition, influenced in part by Arkansas's Wilbur Mills, the chair of the House Ways and Means Committee. Sharing Mills's lack of enthusiasm for general revenue sharing was John W. Byrnes of Wisconsin, the ranking Republican member of the committee. Fiscal conservatism caused Byrnes to look at the federal deficit with alarm and to point out that there was no revenue to share. Eventually, in February 1972, Mills's attitude changed when he became a candidate for the Democratic presidential nomination; he saw the switch as electorally necessary. His reversal confirmed revenue sharing's potential appeal to voters. In contrast to Congress's institutional instinct against revenue sharing, state and local politicians—the beneficiaries of the proposal—favored it. Republican governors, who had increased in number during the 1960s, enthusiastically advocated the measure. Indeed, Nelson Rockefeller promoted the idea so forcefully that Ehrlichman worried that the New York governor rather than the administration would win credit for its authorship.[29] Still, in Congress, Mills's opinion mattered a lot, whereas that of Rockefeller carried little weight.

The nature of the opposition allowed Nixon to sound his antigovernment theme. He tried to frame the debate as being between the advocates of positive reform and the advocates of negative obstructionism. "[W]hen we consider reforms," he told a press conference, "we must remember that they are always opposed by the establishment . . . the establishment of Congress, the establishment of the federal bureaucracy, and also great organizations." Nixon sounded the same antiestablishment theme when discussing the programs in private.[30]

At first sight, more electorally attractive than the idea of government reform was that of tax relief. Charles Colson, especially attentive as ever to the political dimensions of public policy, strongly urged that the White House state the goal of general revenue sharing as reducing the levels of local taxation rather than reversing the flow of government. When the bill ran into congressional difficulties, Colson suggested its replacement with a "Property Tax Relief Act." Even if the proposal failed, the White House would have "a damn good issue which people understand," he wrote. "[W]e become the party trying to help the 66 million homeowners in America—most of them middle class working people who carry the heaviest tax burden and are increasingly restive about it." In fact, when general revenue sharing passed, some local governments deployed the funds to exactly this purpose. Although Nixon recognized the appeal of cutting taxes, Colson's strategy was problematic. Across the country, Democratic governments rather than his administration would secure credit for the cuts. In his public statements about revenue sharing, he referred to the desirability of reducing local taxation, but he maintained an emphasis on the need to reduce the federal government's role.[31]

Even in pursuit of this antigovernment goal and the New Federalism, Nixon almost gave up the fight in response to congressional hostility. Ehrlichman, the president's chief domestic policy adviser, remained enthusiastic about this key component of the new American revolution, however, and although Nixon concluded that cancellation of the plan would help to reduce the budget deficit, he allowed the proposal to continue. Revenue sharing remained under long legislative consideration, its fortunes not to change significantly until Mills's conversion.[32]

The new American revolution was not the crusade of an administration committed to reform. Not only had Nixon not managed in many ways to persuade his party to advocate positive change, but he too privately doubted the political wisdom of that role. In the late spring of 1971, he confided his doubts to his chief of staff, Haldeman. Nixon stated that he was no liberal but a conservative. The programs of his administration were "wrong," with benefits for neither the White House nor the country. Instead, the administration needed "to be much tougher on domestic matters."[33]

Nixon's disenchantment with the new American revolution was linked with a sense that it was not crucial to his fortunes at the ballot boxes. Connally, the recent arrival at the Treasury Department, told senior White House staffers in March that personal factors, such as gossip about the president's daughter, were especially important in electoral politics. "If you gave the average person the choice," he asked, "what would they like to hear—about revenue sharing, taxation, government reorganization, or what Tricia's boyfriend is like?" Nixon shared a similar concern about the value of the reform agenda. It was important "to personalize and conceptualize in broad visionary terms regarding goals, instead of just developing programs and legislation," noted Haldeman of Nixon's thoughts in May. "He said, politically the 'New American Revolution' is a dud. The people don't care how you run the government; they only want it to cost a little less."[34]

HEALTH CARE AND GOVERNMENT REORGANIZATION

Before the announcement of the new American revolution, White House aides had stressed to journalists health care reform's special potential as an administration initiative for the benefit of blue-collar Americans. In 1969, Nixon had spoken of a "massive crisis" that faced the nation's health sector. Escalating costs within the sector had led to concerns about the increase of private insurance premiums and about the government's relatively new financial commitment to Medicare and Medicaid. Medicaid in particular came under scrutiny. By the end of the 1960s, the program was not achieving its planned coverage of the poor because of its dependence on the participation of states, many of which did not create generous schemes. Nevertheless, its expenditure was higher than expected. In sum, the necessary conditions for reform were apparently in place.[35]

But Nixon's proposals for health care reform failed. They did so in ways that again revealed both the lack of Republican enthusiasm for the new American revolution and the administration's inability to steal the momentum of innovation from the Democrats. The February 1971 package included a National Health Insurance Standards Act to ensure that employers offered basic insurance coverage; a Family Health Insurance Plan, a federal scheme to replace Medicaid help for the poor; and a measure to foster the growth of private health maintenance organizations.[36]

Many Republicans hesitated to support the administration's initiatives. The minority members of the House Ways and Means Committee objected to the additional expenses that employers would face; the package was out of step with the party's business constituency. Although the administration secured Republican support for the package, that support was then undercut by the introduction of competing bills promoted by the American Medical Association and by the insurance industry. In addition, shortly before Nixon introduced his measure, Senator Edward Kennedy of Massachusetts had cosponsored the Health Security Act, which sought to create a government-organized national health scheme funded by tax revenues. The overall result was a debate about but eventually no legislative action regarding the problems of increasing medical costs and of inadequate coverage for many poorer Americans. "[D]espite his effort to present a bold stand on health care," two historians of medicine have concluded, "Nixon had been cautious and ambivalent."[37]

No more successful were Nixon's proposals for the reorganization of government. Promised in the State of the Union, a message on reorganization arrived on Capitol Hill in March 1971. The proposals arose from the recommendations of the President's Advisory Council on Executive Reorganization, which was led by businessman Roy L. Ash. All too often, the Ash commission found, many different parts of the executive branch were involved in dealing with the same area of governmental responsibility. Matters of health, for example, involved seven departments and eight agencies. The situation was confusing. In place of this confusion, the proposals within the new American revolution aimed to achieve functional integrity for the federal executive. The key proposal called for the replacement of seven departments with four new ones, the Department of Natural Resources, the Department of Community Development, the Department of Human Resources, and the Department of Economic Affairs. While reorganization won support among previous Democratic occupants of executive positions, it faced a formidable institutional obstacle. It threatened the disruption of existing relations between agencies and the congressional committees responsible for their oversight. "The old organization, while not based on any clear theory, was best justified as an expression of the lobbying or representation concept," noted historian Otis Graham, observing the significant role of interest groups in the existing arrangement. "These groups were not charmed by the proposal for change." By November, Nixon agreed to exclude the Department of Agriculture from the plan on the grounds of strong opposition by farm groups. Intended to ease the passage of the reforms through Congress, the concession merely bolstered other opposition.[38]

The uncertainty of Nixon's commitment to the policies undermined the effectiveness of the way in which the administration sought their implementation in Congress. Frustration arrived too soon; the White House lacked the patience essential to guide an initiative toward enactment. Writer Allen Drury saw this basic failing as a defining characteristic of the Nixon administration, an observation sparked in this case by the administration's treatment of the proposals for executive reorganization. "[A]s in many of his domestic policies to date," Drury wrote, "there is a curious lack of follow-through, a curious inertia that could almost be called disinterest, a curious reluctance, almost, to come to grips with it—to get down to the guts of it—to get into the arena, tear off those nice neat ties, unbutton those nice neat shirts, muss up that nice neat hair and *fight*."[39]

Stronger compatibility between the administration's aims and those of congressional Democrats helped to secure meaningful progress toward the "great goal" of environmental protection. In 1971 and 1972, Nixon sent to Congress an array of proposals, including measures to regulate the dumping of waste in the oceans, to encourage states to engage in land-use planning, to control noise pollution, to offer special protection to coastal areas, and to create guidelines for the state regulation of toxic waste disposal. There were also new initiatives to expand the system of national parks, especially to establish urban recreational areas and to protect wilderness areas. Russell Train, the second administrator of the Environmental Protection Agency, later claimed that Nixon even "upstaged" the Democrats in this area. At the same time, however, Nixon failed to convert many Republicans to environmental activism: economically conservative party members could not enthusiastically greet new examples of business regulation. Moreover, Nixon's activism in this area had limits that revealed his lack of environmentalist zeal and the significance of political expediency rather than personal commitment. Most prominently, in October 1972 he vetoed a bill intended to tackle water pollution, supporting the principle but attacking its price tag.[40]

Absent from the "six great goals" was any commitment to addressing the special needs of minorities. Few votes could be gained in this way, Nixon thought. "Our political types, working the Chicano precincts and the Ghettoes, and Navaho reservations for Republican converts would do well to focus their attention upon the Holy Name Society, the Women's Sodality and the Polish-American Union," observed Buchanan. Nevertheless, as far as substantial policy making was concerned, the electoral imperative did not always triumph. "[I]n the case of Indians," Nixon wrote to Ehrlichman, "a grave injustice has been worked against them for a century and a half and the nation at large will appreciate our having a more active program of concern for their plight." Native American policy became a notable area of reform achievement by the administration, which cast aside the existing emphasis on the assimilation of Native Americans into mainstream society, instead fostering their distinct identity. The new emphasis included the restoration of previously withdrawn tribal status, the encouragement of tribal government, an increase in funding for relevant programs, and a series of bills in favor of tribal land claims.[41]

REORDERING THE PARTY SYSTEM

Few recent presidents had devoted much attention to their party. There was a long-term trend toward concentration on personal, candidate-centered politics rather than on matters partisan. Lyndon Johnson, for example, was the source of great Democratic frustration as a result of his unwillingness strongly to champion party fortunes.[42] During the midterm campaign, Nixon defied this tendency to engage in partisan activity, but the activity was of an idio-syncratic kind. Informed by the desire to rally the silent majority, the cam-paign did not favor the Republican Party but instead opposed "radical liberal-ism." When this campaign ended in relative failure, Nixon abandoned much of his interest in the Republican Party. Nixon's ultimate goal—capturing a new majority—remained the same, but he increasingly did not see the party as compatible with his ambition to reach out both to politicians and to voters of opposing partisan identification. Nixon tried to rearrange the party system in a way that would unlock the strength of this new majority in a number of respects, including fostering a new congressional alliance, selecting a new vice president, promoting a personal campaign organization, and neglecting the existing Republican organization.

Nixon began work on a plan to establish a "new coalition" between Con-gress's Republican leadership and conservative southern Democrats. First, in the aftermath of the 1970 election, as well as meeting with the new Republican senators-elect as a group, Nixon met separately with Conservative James Buck-ley and Democrat Lloyd Bentsen, for whom the president arranged briefings by the State and Defense Departments. Second, Nixon hoped to find many opportunities to work with southern Democratic chairmen and other Demo-cratic leaders whose votes would be important to the administration. He remained eager to ensure that southern Democratic senators such as John Stennis of Mississippi, "who on vote after vote do stick with us," were re-minded of his appreciation.[43]

The final part of the plan was the most innovative. In May 1971 Nixon raised with minority leader Gerald Ford of Michigan and minority whip Les Arends of Illinois a proposal by John Connally for the formation of a congressional coalition between Republicans and conservative Democrats. The chances for such a coalition were more promising in the House than in the Senate. Ford and Arends responded positively to the idea and estimated that about ten Democrats would be prepared to enter such a coalition. Indeed, Ford men-tioned that the House Republican leadership had already taken some steps in this direction.[44] Although the White House commonly sought legislative sup-port for its proposals among opposition members of Congress, Nixon's steps were most unusual. The cooperation he sought was at a notable level of for-mality, approaching an institutionalization of the long-standing conservative coalition that dated from the New Deal.

Another way to shake up the Republican Party was within the executive branch rather than the legislative. Nixon wanted a new vice president on his 1972 ticket, a Democrat rather than a Republican. His candidate was John Connally, who had lived up to Nixon's high expectations both as secretary of the treasury and as a confidant. Shortly after Connally's arrival, Nixon began to contemplate a "national unity ticket" at the time of his reelection. Nixon even toyed with the idea of not waiting until the election but persuading Agnew to resign early, perhaps with the offer of a Supreme Court justiceship. As Ehrlichman pointed out, a fatal problem with this idea was the unlikelihood of a positive Senate response to the vice president's nomination.[45]

Nixon's interest in a new vice president reflected frustration with Agnew as well as enthusiasm about Connally. The political decline of Nixon's "realigner" had been sharp and swift. The stridency of Agnew's participation in the 1970 campaign had damaged his political stock. Although Haldeman looked for ways to improve the vice president's reputation, there was no real change. Author Robert Coles encapsulated misgivings about Agnew in reporting a comment made by a blue-collar worker: "I don't like to hear the Vice President of the United States sounding like I do after I've had a couple of beers." Nixon could be even more dismissive of Agnew's abilities, telling Haldeman that Agnew was "dogmatic, . . . totally inflexible and [saw] things in minuscule terms." Moreover, many governors and party officials believed that "the President's cause would be better served if there were a change in his running mate for 1972." It was thought "almost impossible to make any drastic change in [Agnew's] public image," noted aide Charles McWhorter. Some chairmen even remarked that if Agnew were retained, they hoped he would not campaign in their state.[46]

Nevertheless, enthusiasm for Agnew remained strong among many conservatives, and it saved him. For example, the rightist Young Americans for Freedom (YAF), often hostile to Nixon, pledged support to Agnew, naming him as the organization's preferred candidate for the presidency. To Nixon's concern, Agnew, while urging YAF to support the president, refused to disavow this pledge of confidence. As the YAF endorsement showed, the same rhetoric that alienated mainstream voters made Agnew a leading spokesman for those on the Right. An effort to discard Agnew threatened factional strife. The possibility of change therefore relied on the vice president's personal plans. In July 1971, Bryce Harlow, who had been charged with the task of assessing Agnew's attitudes about his future, reported that there was a three-in-four chance that, in search of other opportunities, he would decide to withdraw from the ticket for reelection.[47] A national-unity ticket in 1972 therefore still seemed possible.

Following the partisan 1970 campaign, Nixon quickly downplayed his Republican identity. He was anxious to secure his reelection and did not see his party, supported by a minority of the electorate, as helpful to his cause. In any case, most Americans did not wish their president to be excessively partisan. Nixon announced to his staff that the coming year would not be "political" inasmuch as he would not attend party functions. The attitude caused frustration within the party. "Our off-year, no politics rule has been tough for [state party chairmen] to swallow," wrote Peter Millspaugh, an aide to Dent. Millspaugh also complained that Nixon was "snubbing important friends" by failing to recognize adequately party leaders on his visits to states—in this case, to Texas, Alabama, and Oklahoma. "These folks aren't buying 'tight schedule,'" Millspaugh noted, "or any other reasons, when all they ask is a momentary handshake."[48]

In the spring of 1971, Nixon established a personal campaign organization, the Committee for the Re-election of the President (CRP but subsequently known more popularly as CREEP). Mainly concerned with the routine management of the presidential campaign, the committee did not address the question of Republican fortunes at large. As Nixon's longtime political adviser, Murray Chotiner, had pointed out, "It is understood . . . that reaching Democrats and Independents will have to be achieved by a separate national committee or campaign as the word 'Republican' may be anathema to the groups we must reach in order to win the election."[49]

As he built up his personal campaign committee, Nixon fashioned a new role for the party organization. In pursuit of a new majority, he reduced the purview of the Republican National Committee under his choice as its new chair, Robert J. Dole, a senator from Kansas. Nixon wanted Dole to act as an administration spokesman, answering partisan attacks, especially in response to the effective Democratic chair, Lawrence O'Brien. Nixon instructed Thomas W. Evans, the party's cochair, to dismantle the pieces of the Republican National Committee (RNC) with responsibility for cultivating groups that he saw as possible recruits for the new majority. He decided that his aides should "go through the committee and knock out all the special-type personnel." Nixon wanted special appeals to constituency groups to originate from a non-Republican but obviously pro-Nixon source. For example, the RNC division for ethnic Americans saw its staffing reduced by three-quarters, while the

Mexican American project and the budget for the cultivation of Catholic voters were both eliminated.[50]

THE NEW ECONOMIC POLICY

As 1971 progressed, the new American revolution did not. Many of the proposals were languishing in legislative torpor, as lengthy discussion continued about their principles and their details. One victim was welfare reform. In mid-1971, a House motion to remove FAP from a comprehensive welfare and Social Security bill was defeated by just 234 to 187, signaling growing opposition among liberal Democrats, who favored a more wide-ranging measure. As with revenue sharing, Nixon often did not respond to the problems of FAP with determination to confront them but with exasperation and a willingness to yield to them, hoping to gain political credit for suggesting, if not achieving, reform.[51]

Democratic discomfort with Nixonian reformism was crucial to the travails of the new American revolution. As the congressional majority, Democrats not only had the votes to decide the revolution's fate but also, significantly, controlled the legislative process under which it was discussed. Still, in many cases, Republicans did not actively promote the programs; as yet, relatively few signs indicated that the party was embracing innovation, as Nixon had urged. But to some extent these woes simply reflected the administration's lackluster commitment both to winning the new American revolution and to selling proposals in Congress. Many Senate Republicans became thoroughly disenchanted with the administration.[52]

The White House had no more success in achieving its goal of prosperity. Inflation as well as unemployment remained high, apparently impervious to governmental interventions. The implementation of monetary policy was imperfect, and its results did not meet expectations. Nixon remained concerned about the poor state of the economy and was eager to take measures to deal with it. In the spring of 1971, the administration identified the states of key electoral value where unemployment was likely to be high in the following November and targeted federal spending to create jobs there, with special attention devoted to California and the troubled aerospace industry. Nixon ordered his subordinates to tell departments that "the President is personally following their action."[53]

In the summer, Nixon decided that he could wait no longer for gradualism to produce the economic conditions necessary for his reelection. The apparent failure of his economic policy to check inflation and unemployment was not the only problem. The nation was suffering from a significant imbalance in foreign trade because of an overvalued dollar, which then became subject to hostile financial speculation. Nixon thought it was time for a major presidential intervention. Following a meeting with his closest economic aides at Camp David, he announced on August 15 a "new economic policy" that embraced a measure he had opposed during his entire political career—controls of prices and wages (an option previously authorized by Congress in 1970 to embarrass Nixon, who at that time was absolutely unwilling to pursue such a policy). The new approach also included the end of the dollar's gold convertibility, the imposition of an import tariff, and a number of tax cuts and exemptions.[54]

The public's massively favorable reaction to the announcement spectacularly affected electoral politics. "The imposition of the controls," Herbert Stein later wrote, "was the most popular move in economic policy that anyone could remember." Thanks to a political-intelligence operation being run by Murray Chotiner, the White House was receiving inside information about the activities of Democratic presidential contenders. Before August 15, leading Democrats saw the state of the economy as Nixon's key electoral weakness. Identifying the economy as "the main issue," George McGovern said, "I don't see anything hopeful that the Administration has done or is even thinking about that will alleviate the economic problems we have at hand." McGovern and other Democrats were convinced that those problems transcended Nixon's recent successes in the realm of foreign policy. "Do you think most voters will care or even remember what Nixon accomplished on the world scene?" asked Wilbur Mills. "I don't. It isn't human nature and it isn't the American nature. If the job market is bad and the whole combination is sour, Nixon's game plan will be on the short end of the score for the elections." Hubert Humphrey, however, reacted more cautiously as conditions worsened in the period before the new economic policy. Humphrey realized that Nixon still had time to improve the economy.[55]

Humphrey's note of caution was vindicated by the events of August 15, a day that subdued leading Democrats' confidence. Henry Jackson even contemplated a withdrawal from the race for the nomination. "At this stage, face it," he reportedly said, "Nixon has it made for a second term." McGovern, by contrast, still saw Nixon as vulnerable because of his inadequate delivery of reform initiatives—the welfare plan and revenue sharing. The Democrats' response in part reflected their difficulty in finding a distinctive and different position after Nixon's sharp change in policy. It also reflected the immediate popularity of the new economic policy. Despite the divergence from Republican orthodoxy, party leaders overwhelmingly supported the new economic policy.[56]

LABOR

Among the people most hostile to the announcement of the new economic policy was George Meany. Meany, the president of the American Federation of Labor and Congress of Industrial Organizations (AFL-CIO), condemned the measures' likely impact on the average wage earner, although the White House maintained that the effects would be positive. Meany claimed that controls held down wage increases, concerns about the inflationary effects of which had helped to precipitate the administration's policy overhaul, but much less stringently controlled prices and business profits. His hostility was exacerbated by the administration's failure to consult with him before the announcement.[57]

Meany's reaction revealed the political difficulty of reducing Republican difficulties with organized labor. But the administration did not meet labor hostility with hostility. Nixon still perceived the potential for allies among labor even as disagreements and conflict remained. At the height of labor opposition to the administration's economic policy, in the fall of 1971, Nixon appeared at the AFL-CIO convention. A number of factors influenced this approach. First, the reaction of labor's rank and file was more favorable than that of the leadership. Nixon realized that his strategy might depend on the encouragement of divisions within labor, separating the leadership from the ordinary members and separating the more favorable from the more hostile unions, to locate segments of support. Second, he knew that he still shared some common ground even with Meany and consequently did not give up hope for friends at the top of organized labor. At Christmas, Meany received a box of cigars from the president.[58]

The White House declined to compete for the labor vote—and, by extension, the blue-collar vote more generally—on economic issues, although the administration avoided active conflict with unions on these questions wherever possible. Instead, it asserted that the lines of partisan competition should

be drawn along related issues of patriotic internationalism overseas and conservative traditionalism at home. Nixon knew that on this basis he could not
woo, for example, the leaders of the United Auto Workers or those of the
Garment Workers; they were, he explained to Colson, "not only hopeless
Democrats, but also hopeless pacifists, as distinguished from Meany who is an
all out Democrat, but a great patriot."[59]

Foreign policy remained a promising foundation for a closer relationship
between the White House and other union leaders. At the end of 1970, Jay
Lovestone reported to Colson the existence of the "biggest block [*sic*] inside
the [AFL-CIO] Council that he [had] ever seen either oppose COPE or impliedly
[*sic*], at least, support Republicans." The reason was foreign policy. The AFL-
CIO elite remained hostile to the domestic agenda yet passed resolutions in
support of foreign policy, especially in Southeast Asia. According to Lovestone,
Meany consistently praised Nixon personally for his international leadership
and blamed what he saw as flawed domestic policy on advisers. When Nixon
met with Meany in November 1970, their discussion therefore focused on
foreign policy. Meany stated his and his organization's support for the president's "forceful" position in such matters. Nixon spoke of his interest in initiatives to help low-income workers as well as his concern about unemployment
and inflation. But Meany seemed rather unresponsive to such conciliatory
words on welfare liberalism.[60] The contours of the relationship between the
administration and organized labor were thus defined.

Nixon believed that the foundation of labor's support was deeper than
shared views on foreign policy. He saw himself as the ally of unionists—middle
Americans—against what he saw as attacks on traditional values. In a July 1971
meeting he explained this view: it was a time of "great moral crisis, a crisis of
character," and "the leaders and the educated class are decadent," Haldeman
recorded Nixon as observing. "When you have to call on the nation to be
strong—on such things as drugs, crime, defense, our basic national position—
the educated people and the leader class no longer have any character, and you
can't count on them." Instead, "[w]hen we need support on tough problems,
the uneducated are the ones that are with us."[61]

Charles Colson's public liaison organization worked hard to cement these
links. Colson's belief in a Republican opportunity with labor was stronger than
that of the White House at large. He hoped that the administration would
explain effectively its concern for issues affecting working Americans, but he
also wanted to create a better relationship with the labor leadership by estab-

lishing contacts among sympathetic union figures, by cultivating potential successors to Meany, by appointing unionists to major positions, and by arranging meetings between labor leaders and senior economic policy makers, for example.[62]

Nixon was ready to be generous to friendly unions. "I think it is very important," he wrote to Colson, "that we get across to the leaders of the labor movement; particularly in the construction trade, the Teamsters, etc., who are our friends, the fact that RN is with them all the way and is going to do everything he can to find a way to help them." Construction workers, the Teamsters, and maritime unions all received benefits from the administration, favors that could be seen as connected to support of Nixon. For example, the administration dropped a bill to prevent transportation strikes through the imposition of compulsory arbitration and supported the extension to the state and local levels of the Davis-Bacon Act, which kept high the wages federal contractors paid on construction projects.[63]

The most prominent example involved the International Brotherhood of the Teamsters. A maverick union that was excluded from the AFL-CIO in 1958 because of corrupt practices, the Teamsters were more conservative in outlook than most of their counterparts. Indeed, the union had departed in 1960 from its normal support for the Democrats by endorsing Nixon's first bid for the presidency.[64] Attorney General Robert F. Kennedy's tireless efforts to eradicate criminal activities within the union further alienated the Teamsters. Those efforts culminated with the prosecution and imprisonment of the union's president, Jimmy Hoffa, for jury tampering and for conspiring to embezzle pension funds.

Hoffa's release was at the top of the Teamster leaders' agenda. Frank Fitzsimmons, the union's acting president, lobbied on behalf of the cause, even though he began to harbor personal misgivings that he would lose influence when Hoffa returned. Shortly before Christmas 1971, Richard Nixon freed Hoffa from jail. An informal condition attached to the early release was that Hoffa should avoid involvement in union politics, ensuring that Fitzsimmons, who had become a friend to the administration and an important labor contact, remained the Teamsters' president. Within months, Hoffa was granted permission to visit Vietnam on a fact-finding tour with obviously political dimensions. Hoffa offered Nixon an early endorsement, even turning up at the Republican convention, while the Teamster leadership continued to insist on the union's political independence until a rather later date.[65]

FOREIGN POLICY AND THE RIGHT

Nixon invested much of his attention in foreign policy. The Vietnam War demanded his time and efforts, as did other events across the world, especially in the Middle East and the Indian subcontinent. But Nixon also pursued an ambitious foreign policy agenda that was intended to reshape and to stabilize international Cold War relations. His administration conducted careful diplomacy to seek agreements with the Soviet Union and to achieve a working relationship with communist China. Nixon believed that the electorate would reward his achievements in the realm of foreign policy.

Since its creation, the People's Republic of China had failed to win the recognition of the United States, which lent its support instead to the nationalist regime in Taiwan. Republican politicians—Nixon hardly the least among them—blamed the Democratic Party under Harry Truman for the "loss" of China. Opposition to communist China remained an article of faith for the American Right. In his vision of global geopolitics after Vietnam, however, Nixon considered China an essential balance to the Soviet Union and thought that the United States should seek rapprochement with the People's Republic. National Security Adviser Henry Kissinger conducted a series of secret talks that allowed Nixon to surprise the nation with the July 1971 public announcement that he would visit Beijing in 1972.[66]

This announcement was one of the great events of Nixon's presidency and even of postwar diplomatic history. Its boldness opened up the possibility that foreign policy might become a positive electoral issue. In the short run, the announcement helped him again to overtake Edmund Muskie in the polls. Then, in October 1971, Nixon made another major foreign policy announcement when he told the American people that he had arranged a summit meeting in Moscow. At the end of 1971, pollster Louis Harris said of the administration's foreign policy, "It just could be Richard Nixon's secret weapon—if he does not wait too long to liquidate U.S. involvement in Vietnam."[67]

A key question was whether this foreign policy could help the party as well as the president. Republican leaders were doubtful, as aide Charlie McWhorter reported. "[T]he President's expertise in foreign policy is regarded as his strongest asset," McWhorter wrote about the mood of Republican governors and party officials, "but there was considerable doubt among GOP leaders whether this would be enough to offset the adverse impact of inflation, unemployment, lack of economic growth and specific difficulties with agriculture." But Nixon had no doubt about détente's importance to his personal fortunes. After announcing his upcoming visit to Moscow, he told Haldeman that "we should really go to work playing the 'Man of Peace' issue all the time, move all the other issues to a lower level and really build that one up, because it's our issue and we have to use it."[68]

Even as Nixon viewed his foreign policy as winning deep support, that policy dismayed many conservatives. The new American revolution had generated some conservative hostility, but Nixon's foreign policy lifted this dissatisfaction to a critical level. The anticommunism of the Republican Right ran deep. Ronald Reagan was not ready publicly to criticize the initiative but privately told Nixon of the difficulties in supporting policies like the opening to China. William Loeb, the strongly right-wing publisher of the *Manchester Union Leader*, had no such qualms about his anticommunist instincts. When Nixon visited New Hampshire in the summer, Loeb wrote an editorial that announced "A Sad Good-Bye to an Old Friend." Loeb described the proposed visit to China as "immoral, indecent, insane and fraught with danger for the survival of the United States."[69]

In December 1971, a group of leading conservatives announced their tentative decision to support a right-wing candidate against Richard Nixon. Known as the Manhattan Twelve, the group included William A. Rusher and William F. Buckley Jr. of *National Review* but boasted no more than vague connections with right-wing congressional Republicans. The president sent Agnew and aide David Keene to meet with Buckley and Rusher, but attempts to persuade the conservatives to drop their insurgency were in vain. The conservatives had a number of policy complaints, but Buchanan determined that the most important were foreign policy issues, notably including a commitment to high defense spending. "[I]f we can provide them with some early proof (line items) of hard, significant, tangible items in the Strategic Weapons and R. & D. budgets of Defense, we can yet abort this thing," he wrote.[70]

There was no compromise. Nixon was not interested in one. These conservatives supported John Ashbrook, a congressman from Ohio, against Nixon for the party's presidential nomination. On announcing his candidacy, Ashbrook issued a list of conditions that, if met, would cause him to stand down. He asked for early confirmation that Spiro Agnew would be renominated as vice president, an indication that welfare reform no longer enjoyed a position of priority on the administration's domestic agenda, an increase in the defense budget, and a side trip to Taiwan after Nixon's visit to Beijing.[71]

In the New Hampshire primary, Nixon faced not only Ashbrook but also Paul "Pete" McCloskey, a liberal antiwar candidate and a congressman from northern California. The president easily contained both challenges without policy compromises. McCloskey won only 2.3 percent of the total primary vote (7.0 percent of the primaries in which he participated, excluding the Illinois write-in poll), and Ashbrook won 5.3 percent (7.9 percent of the primaries in which he participated).[72] Nevertheless, the mere existence of the challenges powerfully signaled that foreign policy, which Nixon identified as advantageous to him in the presidential contest, was an area of minor vulnerability for him within his own party.

The challenges remained irritants of no more than a minor nature. Nixon enthusiastically pursued his policy of détente, gaining high-profile television coverage of his visits to China in February 1972 (shortly before the New Hampshire primary) and to the Soviet Union in May. On the visit to Moscow, in the most important of a number of cooperative measures, he signed the first treaty limiting strategic arms (SALT I), which effectively did not reduce the military capability of either side but did signal both sides' desire to negotiate.[73]

Despite the Right's hostility, Nixon still thought that his foreign policy generally remained popular. While in the Soviet Union, he talked about electoral politics with Haldeman. "[W]e discussed . . . the general political approach that it's not domestic issues that we should spend our time on, that's their issue, not ours," noted Haldeman. "We should concentrate on the international, which is where we make the gains." Nixon was right. The opening to China boosted his popularity. The visit to Moscow then consolidated a widespread sense of optimism about the thawing of the Cold War, together with this surge of support for his presidency. "[T]he President has seized the foreign policy issue and has draped himself successfully with the mantle of peace," observed pollster Lou Harris. Harris saw Nixon's "bold initiatives" as potentially decisive in the election campaign.[74]

VIETNAM

In 1971, Nixon's Vietnam policy proceeded less successfully than his pursuit of détente. The year included the disastrous American-sponsored South Vietnamese invasion of Laos and unsuccessful secret talks in Paris. At the talks, North Vietnam's leaders showed no modification of their negotiating positions despite the administration's hope that its achievement of better relations with China would encourage such flexibility. Nevertheless, throughout 1971, Nixon continued to pursue the war's Vietnamization, even while the fighting in Laos exposed the inadequacy of Thieu's forces. By the middle of the year, the number of American troops in Vietnam was down to 239,200; by the year's end, the number stood at 156,800. Americans suffered 1,105 battle deaths in the first half of the year and 276 in the second.[75]

When progress in negotiations faltered once more and when America's enemy launched a new bombing offensive, Nixon announced on May 8, 1972, the mining of Haiphong Harbor and a major new bombing campaign against the north. In the aftermath of his announcement, he wanted the White House to convey his "courage . . . in going all out for peace in his journey to Peking and in making this decision" and "in rejecting a crass political decision where it would be very easy for him to follow the advice of the bug-outers." He also wanted to convince Americans that "those who were silent or even supported the decisions which sent 549,000 men to Vietnam are now sabotaging the President's efforts to bring our men home and to end the war and win an honorable peace."[76]

Following the start of the new bombing campaign, Nixon's popularity rose to 60 percent. Shortly after Nixon's reelection, Buchanan named May 8, 1972, and August 15, 1971, as key dates in "fashioning the great landslide of 1972." For Buchanan, Nixon's toughness in pursuing peace was crucial to ensuring that the issue of Vietnam would work to his rather than his opponents' advantage. Some further events of 1972 helped Nixon to consolidate this apparent advantage. Toward the end of August, Nixon withdrew the last American battalion of ground combat forces, while peace talks continued. Following the failure of their spring offensive, the North Vietnamese were somewhat more flexible in their approach to negotiations; pressure from the Soviet Union and China played a part in encouraging Hanoi to find a compromise.[77]

YOUTH AND *CHANGING SOURCES OF POWER*

Many contemporaries thought that the Left rather than the Right would pose a more meaningful challenge to Nixon's project. In 1971, a liberal Democratic counterpart to *The Emerging Republican Majority* and *The Real Majority* appeared. The book was Frederick G. Dutton's *Changing Sources of Power*. Dutton argued that the new cohort of American voters would form a radical voice in politics. The ratification of the Twenty-sixth Amendment, which lowered the voting age from twenty-one to eighteen, would increase the influence of the baby boom generation, whose members thought quite differently from their parents, whom Dutton termed the "Silent Generation." Between 1968 and 1980, a huge upheaval would occur, and by the end of this period, one-third of the electorate would be new voters, and they were therefore the key to the political future. Dutton's emphasis on the importance of generational change reflected political scientists' belief that new voters offered the most promising opportunity for movements of insurgency given the durability of party allegiances.[78]

Nixon, of course, disagreed with the Dutton thesis. The president looked for support among America's young voters. After the 1970 elections, Nixon stated that he was "especially concerned about plans for recruiting and utilizing youth, both as campaign enthusiasts and to line up the 18 year old vote." He assigned responsibility for addressing this concern to Charles Colson and Robert Finch. They determined that the Republican creed of individualism might appeal to young people, as would administration achievements such as government reorganization, draft reform, and environmental protection. Nixon did not believe that he could pacify opponents of his policies, especially on Vietnam, but he thought that the initiatives of the new American revolution would convert many young people. The opening to China was another initiative that he saw as valuable in this regard. "What we should try to do," he wrote to Finch, "is put our Democratic opponents in the position of standing for the old politics and a defense of the status quo." Altogether, Nixon's approach resembled that spelled out by Bill Gavin, a U.S. Information Agency official who had worked on the 1968 campaign. "Let the Democrats cozy up to 'youth'; we will treat the new voters as *Americans* first, i.e., we will treat them as seriously as they take themselves," Gavin wrote. But to consolidate this support, Nixon endorsed Finch's proposal to create an unofficial speakers' bureau to communicate with young people. Despite considerable energies devoted to this operation, however, the administration's effort failed.[79]

Unlike Dutton, then, most people in the administration believed that the concerns of youth did not differ substantially from those of the general population; Dutton, among others, might have overestimated the potential for radical change by focusing on the prominent examples of student dissent. In fact, the Twenty-sixth Amendment lowered the average age of the American voter only from forty-seven to forty-four, and the identity of the average voter was largely unchanged, especially because most young people did not fit the stereotype of their generation. Democrats numbered among the fiercest opponents of Dutton's thesis. One was Ben Wattenberg, then an aide to presidential aspirant Henry Jackson. "The notion that the media has created—that these new voters are all liberal arts majors from Berkeley and Harvard—is way off target," he said. Wattenberg pointed out that 7 of the 11 million people between ages eighteen and twenty-one were not in college, and of those receiving higher education, "half either live at home or go to junior college or night school or something like that."[80]

Nevertheless, many young people saw themselves as developing a distinctive culture with values and preoccupations sometimes at odds with the American mainstream. From the White House, Nixon watched the "youth revolution" with some alarm. Engaged by the problem of permissiveness, Nixon blamed parents. "[T]he kids were always screwed up," Nixon told Haldeman, but rather than standing firm, parents now chose to "follow their [children's] lead." In another meeting, the president spoke of American society's responsibility to save the next generation from permissiveness: "[W]e must not destroy the character of children by permissiveness, permissiveness that denies the child the opportunity to look in a mirror and finally realize that the problem is me, not my teachers, not the war, not the environment, but me."[81]

THE EMERGENCE OF A SOCIAL ISSUE AGENDA

The traditional formula of policy in recent American politics was peace, prosperity, and progress. Nixon attended to all three expectations of the electorate. But he also moved beyond the demands of this traditional formula in search of a successful agenda based on new issues. This agenda did not consist of the blue-collar concerns of the Rosow Report; they were addressed no more specifically than in the programs of the new American revolution. Instead, the new agenda reflected Nixon's desire to be identified with social conservatism. By that route, he aimed to mobilize traditionally Democratic groups to support his administration. The fortunes of the radical-liberal campaign in 1970 did not deflect Nixon, who was convinced that the United States was a socially conservative nation, from his determination to reap political benefits from Scammon and Wattenberg's Social Issue.

Despite its absolute centrality to the administration's understanding of the

Social Issue in 1970, the politics of crime was notably absent from Nixon's agenda. The White House sent to Capitol Hill no significant request for legislation on crime. The absence reflected the important dimensions of the legislation passed in 1970. It also revealed the danger of anticrime politics. Crime seemed beyond the reach of tough-minded legislation; statistics revealed at best a decline in the rate at which crime was increasing.[82] It was difficult for Nixon to claim any victory in his war on crime. Moreover, the absence of new anticrime initiatives served as a reminder that Nixon had not managed to create any significant partisan division on the issue. Ever-escalating appropriations for law enforcement were largely uncontroversial; when Nixon asked for more spending on crime, Congress agreed to every cent. Although the $268 million Law Enforcement Assistance Administration appropriation for fiscal year 1970 did not match Nixon's requested $296.5 million, the following years saw increasing requests that were always matched by appropriations. For fiscal year 1973, Nixon requested $850.5 million, which Congress appropriated.

According to popular perception, the nation's problems of law and order were often linked with drug abuse, and law enforcement officials agreed that more than half of street crimes were related to drugs. The forum for the issue's consideration was a national commission chaired by Raymond Shafer, the former Republican governor of Pennsylvania. But the commission's work annoyed Nixon. On a point of crucial importance to society and of political sensitivity—the use of marijuana—the commission offended his social conservatism: it found the occasional use of marijuana harmless and recommended the decriminalization of the private possession, use, and casual sale of the drug. Nixon met with commission members to thank them for their work but also emphasized his disagreement with their findings.[83]

The Calley case provided Nixon with a chance to demonstrate his credentials as a social conservative. In March 1971, a military jury found First Lieutenant William L. Calley Jr. guilty of murder for his role three years earlier in the massacre of three hundred civilians in My Lai, Vietnam. Calley was sentenced to life in jail. The public was horrified by the revelations but also overwhelmingly sympathetic to Calley's plight. Many saw the officer as a patriotic soldier attempting under difficult circumstances to fight for his nation's cause. By mid-May, the White House had received 320,000 pieces of communication on the matter; an assessment of earlier correspondence estimated that it was "99% against the verdict."[84]

Nixon reacted quickly to the verdict, if not so quickly that he did not first take a reading of political and public opinion. He ordered Calley's return to his base pending an appeal. Although the case was not over, the president announced that he would personally review the final sentence, causing the prosecutor to protest this interference in the judicial process. Nixon enjoyed taking a personal interest in the case. After calling Admiral Thomas Moorer, chair of the Joint Chiefs Of Staff, and instructing him to release Calley from the military prison, Nixon told Haldeman, "That's the one place where they say 'yes, sir,' instead of 'yes, but.' "[85]

Nixon agreed with Buchanan that the case was supremely a matter of popular social conservatism. The administration, Buchanan wrote, should be "not reaming Calley, but defending the Army, the process of law in this country, our belief that excesses in combat will not be tolerated—and giving a good scourging to the guilt-ridden, war-crime crowd that is on the other side of our fence, and of the national fence." Nixon welcomed the chance to be "on the side of the people for a change, instead of always doing what's cautious, proper, and efficient." Calley, whose sentence was reduced on appeal from life to twenty and later ten years of imprisonment, would spend less than four years under house arrest before securing parole.[86]

The placing of "fences" in this way encouraged Nixon's identification with traditional Democrats—unionists prominent among them—because of his position on antipermissiveness and patriotism. The Calley case seemed to prove the point. Colson canvassed hard hat reaction to Nixon's intervention in the Calley case and found the response favorable. Thomas W. Gleason, the leader of the longshoremen's union, said that his members were even ready to strike on the issue before the announcement. "[The o]ther guy (Johnson) quit when the going got too rough," read the summary of Gleason's comments, but Nixon had "starch." John H. Lyons of the ironworkers, Frank Rafferty of the painters, and Peter Brennan, the New York builders union leader who had been involved in the 1970 hard hat march on Wall Street, responded in a similarly supportive manner.[87]

BUSING

Despite Nixon's eagerness to establish firmly a reputation as a social conservative, the emergence of a real Social Issue agenda was slow. Nixon heard this judgment firsthand from the coframer of the Social Issue, Richard Scammon, at a January 1972 meeting. Nixon said that he agreed with much of *The Real Majority* and asked Scammon "whether the social issue was still alive." Scammon said yes but suggested that the White House's identification with the issue had been "poor" and "not successful." He spoke of the Social Issue in ways that were much more clear-cut than the diverse set of concerns about American society that were explained in *The Real Majority*. The contemporary manifestations of the Social Issue on the national scene concerned race: Scammon's examples were affirmative measures toward racial integration—that is, busing and scatter-site housing.

Nixon's vision of his majority was different. He explained his political philosophy, which linked patriotism with antipermissiveness. At its heart was a concern with foreign policy, connected with the impact of domestic public opinion on the conduct of such international affairs. Nixon saw the world as dominated by five powers—China, the Soviet Union, Japan, Germany, and the United States. Although America retained marginally its supremacy, disturbing signs of isolationism had appeared in discussions of the country's world role; a resurgence of isolationism would foster global imbalance. Then, rather as he had spoken on the subjects of labor and youth, the president condemned "the intellectual establishment" for its lack of "courage" and "guts." "The President," reported Colson, "said that he thought a bare majority of the country still had the courage, the fortitude to hold strong to do what was right, to see the issues as they really were, to be courageous." Scammon dissented; he argued that what Nixon perceived as the bare majority actually constituted "a large majority." The conversation with Nixon impressed Scammon. "I may find myself voting for Richard Nixon in November," he told Colson after the meeting. "Something I never thought I would ever do."[88]

The exchange between Nixon and Scammon revealed more than a difference between their assessments of the new majority's size: it emphasized their different interpretations of that majority. Scammon discovered his "real majority" in the fears associated with the social upheaval of the 1960s. By 1972 he clearly thought that the main origin of this fear was racial desegregation. Although the president also understood the political importance of social upheaval, Nixon, by contrast, discovered his "silent majority" by seeking to mobilize it in support of his foreign policy and in opposition to antiwar protesters' criticisms. The consequences of this distinction were not, however, significant when Nixon shaped his racial policy. Characterizing his views on race as "if anything, ultra-liberal," Nixon confided his views to Ehrlichman.

"There is nothing that disturbs me more," he wrote, "than to have to appear before the country as a racist, a Wallace type, etc., on this fundamental issue." While he opposed segregation, he also opposed "forced integration," justifying his stance in terms of personal conviction plus public opinion.[89]

In April 1971, the Supreme Court handed down a unanimous decision in the case of *Swann v. Charlotte-Mecklenburg Board of Education*. The Court ruled that the existing methods for desegregation in Charlotte, North Carolina, were inadequate. To achieve a realistic level of desegregation in each district school, the Court demanded more effective measures and endorsed busing as one of these measures. The decision was significant: busing soon began in most southern cities. Lower courts began to hear further cases with even wider-ranging implications. For example, a district court ordered in January 1972 that the desegregation plan for Richmond, Virginia, must involve busing between the city and suburbs even though they were different jurisdictions. In June, however, the circuit court of appeals reversed this decision.

More importantly, the issue went north. Court challenges to segregation in urban areas outside the South pointed out that despite the absence of dual school systems in recent history, the policies of local governments had encouraged de facto racial separation within education. The most sweeping example was Detroit, where Judge Stephen Roth ordered a desegregation plan involving busing across the city and the suburbs; the circuit court upheld the decision. Under the plan, drawn up in 1972, more than 300,000 pupils would take buses to desegregated schools. Roth pointed out that about the same number of children had traveled by bus to school under previous arrangements.[90]

Busing was deeply unpopular among the public. The Harris organization, for example, reported 77 percent opposition in late 1971. But, as pollster Robert Teeter found, opposition constituted "an intense concern only in those areas where bussing [*sic*] [had] been a problem." Nevertheless, politicians could not avoid noticing the strength of opposition in affected areas. In July 1971, Anne Armstrong, the cochair of the RNC, wrote to Nixon that plans for busing in her native Texas were seriously undermining hopes for a Nixon victory there. "If mass bussing [*sic*] is ordered," she argued, "emotions will run so high they cannot be calmed within a year or two." Charles Colson later observed that in its northern incarnation, busing became central to the mobilization of the "white ethnic voter feeling alienated." No issue, he said, was "more sensitive" to such voters in these areas. This sensitivity ensured that busing held Nixon's urgent interest.[91]

"To the extent we can stop this poisonous thing from happening," Nixon told a meeting of Republican congressional leaders, "we ought to do it." Before the *Swann* decision, he instructed Ehrlichman to have "a game plan prepared for a Constitutional Amendment" in case the Court ruled in favor of busing. Given the Supreme Court's rulings, an amendment was the only sure way to stop busing, and Nixon remained interested in the option. Most importantly, he wanted some remedy that he could propose in time for the election and that could "defuse the issue."[92]

In practical terms, Nixon's response to *Swann* was a reluctant acceptance of minimal compliance. Review of desegregation plans by government departments ensured that they met judicial requirements, but no more. Shortly after *Swann*, aide Edward Morgan explained the approach—and its political merits—to Nixon: "If we can keep the liberal writers convinced that we are doing what the Court requires, and our conservative Southern friends convinced that we are not doing more than the Court requires, I think we can walk this tight rope until November, 1972."[93]

George Wallace ensured that the electoral salience of race remained high, making the tightrope walk more perilous. Again campaigning for the Democratic nomination, Wallace used aggressive rhetoric against federal intervention in pursuit of desegregation. Harry Dent argued that a strong administration position on busing was essential; Wallace would then lose "the only leverage issue that remains to him." The effort seemed worthwhile in search of independent and Democratic votes that were essential to reelection. According to Teeter, Wallace's supporters "should be easier to convert than traditional straight Democratic party voters." The Wallaceites' general reaction to the administration's record was much more favorable than that of moderate Democrats, although the Alabamian's supporters were much less likely to see Nixon's economic policy as helpful to working Americans. If those who had favored Wallace were to be mobilized to support Nixon, it would therefore be on the basis of noneconomic issues. Still, according to the same polls, Wallace supporters, like Americans as a whole, did not see busing as an especially important issue unless it touched them directly—unlike such concerns as taxation and Vietnam.[94]

Often attentive to polls, Nixon seemed oblivious to the findings about the salience of the issue, sensing that many who were opposed to busing were reluctant to admit this opposition to pollsters. He felt that it demanded his attention; as Colson noted, even while busing was not the most significant national issue, it was intensely important in certain key areas. Wallace's success at the polls offered Nixon further evidence for this belief. In mid-March, George Wallace won the Florida primary, taking 42 percent of the vote to beat out the rest of the field of twelve Democrats. At the same time, in a nonbinding referendum, Floridians voting convincingly in favor of an antibusing amendment. Just a few days later, Nixon called for the enactment of a "moratorium" on court-ordered busing and, as an alternative remedy for educational inequalities, for a bill that would limit busing and grant special funding to needy schools. Nixon described his approach as moderate, favored by "the majority of Americans of all races [who] want more busing stopped and better education started."[95]

Wallace continued to talk about busing as a key part of his appeal to the electorate until a May assassination attempt left him seriously injured. The shooting took place on a day of primary elections; one was in Michigan, where the plan for busing in Detroit helped Wallace secure 51 percent of the vote, leading Nixon to observe to Ehrlichman that "busing is a potent issue and can make the difference in some northern States which otherwise we would have no chance whatever to win." With Wallace in the hospital rather than on the campaign trail, the busing debate lost some of its urgency. Nixon's proposals did not win enactment. The busing moratorium, an act of dubious constitutionality, was not implemented. The House passed the education bill, but it fell to an October filibuster by Senate liberals. Nevertheless, his proposals and his supporting rhetoric meant that the defeats did not undo Nixon's political point of opposition to busing.[96]

In time, the public policy impact of Nixon's opposition became more clear. The Supreme Court decided the future of busing, and his appointees played a key role in these decisions. In fact, Nixon privately worried that at least some of his appointees, "softened up by the media they read, the communities they live in, the parties they attend, and the very air they breathe on the Potomac," would support "an ultra-liberal decision on both forced integrated housing and in the school cases, including de facto segregation." After all, Chief Justice Warren Burger had voted for busing in *Swann*, although in an unusual move a few months later he circulated a memo to judges emphasizing the limits on the remedy described in the Court's decision. Although Harry Blackmun did not prove to be the strict conservative for whom Nixon had hoped, he had few other grounds for worries. A turning point would arrive in 1974, when the

Detroit case reached the Supreme Court. By that time, Lewis Powell and William Rehnquist had joined Blackmun and Burger on the court. In *Milliken v. Bradley*, Nixon's appointees provided four of the five votes that ruled against busing between school districts. This decision ensured that implementing a desegregation plan in the North involving white-dominated suburbs and minority-dominated central cities would not usually be possible.[97]

RESIDENTIAL DESEGREGATION

The Fair Housing Act of 1968 created a federal commitment to the cause of residential desegregation. The act provided a mechanism by which victims could challenge discriminatory practices in the housing market. The measure also required the Department of Housing and Urban Development (HUD) to run its programs in ways that would promote integration. Nixon viewed the promotion by government of residential desegregation with the same hostility as that of busing. "This country is not ready at this time," he wrote to Ehrlichman, "for either forcibly integrated housing or forcibly integrated education."[98]

When he arrived at HUD as its secretary, George Romney started to create schemes of "open housing," designed to desegregate communities. The reaction where schemes were planned was often hostile. One such community was Blackjack, Missouri, in the suburbs of St. Louis. Blackjack resisted the HUD-supported plan for an integrated housing project for lower- and middle-income families; in response, Romney asked the Justice Department to prosecute. In September 1970, Attorney General John Mitchell refused, thereby calling a halt to Romney's initiative.[99]

A few months later, Nixon, who had already decided that he wanted to remove Romney from the cabinet, looked for a public fight on the issue. The president hoped to use Romney's dismissal to engage in an argument about residential desegregation, thus dramatizing Nixon's opposition. But Romney thwarted the plan. To Nixon's surprise, as Haldeman noted, it "[t]urned out that in the crunch, George would back down on his super-principles, and follow Administration policy about suburb integration, if that would avoid his being tossed out." Without the prospect of a public tussle about the rights and wrongs of affirmative policies of integration, Nixon changed his mind and decided to keep Romney at HUD.[100]

Although the department under Romney developed stricter racial guide-lines for new public housing, their impact was limited, and the implementation of the 1968 act remained imperfect. Housing supported by public funds remained characterized by patterns of racial segregation. Nixon offered no support to the cause, as he demonstrated in his response to another locus of housing controversy, Chicago. In September 1971, a federal appeals court found in the case of *Gautreaux v. Chicago* that the city's housing authority had used discriminatory practices in choosing sites for projects and in assigning tenants. Moreover, HUD was guilty of complicity in these practices, the court found. The judge demanded that the housing authority develop a plan for residential desegregation across the metropolitan area. But Nixon promised Mayor Richard Daley that any proposals to locate public housing in ethnic communities would be resisted despite the court's ruling. The department's practical response was to file an appeal, ultimately unsuccessful, but the process of appeal was time-consuming. Not until 1981 did a limited scheme of desegregation for Chicago's public housing go into effect.[101]

Another case was in New York and involved a plan for public housing in the mostly Jewish Forest Hills neighborhood in Queens. Buchanan advocated forceful presidential intervention to overturn Mayor John Lindsay's decision to build the development there. Adding to the administration's dislike for Lindsay was his recent defection from the Republicans to the Democratic Party. "Scatter-site" housing, Buchanan predicted, threatened to achieve an electoral salience as great as that of busing. Senator James Buckley took the lead in campaigning against the scheme, but his activity focused attention on Lindsay's responsibility for the decision rather than the federal funding for the project. There was no announcement of formal intervention by the administration, but the scale of the project was reduced by half, and a revised plan called for the buildings to be leased to a cooperative organization that would screen tenants.[102]

"While we are not getting blamed, perhaps," Buchanan grumbled, "for being the driving force behind this integrationist mania—we are also forfeiting the political credit that could have been derived from other than a struthious posture on the matter." But Nixon was rarely ostrichlike when dealing with matters political. As in the case of busing, Nixon publicly stated his opposition to residential desegregation. If his position did not satisfy Buchanan, it nevertheless openly slowed the tide of desegregation.[103]

CATHOLICS AND THE SOCIAL ISSUE AGENDA

The Republican Party was the political home of Protestants. The consolidation and expansion of this Protestant support was not an element of the search for a new majority. Outreach to the Protestant community was largely restricted to Nixon's friendship with Baptist preacher Billy Graham, to whom Nixon turned for advice concerning political as well as spiritual matters. Graham encouraged Nixon to include a greater religious content in his speeches, for example. Instead, Nixon was engaged by the possibility of cultivating Catholic support. Catholics traditionally supported the Democratic Party. Indeed, in 1968, Nixon won the votes of only a third of Catholics, no better than the figure achieved by Thomas E. Dewey twenty years earlier. Nevertheless, Catholics now numbered among the traditional Democrats whom Nixon wished to recruit to his new majority. Together with union members and ethnic Americans, Catholics were frequently middle Americans, so a special appeal to Catholics was one method of reaching this elusive target of huge electoral promise. But Nixon also believed that white-collar as well as blue-collar Catholics were potential recruits to his new majority.[104]

Disagreement within the administration about how to target Catholics reflected a division between those who thought that bloc voting was becoming an artifact of political history and those who thought that a last hurrah of Rooseveltian interest groups was possible. This disagreement focused on the question of federal aid for parochial schools. Nixon's decision was never in doubt. In seeking to end the Democratic electoral dominance, in place since Franklin Roosevelt's presidency, Nixon did not reject social groups' importance to electoral calculations.

Parochial schools were a key part of many Catholic communities and were considered very important by many Catholic Americans. But parochial schools often faced economic problems, and some were even closing down as a consequence of lack of funds, reflecting the decline of many inner-city white ethnic communities. The protection of parochial education was a matter of great concern to the Catholic hierarchy. Race motivated some urban Catholics to preserve parochial education, with its mostly white schools. Nixon justified his support for parochial schools, by contrast, on the grounds that they provided educational diversity and offered a yardstick for measuring the effectiveness of the public sector. During a discussion with staff about what issues were emerging in political importance, he stated, "It's vitally important that private schools survive."[105]

Nixon wanted to offer financial aid to parochial schools—"parochaid"—a Republican initiative first seen in the platform of 1968. But the constitutional separation of church and state stood in the way of government promotion of religious education; Nixon cast aside his usual emphasis on strict constitutional constructionism to advocate the permissibility of federal aid to Catholic schools. During his presidency, a key case about state aid for parochial schools, *Lemon v. Kurtzman*, reached the Supreme Court. Nixon ordered Solicitor General Erwin Griswold to file an amicus brief on the side of parochaid, but Griswold refused; Nixon then told Attorney General Mitchell to do so, and he reluctantly complied. As Griswold and Mitchell expected, the Court's June 1971 decision confirmed that direct financial aid was unconstitutional, leaving open only the option of tax relief.[106]

The question of help for parochial schools was an incidental interest of a presidential commission on school finance. For Nixon, the question was central and not incidental. When he met with the commission's chair, Neil McElroy, Nixon emphasized forcefully his special concern about the matter. McElroy accepted only with reluctance Nixon's instructions to appoint Clarence Walton of Catholic University as chair of a panel on nonpublic education. Nixon did not miss further opportunities to remind commission members that he strongly favored a vibrant system of private education.[107]

When parochaid was found unconstitutional in the *Lemon* case, Buchanan's contacts with the Catholic community caused him to alert his colleagues to "a possible Catholic 'break' of sorts with the Administration." Terence Cooke, cardinal of New York, was concerned about the future of Catholic elementary schools. Buchanan did not need to convince Nixon, who already sought to speak to Catholics as Catholics. In August 1971, the president endorsed Cardinal Cooke's call for parochaid during a Knights of Columbus address. Cooke, "deeply upset by the long-term effect of the Burger reasoning" in *Lemon*, subsequently was "favorably disposed" to the rumor that Nixon still hoped to enact a tax credit for parents who sent their children to private schools.[108]

The rumor was true. Although McElroy's commission reported against a tax credit, Nixon refused to endorse the group's findings and instead promoted the favorable report of Walton's panel. All Catholic educational institutions received copies of the report along with a letter from Walton indicating Nixon's support of it. When the 1972 platform was to be written, Nixon instructed his staff to include a strong parochaid plank. Administration polls suggested that a majority of all voters supported parochaid. In the case of Catholics, the support was overwhelming, even if many ordinary Catholics did not share the hierarchy's view of financial aid as critical.[109]

Nixon did not doubt the wisdom of his position, but his staff began to debate the wisdom of the special effort to attract Catholic voters. In the autumn of 1971 John Ehrlichman and the staff of the domestic council challenged the assumption that parochaid was valuable in mobilizing Catholic support for the administration. Roy Morey argued that Catholicism was no longer an active political issue and even that there were "definite risks in attempting to woo Catholics *as* Catholics." Catholic voters were much more concerned about other issues relating to "general economic and social conditions," and many had little interest in the issue of parochaid. Indeed, identification with the issue might prove counterproductive if it generated opposition among the more numerous Protestant voters.[110]

Patrick Buchanan rejected Morey's argument as "remorseless nonsense." Buchanan agreed that differences existed among Catholics but argued that the administration should target "the Catholic social conservatives—the clear majority." Buchanan's enthusiastic support for parochaid was fostered by the belief that the issue would increase Democratic divisions between the socially liberal and the socially conservative. "When RN comes out for aid to parochial schools, this will drive a wedge right down the Middle of the Democratic Party," he wrote. "The same is true of abortion; the same is true of hard-line anti-pornography laws. For those *most* against aid to Catholic schools, *most for* abortion, and an end to all censorship are the New York Times Democrats. And those most violently for aid to Catholic schools and *against* abortion and dirty books, are the Jim Buckley Catholic Democrats."[111]

The discussion about the electoral impact of a Catholic appeal was distorted by the belief that Nixon's Democratic opponent would likely be a Catholic— either Edmund Muskie or Edward Kennedy. Early figures suggested that Nixon's share of the Catholic vote against both Muskie and Kennedy had improved in comparison to the 1968 results but that the vote was apparently unstable. Nixon assumed that Catholics would favor a fellow Catholic candidate and attributed much of Muskie's strength to his Catholicism. On the primary trail, both Muskie and Humphrey strongly endorsed parochial schools, further strengthening White House concerns about the need to dramatize the president's position.[112]

His aides' doubts did not alter Nixon's approach. His instinct was to articulate socially conservative positions, which he believed represented the nation's majority rather than a particular majority among such voter groups as American Catholics. His political opportunism melded with his personal values, he claimed, telling Colson that "[a]ll this business about Catholic schools, it's not politics." The president explained that he could convert to Catholicism except that "everyone would say it was some political gimmick."[113]

The conflict between staff members emerged again when Nixon decided to make a speech in favor of parochaid before the National Catholic Educators Association in Philadelphia in the spring of 1972. Ehrlichman used his responsibility for developing the speech to force its delay or even cancellation. Fighting strongly in its favor, Colson on the day of speech advised Nixon that "[p]reservation of Catholic schools in Philadelphia [was] a public issue not a church issue," because John Krol, the cardinal, had convinced the population that the existence of parochial schools was a major financial benefit to the public school system. A majority of the city's white high school students attended Catholic institutions.[114]

Nixon's new-majority instincts once more won the day, although the concerns of those such as Ehrlichman had some influence. The content was "heavily watered down" on the advice of Connally and others in the White House, but Nixon delivered a speech that won the approval of Krol and Frank Rizzo, Philadelphia's conservative Democratic mayor. "I am irrevocably committed to these propositions: America needs her non-public schools; that those non-public schools need help; that therefore we must and will find ways to provide that help," he said.[115]

As Buchanan noted, the liberalization of abortion laws was another newly emerging issue that was sensitive to socially conservative Catholics—in his phrase, "the Jim Buckley Catholic Democrats." In 1970, Nixon avoided the controversy attached to this issue by insisting that it was properly a matter of concern at the state level. But, in the spring of 1971, he ordered military hospitals to reverse rules that liberalized access to abortion, calling it "an unacceptable form of population control" on the basis of his "personal and religious beliefs." A year later, at the suggestion of Buchanan, Nixon wrote to Cardinal Cooke and expressed opposition to abortion and approval of the New York campaign to repeal the state's liberal abortion law. The letter was leaked and generated some hostile reaction, particularly as a result of Nixon's apparent interference in New York matters. The missive also provided an unequivocal signal of his social conservatism on the matter.[116]

In the campaign, Robert Teeter discovered that Nixon's position on abortion was removed from that of the electorate, while McGovern's view, more liberal, captured the center of public opinion. Teeter did not see Nixon's popularity among Catholics as connected with his public expressions against abortion and advised the president to "avoid this issue if possible unless it becomes absolutely necessary."[117] Nixon generally steered clear of the issue, but he had already managed to clarify his position, especially for the benefit of interested voters.

In one sense, there was no resolution to the internal debate about whether to engineer a distinctive programmatic appeal to the Catholic vote. Nixon's domestic policy staff continued to oppose such an appeal, while his public liaison operation continued to support this approach. In another sense, there was no debate that needed resolution. Nixon wanted to pursue the politics of social conservatism. His aides' arguments against this direction could have no more than a moderating effect. Private opinion polls supported some of those arguments but could not alter Nixon's conviction that his approach represented good politics and good policy.

Nixon's social conservatism caused differences within his staff but was not the source of serious division within the Republican Party, unlike the impact of similar issues on the Democratic Party. The basis of the primary challenges from Republicans was foreign policy, not the Social Issue agenda. When Rita Hauser, a leading Republican from New York, complained about the administration's positions on abortion as well as other issues, Pat Buchanan replied, "he will cost himself Catholic support and gain what, Betty Friedan?"[118]

As Buchanan's dismissive reference to the founder of the National Organization for Women suggests, the Nixon White House was not characterized by much sensitivity to emergent women's issues. Like Hauser, Republican as well as Democratic feminists frequently viewed with alarm the Nixon administration's activities on these issues, which also included federal funding for child care, government appointments for women, and the Equal Rights Amendment, which passed Congress in 1972 with little more than a token endorsement from Nixon. The record was by no means entirely negative; Congress passed equal-rights legislation that secured the administration's acceptance and sometimes even its active support.[119] Nevertheless, recognition of women as a distinct group—whether feminist or not—was largely absent from plans for a new majority.

DIVIDING THE DEMOCRATS

Nixon was not content to rely on the popularity of his record and on the persuasiveness of his political arguments when looking for votes. He resorted to less elevated tactics in search of electoral advantage. His chances for re-election were, of course, related to the strength of his opposition. Disarray within Democratic ranks would weaken that opposition. Moreover, the contenders for the Democratic nomination included politicians who seemed capable of making an effective case against Nixon. If a Democratic candidate revitalized his party's electoral coalition, then the dream of a Nixon majority was at stake.

Nixon was enthusiastic in directing "dirty tricks," activities questionably defended by insiders as a normal part of American electoral politics. For example, in the months immediately following the midterms, the president thought up schemes intended to damage two promising Democrats, Edmund Muskie and Edward Kennedy. Nixon instructed that letters espousing liberal sentiments be sent to leading southern Democrats, purportedly from Muskie supporters. The letters were intended to encourage conservatives to view with suspicion Muskie's moderate reputation. A private detective followed Kennedy during a trip to Paris and obtained photographic evidence of the senator's womanizing. Nixon had the photographs sent to some members of Congress and reporters.[120]

The reach of Nixon's political operation was astonishing, even apparently managing to get Muskie's mother to provide damaging information about him. In April 1971, Murray Chotiner discovered that she was not impressed by the prospect of her son as president: she told Chotiner's agent that current talk of Muskie as "a Lincoln" was "very foolish." Life in Washington had spoiled him, and he had always been "a pretty moody fellow." Indeed, in a Nixon-Muskie contest, she was likely to choose Nixon. "You know, I don't see anything wrong with the President we have," she reportedly commented. "He seems a very nice man."[121]

When the primaries began, the White House stepped up its campaign of dirty tricks against the promising Democratic candidates. In New Hampshire, the conservative *Manchester Union Leader* ran a letter, probably written by Nixon press aide Kenneth Clawson, wrongly claiming that Muskie's wife had insultingly referred to French Canadians as "Canucks." Muskie went to the newspaper's offices to defend his wife but in so doing appeared to cry, thereby damaging his political standing. Further dirty tricks followed. In early April, Patrick Buchanan and Kenneth Khachigian observed that the effort to remove Muskie from the race was showing signs of success. By the end of the month, his position within the Democratic race for the nomination had worsened further and, following a poor performance in the Florida primary, Muskie withdrew his candidacy.[122]

As a candidate for the Democratic nomination, Wallace increased party disunity. But if he stood again as a third-party candidate for the presidency, he would threaten Nixon's position. Administration polls almost invariably revealed that a Wallace candidacy would steal more votes from Nixon than from the Democratic candidate. Wallace was therefore the object of much interest at the White House. In 1970, an investigation by the Internal Revenue Service of Wallace's brother, Gerald, uncovered damaging information, which was leaked, with little effect. The White House then had money sent to Albert Brewer, who was campaigning against Wallace for Alabama's governorship, but Brewer lost. In 1972, to encourage Wallace's primary candidacy and thus Democratic disunity, Harry Dent supplied Wallace's campaign with advice and information.[123]

Despite the serious injuries Wallace had incurred in the May assassination attempt, Nixon still feared that Wallace might decide to run in the presidential election. The president used John Connally and Billy Graham in the effort to dissuade Wallace, telling him that his participation only made a McGovern victory more likely. Nixon also authorized the payment of money to Wallace aides. No deal was concluded, but Wallace, paralyzed by the shooting, did not pursue his campaign.[124]

THE DECLINE OF REFORMISM

The reform agenda remained largely unimplemented. Nixon was unwilling to agree to a more generous form of welfare reform in exchange for liberal congressional support. FAP was finally taken out of an omnibus welfare and Social Security bill at the start of October, during the election season. A key reason for FAP's failure was hostility among more conservative Republicans combined with liberals' desire for a more wide-ranging program. In the Senate vote that finally killed FAP, twenty-four Republican senators voted to do so; the more liberal version of the bill under discussion in the Senate also did not secure administration support. Nevertheless, one piece of welfare reform was saved. The omnibus bill created a federal program offering a guaranteed income to the needy elderly, to the disabled, and to the blind, replacing the federal-state program dating from the New Deal. The reform was important, but its implications were minor in comparison to FAP's ambition. Meanwhile, the health care proposals remained under consideration by Congress, though administration hopes for their progress would ultimately prove to be in vain.

The one major achievement of the new American revolution was general revenue sharing. After long legislative consideration of how to implement revenue sharing, Nixon signed the bill into law in mid-October. Once more, the Republican Party had not been a staunch ally of the administration. In a key June House vote, 57 Republicans voted against revenue sharing, while 113 party members voted for it. On the Democratic side, the vote was 128 against and 110 for. James Reichley has noted that as with welfare reform, Republican opposition was related to members' overall conservatism. The congressional Republican Party had not managed to cast aside its negativism.

If the reform agenda did not transform the Republican Party, it also did not improve relations between Nixon and southern Democrats because opposition to FAP and, to a lesser extent, to revenue sharing was also related to Democrats' ideology. More conservative Democratic legislators thus remained unenthusiastic about the reform agenda. Key obstacles to the administration's FAP proposal were Louisiana's Russell Long, a leading Democrat on the Senate Finance Committee, and Connecticut's Abraham Ribicoff, who had advocated the more generous version of the bill that Nixon had refused to accept. The reform agenda, therefore, did not mobilize a coherent congressional coalition supportive of Nixon.[125] The basis of the often strong relationship between Nixon and conservative Democrats was foreign policy, not Nixonian reformism.

The electoral potential of the new American revolution was slender. In a June 1972 memo cowritten with Khachigian, Buchanan almost gleefully observed the failure of the initiatives against which he had advised. "We have spent countless hours and unrecorded effort selling the bold dynamic 'New American Revolution,' . . . and the returns are, in my judgment, not encouraging," he wrote. It would, Buchanan argued, simply be wasteful to campaign about the administration's "exciting" domestic proposals. Administration polls supported Buchanan's argument suggesting dissatisfaction with the Nixon record in areas such as health, welfare, and the environment but confidence in its foreign policy, including the conduct of the Vietnam War.[126]

A significant source of innovative domestic policy was quite different and separate from the initiatives of the new American revolution. It consisted of Social Security legislation, described by historian Julian Zelizer as "a watershed in public policy." The principal provision of the omnibus act that reformed aid to the needy elderly, disabled, and blind was the expansion of retirement benefits. In addition to increasing benefits by 20 percent (following other increases during the Nixon administration), the measure instituted an automatic cost-of-living adjustment to raise payments in line with inflation. Much of the impetus for change originated with Congress, although Nixon early endorsed indexation as a way "to remove this system from biennial politics." On signing the bill in July, Nixon attacked it as "fiscally irresponsible" for the inclusion of the 20 percent increase. The impossible alternative facing him was to veto the bill, thereby rejecting a popular increase in benefit levels as a campaign approached; moreover, attached to the bill was an increase in the public debt ceiling, which was essential for the government to continue running smoothly. The significance of indexation would become apparent when inflation took serious hold later in the 1970s, resulting in generous increases in benefits that destabilized the Social Security system.[127]

THE RECORD

In early 1972, Agnew told a meeting of Masons that, thanks to the efforts of the Nixon administration, "the end of the era of license is at hand." "Backbones are stiffening all across the land," he said, "against the flouting of laws, traditions and institutions."[128] It is difficult to find much basis for Agnew's claim. Despite his engagement with the problems of permissiveness, Nixon had largely failed to translate this concern meaningfully into action. The successes were few. Because of Vietnamization and the reduction of America's role in the war, the protest movements had lost much of their energy; the nation was undoubtedly calmer in the early 1970s than in the late 1960s. Otherwise, the agenda against permissiveness was limited largely to traditionalist rhetoric, of which the reports of commissions remained a favorite target, and to looking for tokenistic proposals that might be attractive to swing voters, especially among American Catholics.

The new American revolution was largely a failure, while the principal success of the new economic policy lay in demonstrating Nixon's determination to improve the economy. Its practical impact in this regard was less impressive, although other initiatives and developments helped to restore some of the economy's health in 1972. At home, Nixon had managed to push racial policy in a more conservative direction; he had largely reversed the executive branch's commitment to the realization of more genuine equality for African Americans, placing the onus instead on the judiciary. In turn, because of his judicial nominations, he had transformed the Supreme Court into a body less likely to interpret the Constitution in ways that encouraged the enforcement of affirmative and de facto integration, whether in policies of busing, of residential desegregation, or of minority preferences. This was Nixon's answer to the growing disquiet both in the North and the South about the 1960s impetus toward racial equality. One area of genuine accomplishment for the administration was foreign policy. Détente won widespread support with its promise of "a generation of peace."[129] As far as its Vietnam policy was concerned, Nixon managed to convince many that he was dedicated to finding "peace with honor," even if that goal entailed the continuation of conflict.

But the record—as opposed to the rhetoric—of the Nixon administration was unimpressive overall. The administration lacked a sturdy foundation on which to base a new majority. Against a strong opponent, it might not even have been enough to win reelection for Nixon. But Nixon's challenger, George McGovern, was not strong. In the short run, McGovern's shortcomings as a candidate minimized the shortcomings of the administration's record. Indeed, McGovern's problems were significant enough to rekindle Nixon's ambitions regarding the creation of a new majority.

★ FIVE ★

PRESIDENT NIXON FOR PRESIDENT

The Rejection of
the Republican
Party, 1972

★ ★ ★ ★

In 1972, Nixon concentrated on his reelection to the absolute exclusion of the fortunes of other Republicans. Campaign aides told any candidates who raised objections that their best chance of success was a strong showing by the president. But Nixon did not believe that Republicans would win elections in large numbers thanks to his coattails. Instead, he worried about the danger to him if he tried to mobilize a new Republican majority as well as his presidential majority. "[T]he moment I do that," he told Theodore White, "I pull myself down to their level, and . . . part of our problem is that we have a lot of lousy candidates; the good ones will go up with me, the bad ones will go down."[1] In pursuit of the new majority, Nixon was eager to win as many votes as possible from self-identified Democrats; his party, still favored by only a minority of Americans, could not help him in this effort. The connection between president and party was therefore broken. His strategy depended on the rejection of concern for the Republican Party at large.

Nixon's electoral vehicle was not the party but the Committee for the Reelection of the President (CRP). The existence of a personal campaign organization, separate from the national committee, was not a new phenomenon under Nixon. But its significance within the campaign was unprecedented; the administration, according to political scientists Thomas E. Cronin and Michael A. Genovese, achieved "in many ways the ultimate in presidential hostility towards its own party." In some cases, even incumbent Republican senators running for reelection did not benefit from a presidential visit. At best, they could expect instead a visit from Agnew, deployed "to forestall the cries of 'wolf' of Senators in trouble." Unsurprisingly, the result of the White House's rejection strategy was resentment within the party. "All they care about at CRP is Richard M. Nixon," complained one Republican National Committee (RNC) official to a journalist. "They couldn't care less about the Republican Party. Given the chance, they would wreck it."[2] But if Republicans objected to the Nixon campaign, Nixon had grounds to believe that the party deserved little help. Republicans in Congress had not proved to be his dependable allies in his first term. Although Nixon and congressional Republicans rarely disagreed on foreign policy, collective Republican support for the new American revolution was lukewarm at best; this lukewarm attitude poured cold water on Nixon's plans for reform.

In place of the Republican Party, Nixon still contemplated the formation of a new conservative party. This, he thought, was the feasible route to realignment. The right moment to make the move was following the 1972 elections. As late as June, Nixon harbored the hope that Democrat John Connally might take the vice presidential slot in Spiro Agnew's place.[3] Nixon was not, however, able to form a "national unity" ticket for his reelection. Still, Connally was central to Nixon's plans for the campaign as leader of Democrats for Nixon and, beyond that, for the future of the new majority.

MCGOVERN

During Nixon's term as president, some remarkable events took place within the Democratic Party. In the words of political scientist Byron Shafer, they amounted to a "quiet revolution." Lawrence O'Brien summarized them as "the greatest goddamn change since the two-party system."[4] What precipitated the revolution was the outcome of the presidential nominating process in 1968. Many Democratic activists had felt outrage when party leaders chose Hubert Humphrey as the nominee even though Humphrey had participated in no primaries and therefore had won no delegates in open competition. The response to this outrage was the creation of a commission, first under George McGovern and then under Donald Fraser, to revise the nomination process. The new rules decisively moved influence away from party leaders and toward primary voters. In addition, the reforms called for affirmative steps to ensure that convention delegations included members of minorities, young people, and women in numbers reasonably proportionate to their presence in each state.

The contest for the 1972 nomination was fought according to the new rules, and McGovern won. He did so by articulating positions very different from Nixon's. McGovern's candidacy was inspired by opposition to the Vietnam War; he denounced the war, advocated speedy withdrawal, and viewed favorably the idea of amnesty for those who had avoided the draft. On questions of permissiveness, his views were also distinct from Nixon's. McGovern spoke sympathetically about liberalized laws concerning both marijuana use and abortion, even if he did not support such measures outright. Endorsing the idea of a guaranteed income, he was among the liberals in the Senate who criticized the Family Assistance Plan (FAP) as excessively mean, and he mentioned a formula that would set the level of the guaranteed income at $1,000 for each American.[5]

In securing the nomination within a crowded field, McGovern did not need to win an overall majority of Democrats. "I thought that if we started early, and organized at the grass roots, and got the women, the young people, the antiwar crowd, some from labor, and the environmentalists," he said later, "there was enough to win the nomination." The new nominating process proved to be unrepresentative of Democratic adherents, if in a different manner from its predecessor. On average, primary voters were more liberal than voters who supported Democrats in general elections. Nevertheless, McGovern's success indicated a shift leftward within the Democratic Party, a shift that alienated those left behind. While the frustrations with the limited achievements of Great Society liberalism accounted for some of this change, so too did opposition to the Vietnam War and misgivings about Cold War internationalism.[6]

Some of McGovern's most effective opponents were Democrats who had not revised their views in response to the Great Society and to the Vietnam War. Their intervention ensured that the battle for the nomination was bruising. In Nebraska, Humphrey supporters charged that McGovern was the pro-permissiveness candidate of "the three As"—acid, abortion, and amnesty. Later, during the campaign for the California primary, Humphrey launched bitter and damaging attacks on McGovern's proposal for a guaranteed income of $1,000 and on his ideas about foreign policy.[7] Humphrey lost the primary but helped to define McGovern as a radical of the type against which Nixon believed he could campaign most effectively.

Seen from the White House, these events were wonderful. "McGovern's victory is not a popular victory; it is more a coup d'etat of the Democratic Party, where a youthful leftist and suburban leftist elite has deposed and ousted the traditional Catholic and Jewish leadership of the Democratic Party," noted Pat Buchanan. "The fellow is not the people's choice." This meant that the 1972 campaign was the ideal time to mobilize the new majority. "As Barry Goldwater was Lyndon Johnson's gift from the gods," William Safire later wrote, "George McGovern was Richard Nixon's." As McGovern focused his attention on the general rather than the primary electorate, he moved to moderate his positions. The Nixon campaign set out to prevent him from doing so. Shortly before the Democratic National Convention, Agnew denounced "the virus of McGovernism" as "the doctrine of retreat overseas and radicalism at home," linking the senator's views with the "ultra-radical leftist line" of Henry Wallace, the 1948 Progressive candidate. With such accusations of radicalism, Nixon wanted to win the support not only of Democratic voters but also of leading Democrats who had been alienated by McGovern's candidacy.[8]

McGovern shared something with Nixon. Both men believed that current politics was subject to significant long-term change. But McGovern's interpretation of that change differed from Nixon's, of course. Insights into McGovern's strategy were revealed not by *The Emerging Republican Majority* or *The Real Majority* but by *Changing Sources of Power*, whose author, Fred Dutton, became an adviser to the Democratic candidate. While Nixon was engaged by the need to mobilize working Americans of the "silent majority," McGovern wanted to win office by securing the support of those excluded from society's mainstream—the poor and minorities—plus the support of a socially liberal middle class. He thought that his strategy was aided by the Twenty-sixth Amendment, which had lowered the voting age to eighteen.[9] The election was therefore a battle between two visions of America's future and between two interpretations of who constituted the nation's new majority.

THE CONVENTION AND THE ACCEPTANCE OF DIVIDED GOVERNMENT

While factional differences plagued the Democratic Party, Nixon was in near-perfect control of the Republicans. He won his party's nomination with 1,347 of the 1,348 delegates. "The Republican Party's heart," wrote journalist James

Dickenson, "belongs to Nixon," even if Nixon did not return the sentiment. Unity, in noticeable contrast with Democratic disunity, was the theme of the elaborately stage-managed 1972 Republican National Convention. Walter Hickel, whom Nixon had fired as interior secretary in 1970, formally introduced the president. Twelve others joined Hickel in doing so, including the nineteen-year-old mayor of Ayrshire, Iowa; the president of the United Auto Workers' Local 544 in Pittsburgh; a Mobile, Alabama, homemaker; and the wife of Milwaukee's Democratic mayor. The nationally known politicians who spoke for the president were James Buckley, Nelson Rockefeller, and Ronald Reagan (who attracted considerably more audience applause than the New York governor did).[10]

Nixon used his acceptance speech to call for the support of his new majority in favor of his foreign policy and in opposition to "radicalism":

> I ask everyone listening to me tonight—Democrats, Republicans and independents—to join our majority—not on the basis of the party label you wear in your lapel but . . . what you believe in your hearts. . . .
>
> I do not ask you to join our new majority because of what we have done in the past. . . . [T]he choice in this election is not between radical change and no change. The choice . . . is between change that works and change that won't work. . . .
>
> Theirs is the politics of paternalism, where master planners in Washington make decisions for the people. Ours is the politics of people—where people make decisions for themselves. . . .
>
> I ask you, my fellow Americans, to join our new majority not just in the cause of winning an election but in achieving a hope that mankind has had since the beginning of civilization. Let us build a peace that our children and all the children of the world can enjoy for generations to come.[11]

A conventional Republican majority in Congress was most unlikely after the failure of the 1970 midterm campaign. However, Republicans were five seats away from an evenly balanced Senate in which Agnew could cast the deciding vote for organization. The situation was more difficult in the House, where the Republican deficit was forty-five seats. The odds were thus heavily against the overturn of Democratic majorities. Any chance of securing a new-majority Congress depended on partisan defections, usually a rare occurrence. In the Senate, one possible convert was Senator Harry Byrd, formerly a pillar of the Democratic Party in Virginia who had become an independent in 1970. At that time, he had resisted Nixon's efforts to win him for the Republicans. In the House, despite the larger deficit, enough defections to secure a majority did not seem unattainable, provided that Republicans picked up a reasonable number of seats in November.[12] Reaching the moment when the Republican Party was within sight of control was crucial to this possibility, as was dis-affection among conservatives in the congressional Democratic Party.

Gerald Ford, the House minority leader, was hopeful about such gains. "My ambition to become Speaker of the House seemed attainable," he later wrote of this period. In mid-July, he told Nixon of his project "operation switch over," an extension of Connally's earlier proposal for a new congressional coalition. The goal was to persuade Democrats "first, to endorse the P[resident], and second, to vote for a Republican speaker." But Nixon's goal was more cautious. He reacted to Ford's project in a way that revealed the president's lack of enthusiasm for the Republican status quo and his overriding concern with his own fortunes. He urged Republican candidates to "[f]orce the Democrats to back or repudiate McGovern's candidacy" but avoid reference to the Demo-cratic Party when speaking of McGovern, who represented "a minority of his own Party." "There's a defection all over the country regarding the issues, but we make it impossible, if we put it on a Party basis," Nixon said, as chronicled by H. R. Haldeman. Ford secured only some White House help in his project, receiving a letter after the meeting from Charles Colson, who provided the names of four Democratic congressmen who might be responsive.[13]

Nixon was more concerned by the possibility of being dragged down by his identification with the Republican Party than attentive to the ways in which he could improve the chances of the party at large. The White House discouraged even relatively subtle Republican attempts to utilize Nixon's strength in the presidential race. During the campaign, Colson discovered an advertisement in New York that stated, "Vote the Nixon Team—Row A All the Way." He complained to Fred Malek of the CRP: "That's almost as bad as saying 'Vote Republican,'" he wrote. "Everybody knows that Row A is the Republican row. Someone in New York is taking us to the cleaners. This is precisely opposite the strategy I thought everyone was in agreement with. I would imagine this is being done by the Republican organization that wants to get on our coattails, but it sure doesn't help."[14]

Some Republicans had feared that Nixon might reject individual Republi-can candidates outright, as he had done in the "purge" of Senator Charles Goodell in 1970. However, the circumstances of that New York senatorial campaign had been unusual and were unlikely to be repeated elsewhere. Not only had minor-party candidates split the vote, but also Buckley provided a viable candidate who supported many Nixon policies—most importantly, the administration's approach to the Vietnam War. Moreover, few Republican senators facing reelection in 1972 had records considered similarly disloyal to Goodell's. Senator Charles Mathias of Maryland, for example, was seen as one potential victim of a more widespread Nixon purge, but Mathias's term did not expire until 1975.[15] Obvious again were the limitations of a party leader's ability to engage in wholesale party restructuring.

Nevertheless, some liberal Republicans chose to leave the party. The most prominent example was New York Mayor John Lindsay, who became a Democrat in August 1971. Fellow New Yorker Ogden R. Reid also made the move. A former editor-publisher of the *New York Herald Tribune* and ambassador to Israel at the end of the Eisenhower years, Reid was the archetypal eastern-establishment Republican, representing the affluent New York City suburbanites of Westchester County since 1962. In both of these cases, personal ambition played a role, as did dissatisfaction with Nixon's presidency. In Lindsay's case, on the Democratic side he immediately became a presidential contender, if one without much promise. Reid had few opportunities for advancement within the Rockefeller-dominated New York party, and redistricting probably would have left Reid with a difficult renomination battle had he remained a Republican.[16]

In conducting Nixon's candidate-centered campaign, the CRP gained a reputation as the model of a modern political operation (apart, of course, from subsequent discoveries regarding its involvement in the illegalities of Watergate). The reputation was not entirely deserved. Although the CRP had been designed as the campaign arm of the White House, this design did not prevent the emergence of tensions between CRP personnel at 1701 and the presidential staff at 1600 Pennsylvania Avenue. Haldeman worried about the development of a "we/they" attitude because of personal differences and an unwillingness to cooperate. One of Colson's aides described the quality of the CRP's research material as "fairly disgraceful." Nixon too became concerned about the management of the CRP. Some improvement occurred, although certain tensions remained.[17]

The separation between the reelection committee and the party was not always so well defined at the state level. In Indiana, for example, all but "a few key people [worked] simultaneously for both the President and the Governor," and in Ohio, relations between local Republicans and the state CRP were characterized as "excellent." Similarly, Michigan CRP activists worked with Senator Robert Griffin's reelection committee despite "some continuing leadership conflicts." In some other states, the tensions were apparently more pronounced.[18] In these three states, however, where the institutional distinctiveness between Republicans and Nixon activists was less marked than at the national level, that distinctiveness remained.

CONSTITUENCY GROUPS

As a key element of middle America, ethnic Americans were a special target of the Nixon campaign. In fashioning an appeal to this diverse group, Michael Balzano, an aide to Colson, played an important role. Balzano won publicity for his unconventional background: he had dropped out of high school and worked as a garbageman before returning to school and earning a doctorate. He used the publicity about his role in the administration to articulate a message aimed at blue-collar voters. "The president is interested in learning how he can take the outstanding characteristics of these people—work, sacrifice, perseverance, patriotism, etc.—and impart these nation-building traits to all Americans," Balzano commented.[19]

Some of Balzano's work within the White House was policy oriented, involving lobbying for legislation of obvious ethnic interest, such as the encouragement of ethnic studies and the protection of funding for Radio Free Europe and Radio Liberty. His efforts frequently focused on public relations—arranging administration speakers for ethnic events or arguing for the inclusion of ethnic representatives on the president's foreign trips. The memos in support of such moves credited them with powerful potential. If, for example, some leading Polish Americans accompanied Nixon on his visit to Poland following the Moscow summit, Balzano wrote, "it would clinch the Polish vote." Balzano made appearances himself in appropriate ethnic forums. Altogether, encouraging signs indicated that the administration was making inroads into many ethnic Americans' traditional support for Democrats. At the convention of the Polish-American Congress during the campaign, the audience—mostly registered Democratic voters—greeted Sargent Shriver, McGovern's running mate, with indifference. But when Agnew arrived to deliver a speech, the audience warmly welcomed the vice president.[20]

Nixon was not often ready to leave the White House even in pursuit of this significant element of middle America. His activities on the campaign trail were limited, but he did make some appearances intended to appeal to the ethnic vote, including a visit to an Italian American gathering in Maryland. "Every time I'm at an Italian-American picnic," he said, "I think I have some Italian blood." The president also toured the new Museum of American Immigration at Liberty Island in New York, where he spoke about the country's ethnic heritage. While he was there, he posed for photographs with a group of parochial school students. One thirteen-year-old told a journalist of her enthusiasm for Nixon: "He's for America. I can't wait until I'm 18. I hope I get a good guy like Richard Nixon to vote for then."[21]

In addition, Nixon designated October 1 as National Heritage Day, an idea that originated with the RNC's Laszlo Pasztor, who recommended the announcement to provide evidence that the administration was "ethnically aware" and thus to aid the reelection effort in a "nonpolitical" manner. Indeed, although the White House sidelined his office and cut its funding, Pasztor provided a steady flow of suggestions for potential appointees to government advisory committees as well as ideas like National Heritage Day. By 1972, the RNC reported that it had supervised the creation of a thousand local Heritage Councils, with a total membership of 50,000. During the fall campaign, Republican figures attended thirteen separate ethnic events in Chicago alone.[22] The cultivation of ethnic Americans thus had a Republican and not merely presidential dimension.

Nixon did not attempt to win more African American votes, considering it a wasted effort.[23] Although African Americans' preference for the Democratic Party dated from the New Deal, their overwhelming rejection of the Republican Party was much more recent, the product of the exceptional election of 1964. The experimentation with affirmative action, some encouragement of minority business, and the successful desegregation of southern schools were all positive achievements of the administration, but Nixon's campaign made little effort to stress them. Instead, Nixon employed opposition to racial liberalism in search of electoral advantage both in the white South and in affected areas of the North.

McGovern's nomination caused some White House advisers to suggest that the choice provided an opportunity to win over a larger section of the black middle class. Success in such an undertaking would defy the administration's reputation for having halted the civil rights impetus. In 1970, Bishop Stephen

G. Spottswood, chair of the board of directors of the National Association for the Advancement of Colored People, denounced the administration as anti-black, the sort of statement usually voiced only by more radical groups. Reacting to Nixon's position against busing, the organization passed a resolution in July 1972 stating that the president had encouraged "passions of hate and bitterness" among Americans.[24]

In public, campaign aides claimed that Nixon's 12 percent share of the black vote in 1968 could be at least doubled. In June, about two thousand prominent members of the nation's black community attended a strategy meeting held by the CRP's Black Vote Division. At the meeting, Rev. William H. Borders extravagantly praised Nixon as the "statesman of all times . . . whose importance to civilization is almost as Jesus Christ Himself." The organizers' pride in the apparent success of their initiative was marred by participants' complaints that they had been coerced into attending. "My director told me to go to Washington, and I told him I'm not a Republican and didn't want to go," said one official of an Atlanta-based federally funded program. "He said I had to go, that the Republicans would be counting heads and that our program would be up for re-funding soon. I asked him what time the next plane left for Washington."[25]

The Jewish community had stronger anti-Republican traditions. Jews' political importance considerably outweighed their numerical strength as a result of their high degree of political interest, seen in terms of both voter turnout and financial contributions, and their demographic concentration. Jewish Americans maintained a high degree of loyalty to the Democratic Party, however, even when economic interests linked them more naturally to the Republican Party. A limited opportunity was created by the breaking of the bipartisan consensus about American support for Israel and concerns for the fate of Soviet Jews. McGovern's commitment to such issues seemed much less marked than that of his Democratic predecessors. Nixon's commitment was clear, but McGovern attempted to blur the distinction during the campaign.[26]

An appeal to youth was a notable element of the McGovern campaign. In contrast, Nixon and the Republicans made few overtures to young people. Indeed, based on his polling, Robert Teeter advised against any such activity on the grounds that it would encourage further Democratic activity and probably register anti-Republican voters. Still, both the CRP and the RNC unveiled youth programs, each with a different emphasis. The chair of the CRP's Youth Division was William Brock, who attributed his victory in the 1970 Tennessee senatorial election to his success among youth. At the national convention,

Brock's division launched a youth road show that blended music and entertainment with straightforward political propaganda. Nixon attended the debut performance at Miami Beach, where the guest star was Sammy Davis Jr., and later described the evening as "the highlight of the convention." The show then went on tour. Davis, incidentally, was an unusual example of a prominent African American who actively supported Nixon, and the entertainer attracted some criticism from black activists for doing so. But Nixon impressed Davis. Leaving a meeting with the president in the Oval Office, Davis reportedly told his wife, "That man is beautiful; he's got it, baby!"[27]

According to Kenneth Rietz, an aide to Brock, canvassers discovered that parental income was significantly related to young people's voting intentions. When the family income passed $25,000, there was a greater likelihood that the children would vote for McGovern. "College students say Vietnam and the environment [are most important to them]; noncollege, it's 'my home, my family,'" said Rietz. "With noncollege young people those things are very, very important." By contrast, the RNC attempted to forge links with that section of young voters that Rietz appeared to write off. With the intention of appealing to the nation's future elite, the RNC established a "youth issues" team to visit college campuses and hold political discussions. The team debated such issues as a comparison of the Kennedy and Nixon presidencies.[28]

A special Republican committee on delegate selection recommended that state party organizations include young people in proportion to their population in the state. The recommendation demonstrated that a similar desire to represent society sometimes occurred in the Republican Party as well as much more strenuously within the Democrats' McGovern-Fraser hearings on party reform. But the RNC did not adopt the recommendation, and the states did not implement it. Rare were even such symbolic gestures as the choice of nineteen-year-old William Jungbauer, who said that he had already been campaigning for Nixon for twelve years, to represent Minnesota's Electoral College vote for the president.[29]

DEMOCRATS AND THE NEW MAJORITY

Nixon most coveted the heart of the Democratic Party. He sought the support of leading Democrats and of Democratic voters alienated by McGovern and his brand of liberalism. Their support, together with that of independent voters, would create the new majority. For this reason the Nixon campaign did not attack the Democratic Party. Nixon told a meeting of cabinet members and Republican leaders "never [to] blame the Democrats or beat on the Democrats." Indeed, the Republican campaign should avoid the term "Democrats" in favor of "McGovernites."[30]

Nixon wanted to find ways to encourage Democratic division. He read in his news summary that playwright Arthur Miller, a McGovern supporter, had commented, "The Traditional Dem[ocratic] Party no longer exists. We've taken over." He had the statement forwarded to Colson to be sent out to Democratic members of Congress and delegates to the 1968 national convention. In search of sympathetic congressional Democrats, Nixon initiated an effort to force Democratic candidates either to reject McGovern or to link themselves publicly with the party's presidential candidate and policies. Within two weeks of the Democrats' convention, 12 of 29 responding Republican candidates for the Senate and 74 of 148 House candidates reported that their opponents would not work for the national ticket. Because Nixon's campaign emphasized McGovern and his unorthodox brand of Democratic politics, the revelation that their opponents rejected McGovern hardly helped these 86 Republican candidates. But it greatly helped Nixon. A newspaper completed the work for the White House, surveying Democratic candidates for the Senate, House, and state governorships and finding that just under half of them supported McGovern "unequivocally and for the record," and only about a tenth did so "with unbridled enthusiasm."[31]

Nixon preferred to have the backing of dissident rather than defecting Democrats. The symbolism of discontent among loyal partisans was more powerful. After the Democratic convention that nominated McGovern, the White House assigned a high priority to seeking out disenchanted Democrats to oppose McGovern publicly. There was no parallel attempt to win their conversion. It is true that in many cases this effort would have been difficult, but it is even more relevant that it was perceived as politically counterproductive. "In our judgment, . . . it is far better," wrote Pat Buchanan and Ken Khachigian, "for Democrats to stay in their party, and denounce McGovern—than to switch parties now."[32]

John Connally was Nixon's highest-profile Democratic supporter. Connally actually committed himself to changing parties but was asked to wait until after the election. Instead, he led Democrats for Nixon, a group that sought endorsements from leading Democrats whose activism would legitimize support for the president among the rank and file. Rhetoric against McGovern was programmed for the group. An organization of Democrats in support of a Republican presidential candidate was not a new phenomenon, but its centrality to the campaign was unprecedented. Richard Scammon was impressed by its prominence. "The title Democrats for Nixon is a campaign in itself," he told Colson. The group's leaders were concerned that the organization appear autonomous for the sake of public credibility, although Democrats for Nixon was little more than an arm of the CRP. But such was the discontent among some Democrats that Democratic groups in support of Nixon even emerged spontaneously here and there.[33]

Members of Connally's organization were expected to support no Republican but Nixon. The president explained to George Smathers, a former senator from Florida, that joining Democrats for Nixon "only meant supporting the President and that it allowed Democrats to continue to support the Democrat candidates for the House, Senate, state and local office." Many leading Democrats who endorsed Nixon or who proclaimed their neutrality in the election did so because defeating McGovern and his supporters was a necessary precondition to once again dominating the party. Officially neutral in the campaign, George Meany stated his hope that Democratic politicians would understand that no longer could they take labor's support for granted. For others, Connally notably among them, frustrated personal ambition bolstered ideological discontent with McGovern. Nixon offered Connally better chances of advancement, particularly since his base in Texas had started to falter after his departure for Washington.[34]

The avoidance of partisanship not only aided the goal of amassing the largest majority possible but also fostered Nixon's ambition to consolidate a political relationship with southern Democrats. Nixon even publicly admitted his intention. At a news conference, Nixon said that a Republican congressional majority would be hard to achieve in 1972, given the current balance of parties, so he hoped for "a new majority in Congress made up of Republicans and Democrats who support what the President believes in." He spoke of his special debt to some House and Senate Democrats for their foreign policy support.[35]

In his memoirs, Nixon wrote that his support for congressional Democrats extended to withholding help to the Republican candidates who were running against Senators James Eastland in Mississippi and John McClellan in Arkansas, both very supportive of Nixon's foreign policy. In fact, the president told his daughter, Tricia Nixon Cox, to endorse their candidacies during her visit to the South. But Nixon's support for southern Democrats extended still further. In March 1973, Representative Silvio Conte of Massachusetts alleged that in 1972 the White House told the Republican Congressional Committee to make no effort to defeat fifty-five House Democrats on the grounds of their friendliness to the administration. The group included O. C. Fisher of Texas and G. V. "Sonny" Montgomery of Mississippi, who supported Nixon's Vietnam policy in the House Armed Services Committee, as well as veteran southern Democrat Joe Waggonner of Louisiana. The list may have been even longer. In the fall of 1971, Nixon issued to aides a list of seventy-six House Democrats who had supported his conduct of the Vietnam War and whom Nixon would not oppose. He warned members of his cabinet that in making partisan attacks, "we've got to separate the good Democrats from the bad ones—those that support us, especially on national security."[36]

During the campaign, Nixon invited a number of incumbent southern Democrats to the White House for a photo session. On these occasions, Nixon congratulated John Jarman of Oklahoma for "his true American spirit," predicted that Tom Gettys would win by a large margin in his South Carolina district, and talked about football with David Henderson of North Carolina. Other visitors included Fisher and his fellow Texan, Bob Casey, and Floridian Bill Chappell Jr.[37]

Seen another way, Nixon's contribution to the congressional Democratic effort was even greater. His pursuit of his new majority involved the identification and mobilization of Nixon-supporting Democrats. It was a truism of American politics in the period that smaller turnouts favored the Republicans, because Republican supporters were more likely to vote than Democrats were. But in 1972 Nixon felt that a large turnout would increase the size of his new majority. An important theme of the campaign was, as Haldeman described it, to tell the electorate, "Make this the biggest vote in history—whichever side you vote on." The CRP sought to ensure that as many of these voters as possible chose Nixon, even if they also supported Democratic candidates for other offices. Lyn Nofziger, who ran the CRP in California, later described the inevitable result: "[W]e had a lot of protests from candidates and party workers, but we also had our orders from Washington to find and activate our Democratic vote," Nofziger wrote. The reelection committee could only pass on the names of Nixon-supporting Democrats to the Republican candidates.[38]

One special ally among urban Democrats was Frank Rizzo, the mayor of

Philadelphia. When Nixon called to congratulate Rizzo on his election in 1971, Haldeman noted that Rizzo "apparently [was] totally for the P[resident] and in effect told him so." Then, visiting the White House at the start of 1972, Rizzo assured Nixon of his support, which the mayor would announce at Nixon's will, and said he "felt he could deliver Pennsylvania." Nixon asked Rizzo to wait until after the Democratic convention. Both Rizzo and Philadelphia benefited from this support. Soon after the convention, Rizzo was promised $4 million in federal grants for the city police over two years. When John Ehrlichman informed Nixon that the administration was "continuing to devise ways of pumping money into Philadelphia," the president responded, "Good. Go all out." Rizzo also received a federal grant of $1 million for a drug program and help in securing a $6 million grant for a transportation project. Rizzo also wanted money for his city's school system. While the law prevented such additional grants to education, Rizzo was promised $20 million in employment and housing funds. The federal government decided to construct a Social Security building, costing $32 million, on a site recommended by Rizzo and to spend $13 million on improvements to other federal buildings in Philadelphia. Rizzo was also promised further packages of federal spending and the opportunity to announce them. Nixon was richly grateful for Rizzo's support, which included action to ensure that McGovern's visit to Philadelphia was met not only with the mayor's opposition but also with disruptive hecklers.[39]

Independently minded, Rizzo declined an invitation to become vice chair of Democrats for Nixon. The mayor avoided much involvement in the national movement because he faced problems with Philadelphia Democrats. The same problems did not exist across Pennsylvania, because the party was plagued by factional conflict between pro-McGovern and anti-McGovern Democrats that undermined the party's effectiveness, thus helping Republican prospects beyond the presidential level. Harry Dent suggested that Rizzo, widely known and liked in the state, might even run for the Republican gubernatorial nomination in opposition to the local CRP director, Arlen Specter. Another Democratic mayor, Sam Yorty of Los Angeles, similarly won the promise of personal favors in return for supporting Nixon. When Yorty told White House officials that he was concerned about his political future after endorsing Nixon, Colson was authorized in response to offer him the undersecretaryship of any of the armed services. "You can go up to Secretary of the Army," Haldeman wrote, "but it would be much better to avoid that, if we can."[40]

The usual focus of this appeal to Democrats, whether rank-and-file or officeholding, was strictly on an attempt to secure their support for Nixon in the presidential election, not their support for any other Republican or a change in their party affiliation. Some notable exceptions occurred in a few places across the South. One was Louisiana. Clark MacGregor of the CRP asked that "everything possible be done to encourage the possible party change-over" of twenty-four Democratic state legislators who were supporting Nixon. MacGregor requested that when Agnew visited the state, he meet with the legislators to discuss the change.[41]

The situation in Virginia was more promising, so the attempt to convert Virginia Democrats extended beyond Byrd to include his faction within the party. Byrdite Democrats were willing to contemplate conversion not so much out of their enthusiasm for Nixonian Republicanism (although a lack of ideo-logical disagreement was important) as their concern about control of the state party. Virginia Democrats as a whole were turning away from conservatism; their favored candidate for the Senate was William Spong, a moderate opposed to the Byrdites. But many of the state's Republicans did not welcome the prospect of conversions, including Linwood Holton, elected in 1969 as the state's Republican governor and a progressive on racial and other matters. Nevertheless, Harry Dent at the White House certainly welcomed the idea, which he believed would "put Virginia in the GOP column for the next decade or more." Dent suggested intervention in state politics to encourage the selec-tion of a senatorial candidate acceptable to the Byrdites.[42]

While Spong won Democratic nomination, William Scott, a conservative congressman, was the Republicans' selection. Although Scott was not the pre-ferred choice of the Byrdites, the climate within the Democratic Party was clear enough, and it was unsympathetic to them. One delegate to the party's state convention, controlled by pro-McGovern liberals, joked that the conven-tion had agreed "to bus everyone to Canada for free abortions and infusions of marijuana." Still, the truth of factional conflict was stark enough to cause some Democrats to look for a new political home.[43]

Nixon offered one. He invited a group of Virginia Democrats to the White House in August 1972. The group was led by Mills Godwin, a former governor who had formed a 1,200-strong committee of Virginians for the president. Nixon spoke of his admiration for Byrd and "indicated his interest in realign-ment of the political parties along moderate-conservative and liberal lines." After the meeting, Richard Obenshain, chair of the state Republican Party, requested a similar meeting for Virginia Republicans. An invitation was forthcoming, but it included only lunch, a tour of the White House, and a briefing by MacGregor. Virginia Republicans did not meet with Nixon.[44]

The case of Virginia was exceptional. More generally, it was clear that many Democrats who supported Nixon did not identify with the Republican Party, and the reasoning behind the appeal to them had no such long-term aim. "We must convince them that the only way to purge the party of the McGovern influence . . . is to give McGovern the thrashing at the polls he deserves," wrote Dwight Chapin, a Nixon aide. "A Democrat's vote for the President should be considered an 'act of statesmanship.' " In declining to invite Democrats to join the Republican Party, the White House even sought to project the impression that voting for Nixon was the action of a good Democrat. Colson wrote to MacGregor, "[O]ne of the most critical things that we must do in all of our rhetoric is avoid attacking the Democrats or even crediting McGovern as being the candidate of the real Democratic Party." Colson conveyed the same message to George Christian of Democrats for Nixon, and the organization used the line in its hunt for support.[45]

With McGovern as his opponent, Nixon reached deep into the traditional Democratic coalition. Two Democrats who viewed McGovern with dismay offered particularly stark evidence of their party's disarray. One, according to Nixon, was Lyndon Johnson. Nixon sent a report to John Connally of a telephone conversation in which Nixon interpreted Johnson as indicating that he "welcomed" the decision of friends and associates to support the president. "He [said] that he had agreed with most of the positions that I had taken during my tenure in office and that he found himself in sharp disagreement with the nominees of his Party," Nixon wrote to Connally. "He said that he did not want to do anything that would make my job harder and would therefore not discourage any of his friends who wanted to join you in the Democrats for Nixon organization."[46]

Another was George Meany. Sharing a friendly game of golf with George Shultz and Nixon, Meany told the president that organized labor should look beyond labor issues in particular in this election and should oppose McGovern as "bad for America and bad for the world." The leadership of the American Federation of Labor and Congress of Industrial Organizations decided to remain neutral in the presidential election, a decision reflecting its dislike for McGovern but made against the background of the administration's desire to cultivate labor support. The Republican platform praised the labor movement and saluted its "statesmanship." But this neutrality did not extend to other contests. The financial support of the Committee on Political Education, never devoted solely to presidential contests, was targeted at congressional candidates whose records were friendly to labor causes and consequently were mainly Democratic and liberal. Moreover, many more individual unions endorsed McGovern than Nixon.[47]

Nixon's success in gaining the support of traditional Democrats was impressive but limited. It did not in general help the Republican Party more broadly. Indeed, the success potentially represented a unique response to McGovern's candidacy. Many Democrats who supported Nixon were eager to regain influence within their party rather than to join the Republican Party or even a putative conservative party. Moreover, at the elite level, Democrats for Nixon did not always successfully represent the middle-American constituency that Nixon sought. While the problem often escaped Nixon, Douglas Hallett, an aide to Colson, criticized Connally as unrepresentative of most disaffected swing voters. "Frankly, I don't think the Houston Petroleum Club is a very firm footing for a new Republican majority," Hallett wrote. The White House faced a choice, he suggested, between gaining a record for change and becoming "a refuge for antidiluvian [sic] reactionary southern Democrats." Hallett thus echoed McGovern, who sought to contain any damage to his candidacy caused by Democrats for Nixon by dismissing the organization as "Mr. Connally and his exclusive club of oil millionaires." Still, perhaps the most realistic vision for the Republican Party took the guise of exactly such a refuge. Indeed, with the benefit of hindsight, it is possible to see that one district in Mississippi offered a glimpse of the future. After a long career as a southern Democratic stalwart, William S. Colmer, the influential chair of the House Rules Committee, retired. His administrative assistant ran for the seat but did so as a Republican, not a Democrat. Trent Lott won the election.[48]

"PATRIOTISM, MORALITY, RELIGION"

The 1972 presidential election is best remembered for the "dirty tricks" committed by Richard Nixon and his aides in pursuit of victory. The best known of these is, of course, the Watergate scandal, but many other strategies were used during both the primary and presidential campaigns. The tricksters knew few limits. On one occasion, McGovern visited a high school in a Detroit suburb for a rally. An enthusiastic crowd greeted him, as did some unusual hecklers, as one CRP official described to another: "A small group of children whose ages were put at 7–8 were pasting Nixon bumper stickers on the wall . . . and singing 'Nixon Now More Than Ever.' When this activity was discovered, the people in the auditorium became violently hostile, some yelling obscenities at the children. One observer tried to calm down the people around her saying, They're just children! but that had little effect. Finally the kids departed. Although none of them was hurt or humiliated, Ed, I still think you've gone too far this time."[49]

The Watergate burglary was the subject of political discussion during the campaign but did not register as a significant issue until later. Despite Democrats' efforts to suggest otherwise, it proved relatively easy to dismiss the break-in at the Democratic National Committee headquarters as a prank by individuals acting in large part independently of the CRP and the White House. Many voters were, therefore, aware of the crime when they cast their ballots but considered other matters more important than the "caper."[50]

Many voters saw McGovern's mishandling of the Eagleton affair as a more dramatic demonstration of a failure in leadership ability than the burglary was. McGovern had chosen his Senate colleague Thomas Eagleton of Missouri as his running mate, but soon after the convention, controversy swamped Eagleton's candidacy. Journalists discovered that Eagleton had been hospitalized several times for depression and that the treatments had included electroshock therapy. McGovern declared his absolute "one-thousand percent" support for Eagleton but withdrew that support when pressures to do so increased. In the aftermath of the incident, McGovern had difficulty finding a Democrat prepared to join the ticket; Sargent Shriver accepted the position. Polls suggested that the incident damaged McGovern because it caused some voters to see him as unscrupulous, indecisive, or both. At a minimum, this failure to act decisively was unambiguously McGovern's mistake, while Watergate was by no means seen yet as Nixon's criminal responsibility.[51]

As the campaign approached, there was at last some good news about the economy, to the surprise of administration economists. Unemployment fell to 5.5 percent, and real incomes began to increase at a healthy rate. Nixon was also pleased to hear that the rate of increase in consumer prices was low, thanks to the "power of prayer, slightly assisted by seasonal adjustment," in the words of Herbert Stein, the chair of the Council of Economic Advisers. Nixon had paid careful attention to the economy, wanting to ensure that the 1972 elections would not take place, as those in 1970 had, against the background of unfavorable economic conditions—especially in key Electoral College states. And by the time of the election, the president's reputation for running the economy had improved slightly.[52] Although the prosperity created by Nixon's policies was extraordinarily unstable, this problem was not yet obvious.

But when Nixon thought about how to mobilize his coalition of support, he did not think about economic issues. In a strategy meeting, he "made the point that . . . the economic issue is their ground not ours and we should not play to it." Nevertheless, private polls indicated that voters cared about the state of the economy. Skepticism about the recovery remained despite the increase in real income. More tangibly, poll respondents complained about the high prices of goods despite the slow pace of inflation. A number of aides advised Nixon that it was important to address these public concerns. "We continue to be vulnerable on the bread and butter and pocketbook issues," wrote poll analyst Robert Teeter, "and these should receive more emphasis overall."[53]

Nixon disagreed, even describing Teeter's polling as "a disaster." Because of the administration's vulnerability on economic issues, the president knew that the Democratic campaign aimed to emphasize what he described as "class divisions." In response, his campaign had to direct the electorate's attention elsewhere. "The decision in November and our rhetoric," Buchanan noted, "must not focus upon their issues—i.e., 'unemployment' and the unequal economic record of the last four years—it must focus upon our issues—i.e., the extremism, elitism, radicalism, kookism, of McGovern's person, campaign, and programs, against the solid, strong, effective leadership of the President."[54]

Nixon told his cabinet that talk of lower inflation and unemployment was merely defensive. He preferred to attack and to criticize than to defend and to justify. He wanted aggressively to undermine the Democratic position by claiming that McGovern would "raise taxes" and "wreck the economy." As a result, the average voter would then think of economic issues in terms of "McG[overn]'s nutty proposals" rather than "analyzing *our* performance." During campaign speeches, Nixon's discussion of his economic policy was at best general and brief. Material sent out for the use of Nixon spokespeople included the allegation that McGovern's proposals would add at least $99.4 billion to the deficit (the largest addition originating with the proposal to create national health insurance) and the claim that only 17 percent of business economists would vote for McGovern.[55]

The offensive against McGovern extended to his welfare proposals. Nixon finally jettisoned his interest in bold reformism. First, his record of achievement as the American Disraeli was so insubstantial that it offered a flimsy basis for campaigning. Second, economic reality now prevented him from further contemplation of initiatives that involved much more spending. The time was arriving when the growth in spending on Great Society programs would outstrip the growth in government revenues.[56] Because the Democratic Congress remained willing to spend more than Nixon was, Nixon increasingly looked for spending bills to veto. He was therefore preventing rather than promoting new examples of government activism.

McGovern's advocacy of liberal reform provided Nixon with an opportunity to characterize his opponent as a radical who would impose too much taxation. Members of the new majority "are turned off on welfare because it's wrong and because they are anti-elitist," noted Haldeman, "plus they have selfish motives." Campaign aides asked speakers to attack McGovern's welfare plan in tough terms. Ronald Reagan and Nelson Rockefeller received a memo that called the plan "Mr. McGovern's declaration of economic warfare against the American middle class." McGovern's welfare ideas would require excessive taxation, hurting the new middle class, and, moreover, would "permanently divide America into a working class and a welfare class."[57]

On Labor Day, Nixon spoke of his opposition to "the fixed quota system," which he said was emerging both in employment and in politics. He called it "as artificial and unfair a yardstick as has ever been used to deny opportunity to anyone." He implicitly linked McGovern with the advocacy of quotas, especially on the grounds that the Democrats' reformed process for selecting a presidential nominee employed goals of equal representation among state delegates to the national convention. A *New York Times* journalist noted reports that McGovern privately admitted during the discussion of these reforms that they amounted to a quota system.[58] But McGovern, like Nixon, announced his opposition to quotas. That announcement did not change the nature of the Nixon campaign's attacks on the challenger.

The plan to label McGovern a radical on questions of welfare reform and of affirmative action possessed an almost astonishing irony. Milder forms of these policies—FAP and the Philadelphia Plan—had been central pieces of the administration's agenda. But they were quickly forgotten even though, in the case of the Philadelphia Plan, the policy was in operation and was subject to expansion. Nixon denounced quotas yet left in place programs of minority preference. FAP and the Philadelphia Plan were now seen as extraneous to the task of building a new majority. Instead, Nixon sought to reap political benefit from the liberal response to the policy debates he had been instrumental in establishing.[59]

Toward the end of the campaign, talking with Haldeman, Ehrlichman, and Ray Price, Nixon described his new majority as representing "people who care about a strong United States, about patriotism, about moral and spiritual values." He continued, "The real issues of the election are the ones like patriotism, morality, religion—not the material issues. If the issues were prices and taxes, they'd be for McGovern." Nixon similarly told an audience of cabinet members and congressional leaders to "make patriotism and morality the issue and get above the material things." He saw foreign policy as especially salient. This majority, according to Nixon, was united by similar ideas, not, like the Roosevelt coalition, by common economic interest.[60] He thus offered a line of continuity with the "new alignment for American unity" about which he had spoken in 1968.

Although one obvious political response to the relative extremism of McGovern's positions was a centrist countermove that might maximize electoral support, Nixon rejected this idea. "He wants to carve out a clean cut position on the right, away from McGovern," Haldeman noted. Conservative Democrats were Nixon's target; the way to catch them was to "tilt all issues to the right" rather than to blur differences. "The line has to be drawn clearly on the critical issues," said Haldeman, taping his diary after a discussion with Nixon. Nixon believed that the choice was not only between clearly different issues but also between clearly different politicians with different capacities for the presidency. The task of the campaign was to dramatize these differences. Seeking to demonstrate what he saw as his qualities of statesmanship, Nixon spent little time on the campaign trail and delegated much of the responsibility for campaigning to others.[61]

Senate Minority Leader Hugh Scott of Pennsylvania renewed the charge from the Nebraska Democratic primary that McGovern was conducting "the campaign of the three A's: acid, abortion, and amnesty." McGovern tried to escape the tag, which was an unfair summary of his positions. Terence Cardinal Cooke received a letter from McGovern in which the candidate explained his opposition to the liberalized New York abortion law and announced his support for aid to parochial schools, pointing out that Nixon's commitment to the protection of Catholic education had achieved no tangible improvements. Moreover, during a visit to New York, McGovern spoke in support of "the integrity of neighborhoods," seen by Buchanan as "an oblique reference to the

Forest Hills matter." McGovern went on the offensive, too, reminding the electorate of Republican failings, of unemployment, and of unimpressive economic growth. He also spoke of the Vietnam War, which had cost many lives since 1969 while "peace with honor" remained elusive. McGovern, furthermore, claimed that Nixon's was the "most corrupt administration in history."[62]

But it was all too late. McGovern was widely seen as a candidate outside the mainstream of American politics. As Election Day approached, he ran a series of regional telethons to answer voters' questions. Richard Dougherty, an aide, became frustrated by the narrow and unrepresentative nature of the topics always raised: "pot, abortion, amnesty; amnesty, abortion, pot; the one thousand dollars a year for everybody, the 1,000 per cent for Eagleton." McGovern could not change the terms on which many voters viewed him. As Jeb Magruder, the CRP's deputy campaign director, noted shortly after the election, "McGovern was associated with the gay libs, the welfare rights, the black militants, the women's libs, the pot-smokers, the long-haired college kids."[63] Nixon's campaign had worked hard to ensure that this image of McGovern dominated.

The concentration on foreign policy did not relate to the achievements of détente alone but to the progress of Vietnamization too. By winding down the involvement of American forces to a minimal role by the fall of 1972, Nixon undercut the painful controversy that had surrounded the war for so long. At the same time, Nixon had convinced many people that he was doing everything possible to secure peace, both through negotiations, as announced at the start of the year, and through the continued use of force, as demonstrated by the renewed attacks on the north in the spring. "[T]he President was perceived, particularly after May," Magruder said after the election, "as being the most reasonable person in trying to solve the problem that he himself had not created."[64]

McGovern, however, continued to direct outraged criticism at Nixon's Vietnam policy. The war was, McGovern said, the "saddest chapter in our national history." McGovern continued to emphasize his opposition not only to the way in which the administration had conducted the war but also to the larger goal of supporting Thieu's dictatorial regime. "[O]ur own most precious values," he said, "are corrupted by the very government we fight to defend." McGovern pledged to end the war as soon as he became president, ensuring that the withdrawal of American forces was complete within ninety days. According to the Republicans, these proposals ran "contrary to all that America has stood for."[65]

The antiwar basis of McGovern's candidacy did not strengthen it. Nixon thought that his opponent's close association with this cause damaged him. After all, Nixon had long sought to demonize the antiwar movement in identifying and mobilizing the new majority. A clear distinction undoubtedly existed between the two presidential candidates on this as on other issues; popular reaction apparently favored Nixon. The Harris organization reported that on the eve of the Democratic National Convention, voters sounded agreement with Nixon on almost every main issue and that no issue saw greater support for Nixon than "[e]nding U.S. involvement in Vietnam." According to Gallup in mid-October, 58 percent of respondents thought that Nixon would better deal with the war, while only 26 percent preferred McGovern on this question. Teeter wrote that Nixon's handling of the war was "truely [sic] the gut issue in the campaign" and that his position represented the center of public opinion, from which McGovern was far removed. Indeed, pollsters called Nixon's reputation for foreign policy as a whole "invincible."[66]

To emphasize what White House strategists saw as an advantageous difference, Nixon was ready to step down somewhat from his posture of statesmanship to indulge in more aggressive rhetoric. "I think there are those who have faulted this Administration on its efforts to seek peace," he said at a news conference in August, "but those who fault it, I would respectfully suggest, are ones that would have the United States seek peace at the cost of surrender, dishonor, and the destruction of the ability of the United States to conduct foreign policy in a responsible way." In response to McGovern's commitment quickly to end the war, Secretary of Defense Melvin Laird said that the Democratic proposals represented "unconditional surrender" and that the candidate was a "spokesman for the enemy." Agnew described McGovern's views on foreign policy as "pitifully naive."[67]

Television commercials emphasized Nixon's achievements in foreign policy. "Having begun the job of creating the framework for a real and lasting peace in the world," concluded one, "the president is determined to finish it." The message of another, run in the name of Democrats for Nixon, was more aggressive. "[S]howing John Connally sweeping tin soldiers and ships off a table and denouncing McGovern's defense cuts," this ad constituted a uniquely powerful part of the campaign according to Michael Barone. Nixon seemed to agree. He told Connally that his television appearance was a "classic," political television at its best. (Connally returned the compliment by telling Nixon that he had a good radio voice, even the best of the twentieth century.) To call the broadcast to the attention of Nixon supporters, Clark MacGregor sent out a letter describing the commercial as "one of the most effective presentations in the history of American politics."[68]

McGovern's program to end the Vietnam War contained a proposal to offer draft offenders "an opportunity to come home." His opponents called it a policy of amnesty, and it was one of the "three As." The question of amnesty was, according to Teeter, "very significant" as a "'code word' for a set of opinions which [corresponded] directly to beliefs about Vietnam withdrawal." Nixon's position on the issue was an uncompromising rejection of any reassessment of the status of draft avoiders. Urging a schedule of speeches before veterans and labor members, Nixon told Don Johnson, responsible for veterans' affairs with the domestic council, "Kill the hell out of them on amnesty and talk about national defense." Nixon spoke about his opposition to amnesty during campaign appearances. He was also especially eager for his surrogate speakers to campaign on the issue.[69]

The emphasis on foreign policy complemented the cultivation of Democrats. At a breakfast meeting with congressional leaders shortly after Nixon's return from China, Speaker of the House Carl Albert of Oklahoma and House Majority Leader Hale Boggs of Louisiana had pledged to support the president on national security and foreign policy issues, even as the Democrats stepped up attacks on the administration's economic and domestic initiatives. Similarly, George Meany remained critical of Nixon's economic policy despite the labor leader's overall sympathy for the reelection campaign. According to Shultz, Meany said that Nixon was "perfect on foreign policy" and that a stress on this theme was the way to capture labor. And in his statement of endorsement, George Christian, a former press secretary to Lyndon Johnson who joined Democrats for Nixon, said that "a strong international leader" was needed as president. Christian urged Democrats to split their tickets.[70]

The "real issues" to Nixon, then, were "of this being a good country, patriotism and so on." They were the basis of deep division between the Nixon and McGovern campaigns. Theodore White, a veteran observer of American elections, called it a "culture gap" based on different notions of patriotism. "At the White House," White wrote, "the flag button was like a varsity letter—the first team flaunted it." Indeed, as Haldeman noted, Nixon wanted "to get American flags on all of our people and on the bumper strips" and had steps taken to ensure that this happened. While patriotism was "one of the main public thrusts" of the Nixon campaign, at the McGovern campaign it was, by contrast, "a code word for intolerance, war, deception." Feelings about country had no place in the political arena. "Patriotism for the McGoverns," White explained, "was an emotion to be honored in the private places of one's heart." The "culture gap" had an important impact on how the opposing forces viewed politics. "When they discussed the Pentagon, Vietnam, the budget or welfare proposals, the two staffs used roughly the same figures and names, and complementary but antagonistic rhetoric," White observed. "Yet, underneath it all, they were talking from the cultures of two entirely different Americas; style, purpose, values—all separated them."[71]

Under the surface, it was a remarkable time of change for social attitudes. There was a notable liberalization of views toward permissiveness even during the relatively short period of Nixon's presidency. Gallup surveys of public opinion report that between 1969 and 1973, the number of Americans believing that premarital sex was wrong declined from 68 to 48 percent, for example. Similarly, in the same period, the number who found nudity in magazines objectionable declined from 75 to 55 percent. Public support for abortion increased during this period, apparently reaching a high point in around 1973. Attitudes toward drug use were also liberalizing, although they remained hostile overall to any legalization. Against this background, about which the campaign did not always speak with clarity, Nixon decided to "go for all-out square America."[72]

IN THE NATION

On the rare occasions when he took part in active campaigning, Nixon spoke about the importance of values within American society. This emphasis provided a unifying theme for his rhetoric, translating into his practice his thinking about the electoral decisiveness of "patriotism, morality, religion." In Ashland, Kentucky, for example, he spoke about "character" and praised the nation for the "moral and spiritual strength" of its people. In a radio address, he said that he believed in governmental action where needed but criticized those who "have more faith in government than they have in people." Opposition to redistributive policies or to busing, he said, usually was not based on "selfishness" or "bigotry" but on "values to be proud of" regarding work and neighborhood. Along with a belief in strong national defense, such ideas were "the beliefs of a generous and self-reliant people, a people of intellect and character, whose values deserve respect in every segment of our population." The new majority, he claimed, was "forming . . . around a set of principles that is deep in the American spirit." The American people were "united in their continued belief in honest hard work, love of country, spiritual faith."[73]

It is difficult to define with precision the reasons for individuals' voting decisions, but Nixon's approach seemed to work. Economic issues were by no means the most important considerations for many voters, according to interviews conducted by public opinion analyst Samuel Lubell. For example, a firefighter in Rock Island, Illinois, sharply criticized Nixon's economic policy and its apparently favorable treatment of big business. But Nixon's patriotic internationalism was attractive, especially by comparison with the foreign policy of McGovern. "I don't like McGovern's appeasement of the North Vietnamese," the firefighter said. "I'd like to see us out, but with honor. I like to save face." Later, in the Brooklyn community of Canarsie, sociologist Jonathan Rieder met a policeman who voted for Nixon in 1972 solely on the grounds of McGovern's dovish views. "I don't believe in going down on your hands and knees, right or wrong, and begging for forgiveness to an outside power," he said. On a visit to a factory in Columbus, Ohio, McGovern could not convince a Wallaceite Democrat who worked there that the candidate's policies would secure the safe and swift return of prisoners of war. Nixon, the worker maintained, was trying to achieve that goal. "How?" asked McGovern. "By bombing the hell out of people?" "Right," the worker replied. "He should have bombed a hell of a lot more out of 'em."[74]

The offensive against McGovern's welfare proposals also won support among traditional Democrats. McGovern was often perceived as too generous to the poor and underprivileged. "McGovern wants to give them too much," said one voter. "People who work all their lives, all they get is social security. These people who won't work will get more." In communities where race mattered, it could transcend all other considerations. A voter in Queens, New York, told Lubell that he hated Nixon but was thinking about voting for the president. "The one thing I like about Nixon," he said, "is his intervention on the school busing problem." Overall, in late August, a poll suggested that 61 percent of respondents "expressed considerable confidence" in Nixon on the question of "making the government pay more attention to the problems of the working man and his family," whereas only 43 percent voiced similar confidence in McGovern in this regard.[75]

Voters concerned about the state of the economy, however, became more likely to choose McGovern. Lubell found that among supporters of George

Wallace in 1968, Nixon was most unpopular with "those dissatisfied economically." But this group was not nearly numerous enough to undermine the president's appeal. In many cases, other issues were more important, at least for the moment. One Canarsie craftsman later regretted the way in which he neglected economic considerations at a time of relative personal affluence for him. "[T]he hippies were cursing and the blacks were threatening everything we had," he told Rieder. "We forgot we were workers and voted against our interests."[76]

In these ways, Nixon was winning the votes of traditional Democrats to form a new majority. But often he was not gaining their enthusiastic loyalty. Toward the end of the campaign, reports arrived at the White House from aides who had visited important new-majority areas—urban ethnic neighborhoods—to sound out public sentiment. The reports were both encouraging and discouraging. On the one hand, they described widespread support for Nixon, if not for other Republican candidates. On the other, they pointed out that this support was often shallow. "Many of those with whom I spoke," wrote aide Bill Rhatican of his visit to Baltimore, "were looking for a reason to vote for McGovern but were . . . unable to convince themselves to do so."[77]

As the end of the campaign approached, the administration announced fresh progress in peace negotiations with North Vietnam, supporting Nixon's foreign policy focus. The campaign therefore culminated with a strong attack on McGovern's competence and credibility as a potential president, especially as commander in chief. The instructions given to surrogate speakers mentioned McGovern's proposals for taxing and spending but assigned priority to his national-security weaknesses, particularly his policies of "surrender" in Vietnam and amnesty for those who had avoided the draft. Preparing for a television appearance, Connally was told by Colson to call for a "vote of confidence" for Nixon. "[T]hat vote of confidence," Connally said, "will tell Hanoi that the American people are behind this President . . . , it will tell the Soviets, it will tell the Chinese, it will tell the whole world that there is a vote of confidence behind the President and it will strengthen his hand as he deals with the difficult problems that lie ahead for this country."[78]

Similarly, Nixon placed the successful turn in the negotiations at the heart of his election-eve address. He said that issue differences meant that the voters' choice was "probably the clearest choice between the candidates for President ever presented to the American people in this century." Voters could "send a message" to world leaders "that we in the United States seek peace with honor and never peace with surrender." The achievement of peace would allow attention to other matters of concern, and, more than anything else, he offered the promise of peace. "I would . . . urge you to have in mind one overriding issue," he told the voters, "and that is the issue of peace—peace in Vietnam and peace in the world at large for a generation to come."[79]

RESULTS AND REACTIONS

On November 7, Richard Nixon received his vote of confidence from the American electorate. His plurality was the greatest in American history, although Lyndon Johnson eight years earlier had narrowly exceeded Nixon's percentage of the vote, 60.7. He gained 42 percent of the vote among self-identified Democrats, 66 percent among independents, and 94 percent among Republicans. Nixon sought to uncover broader meaning in his victory. In his memoirs, he described his support as "both wide and deep—it was truly a New Majority landslide of the kind I had called for in my acceptance speech in August."[80]

Nixon was proud that he had won over groups that were not traditionally Republican. The nature and not just the extent of his majority was distinctive. The Democratic share of the presidential vote was lower in the once-solid South than outside it, an outcome previously caused in recent years only by Barry Goldwater's 1964 candidacy. A clear indication of McGovern's failure was the voting of American Jews, who still offered 69 percent of their support to McGovern; four years earlier, however, Humphrey had won 93 percent of the Jewish vote. But the Democratic loyalty of African Americans remained strong, and Nixon won 13 percent of nonwhite voters, just a 1 point increase from 1968. Among voters under age thirty, Nixon's support was lower than among older age groups, but at 52 percent it was still stronger than McGovern's. And middle America was an important element of the 1972 new majority. Of voters in union households, 57 percent chose Nixon, as did 60 percent of Catholic voters. Among blue-collar workers, a large demographic group closely associated with the Democratic Party, McGovern attracted just 39 percent of all votes.[81]

But at the moment of Nixon's great triumph there was little else to celebrate for the Republican Party at large. The phenomenon of ticket splitting, so striking in 1968, was becoming an accepted fact of electoral politics. Ticket splitting helped Nixon but victimized other Republican candidates. In the Senate, the Republicans actually lost two seats, offsetting the two gained in 1970. In the House, Republicans posted a net gain of just thirteen seats, restoring the party to exactly the same level as after the 1968 election. Altogether, 25 percent of voters cast ballots in favor of Democratic members of Congress while supporting Nixon. By contrast, just 31 percent voted for Democratic representatives and McGovern. The picture was similarly discouraging for Republicans outside Washington. They lost control of two state legislatures and suffered a net loss of one governorship. Indeed, in the eighteen gubernatorial contests of 1972, the vote for the two parties was roughly equal; in the same states, Nixon had an advantage of 24 percentage points over McGovern.[82]

While Nixon pieced together this impressive victory, he also initiated his downfall because of the Watergate crimes. At one level, it is ironic that a campaign in which Nixon emphasized morality should suffer from this fatal flaw of gross illegalities. Diane Sawyer, a White House press aide before helping Nixon to write his memoirs, later observed that Nixon was incapable of perceiving this contradiction between his politics of morality and the immorality of his politicking.[83]

In the shorter run, the scandal about to destroy his presidency did not hurt Nixon to any significant extent. Some analysts think that the first revelations of Watergate slightly depressed the margin of his victory. Agreeing that Watergate took the edge off the extent of Nixon's victory, Kevin Phillips made the larger claim that Watergate led to a widespread "desire not to round out the Republican equation." Many voters were not impressed by McGovern but were unwilling to see wider gains for the Republican Party. In the absence of the scandal, Republicans would have enjoyed further congressional success, which in turn would have encouraged many southern Democrats to switch parties on the grounds of their ideological similarities, their disagreements with the McGovernite-dominated national party, and their thirst for a new leash of power within a conservative political force. Phillips suggests, therefore, that the Republican majority should have emerged in 1972 and that Watergate arrested this emergence.[84] Phillips's analysis is provocative and presents an intriguing case in favor of his thesis, but it is an unusual interpretation not shared by most observers.

Retrospective analysis of the vote by the Nixon campaign's pollsters, Market Opinion Research, concentrated on the favorable impact of the administration's foreign policy. The organization's polls emphasized again that the incumbent president's great strength was his Vietnam policy, while his great vulnerability was his economic policy. During the campaign, Market Opinion's Robert Teeter had urged Nixon to broaden the foreign policy focus of his appearances and include justification of his economic policies. But after the results, Teeter and his colleague, Frederick Steeper, celebrated Nixon's good luck that McGovern had failed to exploit economic issues. "Instead," they wrote, "he threw down the gauntlet exactly where the Nixon strategists wanted it thrown, i.e., on the war issue and the candidates['] perceived abilities to handle foreign policy generally."[85]

In the eyes of the "real majority" theoretician, Ben Wattenberg, the election had more significant implications than Teeter and Steeper suggested. "It was a referendum on the so-called cultural revolution in this country," Wattenberg said. "It involved many, many facets—busing and defense and welfare and all sorts of things—and a perception of whether this country was doing pretty well or teetering on the brink of failure." The result, Wattenberg concluded, was a rejection of the "new politics" that supported the "cultural revolution."[86] In effect he judged that Nixon's hope of focusing the electorate's attention on the issues of "patriotism, morality, religion" had been realized.

Nixon's victory was certainly impressive. But in larger perspective, the administration's record had fallen far short of its political goals. Some elements of the reformist agenda had finally been achieved—but only some, and these achievements were not central to Nixon's electoral appeal. Nor had they transformed the national perception of the Republican Party, and appropriately so, because Nixon had hardly converted it to the party of "sweeping change" of which he had spoken to congressional Republicans after his new American revolution speech.[87] At the same time, Nixon had hardly devoted a great deal of energy to persuading congressional Republicans to embrace that vision of the party.

Nixon had thus secured his new majority but not his new American revolution. It was time to interpret the mandate. The second term offered an opportunity to deepen the majority's loyalty and perhaps to mobilize it in elections below the presidency. Nixon's interpretation of his mandate did not lead him back to reformism, in which he had won little congressional cooperation and the pursuit of which was likely to be more difficult in the second term. The moment was gone. Instead, Nixon's view would lead him to a renewed emphasis on antigovernment conservatism and to further contemplation of party upheaval.

SIX

FROM NIXON TO REAGAN
The End of the Quest for a New Majority, 1972–1976

On March 7, 1973, Senator Hugh Scott of Pennsylvania telephoned Rose Mary Woods, Richard Nixon's secretary, with some good news for the president. Scott told Woods that the latest poll data from his state suggested that 70 percent of the electorate approved of Nixon's performance, believed to be "the highest approval record ever accorded a President."[1] At the time of his landslide reelection and in the months immediately following it, Nixon achieved a pinnacle of support. But the support of many Americans was about to desert him.

The reason for the impressive poll results in early 1973 was the negotiated end of direct American involvement in Vietnam. When peace talks had stalled in December, Nixon responded by launching a massive bombing campaign against North Vietnam. Talks then resumed, leading to a peace agreement that went into effect on January 27. The peace dividend Nixon enjoyed was to reap the benefits of national satisfaction that American soldiers were no longer participating in the war.

Nixon suffered a spectacular decline because of political scandal. Soon after Scott's conversation with Woods, polls began to show widespread disillusionment stemming from White House involvement in the crimes of Watergate. According to Gallup, the national approval rating for the president dropped to 48 percent in April, 39 percent in July, and 27 percent in October.[2] The scandal increasingly absorbed Nixon's attention, while revelations about its seriousness caused his national base of support to fracture. Watergate quickly sapped the administration's ability to engage in long-range strategic planning or to direct significant, coherent policy making. Eventually, the scandal forced Nixon to concentrate on short-term survival. Finally, when his personal involvement in the attempted cover-up became known the following summer, even his political survival became impossible.

The administration's disintegration was already in place by the end of April 1973. Nixon's key political confidants—H. R. Haldeman and John Ehrlichman—were forced to leave the White House because of Watergate. Charles Colson had left the previous month for the private sector before he, too, became implicated in the crimes.[3] These three aides played an essential role in the Nixon administration and in the new-majority project, and their losses constituted a major blow. After little more than three months, Nixon's bold plans for the second term were, in effect, abandoned.

There was barely any time to work toward Nixon's political goals and time only to contemplate them. Their ambition was almost breathtaking. A month after the landslide, Haldeman enumerated them: "1) to destroy and discredit the old liberal establishment—keep fighting them like they fought us, 2) to build the New Majority including the party, 3) to build the President as he is— the compassionate side, and 4) to re-write the history by building a new establishment across the board, the legacy of what we leave."[4] Patrick Buchanan perceived some urgency in consolidating the allegiance of the 1972 constituency:

> If the President is not to enter the history books as a second political
> Eisenhower—a Republican Regent between Democratic Magistrates—then
> we have to make permanent the new majority that returned the President
> to office. That New Majority essentially consists of the Republican base
> nationally, the Nixon South, the ethnic, blue collar, Catholic, working class
> Americans of the North, Midwest and West.
>
> The danger I see is that the silent majority, which spoke out loud and
> clear November 7th, fell silent again on November 8th. And whose voices
> are again dominant? Those of the liberal media. And the pressure they
> will place upon us will be the same as in the past, to advance the political
> and social interests of the "fashionable minorities"—principally blacks,
> women—and to ignore the ethnics and working class Americans who voted
> Republican for the first time. . . . Our future is the Democratic working
> man, Southern Protestant, and Northern Catholic—and ethnic.[5]

As time ran out for Nixon, he could only ensure better representation of the new American majority within his administration and start work on an ambitious partisan upheaval. In doing so, he tried to make progress toward Haldeman's second and fourth goals.

INSTITUTIONALIZING THE NEW MAJORITY

The first part of the attempt to institutionalize the new majority was to install representatives of key constituency groups in appointive office. Nixon wanted, for example, to recruit members of the "Wallace group" as well as those of the "Labor and Catholic groups." He intended to appoint an Italian American at the Justice Department and to find Catholics for the Supreme Court as well as for the cabinet. These were all ideas for "[b]uilding a New Majority," he explained to Colson shortly after the election. At the vanguard of what was intended to be a new political elite was Peter Brennan, the New York union leader whose involvement with the hard hat march on Wall Street in 1970 had delighted Nixon and had helped to alert him to his blue-collar opportunity. Nixon appointed Brennan secretary of labor. Nixon even told labor leaders that he was considering the appointment of a unionist to a high-level position in every department and agency.[6]

Poor planning undermined the apparently straightforward and foreseeable desire to reward representatives of the new majority. Although Nixon had spoken repeatedly during his first term about the need to create a "new establishment," not until after the election was Fred Malek, responsible for overseeing second-term personnel decisions, instructed to attach priority to new-majority credentials in making appointments. Malek later explained that he was unable to act quickly and effectively in this effort "because Colson convinced the president that we needed to dig deeper and have more ethnics" after many preliminary decisions had been made. Poor implementation sometimes compounded the problem of poor planning. The new transportation secretary, California businessman Claude Brinegar, was, in Haldeman's words, "appointed . . . because he was an Irish Catholic, and two weeks after he was in office, he informed us he was a German Presbyterian."[7]

Nixon wanted a high profile for "some of the loyalists in the New Majority" not only in personnel lists but in official delegations, too. Haldeman told Jeb Magruder, director of the inaugural committee, that it was "imperative that the approach to this Inaugural be one of building recognition and participation of the New American Majority." Beyond the festivities surrounding the inauguration, the administration planned to work "the various New Majority types" into "social events and other Presidential activities over the next four years."[8] In a guest column for Kevin Phillips, Colson compared Nixon's invitations to representatives of his constituency after the election with Andrew Jackson's victory celebrations:

> Christmas time at the White House, 1972, signified the changing of power from the citadels of the Ivy League, the Wall Street law firms and the mass media complex, to Main Street USA. The ordinary folks from the heartland—the shop steward, the electrician, the farmer—were the honored guests of an American President for the first time in generations. . . .
>
> The people filing through the White House the week before Christmas included the head of the Pittsburgh Boilermakers local, officers of the Polish American Congress, an Italian-American priest, Teamster officials, the head of the Policemen's Benevolent Association—the people who really form the heart of the New American Majority. They were the people Candidate Nixon spoke of in his 1968 appeal to the forgotten American—the people he had called the great "silent majority."[9]

A serious effort to confirm Nixon as the leader of "the ordinary folks from the heartland" was under way. It involved a shift in emphasis from the first term, when the Nixon White House had worked hard to identify and mobilize new groups of support. Now the effort was a matter of consolidating the loyalty of Nixon's existing supporters rather than attracting new groups. After all, the constituency had probably reached its broadest extent in the 1972 victory. At this time, Nixon even contemplated the idea that the aggressive political operation built up by Colson to woo the new majority should be "collapsed." Instead, the public liaison office survived Colson's departure, albeit on a smaller basis. William J. Baroody Jr. replaced Colson, assuming duties including building the new majority and getting "people from the New Majority inside the Administration in key appointment positions, appointments to see the President, invitations, etc.," as well as more generally continuing communication with various friendly outside groups.[10]

Nixon's plans for the new majority extended well beyond the choice of officeholders in the executive branch and the distribution of White House patronage. As Buchanan noted publicly at the end of the first term, the goals were great. To consolidate the new majority, Nixon wanted to oversee a complete overhaul of American politics, including "expansion of existing institutions and the creation of new institutions to articulate and defend the values and political beliefs that motivate the Republican Party, the building of new cadres of leadership to implement his own social and political philosophy, not just for the next four years, but over the next two decades."[11]

Nixon began work toward his vision. In the private sector, Colson was to play an important role in building the new establishment that Nixon hoped would accompany his new majority. In private law practice in Washington, Colson was apparently destined to become the Republican Clark Clifford, an elder statesman of considerable influence. On a personal level, Nixon wished to create his own political dynasty. He asked Harry Dent to arrange for the president's brother, Edward Nixon, and his sons-in-law, Edward Cox and David Eisenhower, to run for Congress. Dent later remembered that Nixon even nurtured presidential ambitions for Eisenhower.[12]

It was a time of heady political optimism when the greatest goals seemed within reach. Shortly before he left for the private sector, Colson received a letter from his former aide, Douglas Hallett. "How many times," wrote Hallett, "have we regretted that we had no CBS News, no *Washington Post*, no President of Yale University, no Council on Foreign Relations, no Joe Rauh, no COPE, no Harvard-MIT Joint Center for Urban Studies to develop, sell, and mouth our policies, develop our leaders, and attract our constituency? Perhaps now is the time to do something about it." Colson enthusiastically received Hallett's message of hope.[13]

Kevin Phillips, theoretician of the "emerging Republican majority," was confident enough about the advent of a new political atmosphere to write of its cultural dimensions. The emerging elite of the new majority differed from an old Democratic elite; there was a new "conservative chic." For example, while the universities of the liberal elite were Yale and Harvard, the stereotypical institutions of the new majority were the University of Southern California and the Air Force Academy. Instead of Leonard Bernstein, the new majority preferred the music of Lawrence Welk. The car of the new majority was a Cadillac rather than a Volvo; its food was charcoaled steak, not quiche Lorraine. The new majority, moreover, favored John Wayne over Marlon Brando, *Reader's Digest* over the *New York Review of Books*, and football over baseball. The point was clear. According to Phillips, this new elite was more in tune with ordinary Americans than the "elite liberals" were.[14]

REPUBLICANS

Many Republicans did not share the Nixon circle's delight about the election results. The victory belonged to Nixon, not to the party. Despite the rhetoric of the new majority, the party languished in minority status both in Congress and more generally within the electorate, as measured by polls of party identification. Most congressional Republicans were alarmed by the purely presidential nature of the new majority. Representative John W. Wydler of New York was a rare exception when he wrote to George H. W. Bush, newly appointed as the party's national chair, blaming Republicans who lost for their defeats on the grounds that Nixon had "provided a tremendous advantage to all Republican candidates by running strong for the presidency." Unsurprisingly, Nixon agreed; in fact, he was rather surprised by the extent to which his new majority was a presidential phenomenon. "With only a 55% turn out," Haldeman noted, "we should have won a huge Republican victory." Despite the concentration of his campaign machinery on the race for the presidency, Nixon saw the party's misfortunes as its failure, not his responsibility. He interpreted losses in gubernatorial and state legislative races as revealing "the total ineffectiveness of the Republican party at the lower level" and as showing that "the Party was a terrible drag."[15]

In the words of Buchanan, it was "the age of the ticket-splitter." The problems of the Republican Party, he maintained, were not the concern of Nixon: "If RN sweeps a state by 60% or 65% of the vote and the [Republican] incumbent . . . goes down the tubes, that is *their* fault not *his* fault." The election returns made it clear enough that many Americans preferred Nixon to McGovern but Democratic candidates to Republican candidates for other offices. John Connally read these preferences as indicating a vote in favor of divided government. "[T]he people deliberately set up a split," he told Nixon, according to Haldeman's notes. "The people want to keep the power divided. [Connally] says we shouldn't worry at all about the P[resident] not helping enough. The worst thing he could have done is push for a Republican Congress." A Harris poll supported Connally's view: 50 percent of Americans said that they thought it was better rather than worse to "have a Congress controlled by one party and the White House by another party," but only 29 percent thought this worse rather than better.[16]

The misfortunes of the Republicans at large provoked further contemplation that a new party should be created. During a discussion of political matters—especially important among which was Nixon's desire to ensure that Connally succeed him—Ehrlichman argued that the immediate aftermath of the victory offered the only real opportunity to form the new party. "The P[resident] was intrigued with this as a possibility," Haldeman observed, "recognizing that you can never really go with the P[resident]'s party into a majority and into a viable ongoing party, and that the only hope for making something, probably is to do a new party. The question is whether it can be done and whether we really want to make the effort." Haldeman doubted that the idea would be pursued. Connally himself was "not totally convinced" that a new party offered the most promise for his presidential ambitions but supported the idea "of re-establishing the Republican Party in a different way, with a new name, such as the Republican Independent Party."[17]

Haldeman was right, and Nixon did not form a new party. But the immediate aftermath of the victory did witness a set of initiatives that sought to consolidate the new majority's role within the party system. Nixon thought of reshaping the partisan status quo in three ways. The first was with respect to Congress. He may have taken some steps to encourage the formation of a newly formalized conservative coalition. The second regarded party organization. He tried to revitalize the Republican Party by contemplating the imposition of a far more centralized structure, undercutting the influence of activists closer to the grass roots. The third involved Republican identifiers among politicians and voters. The president tried to encourage Democratic defections, a strategy he had been unwilling to attempt during his reelection campaign. Even together, these three initiatives are not nearly as grand as the formation of a new party. But if Nixon had accomplished them, he would have achieved a significant reordering of the party system.

While Nixon concentrated on his personal fortunes during the 1972 campaign, he continued to hope that the next House of Representatives would be organized on a basis friendly to him. An outright Republican congressional victory obviously was highly unlikely, but a decent set of Republican gains remained possible, and for a time in 1972 Nixon had hoped that his party would pick up enough seats in the House that a number of conservative Democrats would change party affiliation and Republican organization could be achieved. Congressman Bud Shuster of Pennsylvania later recalled a conversation in which a colleague suggested that between fifteen and twenty House Democrats had been approached about switching if the postelection margin was close enough. Bill Timmons, the congressional liaison aide, mentioned the number as seventeen. But the margin was not close enough; the Republican Party performed inadequately in the elections to realize this hope. To gain control of the House, the Republicans needed as many as twenty-six Democrats to switch party allegiance. Despite the disappointing nature of the results and the consequent size of the margin, some observers argued that the prospect was not entirely lost. William Rusher, publisher of *National Review*, later remembered that "the possibility of a continuing coalition of economic and social conservatives" in the House of Representatives was "under serious consideration near the end of 1972." Writer Godfrey Hodgson made a similar claim. "The realignment that nearly happened over the Christmas holidays in 1972–1973," Hodgson noted, "is one of the great untold tales of American politics." He suggested that in early 1973 nearly forty conservative Democratic congressmen discussed seriously with Republicans the possibility of conversion. According to Hodgson, the developing scandal of Watergate rather than the disappointing gains of 1972 ended this chance for a Republican House.[18]

Nixon was certainly interested in the idea of a closer relationship between congressional Republicans and conservative Democrats, even if that relationship fell short of formal union. He talked with Haldeman about "the possibility of going at it like a 'merger'—two companies that don't totally fit together but you still put them together and then you kick out the disparate elements"; alternatively, "at the Congressional level, you build a coalition or fusion group, upset the organization of Congress and go at it that way." Joe Waggonner, a member of the House from Louisiana, publicly speculated about the eventual likelihood of such a coalition. But even in the absence of Watergate, the difficulty of winning the conversion of so many Democrats remained great. As Waggonner later pointed out, the margin between Democrats and Republicans in the House was too wide. Moreover, conservative Democrats generally retained disproportionate influence in Congress thanks to the seniority system, and although other congressional Democrats were starting to challenge that system, the threat to the southerners was not yet serious enough to provoke a major upheaval in party allegiance.[19]

In the absence of a congressional realignment, Nixon wanted to find ways in which his administration could develop a more harmonious relationship with Capitol Hill. He explained to Senate Majority Leader Mike Mansfield plans to hold less frequent meetings with the Republican congressional leadership and perhaps to meet regularly with an alternative "small, bi-partisan group" of legislators. As Nixon had discussed with Connally, the partisan identity of candidates would matter less to future electoral outcomes, so the White House and Congress could not act "on a party versus party basis." "We have an opportunity," noted Haldeman of Nixon's comments, "to think about how we can work with a divided government to find areas to agree and to reduce the partisan thing, and that this can be done if a few sensible people get together to talk and work it out."[20] But Nixon remained an unskilled custodian of executive-legislative relations. Instead of a new era of cooperation within divided government, the 1972 elections led to a bitter phase of institutional conflict.

The need to develop an ongoing electoral vehicle for the new majority again directed Nixon's attention to the Republican Party's problems. "As I began the new term," he wrote in his memoirs, "I had a sense of urgency about the need to revitalize the Republican Party lest the New Majority slip away from us." Despite his neglect of conventional party channels during his own election campaign, he now saw a role for the party in his project. He wanted the Republican National Committee (RNC) "to build upon the 'new majority.'" To do so, he thought that the committee should dedicate itself to campaign management and candidate recruitment. In place of centralizing campaigning functions in the White House, there was now a greater emphasis on cooperation between administration officials and both the congressional campaign committees and the RNC, which "would be upgraded." As Bob Dole's successor as national chair, Nixon selected George H. W. Bush. "He'd do anything for the cause," Nixon noted.[21]

The restructuring of the RNC—orchestrated by Nixon—had bold implications, according to members of the Ripon Society, a liberal Republican group. They saw it as an effort "to dominate the party in a centralized way" by undercutting the role of local parties by centrally controlling the election of candidates. Society members alleged that Nixon sought "the creation of the first national political machine in American history." Political control flowed from money, and the Committee for the Re-election of the President's leftover funds would form the basis of a centralized campaign organization, able to distribute financial and technical resources. "They could have encouraged," wrote Clifford Brown, "the election of candidates who played ball with the team while discouraging the election of others." If this mechanism succeeded in selecting and electing a candidate in 1976, providing a further term in the White House, "the Republican party as a party would have been totally phased out."[22]

The administration certainly hoped to control the party as much as possible. This attitude was exemplified by "relatively heated discussion" in early 1973 about the future of the "Data Base," a computerized list of almost 30 million registered voters in nine large states. Technically sophisticated for the time, it had been developed for the 1972 election at a cost of $1 million and could be used to generate canvassing and specialized mailing lists. Administration staffers were reluctant to see the Data Base turned over to the RNC but instead wanted it to remain under the control of a White House aide. It would be maintained with surplus reelection committee funds, and decisions could be made within the White House about which 1974 and 1976 candidates (including those for the presidency) should have access to this resource. The Nixon administration would thus maintain some capacity of party organization, separate from the national committee. To subdue any criticism within the party, the Data Base was to become the responsibility of a separate entity, and its director should receive an RNC post.[23]

The final part of the postelection partisan upheaval was conversion—the encouragement of Nixon-supporting Democrats to become Republicans. Few did so, as party identification data revealed. John Connally was the highest-profile convert, announcing in May that he was joining the Republican Party and becoming within days a White House adviser. Although Connally's close association with Nixon had probably ended the Texan's chances for further advancement within the Democratic Party, his conversion was a deed of some political bravery, coming as it did at a time when revelations about Watergate were becoming increasingly serious.

Connally seemed to have little enthusiasm for being a Republican. Maintaining his presidential ambitions, he was concerned that he would be damaged by his connection with the scandal-beset administration. His willingness to work for the party was thus limited. Bush reported in June that Connally was refusing to take up any major duties as a spokesman for the administration until the following fall, even though at least 400 Republican groups had extended speaking invitations to him.[24]

Few Democrats followed Connally's example. Even Frank Rizzo, so enthusiastic about Nixon during the campaign, did not switch parties. Nixon hoped in vain that Rizzo might "follow Connally" in joining the Republican Party, especially because the mayor's position among Pennsylvania Democrats was weak. Even in the South, the new-majority effort secured few more converts. Rare examples included Rayford Price, a former speaker of the Texas House of

Representatives and a politician of some promise in the state, who, like Connally, joined the Republican Party. The most sweeping success occurred in Virginia. In February, Richard Obenshain, the Republican state chair, reported that Mills Godwin, a former Democratic governor, had agreed to announce that he would accept the Republican nomination in the 1973 gubernatorial race. Moreover, Godwin agreed that he would not campaign in support of any Democratic candidates. The conversion of other Democrats in the state assembly was then likely in the near future, if not immediately, provided that Republicans guaranteed to honor the defectors' seniority. Godwin "urged patience and flexibility on the part of the Republican Party."[25]

In December 1972, Spiro Agnew traveled to Tallahassee, Florida, for a function called "Operation Switch Over." The name did not refer to John Connally's earlier plan of the same name to win the conversion of conservative Democrats in Congress but to an event designed to welcome Democratic activists in the state who had decided to change party affiliation. Agnew's speech emphasized that the GOP was the party of "individual rights," while the "Democrat [sic] Party [had] increasingly demonstrated a blind spot for the individual." "The Republican philosophy," the vice president said, "holds that Government should act as a catalyst to stimulate the citizen to be productive and self-protective; that public assistance should be provided only where the individual and the private sector have plainly failed." Agnew told the Democrats in his audience that they were being excluded from debate within their national party but would be offered a voice within the Republican Party.[26]

ISSUES AND INSTITUTIONAL CONFLICT

In the final days of the first term, there was a reminder of unfulfilled ambitions. The Department of Health, Education, and Welfare issued a study on "Work in America" that investigated both " 'blue collar blues' and 'white collar woes'—dissatisfaction of workers with their work bordering on despair." William Safire described the study as dealing with "an extremely important sociological subject, going to the heart of the New American Majority."[27] The report was a restatement of the Rosow Report's fundamental concerns about the problems of American workers. In 1969 and 1970, members of the Nixon circle were intrigued by the potential political gains that could accrue as a result of a meaningful response to these problems. But the president and his administration eventually offered little more than sympathetic rhetoric in praise of the American "work ethic" and never engaged in real, tangible activism in this area.

When Nixon spoke of his goals for the second term, his rejection of activism in search of new Republican voters was obvious. During an interview conducted a few days before the election but not published until after it, he spoke again about his desire for a "new American revolution." But the revolution's content differed starkly from that revealed in the State of the Union address less than two years previously. "My approach," he told the interviewer, "is that of a Disraeli conservative—a strong foreign policy, strong adherence to basic values that the nation believes in and the people believe in, and to conserving those values, and not being destructive of them, but combined with reform, reform that will work, not reform that destroys." His aims included the end of "the whole era of permissiveness" and the reduction and reorganization of the federal government.[28]

Nixon therefore discarded many of the "six great goals" of 1971. Out of these ambitions for reform, he now talked only of the straightforwardly conservative goal of executive reorganization, intended to achieve greater efficiency and to challenge the bureaucracy. His domestic formula had again become more recognizably Republican. The disappointing fate of the reform agenda demonstrated that there was no stable foundation of congressional support for Nixonian reformism. Nixon would not devote further energies to it. His second inaugural address reflected the change in tone. "I offer no solutions, no promise of a purely governmental solution for every problem," he said. "We have lived too long with that false hope."[29]

Nixon's plans for the second term followed a new-majority logic. The 1972 elections produced a Democratic Congress, and any efforts to formalize a conservative coalition in the House were unrealistic. The incompatibility between congressional Democrats' and Nixon's goals led to conflict. Nixon's determination to win this institutional conflict involved, in the words of Speaker of the House Carl Albert, an "accelerating usurpation of power by the Executive branch."[30] But Albert and his Democratic colleagues were also determined to win the battle.

In particular, Nixon disagreed with the Democratic Congress about the appropriate levels of government expenditure. His controversial solution was impoundment, the refusal to spend congressionally authorized money if he determined that the consequence of this spending would be inflation or higher taxes. Nixon had made impoundments during his first term, but he escalated their use during his second term in an effort to remove the policy initiative from his congressional opponents. This institutional tussle led to a congressional victory. In 1974, Congress passed the Budget and Impoundment Control Act, making impoundment difficult and creating the Congressional Budget Office to provide economic information independent of the executive branch. In 1975, the Supreme Court ruled against the presidential right of impoundment.[31]

Nixon emphasized the need for government reorganization to undermine the influence of the bureaucracy, which he saw as frequently hostile to his goals. To build a "new establishment," he sought to challenge bureaucrats as part of an old establishment. Following his failure to secure passage of his proposals for governmental reorganization, Nixon decided to implement them by executive action. Nixon designated four cabinet secretaries as "supersecretaries," with overall responsibility for a particular area of domestic policy— natural resources, human resources, community development, and economic affairs. In addition to their cabinet posts, the supersecretaries acted as presidential counselors, with special access to Nixon and to members of the White House staff. The plan further elevated the overall responsibility within the White House of John Ehrlichman for domestic policy and Henry Kissinger for foreign policy. Selected in defiance of Congress's express refusal to approve it, this initiative was one among several intended to assert presidential control throughout the executive branch. Watergate prevented the implementation of these measures, however.[32]

In waging institutional conflict over matters of policy, Nixon lost. Political scandal caused his chances of securing any victory to evaporate. In terms of legislative output, 1973 and 1974 were productive, but the initiative rested almost entirely with Congress.[33] The latest version of the new American revolution proved a hollow dream, just like the first.

The abortive second term was a disappointment not just in terms of frustrated intentions. Unexpectedly, there was bad economic news. "As 1973 began," noted Allen Matusow, "the Nixon White House believed its own rhetoric—that wise policy was guiding America to prosperity without inflation. No one in or out of the government foresaw the approach of the cataclysm." The upturn of 1972 proved to be short-lived because of mistakes in economic policy making and because of external events. Mistakes not only were caused by the tendency to place a priority on political needs in search of electoral success but also revealed the limitations of experts' ability to understand wholly the intricacies of economic developments.[34]

First, price and wage controls, imposed in large part out of political desperation, did not achieve more than short-term success in stabilizing the economy. In the longer term, they failed to undercut inflationary pressures within the economy. Second, in common with many others, government economists misread the situation, believing that expansive measures were appropriate because there was idle capacity within the economy. But there was none, so these expansive measures instead fueled inflation. Third, global problems of scarcity in such areas as food and oil further fed inflation. Inflation topped 8 percent in 1973.[35]

Worse news was still to come. A newly assertive mood among the oil-producing nations of the Middle East caused them to raise their prices, thus turning the problem of scarcity into a still more critical one of escalating costs. The price of oil, as set by the Organization of Petroleum Exporting Countries, climbed on five occasions during 1973. In the middle of the year, it was $2.90 per barrel; by year's end, the price had more than quadrupled to $11.65 per barrel. Deepening the crisis for the United States was an embargo imposed in October by a number of Arab nations as punishment for American aid to Israel in the Yom Kippur War. The embargo remained in place until the following March. Although U.S. dependence on imported oil was relatively small, it was nevertheless great enough to foster an energy crisis of shortages and escalating prices, in turn further increasing inflation.[36]

Even in the absence of any other problems—of which there were, in any case, more and more because of Watergate—the state of the economy posed a major threat to the Nixon administration's popularity and, by extension, jeopardized the new-majority project. Pollster Robert Teeter thought that the economy was "the one issue that could smash the New Majority apart." Teeter echoed the apparently timeless insight popularized by Lloyd Free and Hadley Cantril on the basis of their poll analysis in the 1960s. According to this view, "most people are idealogical [sic] conservatives and operational liberals," he wrote. "That is, they voice concern over big government, high taxes, and government spending, but they also want the federal government to help solve *their* problems and are willing to pay taxes for it."[37]

Cuts in spending were politically troublesome. Public opinion, as sounded out by polling companies, presented politicians with a tricky dilemma. According to Harris, there was widespread agreement with Nixon that inflation must be tackled through reductions in federal spending. But there was often disagreement with recommendations for specific cuts. Indeed, a majority favored increased spending on a number of programs, including job training, hospital construction, rural electrification, and Head Start. When pollsters asked a different question—posing a direct choice between more tax or more programs—the answers were different. Almost three-quarters of respondents preferred less tax, and only 13 percent preferred new programs.[38]

By this point, the electoral imperative was, if not inconsequential, less pressing than when Nixon had weighed policy options in 1971. Richard Howard, now responsible for White House liaison with members of the new majority, complained bitterly that their opinions about economic issues did not receive "proper consideration." "These views are frequently opposite the opinions of Secretary [of the Treasury George] Shultz, Herb Stein, and other economic and domestic advisors to the President," he wrote. "Therefore, many decisions are being made based on the weight of the Economic Advisors, and in my opinion, ignore the desires of the general public." In view of the pressing economic difficulties, Nixon was now ready to propose a budget that would impose widespread cuts on domestic programs.[39]

Two decades later, Nixon, forgetting the array of economic problems that faced the administration, remembered rather inaccurately that 1973 was "so full of promise," both in terms of domestic and foreign policy as well as in terms of changing "the whole establishment":

> I was going to build a new Republican Party and a new majority. . . . I was going to break down elitism in the universities, in the news, in the party. People love to see a president paying attention to them. Yes, a new majority. . . .
>
> And we were going to move the southern Democrats to us. They were ready to go, and with Connally at the top we could have done it. . . .
>
> Nineteen seventy-three was a great time. We had a week before the news of the cover-up business came to me, and then the Watergate bullshit came along.[40]

In Nixon's doomed efforts to fend off the problems of Watergate, the politics of the new majority again became relevant. Many southern politicians, assiduously cultivated by Nixon, were ready to trust the president. At the same time, many Republicans, convinced of Nixon's lack of dedication to party loyalty, were probably more prepared to disengage from the fight to save the president.[41]

DECLINE

The political impact of Watergate was enormously destructive. In 1973 and 1974, revelation after revelation undermined public confidence in the White House. The growth of discontent can be seen in the attitude of the Republican Party at large to Richard Nixon. At the end of 1972, many Republicans viewed Nixon as a major political asset and looked for ways to associate their cause with his personal success. By the end of 1973, Nixon was increasingly a liability, and Republicans sought to contain damage from the administration's identification with criminal activities.

In the aftermath of the 1972 elections, the new majority was the target of Republican ambitions. The party intended "to go forward with programs," wrote Bob Dole, about to step down as national chair, "to win over permanently to the Republican banner many of those formerly straight-ticket-voting Democrats who voted, this year for the first time, for a Republican candidate for office when they cast their vote for the President." George H. W. Bush, Dole's successor, followed these intentions. Bush created a "New Majority Campaign for 1974" within the national committee, and the political activities division organized a number of "New Majority Workshops" to discuss the practicalities of winning "those traditional Democrat ethnic and minority votes."[42]

But, Bush later recalled, his job as national chair became "to serve as a bandage carrier, traveling the country to wrap up party wounds" rather than "to build a new coalition." A clear signal of this massive change in emphasis was his September 1973 proposal to organize a new Republican Coordinating Committee (RCC). It was closely patterned after a similar body that had been convened following Goldwater's disastrous 1964 defeat.[43] The new RCC was a sign of concern with party decline. Bush did not, of course, speak of this accumulating mood of desperation. He did not need to do so for Republicans to understand the need for the RCC.

The proposal had reached Gerald Ford's office some months earlier; the papers of his chief aide, Robert Hartmann, indicate how the idea was inter-

preted. An elaborate nautical analogy captured the Titanic nature of the problems facing the GOP. A new RCC was a good idea because the party had "taken
multiple hits," and the "primary duty of all hands [was] now to keep the ship
afloat." Immediate action was required to "[m]inimize damage to regular
Republican organizations . . . by sealing off the flooded CREEP compartment
and emphasizing its isolation from and antagonism for the traditional Party
apparatus in 1972."[44]

The Nixon White House was thoroughly consumed by scandal. In October
1973, revelations of bribery and corruption forced Spiro Agnew to resign the
vice presidency.[45] Even though Agnew had at one time been the putative
"realigner," his loss was not a serious blow to what remained of the new-
majority project. By contrast, the disgrace of aides Haldeman and Ehrlichman
and ex-aide Colson had much more seriously debilitated Nixon's political
operations. Although Agnew played an important role in 1969 and 1970 in the
identification of the "silent majority," his importance had declined after the
shrill midterm campaign. While Nixon had encouraged Agnew to engage in
controversy to cultivate members of the new majority, the president largely
discarded Agnew when the vice president's success in the politics of polarization became more embarrassing than useful.

Even at this moment of disarray at the heart of his administration, Nixon
still remembered his long-term aspirations. He wanted Connally to be the next
president, and the vice presidency was the right launchpad for a presidential
campaign. But the prospect of a tough confirmation battle caused Nixon to
choose Ford, the House minority leader. Even then, Nixon still managed to
keep sight of his longer-range goal. During the meeting when Nixon informed
Ford of his decision, Ford assured the president that he did not intend to seek
office in 1976 and that he would probably support Connally in that year.[46] On
December 6, 1973, Gerald R. Ford was sworn in as vice president.

As scandal overwhelmed his presidency in 1973 and 1974, Nixon could hardly
escape the conclusion that he now lacked the ability to pursue his new majority.
Nixon's political effectiveness was rapidly disappearing. The best prospect for
his political project was now John Connally in 1976. Nevertheless, Nixon remained bullish. In September 1973, he promised members of the RNC that
he would campaign enthusiastically for Republican candidates the following
year.[47] To increasing numbers of Republicans—formerly desperate for some
practical support from Nixon—the promise sounded like a threat.

If confirmation of Republican problems were needed, then the fall 1973 elections offered it. In New Jersey, the state party shifted rightward in nominating Representative Charles Sandman for the governorship in place of the incumbent, William Cahill. Bush reported that during the campaign Sandman was "properly positioned on the issues ('no tax hike,' 'no bussing [sic],' etc.)" against Democrat Brendan Byrne. But Sandman faced a "tough" fight and won only 31.9 percent of the vote against Byrne's 66.7 percent. Sandman's campaign consultant was F. Clifton White, famous as the leading architect of Barry Goldwater's nomination for the presidency. "We lost the new majority," White concluded. "The peripheral urban ethnics voted for every Democrat in sight." He blamed the loss on Nixon's political decline, which in White's view had halted electoral realignment.[48] New Jersey, which had offered Republican promise in 1969, now presented the opposite signal.

In Virginia, the situation was a little brighter. The conversion of leading Democrats improved the party's prospects. One of them, Mills Godwin, won the governorship for the Republicans by a narrow margin, receiving 50.7 percent of the vote. But many Republicans were unenthusiastic about the campaign on behalf of their former opponent. Despite the cooperation of Linwood Holton, the incumbent Republican governor, more generally Bush found "Republican apathy and in some cases hostility." Moreover, although the new recruits brought with them votes, they did not always bring innovation. The content of Godwin's campaign was that of a politician from the old Byrd machine—which is exactly what Godwin was. According to Bush, the way in which the campaign was fought was poor as well, under "an old-time, old-line Democrat chairman [who was] not in close touch with modern techniques."[49]

Yet another sign of the party's problems was the Democratic capture of Gerald Ford's Michigan congressional seat, which had been strongly Republican. Leading Republicans worried about the electoral impact of Watergate. Nevertheless, in February 1974, Nixon predicted to William Brock that "this would be a bad year for incumbents" and encouraged an attempt "to knock off some Democrat Senators such as [Alan] Cranston [of California], etc." Similarly, when in the same month the president met with the cabinet, his "motivational notes" included a rather unconvincing note of encouragement. "I think the Democrats are going to get some rude shocks come November," his notes read. "Their worst handicap will be overconfidence."[50]

By the end of 1973, every voter category that had moved toward Nixon in 1972 was more strongly reaffirming its commitment to congressional Democrats. The Gallup organization found that the proportion of the electorate identifying itself as Republican had sunk to a twenty-five-year low of 24 percent. The pollsters also found a correlation between falling confidence in the president and falling ratings for his party, although the economy (in terms of the high cost of living) remained the most salient political issue.[51]

FORD

Nixon was accurate in earlier foreseeing 1974 as "a bad year for incumbents"—at least as far as his own tenure in the White House was concerned. That summer, Nixon could no longer escape implication in the crimes of Watergate. He became the first president to resign from office, and Gerald Ford assumed the presidency on August 9, 1974.

Watergate was incontestably a self-inflicted wound, but Nixon interpreted his fall differently. He linked the investigations that led to his resignation with a reaction against his new majority and his hope to create a new establishment. In 1992, talking with his aide, Monica Crowley, he blamed journalistic interest in the story on his intention to challenge a liberal bias within the press. In building the "new conservative majority," he would begin with the press. "I was going to get conservatives in there to take these people on," he told Crowley. "That's why in '72 they had to bring me down. They knew I was after them and that I'd succeed."[52]

Nixon's exit in 1974 had profound implications for American politics, including leaving the legacy of Reaganism. The Republican Party now had a vacuum of leadership, and Ronald Reagan was ready to fill that vacuum, receiving an enthusiastic welcome from many Republican activists. Indeed, at the grass roots, more enthusiasm would build for Reagan than it had for Nixon. After the apparent failure of the new majority, the opportunity had arisen to articulate a new and different vision for the party's future. And while Nixon's conservatism was tempered by pragmatic reformism, Reagan's was more frequently reinforced by principled zeal.

Richard Nixon had managed to keep conservative criticism of his administration in check even while such criticism had limited his ability to engage in imaginative policy making. But Gerald Ford was no Nixon. First, the new president's conciliatory style of politics brought back a sense of stability to the White House but was less effective in quashing any challenges to his leadership, whether from within or outside the party. Second, Ford's legislative career meant that he had not previously tackled the challenge of building a personal constituency across America for the nomination and then for the presidency. National electioneering was new to Ford.

Still another contrast between Nixon and Ford was their approach to policy making. Ford lacked Nixon's bold edge. In a mid-1975 interview, Ford described himself as an internationalist, a fiscal "conservative," and on "social legislation on the domestic side . . . a moderate or middle of the roader."[53] Unlike Nixon, Ford, though not a dogmatic conservative, showed little interest in compromising his fiscal conservatism for the sake of programmatic innovation that might appeal to the electorate. And although Ford shared Nixon's internationalist outlook, the new president had no special expertise in foreign policy, having concentrated in Congress on economic policy.

Ford struggled with an unenviable inheritance from his predecessor. As the midterm elections approached, two issue concerns dominated his administration: the aftermath of Watergate and the economic crisis, which Nixon had failed to solve and which his policies had even exacerbated. Ford ended his short honeymoon period of high popularity when he decided in early September to grant Nixon a pardon, an action that caused widespread outrage. Designed to undermine the continuing political salience of the Watergate scandal, the pardon ensured that its salience remained high in the shorter term.

Beyond Watergate, the poor state of the economy engaged the attention both of Ford and of the electorate. The economy was suffering from inflation, fueled by the high cost of the Vietnam War and by rising world oil prices. Weakness was revealed by other economic indicators, including the Dow Jones Index, the health of the construction industry, the level of gross national product, and the balance of trade. Despite inflation, unemployment remained high. Supported by a conservative group of advisers, Ford unveiled an approach of austerity. In October, Ford called for an income tax surcharge on corporations and the wealthy and for spending cuts of $4.4 billion in Nixon's budget. To encourage a mood of voluntarism, he also launched a campaign called WIN (Whip Inflation Now) to seek ways to keep prices down. The Democratic Congress reacted with scathing hostility to Ford's proposals.[54]

With the midterms approaching, Ford campaigned actively. He traveled 16,685 miles to give eighty-five speeches in twenty days of campaigning. Despite this activity and despite his instinct of loyalty to the party, Ford hesitated to associate himself too closely with the Republican cause. In early appearances, Ford "omitted in his delivered speeches partisan praise of Republicans and criticism of Democrats that had been written into his prepared speeches," noted journalist John Osborne. Ford, no less than Nixon, had decided that it was dangerous to be excessively partisan in legislative races, even though less than a year earlier he had been the leading Republican legislator. But Ford became more anti-Democratic as the campaign progressed. His passion was aroused in defending his conservative economic policy against attacks by his congressional opponents. "It is a Congress, in my judgment, that is stacked against fiscal responsibility," he said in Greenville, South Carolina. "And if [the Democrats] increase their power instead of lose, let me make just one observation: with a veto-proof Congress of the kind of membership they will get, tighten your seatbelts, folks. They will spend the dome of the Capitol right off Capitol Hill."[55]

Ford's passionate defense of fiscal conservatism failed to enthuse the electorate. The election results were extremely poor for the Republican Party, which lost forty-three House seats, three Senate seats, and five governorships. The Democratic Party now enjoyed decisive majorities of 291 to 144 in the House and 61 to 38 in the Senate. In the aftermath of Watergate, these results provided the most compelling evidence yet that no realignment had occurred. Low turnout—just 38 percent—further indicated that this was not a realigning period that dependably saw a heightened interest in politics among the public. For the cabinet, presidential counselor John Marsh prepared an analysis of the reasons for the defeat. He argued that local issues had been decisive in many races, but he confirmed that Democrats had benefited from negative perceptions of the Republican Party not only because of the Watergate scandal but also because of economic problems and the energy crisis.[56]

The Democrats' large majorities in Congress fostered pessimism about the future. At a December 1974 meeting of the RNC executive committee, Robert Teeter pointed out that Republican identification among Americans now stood at just 19 percent. "[P]resent trends indicate," he said, "that in 20–30 years the party will be extinct." A majority of the electorate saw the Republicans as less effective than Democrats at handling most issues and, thanks to Watergate, as untrustworthy. According to Teeter, the only remaining advantage for the party was that it was still considered the more competent custodian of the nation's foreign policy.[57] The results of the 1974 elections had reemphasized the minority status of the Republican Party and the emptiness of the new-majority aspiration.

When confronted in an interview with the worrisome identification figures,

Ford spoke of limited goals for the future. "[T]here's some disillusionment with the Democrats and certainly some with the Republican party as such," he said. "But that doesn't mean that we can't, with good candidates and a good program, retrieve a substantial part of the 40 percent [of self-identified independents]. I'm not sure they're all going to suddenly identify as Republicans but they hopefully would vote Republican and then we can make more progress later on."[58] The statement demonstrated the great contrast between Ford's modest vision and the self-confident, even arrogant, way in which Nixon had contemplated the political future some years earlier.

ISSUES AND THE ECONOMY

The state of the economy gave little reason for confidence. America in the mid-1970s was moving from an era of possibilities and reform to an era of limitations and retrenchment because of the worsening economic situation and the closely connected energy crisis. The administration's response to unemployment and inflation was not dogmatic. Instead, Ford showed pragmatism in his thinking and flexibility in his approach. Moving away from the policy of austerity, he proposed a series of measures aimed at economic stimulus, including a tax cut and rebate and an unbalanced budget including a $2 billion public works appropriation. Ford attempted to connect tax cuts with spending cuts. However, the Democratic Congress passed a number of spending bills that exceeded Ford's budget guidelines, and in response, he vetoed the measures. In total, during his term in office Ford vetoed sixty-six bills, including provisions for housing, education, and public works. Twelve of his vetoes were overridden.

In response to the energy crisis, the administration tried to deregulate domestic oil production and increase levies on imported oil despite the short-run political costs of further price increases. Congressional Democrats argued for more gradual deregulation, a postponement of the tariff increase, and a gasoline tax. The disagreements brought repeated defeats for the administration; eventually, a compromise was found in which both deregulation and the levy increase were approved but would be phased in over a period of time, and domestic oil prices were rolled back before decontrol took effect.[59]

Political attention was thus devoted to the problems of stagflation and to the energy crisis. Less money and time were available to other programmatic developments. The administration was accused of lacking vision. The Democrats, however, certainly did not offer a coherent agenda of governmental goals to contrast with the appearance of an ideologically uncertain administration. "They proposed no major changes in the balance between public and private sectors, no grand expansion of government," Michael Barone noted. The period of reform was finally reaching its end, an end characterized by increasing attention to regulatory matters. In addition to the measures relating to energy and economic stimulus, the major achievements of the Ninety-fourth Congress included laws providing for the deregulation of economic areas (despite Congress's reluctant approval of the domestic oil market's decontrol) and the regulation of other areas, like the environment.[60]

Ford lacked Nixon's relish for foreign policy. The Ford administration's record did not share the glitter of innovation and action that many observers detected during the Nixon years. The problems began with Ford's less authoritative grasp of foreign policy topics—in contrast, for example, with his good knowledge of economic policy. Other problems notably included the assertive nature of Congress, which had become distrustful of executive action in the aftermath of Vietnam. Even Ford's mastery of Congress could not overcome this lack of trust and insistence on a full role for the legislature in the framing of foreign policy. Congress, for example, prevented the administration from helping Turkey in its disagreement with Greece over Cyprus. The administration also failed in attempts to continue American encouragement of talks about the Middle East.

But frustration of its goals did not alone characterize the administration's foreign policy. A very positive public reaction greeted the rescue of an American merchant ship, the *Mayaguez*, from Cambodia in May 1975. Although fifteen marines were killed in the action, the rescue improved Ford's reputation for foreign policy leadership. According to the first major planning document of the presidential campaign, the *Mayaguez* incident was "clearly a turning point in both the perception of [Ford's] ability to handle his job as President and his ability to deal with foreign policy problems."[61]

Nevertheless, the change was not dramatic enough. Most seriously, détente—at the heart of Nixon's foreign policy—seemed to falter and lost public support. Relations with the Soviet Union again became frostier, worsened by congressional attempts to link trade between the two countries with Jewish emigration and by superpower differences concerning Angola's postcolonial regime. Skepticism grew about the wisdom of détente. Ford was criticized when he signed the Helsinki Agreements, which formally accepted post-1945 borders in Europe, although they also included Soviet promises about human rights. He was also criticized when Soviet dissident Alexander Solzhenitsyn visited the United States and the president did not arrange a meeting. Particularly alert to any perceived weakening of America's posture in the Cold War were conservative Republicans, whose support Ford needed for his party's nomination.[62]

CONSERVATIVES

Throughout his administration, Ford faced right-wing criticism. A key precipitant of conservative discomfort was Ford's selection of Nelson Rockefeller as vice president. According to William Rusher, "the conservative movement could only feel that it had been deliberately slapped in the face by the new president." Rockefeller's elevation convinced many conservatives that they needed to work much harder to ensure that the Republican Party moved in their direction. Indeed, conservative activist Richard Viguerie claimed that the nomination was responsible for sparking the emergence of the New Right of the 1970s.[63]

Although Rockefeller's governorship of New York had ended much more conservatively than it began, conservatives remembered his careerlong hostility to their cause. In March 1975, the National Republican Congressional Committee launched a fund-raising effort by sending out a mailing in Rockefeller's name, asking for checks payable to the "Vice President's Special Fund." The response was "a considerable volume of outrageous mail and telephone calls." One Republican sent back Rockefeller's solicitation letter with the handwritten comment, "Since you are running the show, you may pay for it. I remember the 1964 Calif. primary," when Rockefeller conducted a bitter campaign against Barry Goldwater. The name of the fund-raising effort was swiftly changed to the "GOP '76 Victory Fund." Conservative hostility of this kind effectively ended Rockefeller's political career. The prospect of his renomination became implausible. Primarily in response to this right-wing criticism, Rockefeller announced in November 1975 that he would not be Ford's 1976 running mate.[64] But the sacrifice was not great enough to defuse conservatives' conviction that Ford was not and never could be an effective leader in their terms.

Superficially, the growth of conservative criticism is surprising in view of Ford's overall record as president. To prepare Ford for a meeting with a group of Georgia Republicans in June 1975, aide Richard Cheney emphasized the conservative dimensions of Ford's presidency. "I think it can be argued," Cheney wrote, "that your attitude and your approach to government has more consistently reflected conservative Republican principles than any President in the last several decades." As Cheney pointed out, Ford consistently demonstrated a determination to hold down federal spending, recommending, for example, a lower increase in Social Security benefits, limits in federal pay increases, and controls on the cost of food stamps.[65] But conservatives were eager for bolder changes in policy. In the wake of Nixon and his search for a new majority, conservatives had the opportunity to press their case. Many of them believed in the existence of a conservative electoral majority, and they were confident that the Republican Party could and should seek to mobilize such a majority. The modesty of Ford's political aspirations therefore seemed inadequate, his pragmatism unnecessary and objectionable.

The Ford administration was a promising time for conservatives to articulate their demands for three reasons. First, Gerald Ford lacked the political skill of his predecessor in containing their threat. While Nixon largely failed to pursue the conservative agenda, thereby infuriating some conservatives, he managed to keep the scale of open discontent small enough that it did not threaten his leadership. The opposition of the Manhattan Twelve had been rather inconsequential, and despite conservative misgivings, Nixon had enjoyed some success in pursuing his idiosyncratic agenda. He traveled to Beijing and Moscow; he imposed controls on the economy. Conservatives could only watch with frustration and hope for a more favorable future. Still, even Nixon experienced political limitations because of the continuing intraparty power of conservatism, which presented an obstacle to the achievement of important pieces of his agenda, including welfare and health care reform. Within Congress and at the grass roots, conservatives played a significant role in the party. The second reason for Ford's accumulating problems was that this conservative force was continuing to grow, and its political significance was becoming greater both inside and outside the Republican Party. The mid-1970s was a time of remarkable organization by conservative groups.[66]

Third, Nixon's project to build a new majority for the party at large had failed, discrediting this vision and creating an opportunity for an alternative. In 1975, William Rusher claimed the rhetoric of the new majority for the conservative cause in his book, *The Making of the New Majority Party*. Since the 1950s, when he had become publisher of *National Review*, Rusher had been a leading proponent of conservatism, first disappointed by Eisenhower, then enthusiastic about Goldwater, and finally disappointed again by Nixon. Rusher's vision for a new majority relied on a union of economic and social conservatives mobilized in opposition to liberal Democrats. Despite his disappointment with Nixon's record, Rusher saw the presidential victory of 1972 as the first electoral manifestation of this coalition. To Rusher, Rockefeller's nomination was significant because it was "downright counterproductive" to the necessary effort to foster a conservative coalition. Indeed, the nomination encouraged Rusher to write the book; Rusher saw the choice of Rockefeller as a Republican return to a "me-too" strategy that tried "to prize from the Democrats a handful of their moderate liberals, to add to the GOP's economic conservatives." This strategy left no place for the social conservatives, Rusher argued.[67]

This new vision of a new majority was not Rusher's alone: it represented many American conservatives' hopes for political preeminence. Outside signals encouraged these hopes. For example, according to an early 1975 Harris poll, a quarter of voters said that they were likely to support a new political party more conservative than the Republicans. But even while many people agreed on the importance of uniting economic and social conservatives to secure an electoral majority, conservatives disagreed about the detail of this vision. They disagreed about exactly which combination of policies to choose to appeal to these voters. Moreover, conservatives were divided by a strategic disagreement about the Republican Party's place in their plans.[68]

A meeting of the Conservative Political Action Conference in February 1975 revealed both these agreements and these disagreements as well as frustration with the existing Republican Party. Robert Bauman, a Republican congressman from Maryland, attacked the administration's record and Nixon's legacy as insufficiently conservative, calling for a realignment and a new party uniting those seeking "freedom to live their lives without the interference of government." Jesse Helms, a senator from North Carolina, did not explicitly call for the creation of a new party, but he did urge the mobilization of conservatives behind a coherent political force. In contrast, Senator James Buckley of New York emphasized that these efforts should focus on transforming the existing Republican Party. Nevertheless, a surprising number of Republican officeholders joined Bauman in sympathizing with separatist aspirations. In March,

33 of 174 House Republicans failed to sign a pledge of party loyalty that was designed to undermine the third-party movement.[69]

Conservative attention focused on the leadership potential of Ronald Reagan, who had now stepped down as California governor. At the Conservative Political Action Committee meeting, Reagan delivered a speech that emphasized the value of anti-inflation and strong national defense policies. He appeared to reject the idea of a political force outside the Republican Party, however. "Is it a third party we need," he asked the conference, "or is it a new and revitalized second party, raising a banner of no pale pastels, but bold colors which make it unmistakably clear where we stand on all of the issues troubling the people?"[70] Reagan's unwillingness to support the creation of a new party was important. The separatists needed a leader, and Reagan had been the most promising candidate.

Despite Reagan's discouragement of a third party, the separatists continued to investigate the prospect. They organized a Committee on Conservative Alternatives chaired by Helms. This committee created a body to investigate state election laws, a Subcommittee on Independent Conservative Action, and a Subcommittee on Conservative Action in the Major Parties. During the summer, Rusher organized a separate, independent body, the Committee for Freedom of Choice, later known as the Committee for the New Majority.[71]

A newsletter, the *Right Report*, captured the mood among conservatives by stating that Ford was likely "to give conservatives just enough to persuade them that 'good old Jerry' is not bad after all" but was unlikely to placate them after his "many liberal appointments, actions, and programs." The conservatives were "fed up with being taken for granted" and were "in a mood to think the unthinkable, including the formation of a new party." The movement's leaders, including Helms, New Hampshire Governor Meldrim Thomson, and Idaho Senator James McClure, bolstered rank-and-file dissatisfaction and showed a readiness to "put principle before party."[72]

But other leaders were still willing to place party first. Most conservatives still believed that they should stay in the Republican Party. Observed from the White House, the activities were justifiably seen as an attempt to influence the administration's policies in a rightward direction, but differences among conservatives undermined the effectiveness of these efforts. Advocates of a new party were not taken seriously. "[T]he formation of a separatist party appears to have appeal only with the ideologues whose clout with respected GOP leaders is realistically weak," concluded aide Fred Slight.[73] Nevertheless, the extent of conservative dissatisfaction with the administration and the state of the party was serious and posed a formidable threat to Ford's leadership.

FORD AND REAGAN

Gerald Ford faced tough challenges in pursuit of reelection. In the fall campaign, he would need to secure the support of many independents and disillusioned Democrats because the country still had far too few Republicans for a presidential candidate to rely solely on the party's supporters. But to win the Republican nomination for the presidency, Ford would need primary majorities in state after state. And in this task, he would have to contend with the views of voters and political leaders rather more conservative than the general electorate. Though this was not in itself an unusual problem for a Republican candidate, the assertiveness of conservatives made it more troublesome for Ford, who also lacked experience as a national campaigner. The need to cultivate conservatives so assiduously undermined any hope of emulating new-majority politics, which demanded a focus on the more moderate expectations of the electorate as a whole rather than the special interests of the primary constituency.

In domestic policy, a matter of ostensibly secondary importance became an important test of Ford's conservative credentials. Conservatives wanted Ford to veto a common situs picketing bill, which aimed to exempt construction workers from a ban on secondary picketing. Within the climate of the recession, the administration wanted to avoid the alienation of labor unions, so it proposed a bill to allow limited common situs picketing. By the time Congress passed the measure, however, it had attracted the opposition of union leaders, who saw it as too limited. More importantly for Ford, the bill had also attracted the hostile criticism of many Republicans, who saw it as an attack on business rights. Richard Cheney later commented that the White House received more mail on this subject than on any other issue.[74]

The affair revealed again the conservatism of activist Republicans on such issues. Its outcome revealed the fear now within the administration that this conservatism had become strong enough to wrest the nomination away from Ford and hand it to Reagan. Toward the end of 1975, Ford campaign officials reported that leading Republicans nationwide were offering repeated complaints about the common situs proposal. Overall, the campaign organization reported "strongly negative reaction" to the legislation. In the White House, aide Jerry Jones described Ford's original position as a "loser," noting that it would demoralize or completely alienate "conservatives" and "responsible businessmen" who provided crucial financial support and campaign leadership. Any aspirations Ford had for consolidating links with organized labor would not help his primary struggles, Jones pointed out. At the end of 1975, Ford responded to these pressures by vetoing the bill. Campaign chair Bo Callaway congratulated Ford, calling the action a "big plus for us organizationally." The cost of the veto was at least the resignation of Secretary of Labor John Dunlop.[75] Although significant parts of organized labor had already signaled dissatisfaction with the bill, the veto also demonstrated that the administration would not and probably could not attempt to woo labor leaders as Nixon had.

What turned out to be more important to the Reagan challenge was foreign policy. From an early point, Ford's campaign team was aware of the president's relative weakness as a foreign policy leader, urging him "to take strong, positive positions on foreign policy matters" whenever they arose. Ford's lack of foreign policy experience was compounded by the growing skepticism about détente. Opinion polls conducted for the White House prompted analyst Lloyd Free to counsel that "a show of greater toughness toward the Soviet Union, without endangering relationships, could be useful."[76]

Most skeptical of all about détente were conservative Republicans, so the presence of Reagan as a primary opponent sharpened Ford's political difficulty with foreign policy. When Ford contemplated a visit to China, Robert Hartmann advised that the plan should be canceled because of the opportunity it provided for Reagan to appeal to anticommunism. "You will be portrayed as soft on this issue," Hartmann wrote to Ford, "failing to see the magnitude of the clever Communist threat, letting down the hopes of all the Eastern European ethnics at Helsinki, dismantling our military defenses to a dangerous degree through [arms-limitation] negotiations, etc."[77] Nevertheless, at the end of 1975 Ford visited the People's Republic.

In November 1975, Ronald Reagan announced that he would be a candidate. At the start of 1976, many White House staffers believed that Reagan posed a limited threat, although it soon became clear that this belief was dangerously wrongheaded. Nevertheless, Nixon apparently agreed with this view. Before Reagan's announcement, when his candidacy was still a matter of speculation, a message arrived at the White House stating that Reagan, in Nixon's opinion, was "a lightweight and not someone to be considered seriously or feared in terms of a challenge for the nomination."[78] Nixon was wrong. Reagan was far from a lightweight. He almost managed to deny the incumbent president his party's nomination. Reagan's emergence to prominence then helped to set the Republican Party in a new direction, more conservative than the paths advocated by Nixon and by Ford. This success was closely related to criticisms of foreign policy and particularly of détente, on which Nixon had placed so much stress as president and which he identified as so helpful in mobilizing his new majority.

But Reagan suffered some disappointments before uncovering the power of a foreign policy appeal. In New Hampshire, the state with the first primary, Reagan emphasized an antigovernment message, but the Ford campaign exploited concerns about the implications of the challenger's antigovernment approach. There was, for example, alarm about a proposal that Reagan had forwarded to transfer responsibility for funding programs worth $90 billion from the federal to state and local levels—and the alarm was particularly acute in New Hampshire, which had no state income tax. On the day after the primary defeat, strategist John Sears told Reagan, "We didn't quite make it last night. We're going to have to start talking about foreign policy." Pollster Richard Wirthlin agreed with this approach; it would emphasize the contrast between Ford and Reagan.[79]

Reagan launched stinging attacks on the administration's foreign policy, charging that Ford had demonstrated "neither the vision nor the leadership necessary to halt and reverse the diplomatic and military decline of the United States." Henry Kissinger and the policy of détente came in for particularly harsh criticism. "Henry Kissinger's recent stewardship of U.S. foreign policy has coincided precisely with the loss of U.S. military supremacy," Reagan said. "Under Messrs. Kissinger and Ford this nation has become Number Two in military power in a world where it is dangerous—if not fatal—to be second best. . . . All I can see is what other nations the world over see: collapse of the American will and the retreat of American power." Although this strategy scored some success on its launch in Florida, Ford still won the primary there, thanks to announcements of federal spending schemes in the state and to concerns among elderly Americans about Reagan's plans for Social Security.[80]

The contrast between the fortunes of the Reagan campaign before and after the discovery of the foreign policy issue was great. Reagan performed poorly enough in the first few months of 1976 to generate speculation that he might end his candidacy. This speculation remained after the Florida primary, but that defeat had hinted at the strong potential of foreign policy attacks. The Reagan campaign realized that it had found a valuable issue. A Ford source in Reagan's campaign reported that the sentiment there was aggressive. "[I]t was the feeling of the Reagan people that they were going to do a lot more to generate national headlines, and that Reagan was going to say 'interesting things' about the President on a daily basis from now on," the source reported. "Rather than discuss their own programs they will attack us."[81]

The foreign policy emphasis scored greater success in North Carolina, where Reagan posted an unusual victory over an incumbent. He discovered that his strongest applause line there concerned the future of the Panama Canal Zone. It was rumored that in its continuing negotiations with Panama about the zone, the administration had offered to give up sovereignty. Although the information was no more than a completely unsubstantiated rumor, Reagan productively placed it at the center of his attacks on administration foreign policy. "When it comes the Canal," Reagan said time and again, "we built it, we paid for it, it's ours and we should tell [Panamanian dictator Omar] Torrijos and Company that we are going to keep it!"[82]

Within the White House, Reagan's success was considered to be strongly linked with such rhetoric. Polling seemed to provide concrete evidence of the effectiveness of such words. For example, just before Reagan delivered a major foreign policy speech in Texas, 45 percent of the state's primary voters had favored Ford and 28 percent Reagan, with no perceived difference between the candidates on the subject. By contrast, a day after the speech, Reagan had increased his support across the state by 5 points, and Ford's support had fallen to 37 percent.[83]

The Ford campaign tended not to respond with equally strong attacks on Reagan. However, campaign managers Stuart Spencer and Peter Kaye strongly emphasized the connection between Reagan's unpopular domestic proposals and his primary failures. "Our political fortunes began to drop," they commented, "when we let up on Reagan, on the $90-billion plan [for saving money by transferring federal programs to the states for their administration or termination], on his Social Security stands etc." Kaye and Spencer advocated a similarly strong attack on foreign policy, playing on a fear "of a President

Reagan with his bellicose statements, as a commander-in-chief and with his finger on the nuclear button." But rhetoric of this kind became notable only in California at the end of the primary season.[84]

Reagan also emphasized cultural issues, denouncing permissiveness, abortion, and gun control and speaking of his personal religious faith. "[T]his country is hungry for a spiritual revival," he said in a June interview. As president, he would "take advantage of every opportunity to stress moral values," he pledged. One result of Reagan's cultural conservatism, the White House noted, was to secure the enthusiastic support of right-wing single-issue groups, which were helpful in mobilizing voters. Many of these groups were connected with right-wing organizer Richard Viguerie, and their members were often not loyal partisan identifiers but were committed to particular issues, such as opposition to abortion and gun control. "We are in real danger," warned an unsigned memo circulated in the White House, "of being out-organized by a small number of highly motivated *right wing nuts*." The danger was especially strong in some states, including Utah, Texas, and Arizona, according to Rogers Morton, the president's campaign manager.[85]

Reagan appealed to conservative Democrats in states that allowed crossover primary voting, such as Tennessee, Arkansas, and Texas; local officials of the President Ford Committee (PFC) tried to deter such voters. In a July television address, Reagan pointed with pride to the Democratic and independent votes he was winning. "It indicates," he said, "the issues I was talking about—our basic values, Washington's excesses, our declining national defense—all go beyond party lines; that there is a new coalition, a new majority across this land ready to answer the nation's needs."[86]

While Republicans argued about foreign policy, public confidence in their party's custody of the economy remained low. In January 1976, Foster Chanock, an aide to Cheney, noted that the only break in this negative perception throughout the postwar years had occurred in 1971 and 1972. Nixon's program of controls was responsible for creating a unique change in political attitudes and for temporarily undermining this long-standing Democratic advantage. The change was soon reversed. By March 1975, only 14 percent of people surveyed had more confidence in the Republicans as custodians of the economy. Robert Teeter had already described the connection between confidence about the economy and the potential for greater electoral achievement: "It is not going to be possible to re-build 'the new majority' from 1972 with a Republican President in a recession," Teeter wrote to Spencer. "Too many of the new majority were Democrats who came over on the social issues and who are now far more concerned with economic issues, [and] are a long way from the President's position [on] them."[87]

Reagan's challenge did not address these problems with the electorate but was nevertheless serious enough that the party's nominee was not chosen until the convention at Kansas City. The strength of the challenge was demonstrated in the convention's adoption of a platform plank about "morality in foreign policy." The platform, the party's official statement about the campaign, in essence contained an articulation of Reagan's critique of the administration's foreign policy. It was toned down enough so that it did not overtly undermine the administration's authority, but its message was clear. It criticized détente, Ford's refusal to meet with Alexander Solzhenitsyn, the Helsinki Pact, and unilateral nuclear-testing bans; it even included an oblique criticism of the Panama Canal negotiations.[88]

THE PARTY AND THE SEPARATISTS

The demands of the campaign against Reagan forced Ford to devote special attention to the party. The opposing candidates' delegate tallies became so evenly matched that it was important to woo every possible uncommitted delegate, and Ford worked hard to do so. He wrote, telephoned, and even met with individual delegates in pursuit of their votes. The Ford campaign argued that the president was not only the most electable candidate but also the best Republican, most likely to secure the election of fellow Republicans.[89]

The argument was convincing. It was reasonable to expect that Ford's campaign would be more party centered and less candidate centered than the new-majority campaign of 1972. After all, Ford was a loyal Republican, and he had viewed with frustration Nixon's unwillingness to help the party. Speaking to the RNC in early 1975, Ford made the point explicit: "I pledge to you now—that I will be in the middle of the 1976 campaign not only for the Presidency but on behalf of Republican candidates for the House as well as the Senate and for state governors and other elective offices across the country. I've been doing this for a good many years and I'm too old to change my good habits now." In fact, Ford did break with his habits. The campaign of 1976 was as candidate centered as that of 1972 and was run under the auspices of a personal organization, the PFC. Advisers told Ford that any help to Republicans undermined the effort to reach independents and ticket-splitting Democrats. "The President must not campaign for GOP candidates," the PFC plan stated bluntly.[90]

Meanwhile, the conservatives who had completely rejected the Republican Party continued their separatist efforts. William Rusher and his allies decided to make an effort to take over the American Independent Party, George Wallace's 1968 electoral vehicle, as the basis of a new conservative party. Rusher hoped that the movement would secure ballot positions in all fifty states and field a candidate strong enough to draw 5 percent of the vote, the figure needed to qualify the party for federal election funding in 1980. As far as many conservatives were concerned, the ideal candidate remained Reagan.

The separatists were aware that a third candidate made Democratic victory more likely. According to the *Right Report*, the presence of a strong independent conservative alternative "would almost certainly doom the Ford ticket in November." White House aides recognized the dangerous hostility of these moves. "[T]he entire third party effort . . . is based upon a desire to defeat the Republican Party in November," wrote Coleman Andrews in July, "since the leaders of the third party movement believe that their desires and the desires of the new majority can best be gained through a new party structure rather than through an evolution of the old Republican party."[91]

Ultimately, the danger was not so great. The separatists' effort to take over the American Independent Party failed. Its convention did not choose a candidate that fitted Rusher's criteria. Indeed, the nominee alienated both Rusher and Viguerie as well as many other conservative activists. In this test of an alliance between economic and social conservatives, a group of rather extreme social conservatives refused to make common cause with the dissident Republicans. The convention nominated Lester Maddox, the former governor of Georgia and, in Rusher's words, a "notorious racist." Maddox held views more extreme than those of Wallace. Indeed, Maddox attacked Wallace, who had flirted again with national politics in 1976 but whose speeches often lacked their earlier passion and energy. Stating that Wallace was "no longer in the conservative movement," Maddox criticized the former governor of Alabama in remarkable ways that revealed more about Maddox's extremism than about Wallace's views. "He is now speaking for the liberal-radical establishment," Maddox said. "He is now associating himself with pointy headed liberals." Maddox languished far from the mainstream and was irrelevant to the presidential campaign overall. The inheritor of Rusher's efforts for a new-majority party in 1976, Maddox won just 170,531 votes nationwide.[92]

THE CAMPAIGN

The 1976 campaign raised a crucial question about the fate of Nixon's new majority. As president, Nixon had envisioned the creation of a long-term majority, not simply one that would win him reelection in 1972. Now was the first opportunity to test the idea, to discover whether many of Nixon's non-Republican supporters would vote for Ford.

Democratic candidate Jimmy Carter, a former governor of Georgia, differed completely from George McGovern. While opposition to the Vietnam War shaped most profoundly McGovern's presidential candidacy, national reactions to Watergate formed the background of Carter's candidacy. On the Democratic campaign trail, Carter emphasized his status as an outsider to Washington politics. "I will never lie to you," he pledged to his audiences. According to speechwriter Patrick Anderson, Carter and his senior advisers were "anti-issues," preferring to focus on " 'themes'—honesty, compassion, trust."[93]

Similarly, Carter secured his party's nomination by putting together a coalition that differed from McGovern's. Indeed, Carter was the choice of many "Nixon Democrats," winning more support among Democrats who had voted for Nixon in 1972 than among those who had chosen McGovern. Moreover, polls conducted during the primary season indicated that as many as four in ten of Carter's supporters would vote for Ford if Carter were not nominated. At the same time, Democratic regulars and liberals—less likely to defect and support a Republican in the presidential contest—were unenthusiastic about Carter.[94] His emergence proved that the reform of the Democratic nominating process, which had been modified in certain respects after 1972, did not necessarily produce a liberal.

Carter posed a much stronger challenge to Ford than McGovern did to Nixon. Demographically and attitudinally, Carter's appeal undermined two essential areas of new Republican strength at the presidential level: in regional terms, the South; in issue terms, social conservatism. A born-again Southern Baptist, he spoke of the importance of religion in American society and politics. In contrast with his predecessor as Democratic nominee, Carter energetically advocated conservative positions on many social issues. Taken as a whole, his views represented a belief in America's greatness, a potential betrayed by current leaders; according to Anderson, Carter sought to present himself as "a decent man who believed America could be great again."[95] Carter therefore emphasized some attitudes that resembled those placed by Nixon at the heart of his appeals in 1970 and 1972 in the hope that they would become a core Republican advantage.

Private poll analysis conducted after the conventions made for gloomy reading at the White House. It revealed the power of Carter's appeal on the issues. As Martin Schram reported, Robert Teeter found that voters placed Carter "slightly to the left of center . . . on social-economic matters" and slightly to the right of center on foreign policy and national security matters, summarized by Teeter as "Traditional American Values." In this way, Carter was close to the greatest number of voters. By contrast, Ford was seen as somewhat conservative in the former category but "just to the *liberal* side . . . on the national security (Traditional American Values) scale." Both of these positions categorized Ford as more distant from the electorate as a whole. The Ford campaign sought to make the electorate see the president as more conservative—and Carter as more liberal—in the area of foreign policy and see Ford as more liberal on social-economic issues. When Ford's campaign plan stated its aim to win over independents and Democratic ticket splitters, it outlined a way to achieve the goal simply: "Strive to create the perception of the President as a conservative on social issues and moderate on economic issues."[96]

Most bluntly, in its television incarnation, the campaign emphasized social conservatism blended with an internationalist and patriotic view of foreign policy. The patriotism was encapsulated by the campaign song, "Feelin' Good about America." Teeter told the PFC advertising team what themes to promote: "Love of family. Love of God. Love of country. Pride in yourself." His desire to focus the advertising on this kind of conservatism caused him to tell advertising official Malcolm MacDougall, "America seems to be considerably to the right of Barry Goldwater." Teeter was, nevertheless, exaggerating somewhat. In one important sense, Americans were not to Goldwater's right. A majority of the electorate favored at least some economic moderation; Americans wanted "a conservative government, but one tempered with compassion for all the people," MacDougall noted.[97]

The economy's poor performance since Nixon's reelection was a problem for Ford. Carter attacked the record, as did his running mate, Walter Mondale, with even more enthusiasm. Ford not only sought to defend the record but looked for new proposals that would allow him to add some moderate activism to the campaign's overall conservative thrust. On vacation in Vail, Colorado, after the convention, Ford announced his issues for the campaign. In addition to peace, they included jobs, "an accelerated home ownership program," "quality health care that is affordable to the American people," crime, and "better recreation facilities," such as improvements to the national parks. Even after Ford made these comments, Teeter eagerly sought further similar initiatives. Although voters did identify Ford with anti-inflation efforts, Teeter wanted to find measures where Ford could be "seen as being *for* something that will help people."[98] But there was not enough time to change fundamentally the administration's record.

The campaign aimed not only to improve the electorate's perception of Ford but also to damage its perception of Carter. In July, Richard Moore, a former Nixon aide, had impressed on Ford staffer Michael Raoul-Duval the need to do this: the presidential race was at that time between a liberal and a conservative, but it should be "between [the] far left and [the] *middle*."[99] In making this characterization of the content, Moore did not give credit to the conservative aspects of Carter's appeal. But Moore's message was undoubtedly clear. Ford's chances for victory would be much improved if his candidacy could be contrasted with that of an opponent seen to have views as similar as possible to McGovern's.

But Carter tended to thwart attempts to categorize him as a McGovern-like liberal in either economic or social terms. Carter showed his determination to be a different kind of Democrat in choosing Warm Springs, Georgia, as the location for launching his campaign. By traveling to Franklin Roosevelt's favorite vacation spot, Carter rejected the traditional place for the launch of Democratic campaigns—Cadillac Square in Detroit, a symbol of labor America. In his speech, Carter paid tribute to Roosevelt, compared Ford with Herbert Hoover, and quoted Harry Truman to claim that the Republican Party was the party of the rich. The Democratic candidate therefore linked himself with a party tradition of great success. At the same time, he spoke of a choice between work and welfare in which Americans should choose work and therefore distanced himself from less popular positions associated with more recent Democrats. Moreover, Carter was notably slow to speak out for newer Democratic interest groups, such as feminists and environmentalists. By contrast, while Carter was not the preferred Democratic candidate of organized labor, he nevertheless secured some useful support from this source during the fall campaign.[100]

Because of Carter's southern identity, the Ford campaign could not rely on the region's electoral votes. Most southern states were classified as "low priority." Unlike Nixon, Ford had little realistic chance to win the conversion of southern Democrats when the presidential candidate was a fellow southerner. There was one exception. Ford's campaign discovered that Louisiana Congressman Joe Waggonner was reluctant to endorse Carter. Ford telephoned Waggonner to ask for his endorsement and to invite him to join the Republican Party. Even in this case, the possible opportunity was the result of alienation from Carter rather than enthusiasm about Ford, and the Democrats contributed to the opening by threatening Waggonner with the loss of congressional seniority if he did not endorse Carter. Even in this case, however, the approach failed: Waggonner offered to support Ford, but only in private.[101]

The preoccupation with social conservatism outlived Nixon. On these questions, Ford articulated positions more conservative than Carter's. But the difference was marginal. "Carter's relative social conservatism," observed Wilson Carey McWilliams, "lessened the impact of such issues," even while they remained important to the electorate.[102] Two important examples of these issues in 1976 were abortion and amnesty, two-thirds of the "three As" formula by which Hugh Scott had described the 1972 anti-McGovern strategy.

Questions about abortion rights were, in fact, much more prominent in 1976 than 1972 thanks to the Supreme Court's 1973 decision in *Roe v. Wade*. That decision held that women had a fundamental, constitutionally protected right to an abortion, balanced by state interests in the mother's health and in the potential life of the fetus. The decision was controversial and led to intense political activity by antiabortion—or "prolife"—campaigners. In 1972, abortion had been largely absent from national political debate; in 1976, the candidates were forced to address the issue.

Ford declared antiabortion views but at different times during the primary season advocated different remedies—a constitutional amendment or a legislative approach. Despite some uncertainty, Ford's advisers recommended a position that did not openly oppose abortion rights but questioned the appropriateness of the Supreme Court's intervention in the matter. Irving Kristol, a neoconservative intellectual and an informal administration adviser, estimated that the prolife bloc included between 1 and 2 million voters and advised

Ford to meet their concerns. "He ought to declare," wrote Kristol to Robert Goldwin at the White House, "that in this heterogeneous nation . . . such 'moral' issues as abortion, pornography, and capital punishment should be a matter for the states to deal with."[103] Kristol therefore argued that Ford should seek to overturn a series of rulings by the Supreme Court that set out national standards on these matters.

The Republican Party platform included a proposal for an antiabortion amendment. By contrast, the Democratic Party officially supported abortion rights. But Jimmy Carter's position was less clearly supportive. Carter announced that he opposed abortion and that as president he would attempt to restrict it but would not support a constitutional amendment. A group of Catholic bishops criticized this position as "disappointing." Ford met with the bishops, who were not completely satisfied with his position but preferred it to Carter's.[104]

Prolife activists greeted the antiabortion plank as "a major victory," even while most dedicated social conservatives preferred Reagan. Still critical of Ford's reluctance to campaign openly against abortion, a prolife newsletter nevertheless exulted about the prominence their cause had gained. "[A]bortion will unquestionably be a major issue—national and local—in the campaign ahead, and seems certain to be *the* moral issue facing Americans in the years to come—an enormous advance nobody would have *dared* to predict." The newsletter attributed the inclusion of the platform plank to the Ford forces' desire to placate their intraparty opponents.[105]

The Ford campaign noticed the potential importance of groups like the prolifers in mobilizing support. The campaign's plan underscored the need to appeal to religious groups and to what it called " '[a]nti' groups such as gun control, abortion, busing." Despite Ford's lukewarm ambiguity on abortion, Marjory Mecklenburg, a prolife activist, joined the PFC. From there she contacted her colleagues in the prolife movement, supplying them with material about the candidates' positions and attempting to persuade them to work for the Republican cause. "You have an opportunity to make a significant difference in the outcome of the presidential election and thereby establish the prolife movement as a potent political force in this nation," she wrote. Mecklenburg also acted as the in-house advocate against abortion, writing to campaign manager Stuart Spencer to urge stronger rhetoric by Ford on this topic.[106]

Another social issue under debate in 1976 was the question of amnesty for those who had evaded the Vietnam War draft. Domestic reaction to the war had been one of the most important manifestations of social conservatism in the first few years of the Nixon administration. Now there were disagreements about whether to pardon draft dodgers. As on abortion, Ford's position on amnesty did not satisfy the more conservative. They opposed his creation of the Presidential Clemency Board, chaired by Nixon's bête noire, Charles Goodell, although the board created a fairly tough procedure by which to achieve rehabilitation. Carter's position on the issue was more liberal, if not liberal enough to satisfy all Democrats. "I do not favor a blanket amnesty," Carter told the convention of the American Legion, "but for those who violated Selective Service laws I intend to grant a blanket pardon." He explained that although an amnesty meant "that what you did is right," a pardon meant "that what you did—right or wrong—is forgiven." The American Legion audience reacted with hostility, but the stance apparently alienated few members of the wider public.[107] Carter seemed to have defused the issue.

Despite Ford's requests, Reagan campaigned little for the president. Instead, the former California governor remained an articulate advocate of the conservative aspects of the platform, speaking on behalf of conservative congressional candidates. Other, less consequential, conservatives more openly continued their opposition to Ford. At least one Reagan enthusiast organized an unofficial write-in campaign.[108] Reagan's negative legacy thus remained.

In the aftermath of Vietnam, issues of foreign policy attracted less attention than in either 1968 or 1972. The most prominent campaign incident concerning foreign policy was to Ford's detriment. During a television debate with Carter, Ford insisted that no Soviet domination of Eastern Europe existed; after the debate, he compounded his political problem by being reluctant to admit the mistake. Not surprisingly, this campaign event delighted the Democrats because it consolidated attack rhetoric by Carter that essentially echoed that by Reagan during the primaries. Reagan had accused Ford of a lack of leadership on foreign policy, criticizing issues such as Kissinger's performance as secretary of state and the conduct of negotiations on the Panama Canal Zone. Carter's repetition of these criticisms during the foreign policy debate evoked a favorable response from a panel of voters whose reactions Ford campaign officials were monitoring. The panel also responded positively, however, when Ford spoke about other elements of his record, including discussion of the *Mayaguez* incident. Despite the mixed record and despite damaging intraparty criticism, Ford of course could point to more foreign policy experience than Carter. Ford's campaign exploited doubts about his opponent.[109]

The Ford campaign's final drive omitted overt appeals to cultural issues. For the last two weeks, spokespeople were urged to concentrate on "trust," "peace," "spending" (arguing that Ford was likely to lower taxes and Carter to raise them), and "record." "Gerald Ford has a proven record of achievement," their list of talking points read. "You know where he stands. He is solid, reliable, an honest and trustworthy man. Jimmy Carter? He is fuzzy on almost every issue, he waffles and has no record of accomplishment. . . . He is unpredictable and a mystery. Voting for Carter would be taking a chance, gambling on America's security and safety."[110] If thinking about the 1976 campaign began with personal characteristics, it thus also ended with them. Certain, perhaps vague, doubts about Carter's qualities had emerged during the campaign, as these comments indicate, and Ford strategists wanted to exploit these doubts, which were encouraged by a *Playboy* interview with Carter that seemed to undermine his morally pristine image.

At the end of the campaign, Robert Teeter again mapped out voters' perceptions of the candidates' positions and discovered that these perceptions had changed. Carter was now seen as more liberal than he had been earlier in the campaign with respect to "Traditional American Values"—the scale dominated by foreign policy concerns. Ford was seen both as more liberal on the economic-welfare scale and as more conservative on the "Traditional American Values" scale than the previous polling had suggested. In short, he was now closer to the views of the electorate at large.[111]

RESULTS

The last Gallup poll before the election showed the Ford campaign's success in associating Republican presidential strengths with Ford and its less pronounced success in associating Democratic presidential weakness with Carter. Ford received a statistically insignificant 1 point edge over Carter. But, in the end, the strategy was not quite successful enough. On election day, Ford narrowly lost, winning 48.0 percent of the popular vote against Carter's 50.1 percent. Ford won four of his eight targeted big states (New Jersey, Michigan, Illinois, and California) and accumulated 240 electoral votes to Carter's 297.[112] Carter's coattails were almost as hopelessly short as Nixon's. In the House, the balance of seats at 292–143 remained almost the same as after the 1974 elections. Seen one way, this was a real success for a losing Republican ticket; seen another, it still meant that the Democrats had held onto their impressive 1974 gains. In the Senate, incumbency was not similarly powerful, and many senators lost their reelection efforts. But in the resulting shuffle, the net effect was insignificant: at 62–38, the complexion of the Senate was no different from that before the elections.

The results offered strong evidence that no Republican realignment had taken place. Data about party identification provided still more evidence, suggesting, in fact, that the Democratic margin over the Republicans had achieved new heights. The number of independent voters had grown at the expense of the Republican Party, which could no longer claim pluralities even among business executives or college graduates. Writing in 1978, scholar Everett Carll Ladd Jr. observed that outside the presidency, the Democrats had become the "everyone party."[113]

But Ladd's exception was significant. Electoral politics were now different, at least for the presidency. Patrick Caddell, pollster to Carter as previously to McGovern, made exactly this point to the new president. Caddell disagreed with those analysts who saw in Carter's victory a revitalization of the old Democratic coalition. "Carter's performance among traditional [Democratic] groups," Caddell wrote, "is impressive when compared to McGovern's showing in 1972, but when placed in long-term historical perspective it simply cannot explain the victory." Instead, he claimed, the victory relied on inroads into traditionally Republican groups: white Protestants, better-educated white-collar workers, and rural and small-town voters.[114]

Caddell's observation implied that even in defeat, Ford, like Nixon, had won over important sections of middle America, traditionally Democratic constituencies. One was the South. Of the southern states, Ford won only Virginia, but even native son Carter could not secure a majority among southern whites; African Americans provided the margin of his victories there. Another was blue-collar America. Nationally, Carter did not restore large majorities in support of a Democratic candidate for president among working-class whites. While blue-collar urban Catholics, key members of Nixon's new majority, were less likely to vote for Ford than for Nixon, they were also less likely to vote for Carter than for Truman or Johnson.[115]

The Democratic coalition's modified fortunes reflected the inadequacy for presidential-election purposes of the bread-and-butter issues on which Democrats had built and maintained that coalition for a generation. Caddell argued that to secure reelection, Carter had to accomplish a complicated political maneuver. On the one hand, he needed to maintain support among Americans for whom tangible economic self-interest remained an important factor in motivating a Democratic vote. On the other hand, he needed to reach voters who thought differently and who cared about other issues. These younger Americans were often "social liberals and economic conservatives" and were engaged about new issues, including "the 'counterculture' and issues such as growth versus the environment."[116] As this analysis confirmed, a change had taken place among the issues around which American electoral politics revolved. But as time and experience would prove, the coalition Caddell described was difficult to assemble. It was not at all easy to simultaneously appeal to the former group, characterized by Richard Scammon and Ben Wattenberg as economic liberals and social conservatives, and to the latter group of social liberals and economic conservatives.

Although no realignment had taken place, there was a new battleground for the presidency. This battleground was more conducive to Republican success than the arena that had lasted for a generation beginning in 1932. In the end, Nixon was right. He was right to see that middle America—the vague composite of traditional Democratic strongholds—was more open than before to Republican cultivation. He was right, too, to view different issues as newly important. Economic issues mattered in national contests, but so did others. In 1960, when Nixon first tried for the presidency, the "Social Issue" did not exist, and the role of race in national politics was relatively minor. At that time, the differences between Democrats and Republicans on questions of foreign policy, while apparently significant, left largely intact a consensus about the need vigorously to wage the Cold War. By contrast, when he was president, his opposition to permissiveness and to racial liberalism and his patriotic internationalism all possessed crucial importance.

Nixon was also wrong. He played the new battleground of national politics with successful consequences for his own electoral fortunes. But in thinking about the future of American politics as dominated at all levels by a new conservative party, he was mistaken. After Nixon, there was no single majority party. While Republicans enjoyed greater success in winning the presidency, Democrats retained great support at congressional and other levels of electoral politics.

∗ CONCLUSION ∗

The Nixon administration marks a turning point in recent American history, when political conservatism achieved new dominance following a long period of liberal ascendancy. But it does not mark a realignment of American politics. The quest for a new majority did not find one; despite Nixon's success in persuading supporters of the Democratic Party to vote for his presidential candidacy in 1972, he did not enjoy any similar success in boosting the fortunes of the Republican Party as a whole. Not until the 1980s and 1990s would Republicans challenge the Democrats in terms of the proportion of Americans who preferred the party and in terms of representation in Congress. Indeed, the absence of a realignment encouraged many scholars to question the paradigm's utility in understanding electoral change.[1]

Nixon's quest for a new majority was thoughtful. With the help of his aides, he carefully analyzed social and political trends. A belief in the realigning potential of these trends animated his administration, informed the creation of public policy, and encouraged the development of many initiatives to forge better relationships with individual groups within his target constituency. To argue that the search for a new majority should be central to any understanding of the Nixon White House is not to argue that electoral expediency was the key factor that determined its policies, however. A compelling feature of the new-majority project was Nixon's belief that his political concerns matched those of the middle Americans whose votes he sought. His rhetoric about the importance of traditional values, for example, reflected a conviction that the questioning of those values in contemporary society was a destructive force. Most significantly, Nixon believed that the public would support his reinvention of internationalism in foreign policy provided that he packaged his ideas with an appropriate emphasis on their patriotic rationale. To a great extent, the silent majority that provided essential backing for his Vietnam policy became the cornerstone of his new majority. In general, then, Nixon did not need to worry that cultivation of the new majority demanded neglect of his goals in public policy.

Despite its thoughtfulness, the quest was flawed. The most infamous of these flaws involved the rawest edge of the new-majority strategy, aiming to encourage and to exploit weaknesses within the Democratic Party, even through the dirtiest of political dirty tricks—aberrations in pursuit of victory and abuses of power that would eventually bring Nixon down. But other flaws existed, too, notably Nixon's cultivation of middle America—the key to the quest, because this entity included the votes that could switch electoral dominance from the Democrats to the Republicans. Among those offering advice to Nixon were George Shultz, Jerome Rosow, and Daniel Patrick Moynihan, all of whom recommended government activism to tackle the economic concerns of upper-working-class and lower-middle-class Americans. Kevin Phillips, author of *The Emerging Republican Majority*, and Richard Scammon and Ben Wattenberg, authors of *The Real Majority*, advocated similar paths among other suggestions for achieving a majority. The most sweeping statement of how middle America's economic concerns might translate into public policy was the 1970 Rosow Report. It offered no more than the starting point for discussion, but the implications of its thinking were clear. By seriously addressing this pocketbook anxiety and workplace malaise, the Republican Party would no longer be "the party of the small-town banker," in Scammon and Wattenberg's words. Instead, the Republicans might become the party of middle America on the grounds of their programmatic ambitions. But the path indicated by the Rosow Report was a path not taken. And Nixon did not develop his plan to win a new majority in the company of Shultz, Rosow, and Moynihan. Instead of the policy thinkers, Nixon shaped his understanding of the middle-American opportunity with the electoral politicians, particularly H. R. Haldeman and Charles Colson.

Nixon did not reject the thesis that economic activism was important for winning a new majority. He agreed that electoral promise lay in becoming the "American Disraeli." His reform-oriented impulse resulted in the proposal of the Family Assistance Plan and, more broadly, in the early 1971 announcement of the new American revolution, which included welfare reform among a wealth of other measures. But his administration's commitment to reformism was uncertain, ambivalent, and apathetic. Those qualities were fatal to its prospects, and much of the agenda fell to defeat. Although the achievements were great enough for the administration to acquire retrospective credit for its reforms, the accomplishments were not sufficiently substantial to challenge at the time the Republican Party's powerfully pervasive reputation for laissez-faire conservatism, responsive to a business elite rather than to middle Americans.

Even in the hands of a more enthusiastic salesman than Nixon, ideas such as Rosow's would have been a tough sell to many Republicans. They could not welcome the economic activism that Nixon embraced. Congressional Republicans had difficulty understanding why they should support Nixon's initiatives, planned with a national constituency in mind, when they needed to win reelection by appealing to their state or district constituencies. One Republican member of Congress perfectly explained the point, the logic of which, he suggested, people at the White House failed to understand: "When I took my oath of office, I took it because millions of voters in my state had pulled a little green cloth across the booth and marked my name. My first obligation is to them. My second is to my colleagues here in this body, and *then* my obligation is to the President."[2] As legislative representatives of a party usually dedicated to the principles of economic conservatism, the lack of enthusiasm among many of them for the reformism of the new American revolution was unsurprising. The ranks of activists and loyal Republican voters—to whose support congressional politicians owed their careers—contained relatively few of the reform-minded sympathies with which Nixon flirted.[3] The consequences of the failure to achieve the agenda for reform were great. Nixon became a politician of middle America, but most elected officials within his party did not.

In failing to follow the path suggested by the Rosow Report, Nixon found other ways to mobilize a new majority. Exploiting a new climate within politics, he relied primarily on four factors: the foreign policy of assertive internationalism, wrapped in patriotism, through which Nixon identified his silent majority; mostly rhetorical attacks on his bugbear of permissiveness, which Scammon and Wattenberg handily summarized as the Social Issue; opposition to racial liberalism, which Kevin Phillips had emphasized in *The Emerging Republican Majority*; and special appeals to various groups, notably Catholics. The quest for a new majority did not therefore include what many early analysts had identified as essential to its success, domestic reformism. Particularly important among the four aspects of the quest was the defense of Nixon's foreign policy, which would produce a majority rallied around the flag and supporting Nixon's search for "peace with honor" in Vietnam.

The result of this quest was the missing realignment of American politics.

Contemporary observers watched and waited for the emergence of a new majority party, but it did not arrive. It is true that American politics assumed a more conservative cast in 1968 and thereafter; it is also true that the center of national debate during campaigns often moved away from the Economic Issue and toward the Social Issue. Nixon, moreover, stood at the forefront of this trend, attempting to stress the concerns of "patriotism, morality, religion" with a conviction that they offered a route to electoral victory. While politics changed, however, this change did not constitute a realignment. The Democratic Party remained powerfully successful, as shown both by data of partisan identification and by results for most elections below the presidency. Its presidential candidates from George McGovern to Michael Dukakis could not replicate this success; even Jimmy Carter's 1976 victory was smaller than that of the party at large. While many middle Americans were ready to vote for Republican candidates for the presidency, rather fewer did so in congressional and other elections.

The way in which the Nixon White House conducted its new-majority strategy offers explanations for these divided outcomes—Republican strength at the presidential level but Democratic strength at other levels. During his 1972 reelection campaign, Nixon saw the electoral formula of "patriotism, morality, religion" as the key to his victory. But this advantage was hard to share. These issues were frequently less powerful within individual states and districts. Bread-and-butter issues still mattered and could easily dominate a congressional contest even as questions of foreign policy moved votes for the presidency. And the great failure of the Nixon administration was its inability to create a more positive record for domestic policy making and to emphasize reform-minded goals during campaigns.

Even if the politics that made Nixon popular also emerged as important on a local level, it did not necessarily spell problems for congressional Democrats in fighting off Republican challenges. Local politicians inevitably responded to their constituencies' needs and concerns. The Nixon strategy often presupposed a willing foil who could be characterized as dedicated to the more unpopular pieces of liberalism. But in 1970 most congressional Democrats convincingly cast aside the accusations of radical liberalism, and in 1972 many disassociated themselves from McGovernism.

The success of many congressional Democrats led to the failure of the most ambitious plans for a new majority. The Democrats maintained their majorities in Congress, while more American voters still saw themselves as Democrats than as Republicans. The enduring persistence of Democratic majorities suggests another conclusion about the pursuit of the new majority. Richard Nixon assembled a presidential majority not only because of the electoral strategy that his administration designed and executed but also because of the electoral strategy that his Democratic opponent pursued. In 1972, at the height of his rhetoric about a new majority, Nixon benefited from a series of problems that plagued the Democrats. First, the process of presidential nomination left the party bitterly divided. Second, the general electorate by no means saw the winner of that process, George McGovern, as the most attractive of the party's candidates. Third, McGovern failed to emphasize his strengths and Nixon's weaknesses in a campaign that was at best lackluster. The Democratic Party clearly repeated these mistakes in subsequent presidential contests, thus allowing Republican candidates an easier route to the White House in following decades.

Nevertheless, the accomplishments of the new-majority project should not be understated. Its success did not rest on Democratic mistakes alone. The Nixon administration's perception of a political opportunity fostered a creative outpouring of ideas for finding and developing a new majority. Some of these ideas were flawed, and some would fail, but innovation and insight also resulted. Consequently, stronger ties were established between a Republican politician and sections of the American electorate that had previously viewed the party's candidates with skepticism at best. Richard Nixon in 1972 achieved a personal triumph of enormous proportions thanks, at its moment of greatest success, to the quest for a new majority.

⋆ NOTES ⋆

ABBREVIATIONS

BE Files
   White House Central Files—Subject Files: BE Business-Economics, Nixon
   Presidential Materials Project, National Archives, College Park, Md.

Buchanan Files
   White House Special Files—Staff Member and Office Files, Patrick J. Buchanan,
   Nixon Presidential Materials Project, National Archives, College Park, Md.

Colson Files
   White House Special Files—Staff Member and Office Files, Charles W. Colson, Nixon
   Presidential Materials Project, National Archives, College Park, Md.

Confidential Files
   White House Special Files—Central Files (Confidential Files), Nixon Presidential
   Materials Project, National Archives, College Park, Md.

Dent Files
   White House Special Files—Staff Member and Office Files, Harry S. Dent, Nixon
   Presidential Materials Project, National Archives, College Park, Md.

Ehrlichman Files
   White House Special Files—Staff Member and Office Files, John D. Ehrlichman,
   Nixon Presidential Materials Project, National Archives, College Park, Md.

GRFL
   Gerald R. Ford Library, Ann Arbor, Mich.

Haldeman Diaries
   H. R. Haldeman, *The Haldeman Diaries: Inside the Nixon White House*, complete
   multimedia ed. (Santa Monica, Calif.: Sony Electronic, 1994)

Haldeman Files
   White House Special Files—Staff Member and Office Files, H. R. Haldeman, Nixon
   Presidential Materials Project, National Archives, College Park, Md.

Haldeman Notes
   Papers of the Nixon White House, microfiche, part 5: *H. R. Haldeman: Notes of White
   House Meetings, 1969–1973* (Frederick, Md.: University Publications of America, 1989)

Hartmann Files
   Robert T. Hartmann Files, Gerald R. Ford Library, Ann Arbor, Mich.

Hartmann Papers
   Robert T. Hartmann Papers, Gerald R. Ford Library, Ann Arbor, Mich.

Hodgson Records
   General Records of the Department of Labor, Office of the Secretary (RG 174): Records of Secretary James D. Hodgson, 1970–72, National Archives, College Park, Md.

Jones Files
   Jerry H. Jones Files, Gerald R. Ford Library, Ann Arbor, Mich.

LC
   Manuscript Division, Library of Congress, Washington, D.C.

NPMP
   Nixon Presidential Materials Project, National Archives, College Park, Md.

NYT
   New York Times

President's Office Files
   White House Special Files—Staff Member and Office Files, President's Office Files, Nixon Presidential Materials Project, National Archives, College Park, Md.

President's Personal Files
   White House Special Files—Staff Member and Office Files, President's Personal Files, Nixon Presidential Materials Project, National Archives, College Park, Md.

Taft Papers
   Robert Taft Jr. Papers, Manuscript Division, Library of Congress, Washington, D.C.

Teeter Papers
   Robert Teeter Papers, Gerald R. Ford Library, Ann Arbor, Mich.

USN
   U.S. News and World Report

WP
   Washington Post

WSJ
   Wall Street Journal

INTRODUCTION

1. *NYT*, April 28, 1994, A2.
2. Wicker, "Richard M. Nixon," 251, 254. A challenge to the conventional wisdom about Nixon's early career nevertheless offers further evidence that the perception of Nixon as devious and manipulative was widespread; see Gellner, *Contender*.

3. Key, "Theory"; Key, "Secular Realignment"; Shafer, "Notion"; Lubell, *Future of American Politics*, 210–17. A particularly effective description of theories concerning realignments is Sundquist, *Dynamics*, 1–47.

4. See, for example, *Reporter*, November 7, 1963, 23–26; *Fortune*, September 1, 1967, 95–97, 162–66.

CHAPTER ONE

1. Goldberg, *Goldwater*, 150.

2. Goldwater, *Conscience*.

3. Leuchtenburg, *Franklin D. Roosevelt*, 4.

4. Brennan, *Turning Right*, 63; Polsby, "Strategic Considerations," 1289–92; Morris, *Dutch*, 315; Harlow memo, December 28, 1960, box 53, Dwight D. Eisenhower Diary Series, Ann Whitman File, Dwight D. Eisenhower Library, Abilene, Kansas.

5. *Harper's*, January 1965, 56–63.

6. Converse, Clausen, and Miller, "Electoral Myth," 322–28; Schlafly, *Choice*.

7. Goldwater with Casserley, *Goldwater*, 189–90.

8. Andrew, *Lyndon Johnson*, 12–16, 23–31, 64–72.

9. Free and Cantril, *Political Beliefs*, 5–6, 28, 161.

10. Goldberg, *Goldwater*, 215–16.

11. Carmines and Stimson, *Issue Evolution*, 47.

12. Faber, *Road*, 195; Goldberg, *Goldwater*, 216.

13. Faber, *Road*, 204; Jamieson, *Packaging*, 198–204; Converse, Clausen, and Miller, "Electoral Myth," 331–32.

14. Goldberg, *Goldwater*, 155.

15. Ibid., 202, 221, 229–31.

16. Brennan, *Turning Right*, 98–99.

17. Califano, *Triumph and Tragedy*, 55; Chester, Hodgson, and Page, *American Melodrama*, 271.

18. Hodgson, *World Turned Right Side Up*, 105; Black and Black, *Rise*, 209; Carter, *Politics*, 202–25.

19. Frymer and Skrentny, "Coalition-Building," 137–50; Carmines and Stimson, *Issue Evolution*, 61–106.

20. Brennan, *Turning Right*, 88–89.

21. Klinkner, *Losing Parties*, 122–23; Brennan, *Turning Right*, 102–3, 138–41.

22. *Commonweal*, March 19, 1965, 781.

23. Converse, *Dynamics*, 67–119.

24. Carter, *From George Wallace to Newt Gingrich*, 9; Weisbrot, *Freedom Bound*, 222–65.

25. Schulzinger, *Time*, 182.

26. Woods, *Fulbright*, 106–32.

27. Schulzinger, *Time*, 215–45.

28. Lunch and Sperlich, "American Public Opinion," 25–32; Converse and Schuman, "'Silent Majorities,'" 24.

29. Mayer, *Changing American Mind*, 425.

30. Davies, *From Opportunity to Entitlement*, 30–53.

31. Burner, *Making Peace*, 178–79; *NYT*, September 8, 1968, sec. 4, p. 14; *USN*, June 3, 1968, 52.

32. Stein, *Presidential Economics*, 118–22; *USN*, June 3, 1968, 54; *Harper's*, August 1969, 27–28.

33. Davies, *From Opportunity to Entitlement*, 235–43.

34. F. P. Graham, "Contemporary History," 487–502; Walker, *Popular Justice*, 195.

35. Walker, *Popular Justice*, 201–5; Califano, *Triumph and Tragedy*, 153–54, 185–88.

36. Mayer, *Changing American Mind*, 19–21, 358–59; F. P. Graham, "Contemporary History," 496.

37. *Newsweek*, November 13, 1967, 74.

38. Matusow, *Unraveling*, 275–307; Mayer, *Changing American Mind*, 385–88; Musto, *American Disease*, 251–54; Brennan, *Turning Right*, 118.

39. Blum, "Politics"; McCloskey, *American Supreme Court*, 153–66; English and the Staff of the *Daily Express*, *Divided*, 343.

40. *Saturday Evening Post*, April 20, 1968, 38–51.

41. Califano, *Triumph and Tragedy*, 254; *Saturday Evening Post*, May 4, 1968, 12, 16.

42. *NYT*, November 6, 1966, 1; Reinhard, *Republican Right*, 216–17; Rae, *Decline and Fall*, 86–87; Witcover, *Resurrection*, 175.

43. *Fortune*, September 1, 1967, 96.

44. Davies, *From Opportunity to Entitlement*, 162–73.

45. *Harper's*, February 1965, 39–45; Drucker, "Notes"; Rodgers, "Seventh American Revolution"; Gillon, *Democrats' Dilemma*, 103.

46. Rae, *Decline and Fall*, 81.

47. Lesher, *George Wallace*, 395, 413; Kazin, *Populist Persuasion*, 233–37.

48. Wills, *Nixon Agonistes*, 17.

49. *New Republic*, September 17, 1966, 12–18.

50. *Reporter*, August 10, 1967, 23.

51. Rather and Gates, *Palace Guard*, 194; *Time*, September 22, 1967, 24.

52. Hess and Broder, *Republican Establishment*, 189–93; White, *Making 1968*, 57–60, 69–73.

53. Wills, *Nixon Agonistes*, 246–47; Garment, *Crazy Rhythm*, 134.

54. Safire, *Before the Fall*, 49–50; *New Republic*, July 13, 1968, 19.

55. Wills, *Nixon Agonistes*, 73–75; *New Republic*, June 8, 1968, 4.

56. Nixon to Haldeman, November 30, 1970, box 2, President's Personal Files.

57. Dent, *Prodigal South*, 81–104; Rusher to Ashbrook, August 23, 1968, box 7, William A. Rusher Papers, LC.

58. Witcover, *Year*, 306.

59. *NYT*, August 9, 1968, 34; *New Republic*, August 17, 1968, 6; Witcover, *Year*, 355–96.

60. Burner, *Making Peace*, 213.

61. White, *Making 1968*, 189; McGinniss, *Selling*, 16–17; Converse et al., "Continuity."

62. Chester, Hodgson, and Page, *American Melodrama*, 609–10; White, *Making 1968*, 325.

63. Chester, Hodgson, and Page, *American Melodrama*, 680–84; *NYT*, September 8, 1968, sec. 4, p. 14; Schulzinger, *Time*, 243; Barone, *Our Country*, 448–49.

64. Chester, Hodgson, and Page, *American Melodrama*, 280; Lipset, "George Wallace"; Chester, Hodgson, and Page, *American Melodrama*, 652–58.

65. Thurber, *Politics*, 211–13, 311.

66. Solberg, *Hubert Humphrey*, 372–88; White, *Making 1968*, 446–47; Thurber, *Politics*, 217.

67. Lubell, *Hidden Crisis*, 153–54; Safire, *Before the Fall*, 58; Rowland Evans and Robert Novak, "Inside Report," quoted in Rutgers University Press advertisement, *Yale Review* 57 (Summer 1968): inside cover.

68. Page and Brody, "Policy Voting"; Witcover, *Year*, 396–444.

69. Converse et al., "Continuity," 1084–85, 1101–5; Hixson, *Search*, 124.

70. Small, *Presidency*, 30.

71. *USN*, September 16, 1968, 34.

CHAPTER TWO

1. White, *Making 1968*, 492; *New Republic*, October 12, 1968, 16.

2. Genovese, *Nixon Presidency*, 23.

3. *Harper's*, March 1970, 46.

4. Glad and Link, "President Nixon's Inner Circle," 26; Nixon, *RN*, 496.

5. Magruder, *American Life*, 81.

6. *New Republic*, November 16, 1968, 11.

7. Bowles, *White House*, 184–87; Genovese, *Nixon Presidency*, 35–36.

8. Drury, *Courage*, 87, 49, 184–87, 230, 244–45, 249–50; Rather and Gates, *Palace Guard*, 232.

9. *Atlantic*, April 1970, 4–14; Small, *Johnson*, 168; Stein, *Presidential Economics*, 134–35.

10. Nixon to Ehrlichman, January 25, 1969, box 1, President's Personal Files.

11. Ehrlichman, *Witness*, 239; Klein, *Making It*, 107.

12. Buchanan to Colson, January 12, 1972, box 9, Buchanan Files; Haldeman notes "on presidential approval from Roper essay," January 18, 1971, box 117, Haldeman Files.

13. Jacobs and Shapiro, "Rise"; Buchanan to Ehrlichman, Haldeman, and Colson, September 23, 1971, box 1, Buchanan Files.

14. *Atlantic*, October 1970, 51.

15. Parmet, *Richard Nixon*, 578; *Time*, August 8, 1969, 43; *Newsweek*, October 6, 1969, 28–73; *Time*, January 5, 1970, 10–17; Haldeman Diaries, December 31, 1969.

16. Hixson, *Search*, 146.

17. *Time*, August 8, 1969, 42, November 9, 1970, 68–78.

18. Hixson, *Search*, 147; Parker, "Myth"; Berg, "1968," 402.

19. *Time*, August 8, 1969, 42.

20. *USN*, November 24, 1969, 54–55; Pettigrew and Riley, "Social Psychology."

21. *Harper's*, December 1970, 109; Armbruster with Yokelson, *Forgotten Americans*, 19–172.

22. Pete Hamill, "The Revolt of the White Lower Middle Class," *New York*, April 14, 1969, 24–29.

23. Chapin to Haldeman, May 16, 1969, Flanigan to Bull, June 9, 1969, Behrens to Bull, June 10, 1969, Bosco to Cole, July 25, 1969, box 46, BE Files.

24. Shultz to Nixon, June 26, 1969, box 46, BE Files; Rosow to Shultz, April 16, 1969, box 154, General Records of the Department of Labor, Office of the Secretary (RG 174), Records of Secretary George P. Shultz, 1969–70, National Archives, College Park, Md.

25. Rosow to Shultz, April 16, 1969, box 154, Shultz Records.

26. Blount to Bull, June 18, 1969, Warren to Blount, June 16, 1969, box 46, BE Files.

27. *NYT*, June 4, 1970, 31, January 2, 1970, 16.

28. Safire to Ehrlichman, July 17, 1969, box 1, Dent Files.

29. Evans and Novak, *Nixon*, 322–23; Scammon and Wattenberg, *Real Majority*, 57; Kevin P. Phillips, "Middle America and the Emerging Republican Majority," box 8, Dent Files.

30. Phillips, "Middle America."

31. Shafer, "Notion," 40; Phillips, *Emerging*, 37.

32. Phillips, *Emerging*, 471.

33. *Commentary*, November 1969, 65–70, annotated by Phillips, box 8, Dent Files; Phillips, *Emerging*, 23–24.

34. Phillips, *Emerging*, 470, 286–89, 464.

35. *NYT*, November 22, 1969, 24; McLaughlin to Peterson, October 6, 1969, box 6, Dent Files; *New Republic*, December 20–27, 1969, 4; Rusher to Phillips, August 18, 1969, box 71, William A. Rusher Papers, LC.

36. *NYT*, December 25, 1969, 34, September 27, 1969, 14; Safire to Ehrlichman, July 25, 1969, Mitchell to Ehrlichman, July 29, 1969, box 30, Ehrlichman Files.

37. Kimball, *Nixon's Vietnam War*, 87–165.

38. *Esquire*, May 1969, 128.

39. *Newsweek*, September 8, 1969, 29; Epstein, "Krogh Files," 102.

40. *Newsweek*, September 8, 1969, 32–33; Epstein, "Krogh Files," 104.

41. Wilkinson, *From Brown to Bakke*, 116; Lubell, *Hidden Crisis*, 172–81.

42. Haldeman Notes, August 4, 1970.

43. Greenberg, *Crusaders*, 384–87; Dent, *Prodigal South*, 134.

44. Dent, *Prodigal South*, 121–56; Panetta and Gall, *Bring Us Together*, vii–x; Murphy and Gulliver, *Southern Strategy*, 65–70; Dent to Nixon, January 13, 1970, box 4, President's Office Files.

45. H. D. Graham, *Civil Rights Era*, 322–25.

46. H. D. Graham, "Richard Nixon," 103; *NYT*, September 30, 1969, 27; Kotlowski, *Nixon's Civil Rights*, 106–8; Brown to Ehrlichman and Garment, January 14, 1970, box 18, Ehrlichman Files; Hoff, *Nixon Reconsidered*, 92.

47. Hoff, *Nixon Reconsidered*, 95–97; Orfield, *Congressional Power*, 81–82, 88–90.

48. Kotlowski, "Trial," 72–82.

49. Haldeman Diaries, November 21, 1969; John Osborne notes, December 16, 1969, box 22, John Osborne Papers, LC.

50. Wicker, *One of Us*, 497.

51. Murphy and Gulliver, *Southern Strategy*, 135–39.

52. Colson to Chapin, November 25, 1969, box 39, Colson Files; *NYT*, December 7, 1969, sec. 4, p. 10; *NYT*, December 7, 1969, 60.

53. Nixon, *RN*, 414; Garment notes, July 9, 1971, box 1, Leonard Garment Papers, LC.

54. Nixon, *Public Papers* (1969), 1–4.

55. Moynihan, *Politics*, 103; Safire, *Before the Fall*, 218–31; *NYT*, August 17, 1969, sec. 4, p. 12.

56. Hoff, *Nixon Reconsidered*, 66.

57. Hodgson, *Gentleman*, 159–73.

58. Moynihan to Nixon, May 17, 1969, box 46, BE Files; Davies, *From Opportunity to Entitlement*, 219.

59. Burke and Burke, *Nixon's Good Deed*, 125–28; Wicker, *One of Us*, 418–24; Ehrlichman, *Witness*, 181–82.

60. Matusow, *Nixon's Economy*, 38–39; Stein, *Presidential Economics*, 198.

61. *Harper's*, October 1969, 92; *Congressional Quarterly Almanac* 25:108.

62. Moynihan, *Politics*, 156.

63. Burke and Burke, *Nixon's Good Deed*, 146–50.

64. Friedman and Levantrosser, *Watergate*, 326; Flippen, *Nixon*.

65. Nixon, *Six Crises*, 303, 309–11; *Harper's*, March 1970, 48.

66. Matusow, *Nixon's Economy*, 17; Thompson, *Nixon Presidency*, 93.

67. Matusow, *Nixon's Economy*, 12–43.

68. Stein, *Presidential Economics*, 137; Matusow, *Nixon's Economy*, 43–51.

69. *NYT*, July 13, 1969, 54.

70. Cole to Dent, October 6, 1969, box 8, Dent Files.

71. DeBenedetti with Chatfield, *American Ordeal*, 253.

72. Ibid., 248–58.

73. Lunch and Sperlich, "American Public Opinion," 25, 28; *Harper's*, December 1970, 49.

74. Small, *Presidency*, 70; *NYT*, November 4, 1969, 16; Nixon to Haldeman, November 30, 1970, box 2, President's Personal Files.

75. DeBenedetti with Chatfield, *American Ordeal*, 259–68; Buchanan to Nixon's files, November 30, 1972, box 2, Buchanan Files.

76. Rieder, *Canarsie*, 155–57; Appy, *Working-Class War*, 22–43; Ransford, "Blue Collar Anger."

77. Opinion Research Corporation poll, forwarded by Derge to Nixon, July 3, 1970, box 376, Haldeman Files.

78. Brown to Dent, Ehrlichman, Harlow, and Magruder, February 10, 1970, box 8, Dent Files; Klein, *Making It*, 200.

79. Small, *Presidency*, 76, 179–80.

80. *USN*, November 17, 1969, 19; Coyne, *Impudent Snobs*.

81. Haldeman Diaries, November 11, 1969; Rather and Gates, *Palace Guard*, 254–57.

82. Haldeman Diaries, November 13, 1969.

83. Evans and Novak, *Nixon*, 317–18; Haldeman Diaries, November 18, 1969.

84. Nixon to Buchanan, April 21, 1970, box 2, President's Personal Files.

85. *NYT*, November 30, 1969, sec. 4, p. 2.
86. Haldeman Diaries, November 4, 1969, January 8, 1970.
87. *USN*, January 19, 1970, 32–33.
88. *USN*, November 17, 1969, 40; Billington, *Political South*, 163.
89. *USN*, November 17, 1969, 35; John Deardourff and Doug Bailey to Morton, November 10, 1969, box 13, Elly Peterson Papers, Bentley Historical Library, University of Michigan, Ann Arbor.
90. Parmet, *Richard Nixon*, 430; Scammon and Wattenberg, *Real Majority*, 273.
91. Broder, *Party's Over*, 192.
92. *NYT*, March 1, 1970, 28, February 13, 1970, 18.
93. Haldeman Diaries, January 12, 1970.
94. *USN*, May 11, 1970, 24.
95. Haldeman Diaries, July 9, 1970.
96. Haldeman Diaries, May 4, 10, 20, 1970; *Fortune*, September 1970, 156.
97. *NYT*, May 24, 1970, sec. 4, p. 2; Colson to Nixon, May 26, 1970, box 26, Colson Files.
98. Bull to Colson, May 22, 1970, box 69, Colson Files; Huston to Harlow, Dent, Nofziger, Chotiner, Haldeman, and Ehrlichman, May 13, 1970, box 139, Haldeman Files; Jeffreys-Jones, *Peace Now!*, 202–3.
99. Small, *Presidency*, 80–81.
100. Charles W. Colson Oral History Interviews, NPMP; Jerome M. Rosow, "The Problems of Lower-Middle-Income Workers," in Levitan, *Blue-Collar Workers*, 78; Kissinger to Nixon, April 8, 1969, box 5, President's Personal Files; Colson to Haldeman, July 28, 1970, box 61, Haldeman Files; Davies, *From Opportunity to Entitlement*, 221.
101. Colson to Haldeman, July 28, 1970, box 61, Haldeman Files.
102. Rosow, "Problems," 76–94.
103. Jerome M. Rosow, "Directions for Action," in Levitan, *Blue-Collar Workers*, 342–50.
104. *USN*, July 20, 1970, 18–20; *Time*, November 9, 1970, 72.
105. Huston to Dent, August 11, 1970, box 293, Haldeman Files; Stein to Shultz, April 21, 1970, box 11, Hodgson Records.
106. Richard Nathan to Arnold Weber, n.d., box 39, Colson Files; Hodgson to Nixon, August 25, 1970, box 11, Hodgson Records.
107. Howard L. Reiter, "Blue-Collar Workers and the Future of American Politics," in Levitan, *Blue-Collar Workers*, 101.
108. Reichley, *Conservatives*, 138–48; *Atlantic*, April 1970, 14.
109. Rather and Gates, *Palace Guard*, 109.
110. *NYT Magazine*, May 17, 1970, 106.
111. *Fortune*, December 1969, 126; *Commentary*, November 1969, 69–70, box 8, Dent Files.

CHAPTER THREE

1. *National Observer*, October 26, 1970, 1, 9; *Atlantic*, October 1970, 54–56.
2. Haldeman Notes, July 10, 11, 1970.

3. *Atlantic*, October 1970, 55–56; Haldeman Diaries, September 26, 1970; Haldeman to Harlow, September 26, 1970, box 64, Haldeman Files; Nixon to Haldeman, September 21, 1970, box 2, President's Personal Files.

4. Haldeman Diaries, July 9, 1970; Haldeman to Chotiner and Dent, July 11, 1970, box 60, Haldeman Files; Haldeman Notes, July 11, 1970; *Atlantic*, October 1970, 56; Haldeman Notes, August 13, 1970.

5. Haldeman Diaries, July 11, 1970; Magruder, *American Life*, 164; Buchanan to Nixon, August 24, 1970, annotated by Nixon, box 6, President's Personal Files; Haldeman Diaries, July 11, 1970.

6. Manley, "Conservative Coalition," 86–90; Sinclair, *Congressional Realignment*, 116–24.

7. Sinclair, *Congressional Realignment*, 131–49.

8. Reichley, *Conservatives*, 80–86.

9. Evans and Novak, *Nixon*, 122–29.

10. Matusow, *Nixon's Economy*, 55–78; O'Brien, *No Final Victories*, 288.

11. Ambrose, *Nixon*, 2:391; *Time*, November 9, 1970, 68–78; *WSJ*, October 7, 1970, 1.

12. Matusow, *Nixon's Economy*, 79; Haldeman Notes, September 2, 1970.

13. *NYT*, October 23, 1970, 46.

14. Scammon and Wattenberg, *Real Majority*, 35–58.

15. Wattenberg interview.

16. Scammon and Wattenberg, *Real Majority*, 292.

17. "The Elections of '70 & '72," unsigned, n.d., box 342, Haldeman Files; Haldeman Notes, September 1, 1970; Haldeman Diaries, August 31, 1970.

18. Buchanan to Nixon, August 24, 1970, annotated by Nixon, box 6, President's Personal Files.

19. Higby to Magruder, September 14, 1970, box 64, Haldeman Files; Magruder, *American Life*, 144–45; Morton to leading Republicans, September 25, 1970, annotated by Colson, box 107, Colson Files.

20. Haldeman Diaries, August 31, 28, 1970.

21. Haldeman to Buchanan, July 13, 1970, box 61, Haldeman Files; Haldeman to Keogh, July 13, 1970, box 62, Haldeman Files; Nixon to Haldeman, September 21, 1970, box 2, President's Personal Files.

22. Haldeman to Mitchell, July 25, 1970, box 115, Haldeman Files.

23. Reichley, *Conservatives*, 80–96.

24. Nixon to Haldeman, April 13, 1970, box 138, Haldeman Files.

25. *National Observer*, October 12, 1970, 1; Evans and Novak, *Nixon*, 319.

26. Dent to Nixon, December 22, 1969, box 4, President's Office Files.

27. Bartley and Graham, *Southern Politics*, 146–47; Nixon to Rebozo, April 21, 1970, annotated by Nixon, and Nixon to Dent, April 21, 1970, box 2, President's Personal Files; Lesher, *George Wallace*, 463; Murphy and Gulliver, *Southern Strategy*, 148; Evans and Novak, *Nixon*, 321.

28. Nixon to Haldeman, December 1, 1969, box 138, Haldeman Files; *WP*, July 6, 1976, A1, A6; *WP*, July 7, 1976, A2; *Economist*, September 26, 1970, 47.

29. Brown to Ehrlichman, Finch, and Haldeman, September 8, 1970, box 66, Haldeman Files.

30. Harlow to Nixon, September 8, 1970, annotated by Nixon, box 7, President's Office Files.

31. Safire, *Before the Fall*, 318–19.

32. Nofziger to Haldeman, September 17, 1970, box 65, Haldeman Files.

33. *Economist*, October 17, 1970, 51.

34. *Congress and the Nation*, 3:256–77.

35. *Time*, October 19, 1970, 10–11; Bud Krogh to Richard Moore et al., September 25, 1970, box 65, Haldeman Files.

36. Cole to Ehrlichman, August 4, 1970, Buchanan to Ehrlichman, August 19, 1970, box 1, FG 95 Commission on Obscenity and Pornography, White House Central Files—Subject Files, NPMP.

37. Haldeman to Buchanan, September 7, 1970, Brown to Colson, September 7, 1970, Colson to Brown, September 14, 1970, box 1, FG 95 Files; Heineman, *God*, 48.

38. Safire, *Before the Fall*, 322.

39. *National Review*, January 27, 1970, 56.

40. *WSJ*, October 27, 1970, 22.

41. Flemming to Nixon, October 22, 1969, box 47, Confidential Files.

42. Sweeney, "Southern Strategies."

43. Bone, "1970 Election," 351–52; Hainsworth, "1970 Election," 303–6.

44. *NYT*, August 31, 1970, 1, 55; *WP*, August 31, 1970, A1, annotated by Haldeman, box 77, Colson Files.

45. Haldeman Diaries, September 7, 1970; transcript of Nixon and Meany, September 7, 1970, box 11, Hodgson Records; *NYT*, September 7, 1970, 1, 12.

46. Safire, *Before the Fall*, 324; *NYT*, September 7, 1970, 1, 12.

47. Colson to Haldeman, September 14, 1970, box 7, President's Office Files; Brown to Ehrlichman, September 26, 1970, box 77, Colson Files.

48. Brown to Shultz, Brown to Dent and Chotiner, Brown to Flemming, Brown to Klein, September 26, 1970, box 77, Colson Files.

49. Haldeman Notes, July 11, 1970; *USN*, April 28, 1969, 14–15; *NYT*, October 21, 1970, 54.

50. *USN*, April 28, 1969, 14–15; Chotiner to Pasztor, July 14, 1970, Colson to Magruder, September 29, 1970, box 107, Colson Files.

51. Ambrose, *Nixon*, 2:375–77; *National Observer*, March 2, 1970, 10; *Economist*, October 3, 1970, 50.

52. Coyne, *Impudent Snobs*, 360–427.

53. *WP*, September 25, 1970, A25.

54. Ehrlichman, *Witness*, 186.

55. Ehrlichman to Nixon, October 21, 1970, annotated by Nixon, box 23, Ehrlichman Files; Ehrlichman, *Witness*, 187, 194.

56. *Saturday Review*, September 26, 1970, 8, 12; Chotiner to staff secretary, October 12, 1970, box 65, Haldeman Files; Haldeman to Chotiner, September 14, 1970, box 64, Haldeman Files.

57. Haldeman to Chotiner, September 7, 1970, box 64, Haldeman Files.

58. Solberg, *Hubert Humphrey*, 418–19.

59. Haldeman to Chotiner, September 24, 1970, box 64, Haldeman Files.

60. *WSJ*, September 16, 1970, 1.

61. *NYT*, July 11, 2000, A1, A20–21; Bartley and Graham, *Southern Politics*, 157–58.

62. Transcript, WCPO-TV debate, October 3, 1970, box 304, Taft Papers.

63. *National Observer*, September 6, 1971, 5; *NYT*, November 9, 1970, 41; Bartley and Graham, *Southern Politics*, 147; Jonas and Jones, "1970 Election"; Richard, "1970 Election," 363–68; *Economist*, October 31, 1970, 44–45.

64. Coyne, *Impudent Snobs*, 368; Haldeman to Colson, September 26, 1970, box 64, Haldeman Files.

65. Haldeman Notes, July 10, 1970; Morgan to Nixon, August 27, 28, 1970, box 7, President's Office Files; Kotlowski, *Nixon's Civil Rights*, 21–43.

66. *Fortune*, September 1970, 156; Nixon, *Public Papers* (1970), 970.

67. Carter, *From George Wallace to Newt Gingrich*, 42.

68. Haldeman Diaries, July 9, 1970; Haldeman Notes, July 10, 1970; Nixon, *RN*, 244.

69. Bundy, *Tangled Web*, 179–91; *Economist*, September 26, 1970, 48.

70. Ambrose, *Nixon*, 2:388–90; Haldeman Diaries, October 8, 1970.

71. Haldeman Diaries, October 8, 1970; William J. Graham Jr. to Taft, August 18, 1970, box 303, Taft Papers.

72. Haldeman Diaries, October 4, 1970.

73. Derge to Haldeman, October 13, 1970, box 403, Haldeman Files; Haldeman Diaries, October 12, 1970.

74. Safire, *Before the Fall*, 328–34; "Suggested Basic Campaign Text," October 13, 1970, box 61, President's Personal Files.

75. *National Observer*, November 2, 1970, 4; *NYT*, October 28, 1970, 43.

76. Evans and Novak, *Nixon*, 338–39; Nixon notes, n.d., box 61, President's Personal Files; *NYT*, November 30, 1970, 41.

77. Nixon statement, October 24, 1970, box 1, FG 95 Files.

78. Evans and Novak, *Nixon*, 341–42; Chotiner to Haldeman, n.d., box 123, Haldeman Files; Haldeman Diaries, October 29, 1970; *NYT*, October 30, 1970, 68.

79. Nixon speech, October 31, 1970, box 65, Haldeman Files.

80. Magruder, *American Life*, 155; Haldeman Notes, November 2, 1970.

81. *Time*, November 16, 1970, 12; Matusow, *Nixon's Economy*, 82.

82. *USN*, November 16, 1970, 20–22, 31; *Congressional Quarterly Almanac* 26:1073, 1076; DeBenedetti with Chatfield, *American Ordeal*, 293.

83. *Congressional Quarterly Almanac* 26:1071, 1077; Haldeman to Chotiner and Dent, September 7, 1970, box 64, Haldeman Files; Haldeman Diaries, November 4, October 26, 1970.

84. *Newsweek*, November 16, 1970, 24–30; *Time*, November 16, 1970, 14–24; Haldeman Notes, November 5, 1970; Lukas, *Nightmare*, 1.

85. Haldeman Notes, November 2, 1970; Haldeman Diaries, November 4, 1970; unsigned, n.d., Finch to party leaders, November 7, 1970, box 342, Haldeman Files.

86. Burnham, *Critical Elections*, 91–134.

87. When he wrote the preface to the book's paperback edition, published in January 1970, however, Phillips stressed more unambiguously that his theory applied only to

electoral politics for the presidency (*The Emerging Republican Majority* [Garden City, N.Y.: Anchor, 1970], 22).

88. *WSJ*, November 11, 1970, annotated by Nixon, box 8, President's Office Files; *National Observer*, November 9, 1970, 16.

CHAPTER FOUR

1. Price to Nixon, November 13, 1970, box 8, President's Office Files; Safire, *Before the Fall*, 541.
2. *NYT*, April 11, 1971, sec. 6, pp. 7−9, 52−54; Dwight Chapin to Colson, March 8, 1971, box 46, Confidential Files; Schulzinger, *Time*, 289−90; DeBenedetti with Chatfield, *American Ordeal*, 298−311.
3. Matusow, *Nixon's Economy*, 84−94; *WP*, March 26, 1971, A27.
4. Evans and Novak, *Nixon*, 344−45; White, *Making 1972*, 75.
5. Lukas, *Nightmare*, 146−68; *WP*, October 30, 1997, A19.
6. Haldeman Diaries, August 9, 1970; Kazin, *Populist Persuasion*, 248−55.
7. Haldeman Diaries, June 9, 1971; Milkis, *President*; Haldeman Diaries, April 6, 9, 1971; Kutler, *Wars*, 161−84; Nixon to Haldeman, November 22, 1970, box 164, Haldeman Files; Magruder, *American Life*, 112; Nixon to Haldeman, March 2, September 21, 1970, box 2, President's Personal Files.
8. Hodgson, *World Turned Right Side Up*, 120−23.
9. Moynihan to Nixon, November 13, 1970, box 8, President's Office Files; Haldeman Diaries, November 16, 1970; Magruder, *American Life*, 87−89; Haldeman to Colson, July 13, 1970, box 273, Haldeman Files.
10. Huston to Haldeman, December 1, 1970, box 163, Haldeman Files; Haldeman to Buchanan, December 30, 1970, box 67, Haldeman Files; Phillips interview.
11. Safire, *Before the Fall*, 541; Nixon to Haldeman, December 1, 1970, box 2, President's Personal Files.
12. Transcript of Republican Governors Conference, December 14, 1970, box 91, Hartmann Papers.
13. Rosow left the administration in June 1971. Lily Mary David to Hallett, June 4, 1971, box 39, Colson Files; Hodgson memo, June 7, 1971, box 148, Hodgson Records; *Congress and the Nation*, 3:453; Noble, *Liberalism*, 89−98.
14. Reichley, *Conservatives*, 148−49; Ehrlichman to Domestic Council, October 12, 1970, box 11, Hodgson Records; *WSJ*, November 5, 1970, 22; *NYT*, January 7, 1971, 1; *NYT*, January 24, 1971, sec. 4, p. 1.
15. Nixon, *RN*, 533; *NYT*, January 23, 1971, 12.
16. Klein, *Making It*, 330.
17. Safire to Alexander Butterfield, January 27, 1971, Lee Huebner to Butterfield, January 28, 1971, box 84, President's Office Files; Buchanan to Ronald Ziegler, January 29, 1971, box 1, Buchanan Files.
18. Dent, *Prodigal South*, 244.
19. Buchanan to Haldeman, January 14, 1971, box 9, President's Office Files.
20. Garment, *Crazy Rhythm*, 212.

21. Haldeman Diaries, January 17, 1971.

22. Colson to Nixon, November 19, 1970, box 127, Colson Files; Nixon to Haldeman, November 22, 1970, box 164, Haldeman Files.

23. Transcript of Republican Governors' Conference, December 14, 1970, box 91, Hartmann Papers; Matusow, *Nixon's Economy*, 2, 88, 84; McCracken, "Economic Policy," 172.

24. Huebner memo, January 28, 1971, box 84, President's Office Files.

25. Matusow, *Nixon's Economy*, 87–104; Stein, *Presidential Economics*, 173.

26. Haldeman Notes, January 10, 1972; Colson to Ehrlichman, April 9, 1971, box 99, Colson Files.

27. Stein, *Presidential Economics*, 199.

28. Nixon, *RN*, 533; Conlan, *New Federalism*, 31–64.

29. *Congressional Quarterly Weekly Report* 29 (1971), 983; Zelizer, *Taxing*, 333; Dent to Ehrlichman, December 14, 1970, box 11, Dent Files; Ehrlichman to Nixon, January 4, 1971, box 83, President's Office Files.

30. J. R. Greene, *Limits*, 63; Harper, "Domestic Policy Making," 51.

31. Nixon to Ehrlichman, January 14, 1971, box 18, Ehrlichman Files; Buchanan to Nixon, February 16, 1971, box 1, Buchanan Files; Nathan et al., *Monitoring Revenue Sharing*.

32. Ehrlichman, *Witness*, 183–84.

33. Haldeman Diaries, June 2, 1971.

34. Reston, *Lone Star*, 389–94; Haldeman Diaries, May 13, 1971.

35. *WSJ*, November 5, 1970, 22; Cunningham and Cunningham, *Blues*, 168–86.

36. *Congress and the Nation*, 3:562–71.

37. Nathan, "Retrospective," 161–62; *Congress and the Nation*, 3:562–71; Cunningham and Cunningham, *Blues*, 190.

38. O. L. Graham, *Toward a Planned Society*, 209–13.

39. Drury, *Courage*, 312.

40. Train, "Environmental Record," 188–96; Ehrlichman to Haldeman, November 6, 1971, box 117, Haldeman Files; Hoff, *Nixon Reconsidered*, 24–29.

41. Nixon to Ehrlichman, November 30, 1970, box 164, Haldeman Files; Buchanan to Nixon, October 24, 1971, box 1, Buchanan Files; Hoff, *Nixon Reconsidered*, 27–44.

42. Milkis, *President*, 228–38; Gould, "Never."

43. Timmons to Nixon, November 16, 1970, box 83, President's Office Files; Timmons to Nixon, November 16, 1970, box 8, President's Office Files; Haldeman to Chapin, November 27, 1970, box 67, Haldeman Files; Hoff, *Nixon Reconsidered*, 80.

44. Haldeman to file, May 5, 1971, box 85, President's Office Files.

45. Safire, *Before the Fall*, 505–8; Haldeman Diaries, April 7, May 22, 1971; Ambrose, *Nixon*, 2:457, 469; Thompson, *Nixon Presidency*, 144.

46. Haldeman to Nixon, December 1, 1970, annotated by Nixon, box 83, President's Office Files; Price to Nixon, November 5, 1971, box 117, Haldeman Files; Haldeman Diaries, July 20, 1971; McWhorter to Flemming, July 26, 1971, box 46, Confidential Files.

47. Buchanan to Nixon, July 23, 1971, box 1, Buchanan Files; Schneider, *Cadres*, 150–51; Haldeman Diaries, September 13, July 9, 1971.

48. Haldeman to Chapin, November 30, 1970, box 46, Confidential Files; Millspaugh to John Evans, May 26, 1971, Millspaugh to Dent, June 4, 1971, box 2, White House Special Files—Staff Member and Office Files, Peter E. Millspaugh, NPMP.

49. CRP press release, May 11, 1971, box 12, Michigan Republican State Central Committee Papers, Bentley Historical Library, University of Michigan, Ann Arbor; Chotiner to Nixon, November 10, 1970, box 66, Haldeman Files.

50. Evans and Novak, *Nixon*, 362–64; Haldeman Diaries, December 24, 1970, January 10, 1971; Haldeman to file, January 23, 1971, box 163, Haldeman Files; Pasztor to Colson, May 3, 1971, Pasztor to Richard Richards, April 29, 1971, box 2, Colson Files; Krickus, *Pursuing*, 256–58.

51. Reichley, *Conservatives*, 149; Haldeman Diaries, July 20, November 7, 1970, October 27, 1971.

52. Ehrlichman to Nixon, August 1, 1972, box 47, Confidential Files.

53. Matusow, *Nixon's Economy*, 102–6; Weinberger and Flanigan to Nixon, June 15, 1971, annotated by Nixon, box 12, President's Office Files.

54. Matusow, *Nixon's Economy*, 126–55.

55. Stein, *Presidential Economics*, 180; Chotiner to Mitchell, July 27, August 2, 1971, box 303, Haldeman Files.

56. Chotiner to Mitchell, August 30, 1971, box 303, Haldeman Files; Tom Evans to Haldeman, August 27, 1971, box 144, Haldeman Files.

57. Ambrose, *Nixon*, 2:459; Chotiner to Mitchell, August 23, 1971, box 303, Haldeman Files.

58. Cowie, "Nixon's Class Struggle"; *NYT*, November 28, 1971, 80; I. Irving Davidson to Woods, January 18, 1972, box 7, President's Personal Files.

59. Matusow, *Nixon's Economy*, 110; Nixon to Colson, March 8, 1971, box 140, Haldeman Files.

60. Colson to Haldeman, December 17, 1970, box 67, Haldeman Files; Colson to Haldeman, February 16, 1971, Hodgson to Butterfield, December 7, 1970, box 77, Colson Files.

61. Haldeman Diaries, July 21, 1971.

62. Colson to Nixon, March 15, 1971, box 9, President's Office Files; Colson notes, n.d., box 77, Colson Files.

63. Nixon to Colson, March 8, 1971, box 140, Haldeman Files; *NYT*, December 4, 1972, 39; Ripon Society and Brown, *Jaws*, 179–82.

64. *Congress and the Nation*, 3:719.

65. Brill, *Teamsters*, 104–5; Colson to Haldeman, February 20, 1971, box 294, Haldeman Files; Ripon Society and Brown, *Jaws*, 181; Ambrose, *Nixon*, 2:491–92; White, *Making 1972*, 323.

66. Hoff, *Nixon Reconsidered*, 194–200.

67. Harris speech, December 2, 1971, box 69, Colson Files; Bundy, *Tangled Web*, 240–41.

68. McWhorter to Flemming, July 26, 1971, box 46, Confidential Files; Haldeman Notes, July 25, 1971; Haldeman Diaries, October 12, 1971; Haldeman to Frank Leonard et al., October 13, 1971, box 168, Haldeman Files.

69. Haldeman Notes, October 26, 1971; Cash, *Who*, 321–22.

70. *NYT*, December 7, 1971, 30, December 17, 1971, 15; Buchanan to Mitchell and Haldeman, December 15, 1971, box 3, Buchanan Files.

71. Haldeman Notes, December 29, 1971; *NYT*, December 30, 1971, 1, 9.

72. May and Fraser, *Campaign '72*, 296–97.

73. J. R. Greene, *Limits*, 118–19.

74. Haldeman Diaries, May 27, 1972; Teeter to Haldeman, February 2, 1972, box 1, Teeter Papers; Bundy, *Tangled Web*, 331–32; Harris speech, April 25, 1972, box 69, Colson Files.

75. Bundy, *Tangled Web*, 296–98; Small, *Johnson*, 215.

76. Nixon to Haldeman, May 7, 1972, box 75, President's Personal Files.

77. J. R. Greene, *Limits*, 96–102; Buchanan, *New Majority*, 55; Small, *Presidency*, 90.

78. Dutton, *Changing Sources*, 15–56; Andersen, "Generation," 74–77, 93–95.

79. Haldeman Diaries, November 26–29, 1970; Haldeman to Finch, December 2, 1970, box 44, White House Central Files—Staff Member and Office Files, Robert Finch, NPMP; Nixon to Finch, January 18, 1971, box 43, Finch Files; Haldeman to Finch, February 2, 1971, box 44, Finch Files; Colson to Nixon, July 28, 1971, annotated by Nixon, and Finch and Colson to Haldeman, December 9, 1970, Colson Files; Colson to Nixon, March 22, 1971, box 10, President's Office Files; Bill Gavin to Frank Shakespeare, June 14, 1971, box 46, Confidential Files; Finch to Nixon, April 8, 1971, annotated by Nixon, box 44, Finch Files; Hallett to Colson (three memos), August 10, 1971, box 7, Colson Files; Colson to James McLane, August 10, 1971, McLane to Nixon, August 25, December 7, 1971, Hallett to Colson, n.d., box 125, Colson Files.

80. *NYT*, December 26, 1971, 45.

81. Haldeman Diaries, December 24, 1970, April 22, 1971.

82. *Congress and the Nation*, 3:277–86; Krogh to Ehrlichman, September 27, 1972, box 5, White House Special Files—Staff Member and Office Files, Egil M. Krogh, NPMP.

83. *Congress and the Nation*, 3:256–58; Krogh to Nixon, March 20, 1972, box 1, White House Central Files—Subject Files, FG 308 Commission on Marihuana and Drug Abuse, NPMP.

84. Dean to Ehrlichman, Colson, and Ziegler, May 10, 1971, Bill Hopkins memo, April 5, 1972, box 115, Haldeman Files.

85. Haldeman Diaries, March 31, 1971; Schell, *Time*, 147–48; Haldeman Diaries, April 1, 1971.

86. Jon Huntsman to Buchanan, April 15, 1971, box 3, Buchanan Files; Haldeman Diaries, April 1, 1971; Hoff, *Nixon Reconsidered*, 222; Appy, *Working-Class War*, 277.

87. Colson to Haldeman, April 2, 1971, Cashen to Colson, April 2, 1971, box 2, Colson Files.

88. Colson to Nixon's file, January 28, 1972, box 24, Colson Files.

89. Nixon to Ehrlichman, January 28, 1972, box 20, Ehrlichman Files.

90. White, *Making 1972*, 112–14; Wilkinson, *From Brown to Bakke*, 134–54, 193–200, 216–22.

91. Teeter to Haldeman, February 2, 1972, box 1, Teeter Papers; Armstrong to Nixon, July 30, 1971, box 47, Confidential Files; Charles W. Colson Oral History Interviews, NPMP; Wicker, *One of Us*, 397.

92. Buchanan to Nixon's file, March 29, 1972, box 2, Buchanan Files; Nixon to Ehrlichman, February 8, 1971, box 3, President's Personal Files; Morgan to staff secretary, January 14, 1972, annotated by Nixon, box 16, President's Personal Files.

93. Morgan to Nixon, May 24, 1971, box 11, President's Office Files.

94. Magruder to Mitchell, January 28, 1972, box 401, Haldeman Files; Robert Teeter to Mitchell, April 11, 1972, box 1, Teeter Papers.

95. Nixon to Ehrlichman, May 17, 1972, box 24, Ehrlichman Files; Carter, *Politics*, 422–26; Reichley, *Conservatives*, 197–98.

96. Carter, *Politics*, 426, 431–34, 437, 445; Nixon to Ehrlichman, May 17, 1972, box 24, Ehrlichman Files; Reichley, *Conservatives*, 197–99.

97. Nixon to Ehrlichman, January 28, 1972, box 20, Ehrlichman Files; Wilkinson, *From Brown to Bakke*, 147–49; Gary Orfield, "Turning Back to Segregation," in Orfield, Eaton, and Harvard Project, *Dismantling*, 9–13.

98. Nixon to Ehrlichman, January 28, 1972, box 20, Ehrlichman Files.

99. Quadagno, *Color*, 107–10.

100. Haldeman Diaries, March 18, November 7, 13, December 2, 1970, January 2, 1971.

101. Gary Orfield, "Segregated Housing and School Resegregation," in Orfield, Eaton, and Harvard Project, *Dismantling*, 310–12; Massey and Denton, *American Apartheid*, 190–91; Ehrlichman, *Witness*, 196.

102. Buckley, *If Men Were Angels*, 22–23; Buchanan to Colson and Rhatican, February 3, 1972, box 7, Colson Files; Buchanan to Colson, January 12, 1972, box 9, Buchanan Files; Larry Goldberg to Colson, February 12, 1972, box 7, Colson Files.

103. Buchanan to Cole, August 31, 1972, box 2, Buchanan Files; Nixon, *Public Papers* (1971), 11–12, 464, 973.

104. Haldeman Diaries, December 15, 1970, February 7, August 10, 1971, September 16, 1972; Haldeman to Nixon's file, March 9, 1972, box 163, Haldeman Files; Martin, *With God*, 146; Prendergast, *Catholic Voter*, 155; Nixon to Haldeman, November 22, 1970, box 164, Haldeman Files.

105. McGreevey, *Parish Boundaries*, 215, 234–36; Prendergast, *Catholic Voter*, 159; Krickus, *Pursuing*, 284–85; Safire, *Before the Fall*, 554.

106. Prendergast, *Catholic Voter*, 156–57; Safire, *Before the Fall*, 553–59; Haldeman Diaries, August 18, 1970.

107. Moynihan to Safire, November 7, 1969, Colson to Ehrlichman, April 6, 1970, Colson to Nixon, April 10, 1970, box 1, White House Central Files—Subject Files, FG 273 President's Commission on School Finance, NPMP; John F. Evans to file, May 4, 1971, box 85, President's Office Files.

108. Thomas Patrick Melady to Buchanan, September 27, 1971, Buchanan to Ehrlichman, Haldeman, and Colson, September 29, 1971, box 46, Colson Files; Nixon, *Public Papers* (1971), 894–95; Melady to Buchanan, September 27, 1971, box 46, Colson Files.

109. Flanigan to Nixon, January 21, 1972, box 37, White House Special Files—Staff Member and Office Files, Special Staff Files, NPMP; Lew Engman to Nixon, April 19, 1972, and Engman to Cole, May 27, 1972, box 1, FG 273 Files; Haldeman Diaries,

June 22, 1972; Strachan to Ziegler, April 12, 1972, box 302, Haldeman Files; Krickus, *Pursuing*, 390.

110. Morey to Cole and Harper, September 16, 1971, box 338, Haldeman Files.

111. Buchanan to Ehrlichman, Haldeman, and Colson, September 23, 1971, box 3, Buchanan Files.

112. Colson to Buchanan, October 20, 1971, box 46, Colson Files; Colson to Nixon, January 20, 1972, Bruce Kehrli to Colson and Haldeman, January 10, 1972, box 9, Colson Files; Colson to Ehrlichman, April 12, 1972, box 7, Colson Files.

113. Colson, *Born Again*, 64.

114. Haldeman Diaries, March 30, April 3, 1972; Colson to Nixon, April 6, 1972, box 46, Colson Files; McGreevey, *Parish Boundaries*, 237–38.

115. White, *Making 1972*, 306; Haldeman Diaries, April 4, 6, 1972.

116. Nixon, *Public Papers* (1971), 500; Safire, *Before the Fall*, 558.

117. Teeter to Haldeman, August 11, 1972, box 1, Teeter Papers.

118. Buchanan to Hauser, January 10, 1972, box 2, Buchanan Files.

119. Kotlowski, *Nixon's Civil Rights*, 222–58.

120. Haldeman Diaries, July 21, 1969; Magruder, *American Life*, 196; Haldeman Diaries, November 25, December 5, 1970.

121. Chotiner to Mitchell, April 13, 1971, box 303, Haldeman Files.

122. Small, *Presidency*, 254–55; Genovese, *Nixon Presidency*, 183.

123. Thomas W. Benham to Haldeman, November 21, 1971, May 17, 1972, box 281, Haldeman Files; Carter, *Politics*, 384–92, 432–33.

124. Carter, *Politics*, 445–50; Haldeman Diaries, July 14, 20, 25 1972.

125. Reichley, *Conservatives*, 144–51, 160–64; Hoff, *Nixon Reconsidered*, 138.

126. Buchanan and Khachigian to Haldeman, June 18, 1972, box 299, Haldeman Files; Gordon Strachan to Ziegler, April 12, 1972, box 302, Haldeman Files.

127. Zelizer, *Taxing*, 317–46.

128. *NYT*, January 10, 1972, 21.

129. Magruder, *American Life*, 163.

CHAPTER FIVE

1. White, *Making 1972*, 403.

2. Davis, *President*, 128–30, 136; Cronin and Genovese, *Paradoxes*, 210; David Parker to Haldeman, August 8, 1972, box 400, Haldeman Files; Woodward and Bernstein, *All the President's Men*, 29.

3. Haldeman Diaries, January 17, June 12, 1972; Ehrlichman, *Witness*, 232–33 Haldeman Diaries.

4. Shafer, *Quiet Revolution*; May and Fraser, *Campaign '72*, 4.

5. Parmet, *Democrats*, 300–304.

6. Strober and Strober, *Nixon*, 262; Radosh, *Divided*, 133–80.

7. Heineman, *God*, 60; White, *Making 1972*, 165–71.

8. Buchanan to MacGregor and Haldeman, July 14, 1972, box 299, Haldeman Files;

Safire, *Before the Fall*, 641; Parmet, *Democrats*, 300–304; *NYT*, June 27, 1972, 23; Nixon to Mitchell, June 6, 1972, Nixon to Buchanan, June 10, 1972, box 4, President's Personal Files.

9. Gillon, *Democrats' Dilemma*, 137.

10. *NYT*, August 23, 1972, 1, 26; *National Observer*, September 2, 1972, 6; *NYT*, August 3, 1972, 20.

11. White, *Making 1972*, 257–58.

12. Howard to staff secretary, August 2, 1972, box 4, Howard Files; Dent to file, December 11, 1970, box 83, President's Office Files; Richard K. Cook to Timmons, October 12, 1972, box 19, President's Office Files.

13. Ford, *Time*, 96; Haldeman Diaries, July 21, 1972; Colson to Ford, July 21, 1972, box 16, Colson Files.

14. Colson to Malek, October 10, 1972, box 48, Colson Files.

15. Milkis, *President*, 228.

16. White, *Making 1972*, 93–113; *NYT*, March 22, 1972, 1, 34.

17. White, *Making 1972*, 341–51; Haldeman to Ehrlichman, March 17, 1972, box 18, Ehrlichman Files; Hallett to Colson, July 21, 1972, box 115, Colson Files; Haldeman Diaries, June 14, 1972; Rhatican to Colson and Malek, June 6, 1972, Rhatican to Colson, August 7, 1972, box 10, Colson Files.

18. Don Mosiman to Malek, November 30, 1972, Charles D. Ross report, November 28, 1972, box 276, Haldeman Files.

19. UPI article, April 17, 1972, box 5, Colson Files.

20. Balzano to Colson, April 3, 1972, box 5, Colson Files; Harry J. Hogan to Balzano, April 21, 1972, box 1, White House Central Files—Staff Member and Office Files, Michael Balzano, NPMP; Balzano to Colson, n.d., April 18, 1972, box 5, Balzano Files; Colson to Balzano, May 24, 1972, box 5, Colson Files; *NYT*, October 8, 1972, 50.

21. Krickus, *Pursuing*, 255; B. Greene, *Running*, 136–39; *NYT*, September 27, 1972, 35.

22. Pasztor to Dent, May 24, 1972, Pasztor and John F. Burgess to Colson, June 9, 1972, Balzano to Nixon, August 2, 1972, box 5, Balzano Files; *NYT*, September 24, 1972, 46.

23. Nixon to Ehrlichman, November 30, 1970, box 164, Haldeman Files.

24. Unsigned, n.d., box 8, Buchanan Files; *WP*, July 17, 1970, A17, July 5, 1972, A3.

25. *NYT*, June 12, 1972, 30.

26. Levy and Kramer, *Ethnic Factor*, 95–122; Ambrose, *Nixon*, 2:583, 616; Parmet, *Democrats*, 304.

27. Magruder, *American Life*, 182, 185; *NYT*, October 17, 1972, 50, 29; Nixon, *RN*, 678; B. Greene, *Running*, 203; John Osborne interview with Henry Cashen, December 14, 1972, box 22, John Osborne Papers, LC.

28. *NYT*, October 22, 1972, 50.

29. Ibid., December 5, 1971, 42, June 27, 1972, 18.

30. Haldeman Diaries, July 21, 1972.

31. News summary, July 21, 1972, annotated by Nixon, box 41, President's Office Files; Haldeman Diaries, July 21, 1972; Colson to staff secretary, July 31, 1972, box 9, Colson

Files; Colson to Howard, August 28, 1972, box 8, Colson Files; Republican National Committee, "Answerdesk '72," October 3, 1972, box 313, Taft Papers.

32. Buchanan and Khachigian to Haldeman and MacGregor, July 7, 1972, box 99, Colson Files.

33. Haldeman Diaries, June 12, 1972; Buchanan to Nixon, October 23, 1972, box 300, Haldeman Files; E. D. Failor to MacGregor, July 5, 1972, box 55, Colson Files; Haldeman memo, July 25, 1972, box 137, Haldeman Files; Jamieson, *Packaging*, 301–3; transcript, Colson conversation with Scammon, September 30, 1972, box 104, Haldeman Files; Michael R. Gardner to Colson, July 7, 1972, box 55, Colson Files; Colson to Connally, July 31, 1972, box 55, Colson Files.

34. Nixon to Connally, July 24, 1972, box 4, President's Personal Files; *NYT*, November 13, 1972, 27; *Nation*, December 4, 1972, 559–61.

35. Nixon, *Public Papers* (1972), 838.

36. Nixon, *RN*, 669; Haldeman Diaries, September 26, 1972; *WP*, March 21, 1973, A6; Dent, *Prodigal South*, 223; Price to file, November 5, 1971, box 119, President's Personal Files.

37. John E. Niedecker to file, September 12, 14, 18, 19, 21, 1972, box 89, President's Office Files.

38. Haldeman to Colson, September 21, 1972, box 6, Buchanan Files; Nofziger, *Nofziger*, 151.

39. Haldeman Diaries, November 3, 1971, January 24, 1972; Krogh to Ehrlichman, July 18, 1972, Ehrlichman to Nixon, July 20, 1972, annotated by Nixon, box 18, President's Office Files; Krogh to Cole, September 13, 1972, box 5, White House Special Files— Staff Member and Office Files, Egil M. Krogh, NPMP; Cole to Nixon, September 14, 1972, box 318, Haldeman Files.

40. Colson to Ehrlichman, August 9, 1972, Colson to Gardner, August 12, 1972, box 55, Colson Files; Dent to Nixon, October 19, 1972, box 19, President's Office Files; Colson notes, July 28, 1972, box 16, Colson Files; Haldeman to Colson, August 7, 1972, box 112, Haldeman Files.

41. J. Marsh Thomson to Agnew, September 22, 1972, box 9, subseries 8, series 3, Agnew Papers.

42. Bartley and Graham, *Southern Politics*, 177–78; Dent to Nixon, December 2, November 27, 1970, box 8, President's Office Files; Dent to Mitchell, March 8, 1972, Timmons to Dent, March 18, 1972, box 47, Confidential Files.

43. Bass and DeVries, *Transformation*, 355, 360; Bartley and Graham, *Southern Politics*, 177.

44. Dent to file, August 7, 1972, box 89, President's Office Files; Richard D. Obenshain to Colson, August 9, 1972, Colson to Dent, August 16, 1972, Dent to Colson, August 17, 1972, Howard to Obenshain, August 18, 1972, box 115, Colson Files.

45. Chapin to Colson, October 4, 1972, box 55, Colson Files; Colson to MacGregor, July 20, 1972, box 48, Colson Files; Colson to Christian, October 10, 20, 1972, box 55, Colson Files; Buchanan to Haldeman, Ehrlichman, and Colson, October 26, 1972, box 70, Colson Files.

46. Nixon to Connally, July 24, 1972, box 4, President's Personal Files.

47. Shultz to file, August 8, 1972, box 89, President's Office Files; White, *Making 1972*, 319–20, 467–68; Ripon Society and Brown, *Jaws*, 173.

48. Hallett to Colson, August 10, 1972, box 99, Colson Files; McGovern, *American Journey*, 34; *WP*, March 6, 1973, A20; Black and Black, *Rise*.

49. Art Amolsch to Edward D. Failor and Albert E. Abrahams, October 26, 1972, box 345, Haldeman Files.

50. Barone, *Our Country*, 507.

51. Wilson and Williams, "Mr. Nixon's Triumph," 188–91.

52. Matusow, *Nixon's Economy*, 189; Stein to Nixon, July 20, 1972, annotated by Nixon, box 18, President's Office Files; Peter Flanigan and Caspar Weinberger to Nixon, June 15, 1971, annotated by Nixon, box 12, President's Office Files; Nixon to Ehrlichman, June 2, 1971, box 3, President's Personal Files; Peter Peterson to Nixon, October 24, 1972, box 19, President's Office Files.

53. Matusow, *Nixon's Economy*, 212–13; Haldeman Diaries, July 6, 1972; Garrish to Porter, June 22, 1972, box 1, Teeter Papers; Peterson to Nixon, August 19, 1972, box 69, Colson Files; Howard to Colson, September 27, 1972, box 99, Colson Files; MacGregor to Haldeman, June 29, 1972, box 117, Haldeman Files; Peterson to Nixon, August 19, 1972, box 69, Colson Files; Teeter to MacGregor, July 15, September 28, 1972, box 1, Teeter Papers.

54. Haldeman Diaries, October 10, 1972; Haldeman Notes, July 21, 1972; Buchanan to Nixon, August 6, 1972, box 117, Haldeman Files.

55. Haldeman Notes, August 8, 18, 1972; Nixon, *Public Papers* (1972), 1115–20, 1121–27, 1129–34; Patrick E. O'Donnell to administration spokespeople, September 15, 1972, Colson to administration spokespeople, September 29, 1972, box 312, Taft Papers.

56. Matusow, *Nixon's Economy*, 204–6.

57. Haldeman Diaries, September 6, October 14, 1972; unsigned to Reagan and Rockefeller, August 18, 1972, box 2, Buchanan Files.

58. Belz, *Equality Transformed*, 95; *NYT Magazine*, September 10, 1972, 29.

59. Belz, *Equality Transformed*, 93–97.

60. Price, *With Nixon*, 121–22; Haldeman Diaries, October 10, July 6, October 14, 1972.

61. Haldeman Diaries, June 2, 9, 16, July 17, 1972; Ehrlichman, *Witness*, 179; Nixon to Haldeman, August 14, 1972, box 4, President's Personal Files; Haldeman to Colson, September 21, 1972, box 6, Buchanan Files.

62. O'Brien, *No Final Victories*, 340; Parmet, *Democrats*, 304; McGovern, *American Journey*, 140; Buchanan to Cole, August 31, 1972, box 2, Buchanan Files; Ambrose, *Nixon*, 2:620.

63. Dougherty, *Goodbye*, 237; May and Fraser, *Campaign '72*, 235.

64. B. Greene, *Running*, 241; May and Fraser, *Campaign '72*, 229.

65. McGovern, *American Journey*, 109–18; Republican National Committee talking paper, October 23, 1972, box 313, Taft Papers.

66. Haldeman Diaries, June 16, 1972; Harris article, July 17, 1972, box 399, Haldeman Files; Jamieson, *Packaging*, 318; Teeter to Haldeman, August 15, 1972, box 1, Teeter Papers; *NYT*, September 27, 1972, 34.

67. Ambrose, *Nixon*, 2:602; DeBenedetti with Chatfield, *American Ordeal*, 341; *NYT*, October 19, 1972, 53.

68. Jamieson, *Packaging*, 295; Barone, *Our Country*, 507; Ehrlichman notes, October 17, 1972, in *Papers of the Nixon White House*, microfiche, part 3, *John Ehrlichman*; MacGregor form letter, October 17, 1972, box 312, Taft Papers.

69. DeBenedetti with Chatfield, *American Ordeal*, 341; Teeter to Haldeman, August 15, 1972, box 1, Teeter Papers; Nixon, *Public Papers* (1972), 978, 1019, 1061, 1118–19, 1126; Ambrose, *Nixon*, 2:620.

70. MacGregor to file, March 8, 1972, box 89, President's Office Files; Colson notes, August 3, 1972, box 16, Colson Files; Ehrlichman memo, August 25, 1972, box 28, Ehrlichman Files; news summary, August 3, 1972, annotated by Nixon, box 42, President's Office Files.

71. Haldeman Diaries, October 10, 1972; White, *Making 1972*, 291–92; Haldeman Diaries, September 12, 1972; Haldeman memo, September 12, 1972, box 112, Haldeman Files; Magruder to MacGregor, September 15 1972, box 320, Haldeman Files.

72. Haldeman Notes, June 9, 1972; Mayer, *Changing American Mind*, 36, 385, 41–42, 38, 392, 132.

73. Nixon, *Public Papers* (1972), 1041, 997–1000, 1057.

74. Lubell, *Future while It Happened*, 84; Rieder, *Canarsie*, 158; *NYT*, September 21, 1972, 40.

75. Lubell, *Future while It Happened*, 58, 95; Stewart, *One Last Chance*, 21.

76. Lubell, *Future while It Happened*, 114; Rieder, *Canarsie*, 251.

77. Steve Karalekas to Colson, October 25, 1972, Mel Stephens to Colson, October 27, 1972, Rhatican to Colson, October 26, 1972, box 18, Colson Files.

78. Colson to surrogates, October 23, 1972, box 70, Colson Files; conversation transcript, October 31, 1972, box 55, Colson Files.

79. Nixon, *Public Papers* (1972), 1138–39.

80. White, *Making 1972*, 365; A. H. Miller et al., "Majority Party," 768; Nixon, *RN*, 716–17.

81. W. E. Miller and Traugott, *Data Sourcebook*, 316; Stanley and Niemi, *Vital Statistics*, 77.

82. Stanley and Niemi, *Vital Statistics*, 90; W. E. Miller and Traugott, *Data Sourcebook*, 336; Stewart, *One Last Chance*, 18.

83. Osborne interview with Diane Sawyer, June 1, 1978, box 22, John Osborne Papers.

84. Barone, *Our Country*, 509; White, *Making 1972*, 398–400; Phillips interview; Phillips, *Post-Conservative America*, 57–59.

85. Steeper and Teeter, "Comment," 806–13.

86. May and Fraser, *Campaign '72*, 233.

87. Memo, Buchanan to Ziegler, January 29, 1971, "January 1971," box 1, Buchanan Files.

CHAPTER SIX

1. Woods to Nixon, March 7, 1973, box 15, President's Personal Files.

2. Barone, *Our Country*, 517.

3. Rather and Gates, *Palace Guard*, 355–56; Colson, *Born Again*, 91, 96–97.

4. Haldeman memo, December 12, 1972, box 112, Haldeman Files.

5. Buchanan to Nixon, November 10, 1972, in Oudes, *From the President*, 561–62.

6. Haldeman memo, November 12, 1972, box 112, Haldeman Files; Haldeman Diaries, November 11, 1972; Colson notes, November 13, 1972, box 16, Colson Files; Rather and Gates, *Palace Guard*, 350–51.

7. Strober and Strober, *Nixon*, 271; Haldeman with DiMona, *Ends*, 175.

8. Nixon to Haldeman, January 1, 1973, box 4, President's Personal Files; Haldeman to Magruder, November 13, 1972, box 125, Haldeman Files; Haldeman to Colson, January 5, 1973, box 273, Haldeman Files.

9. Colson article, January 10, 1973, box 17, Colson Files.

10. Buchanan to file, November 30, 1972, box 2, Buchanan Files; Haldeman talking points, December 15, 1972, box 168, Haldeman Files.

11. Buchanan, *New Majority*, 77.

12. Haldeman Diaries, November 10, 15, 1972; *WP*, February 15, 1973, A21, June 25, 1986, D3; Haldeman Diaries, December 10, 1972.

13. Hallett to Colson, November 30, 1972, Colson to Buchanan, December 8, 1972, box 5, Colson Files.

14. *Harper's*, June 1973, 66–70.

15. Wydler to Bush, March 2, 1973, box 48, Confidential Files; Haldeman memo, November 13, 1972, box 112, Haldeman Files; Haldeman Diaries, November 13, 1972.

16. Buchanan to Haldeman, December 21, 1972, box 2, Buchanan Files; Haldeman Diaries, November 17, 1972; Harris press release, January 25, 1972, box 17, Colson Files.

17. Haldeman Diaries, December 1, 5, 1972.

18. Reichley interview with Bud Shuster, October 6, 1977, box 2, A. James Reichley Interviews, GRFL; Reichley interview with William Timmons, November 29, 1977, box 1, Reichley Interviews; Rusher, *Rise*, 251; Hodgson, *World Turned Right Side Up*, 123–27.

19. Haldeman Diaries, December 2, 1972; *WSJ*, April 13, 1973, 1, 20, March 30, 1973, 1; Reichley interview with Joe Waggoner, February 8, 1978, box 2, Reichley Interviews; Hodgson, *World Turned Right Side Up*, 293–94, 328.

20. Haldeman to Timmons, December 16, 1972, box 168, Haldeman Files.

21. Nixon, *RN*, 769; Timmons to file, November 28, 1972, box 90, President's Office Files; Haldeman memo, January 8, 1973, box 112, Haldeman Files; Buchanan to file, November 30, 1972, box 2, Buchanan Files; Ehrlichman notes, November 14, 1972, in *Papers of the Nixon White House*, microfiche, part 3, *John Ehrlichman*.

22. Ripon Society and Brown, *Jaws*, 236–39.

23. Howard to Haldeman, February 20, 1973, box 6, Howard Files; Howard to Haldeman, April 5, 1973, box 5, Howard Files.

24. Reston, *Lone Star*, 453–54; Woods to Nixon, June 19, 1973, box 6, President's Personal Files.

25. Colson to Howard, December 22, 1972, box 8, Colson Files; Bush to Nixon, March 8, 1973, annotated by Nixon, and Kehrli to Haldeman, March 13, 1973, box 21, Presi-

dent's Office Files; *WP*, May 15, 1973, A4; Ed DeBolt and Jim Galbraith to Bush, February 22, 1973, box 20, President's Office Files; Flanigan to Nixon, February 26 1973, box 47, Confidential Files.

26. Agnew speech, December 12, 1972, box 10, subseries 7, series 3, Agnew Papers.

27. Safire to Nixon, December 22, 1972, box 6, Howard Files.

28. Ambrose, *Nixon*, 3:12–13.

29. Nathan, *Plot*, 63–84.

30. Sundquist, *Decline*, 1.

31. Small, *Presidency*, 200–201.

32. Nathan, *Plot*, 67–69; Hoff, *Nixon Reconsidered*, 74; Genovese, *Nixon Presidency*, 31.

33. Jones, *Presidency*.

34. Matusow, *Nixon's Economy*, 219–20.

35. Stein, *Presidential Economics*, 182–83; Matusow, *Nixon's Economy*, 216–34, 241–55.

36. Kunz, *Butter and Guns*, 223–42.

37. Higby to Haldeman, March 13, 1973, Teeter to Higby, March 19, 1973, box 170, Haldeman Files.

38. Harris press release, February 26, 1973, Market Opinion Research press release, March 21, 1973, box 170, Haldeman Files.

39. Howard to Haig, May 7, 1973, box 5, Howard Files; Matusow, *Nixon's Economy*, 215–19.

40. Crowley, *Nixon Off the Record*, 149.

41. Safire, *Before the Fall*, 549.

42. *Monday* (Republican National Committee newsletter), November 20, 1972, box 92, Hartmann Papers; *NYT*, February 28, 1973, 14; Republican National Committee leaflet, n.d., box A184, Gerald R. Ford Congressional Papers, GRFL.

43. Bush with Gold, *Looking Forward*, 121, 123; Bush to Ford (form letter), October 1, 1973, box 90, Hartmann Papers.

44. Unsigned memo, May 15, 1973, box 90, Hartmann Papers.

45. Cohen and Witcover, *Heartbeat*.

46. Nixon, *RN*, 925–26; Cannon, *Time and Chance*, 210–11.

47. *Republican Congressional Committee Newsletter*, September 17, 1973, box 229, Gerald R. Ford Vice-Presidential Papers, GRFL.

48. Kehrli to Parker, February 16, 1973, box 47, Confidential Files; Bush to Nixon, October 1, 1973, box 23, President's Office Files; *WP*, December 2, 1973, A8.

49. Lamis, *Two-Party South*, 154–55; Roland, *Improbable Era*, 95–96; Bush to Nixon, October 1, 1973, box 23, President's Office Files.

50. Bush to Nixon, December 10, 1973, box 47, Confidential Files; transcript, press conference with Brock, Bush, Michel, December 11, 1973, box 229, Ford Vice-Presidential Papers; Tom Korologos to file, February 13, 1974, box 93, President's Office Files; Parker agenda, February 21, 1974, box 26, President's Office Files.

51. *WP*, December 2, 1973, A1, A8.

52. Crowley, *Nixon in Winter*, 306.

53. Transcript, Ford interview, June 30, 1975, box 41, James M. Cannon Files, GRFL.

54. J. R. Greene, *Presidency*, 67–72.

55. Ibid., 55; Osborne, *White House Watch*, 24–25; Pat Lindh to Armstrong, September 18, 1974, box 1, Political Affairs, White House Central Files Subject File, GRFL.

56. Stanley and Niemi, *Vital Statistics*, 90; *USN*, November 18, 1974, 20; *Congressional Quarterly Almanac* 30:839; cabinet minutes, January 8, 1975, box 3, James E. Connor Files, GRFL. The Senate race in New Hampshire was undecided; the rerun in September 1975 was won by the Democratic candidate.

57. Anderson to Hartmann, December 9, 1974, box 3, John T. Calkins Files, GRFL.

58. *Washington Star*, February 16, 1975, box 149, Hartmann Papers.

59. J. R. Greene, *Presidency*, 67–81.

60. Barone, *Our Country*, 541; Mayhew, *Divided*, 66–67.

61. Unsigned campaign plan, August 29, 1975, box 23, Jones Files.

62. Teeter and Spencer to Cheney, November 12, 1975, box 5, A. James Reichley Files, GRFL.

63. Rusher, *Rise*, 264; Gottfried, *Conservative Movement*, 98–99.

64. Barone, *Our Country*, 531–32; Roger W. Hooker Jr. to Cannon, March 19, 1975, David A. Cole to Calkins, March 25, 1975, box 27, Hartmann Files; Rockefeller interview by Hartmann, December 2, 1978, box 199, Hartmann Papers.

65. Cheney to Ford, June 13, 1975, box 19, Richard B. Cheney Files, GRFL.

66. Himmelstein, *To the Right*, 80–151.

67. Rusher, *Making*; Rusher, *Rise*, 263–64.

68. Polls report, April 1975, box 163, Hartmann Papers; Crawford, *Thunder*, 124.

69. *WP*, March 14, 1975, A9.

70. *New Guard*, April 1975, box 21, Agnes M. Waldron Files, GRFL.

71. Rusher, *Rise*, 272, 275–76.

72. *Right Report*, May 19, 1975, box 28, Hartmann Files.

73. Slight to Jones, June 6, 1975, box 16, Cheney Files.

74. J. R. Greene, *Presidency*, 97.

75. Thorsness to Callaway, October 29, November 19, 1975, box 5, Rogers C. B. Morton Files, GRFL; Callaway to Ford, November 28, 1975, box 14, Cheney Files; Jones to Cheney, November 21, 1975, box 19, Jones Files; Callaway to Ford, January 12, 1976, box 14, Cheney Files; J. R. Greene, *Presidency*, 97–98.

76. Unsigned campaign plan, August 29, 1975, box 23, Jones Files; Free to Stuart Spencer, December 2, 1975, box 4, Foster Chanock Files, GRFL.

77. Hartmann to Ford, October 25, 1975, box 39, Hartmann Files.

78. Kolodny, "1976 Republican Nomination," 590; Jones to Rumsfeld and Cheney, September 26, 1975, box 25, Jones Files.

79. Witcover, *Marathon*, 398.

80. Ibid., 401–2; J. R. Greene, *Presidency*, 164.

81. Wayne Valis for record, March 10, 1976, box 25, Jones Files.

82. J. R. Greene, *Presidency*, 164–65.

83. Raoul-Duval notes, April 19, 1976, box 14, Michael Raoul-Duval Papers, GRFL.

84. Spencer and Kaye to Morton, May 5, 1976, box B10, President Ford Committee Records, GRFL; Witcover, *Marathon*, 459–60.

85. Godfrey Sperling interview, *Christian Science Monitor*, June 3, 1976, box 23, Raoul-

Duval Papers; unsigned, n.d., box 25, Jones Files; Morton to Ford, May 11, 1976, box 15, Cheney Files.

86. Morton to Ford, May 11, 1976, box 15, Cheney Files; Citizens for Reagan news release, July 6, 1976, box 23, Raoul-Duval Papers.

87. Chanock to Cheney, January 12, 1976, box 22, Jones Files; Teeter to Spencer, December 12, 1975, box 4, Chanock Files.

88. Witcover, *Marathon*, 485–86.

89. Ford to Alaska Republican State Convention delegates, May 17, [1976], box 4, Morton Files; Nessen, *It Sure Looks Different*, 222; Cheney to Gergen, June 7, 1976, box 19, Waldron Files; Waldron to Gergen, June 10, 1976, box 3, Political Affairs, White House Central Files Subject File.

90. *First Monday* (Republican National Committee magazine), April 1975, box 24, Hartmann Files; unsigned campaign plan, n.d., box 1, Dorothy E. Downton Files, GRFL.

91. *Right Report*, July 2, 1976, box 16, Cheney Files; Andrews for the record, July 28, 1976, box B10, President Ford Committee Records.

92. Rusher, *Rise*, 275–89; Carter, *Politics*, 457; *WP*, August 24, 1976, A3.

93. Anderson, *Electing*, 103.

94. Orren, "Candidate Style."

95. Adee, "American Civil Religion," 78–79; Anderson, *Electing*, 23.

96. Schram, *Running*, 269–70; unsigned campaign plan, n.d., box 1, Downton Files.

97. MacDougall, *We Almost Made It*, 35, 44, 50, 70.

98. Gillon, *Democrats' Dilemma*, 175–76; Ford remarks, August 27, 1976, box 26, Hartmann Files; Teeter to Alan Greenspan, September 8, 1976, box 4, Chanock Files.

99. Raoul-Duval notes, July 23, [1976], box 16, Raoul-Duval Papers.

100. Witcover, *Marathon*, 545; Anderson, *Electing*, 101, 106, 119; Dark, *Unions*, 100–103.

101. Unsigned, n.d., box 161, Hartmann Papers; Barbour and Skip Watts memo, n.d., annotated by Ford, October 12, [1976], box 18, Cheney Files.

102. McWilliams, "Meaning," 155–56.

103. Kirk Emmett to Goldwin, August, 5 1976, box 3, Robert A. Goldwin Files, GRFL; Richard S. B. Rannon to Gergen, July 17, 1976, box 1, David R. Gergen Files, GRFL; Kristol to Goldwin, July 21, 1976, box 3, Goldwin Files.

104. Witcover, *Marathon*, 549, 551.

105. "Lifeletter '76," August 23, 1976, box 1, Gergen Files.

106. Unsigned strategy document, n.d., box 1, Downton Files; Marjory Mecklenburg to prolife groups, n.d., Mecklenburg to Spender, September 21, October 21, 1976, box C25, President Ford Committee Records.

107. *Washington Star-News*, March 2, 1975, box 164, Hartmann Papers; *Presidential Campaign 1976*, vol. 1, part 1, p. 517; Witcover, *Marathon*, 526.

108. Unsigned for Ford, n.d., box 18, Cheney Files; Witcover, *Marathon*, 628; newsletter, "Don't Despair: Vote for Reagan Nov. 2," n.d., box 23, Raoul-Duval Papers.

109. Schram, *Running*, 319; Chanock to Duval, October 1, 1976, box 16, Raoul-Duval Papers; Witcover, *Marathon*, 657.

110. Unsigned "talking points," October 20, 1976, box F4, President Ford Committee Records.
111. Schram, *Running*, 367.
112. Ibid., 359, 366.
113. Ladd, "Shifting Party Coalitions," 83–88.
114. Abramson, "Class Voting"; Sundquist, *Dynamics*, 419; Ladd, "Shifting Party Coalitions," 101.
115. Ladd, "Shifting Party Coalitions," 90–100.
116. Ibid., 102; Gillon, *Democrats' Dilemma*, 178–79.

CONCLUSION

1. Shafer, *End of Realignment?*; Mayhew, *Electoral Realignments*.
2. Drury, *Courage*, 245.
3. McGirr, *Suburban Warriors*, is a particularly effective exploration of the ideas and activism of grassroots conservatives.

⋆ BIBLIOGRAPHY ⋆

MANUSCRIPT SOURCES

Abilene, Kansas
  Dwight D. Eisenhower Library
    Dwight D. Eisenhower Diary Series, Ann Whitman File (Papers of Dwight D. Eisenhower as President of the United States)
Ann Arbor, Michigan
  Bentley Historical Library, University of Michigan
    Michigan Republican State Central Committee Papers
    Elly Peterson Papers
  Gerald R. Ford Library
    John T. Calkins Files
    James M. Cannon Files
    Foster Chanock Files
    Richard B. Cheney Files
    James E. Connor Files
    Dorothy E. Downton Files
    Gerald R. Ford Congressional Papers
    Gerald R. Ford Vice-Presidential Papers
    David R. Gergen Files
    Robert A. Goldwin Files
    Robert T. Hartmann Files
    Robert T. Hartmann Papers
    Jerry H. Jones Files
    Rogers C. B. Morton Files
    President Ford Committee Records
    Michael Raoul-Duval Papers
    A. James Reichley Files
    A. James Reichley Interviews
    Robert Teeter Papers
    Agnes M. Waldron Files
    White House Central Files Subject File

College Park, Maryland
  National Archives
    General Records of the Department of Labor, Office of the Secretary (RG 174):
      Records of Secretary George P. Shultz, 1969–70; Records of Secretary James D.
      Hodgson, 1970–72
    Nixon Presidential Materials Project
      Oral History Interviews: Charles W. Colson
      White House Central Files—Staff Member and Office Files: Michael Balzano;
        Robert Finch
      White House Central Files—Subject Files: BE Business-Economics; FG 95 Com-
        mission on Obscenity and Pornography; FG 273 President's Commission on
        School Finance; FG 308 Commission on Marihuana and Drug Abuse
      White House Special Files—Central Files (Confidential Files)
      White House Special Files—Staff Member and Office Files: Patrick J. Buchanan;
        Charles W. Colson; Harry S. Dent; John D. Ehrlichman; H. R. Haldeman; W.
        Richard Howard; Egil M. Krogh; Peter E. Millspaugh; President's Office Files;
        President's Personal Files; Special Staff Files
  Special Collections, University of Maryland Libraries
    Spiro T. Agnew Papers
Washington, D.C.
  Manuscript Division, Library of Congress
    Leonard Garment Papers
    John Osborne Papers
    William A. Rusher Papers
    Robert Taft Jr. Papers

INTERVIEWS

Phillips, Kevin P., Oxford, England, April 28, 1995.
Wattenberg, Ben J., Washington, D.C., April 25, 1996.

PRINTED PRIMARY SOURCES

Ford, Gerald R. *Public Papers of the Presidents of the United States: Gerald R. Ford*. 6 vols.
  Washington, D.C.: U.S. Government Printing Office, 1975–79.
Haldeman, H. R. *The Haldeman Diaries: Inside the Nixon White House*. Complete mul-
  timedia ed. Santa Monica, Calif.: Sony Electronic, 1994.
McGovern, George. *An American Journey: The Presidential Campaign Speeches of George
  McGovern*. New York: Random House, 1974.
Nixon, Richard. *Public Papers of the Presidents of the United States: Richard Nixon*. 6
  vols. Washington, D.C.: U.S. Government Printing Office, 1971–75.
Oudes, Bruce, ed. *From the President—Richard Nixon's Secret Files*. New York: Harper
  and Row, 1989.
Papers of the Nixon White House, microfiche, part 3, *John Ehrlichman: Notes of Meetings*

with the President, 1969–1973, and part 5, *H. R. Haldeman: Notes of White House Meetings, 1969–1973*. Frederick, Md.: University Publications of America, 1988, 1989.

The Presidential Campaign 1976. 2 vols. Washington, D.C.: U.S. Government Printing Office, 1978.

NEWSPAPERS AND PERIODICALS

The Atlantic
Commonweal
Congressional Quarterly Weekly Report
The Economist
Esquire
Fortune
Harper's
Human Events
Los Angeles Times
The Nation
National Observer
National Review
New Republic
Newsweek
New York
The New Yorker
New York Times
The Reporter
Saturday Evening Post
Saturday Review
Time
U.S. News and World Report
Wall Street Journal
Washington Post

SECONDARY SOURCES

Abramson, Paul R. "Class Voting in the 1976 Presidential Election." *Journal of Politics* 40 (1978): 1066–72.

Adee, Michael J. "American Civil Religion and the Presidential Rhetoric of Jimmy Carter." In *The Presidency and Domestic Politics of Jimmy Carter*, edited by Herbert D. Rosenbaum and Alexej Ugrinsky, 73–82. Westport, Conn.: Greenwood, 1994.

Ambrose, Stephen E. *Nixon.* Vol. 2, *The Triumph of a Politician 1962–1972*, and vol. 3, *Ruin and Recovery 1973–1990*. New York: Simon and Schuster, 1989, 1991.

Andersen, Kristi. "Generation, Partisan Shift, and Realignment: A Glance Back at the New Deal." In *The Changing American Voter*, by Norman H. Nie, Sidney Verba, and John R. Petrocik, 74–95. Cambridge: Harvard University Press, 1976.

Anderson, Patrick. *Electing Jimmy Carter: The Campaign of 1976*. Baton Rouge: Louisiana State University Press, 1994.

Andrew, John A., III. *Lyndon Johnson and the Great Society*. Chicago: Dee, 1998.

Appy, Christian G. *Working-Class War: American Combat Soldiers and Vietnam*. Chapel Hill: University of North Carolina Press, 1993.

Armbruster, Frank E., with Doris Yokelson. *The Forgotten Americans: A Survey of Values, Beliefs, and Concerns of the Majority*. New Rochelle, N.Y.: Arlington House, 1972.

Balzano, Michael P., Jr. "The Silent Versus the New Majority." In *Richard M. Nixon: Politician, President, Administrator*, edited by William F. Levantrosser and Leon Friedman, 259–82. Westport, Conn.: Greenwood, 1991.

Barone, Michael. *Our Country: The Shaping of America from Roosevelt to Reagan*. New York: Free Press, 1990.

Bartley, Numan V., and Hugh D. Graham. *Southern Politics and the Second Reconstruction*. Baltimore: Johns Hopkins University Press, 1975.

Bass, Jack, and Walter DeVries. *The Transformation of Southern Politics: Social Change and Political Consequence since 1945*. New York: Basic Books, 1976.

Belz, Herman. *Equality Transformed: A Quarter-Century of Affirmative Action*. New Brunswick, N.J.: Transaction, 1991.

Berg, Manfred. "1968: A Turning Point in American Race Relations?" In *1968: The World Transformed*, edited by Carole Fink, Philipp Gassert, and Detlef Junker, 397–420. Cambridge: Cambridge University Press, 1998.

Billington, Monroe Lee. *The Political South in the Twentieth Century*. New York: Scribner's, 1975.

Black, Earl, and Merle Black. *The Rise of Southern Republicans*. Cambridge: Harvard University Press, 2002.

Blum, John Morton, "The Politics of the Warren Court." In *Liberty, Justice, Order: Writings on Past Politics*, by Blum, 323–61. New York: Norton, 1993.

Bone, Hugh A. "The 1970 Election in Washington." *Western Political Quarterly* 24 (1971): 350–61.

Bowles, Nigel. *The White House and Capitol Hill: The Politics of Presidential Persuasion*. Oxford: Clarendon, 1987.

Brennan, Mary C. *Turning Right in the Sixties: The Conservative Capture of the GOP*. Chapel Hill: University of North Carolina Press, 1995.

Brill, Steven. *The Teamsters*. New York: Simon and Schuster, 1978.

Broder, David S. *The Party's Over: The Failure of Politics in America*. New York: Harper and Row, 1972.

Buchanan, Patrick J. *The New Majority: President Nixon at Mid-Passage*. [Philadelphia?]: Girard Bank, 1973.

Buckley, James L. *If Men Were Angels: A View from the Senate*. New York: Putnam, 1975.

Bundy, William. *Tangled Web: The Making of Nixon's Foreign Policy, 1968–1974*. New York: Hill and Wang, 1998.

Burke, Vincent J., and Vee Burke. *Nixon's Good Deed: Welfare Reform*. New York: Columbia University Press, 1974.

Burner, David. *Making Peace with the 60s*. Princeton: Princeton University Press, 1996.

Burnham, Walter Dean. *Critical Elections and the Mainsprings of American Politics*. New York: Norton, 1970.

Bush, George, with Victor Gold. *Looking Forward*. 1987; London: Bodley Head, 1988.

Califano, Joseph A., Jr. *The Triumph and Tragedy of Lyndon Johnson: The White House Years*. New York: Simon and Schuster, 1991.

Cannon, James. *Time and Chance: Gerald Ford's Appointment with History*. New York: HarperCollins, 1994.

Carmines, Edward G., and James A. Stimson. *Issue Evolution: Race and the Transformation of American Politics*. Princeton: Princeton University Press, 1989.

Carter, Dan T. *From George Wallace to Newt Gingrich: Race in the Conservative Counterrevolution, 1963–1994*. Baton Rouge: Louisiana State University Press, 1996.

———. *The Politics of Rage: George Wallace, the Origins of the New Conservatism, and the Transformation of American Politics*. New York: Simon and Schuster, 1995.

Cash, Kevin. *Who the Hell Is William Loeb?* Manchester, N.H.: Amskoeag, 1975.

Chester, Lewis, Godfrey Hodgson, and Bruce Page. *An American Melodrama: The Presidential Campaign of 1968*. London: André Deutsch, 1969.

Cohen, Richard T., and Jules Witcover. *A Heartbeat Away: The Investigation and Resignation of Vice President Spiro T. Agnew*. New York: Viking, 1974.

Colson, Charles W. *Born Again*. London: Hodder and Stoughton, 1976.

Congress and the Nation: A Review of Government and Politics. Vol. 3, 1969–1972, and vol. 4, 1973–1976. Washington, D.C.: Congressional Quarterly, 1973, 1977.

Congressional Quarterly Almanac, vols. 25–32 (1969–1976). Washington, D.C.: Congressional Quarterly, 1970–76.

Conlan, Timothy. *New Federalism: Intergovernmental Reform from Nixon to Reagan*. Washington, D.C.: Brookings Institution, 1988.

Converse, Philip E. *The Dynamics of Party Support: Cohort-Analyzing Party Identification*. Beverly Hills, Calif.: Sage, 1976.

Converse, Philip E., Aage R. Clausen, and Warren E. Miller. "Electoral Myth and Reality: The 1964 Election." *American Political Science Review* 59 (1965): 321–36.

Converse, Philip E., Warren E. Miller, Jerrold G. Rusk, and Arthur C. Wolfe. "Continuity and Change in American Politics: Parties and Issues in the 1968 Election." *American Political Science Review* 63 (1969): 1083–1105.

Converse, Philip E., and Howard Schuman. " 'Silent Majorities' and the Vietnam War." *Scientific American* 222 (June 1970): 17–25.

Cowie, Jefferson. "Nixon's Class Struggle: Romancing the New Right Worker, 1969–1973." *Labor History* 43 (2002): 257–83.

Coyne, John R., Jr. *The Impudent Snobs: Agnew vs. the Intellectual Establishment*. New Rochelle, N.Y.: Arlington House, 1972.

Crawford, Alan. *Thunder on the Right: The "New Right" and the Politics of Resentment*. New York: Pantheon, 1980.

Cronin, Thomas E., and Michael A. Genovese. *The Paradoxes of the American Presidency*. New York: Oxford University Press, 1998.

Crowley, Monica. *Nixon in Winter: The Final Revelations*. London: Tauris, 1998.

——. *Nixon Off the Record*. New York: Random House, 1996.

Cunningham, Robert, III, and Robert M. Cunningham Jr. *The Blues: A History of the Blue Cross and Blue Shield System*. De Kalb: Northern Illinois University Press, 1997.

Dark, Taylor E. *The Unions and the Democrats: An Enduring Alliance*. Ithaca: Cornell University Press, 1999.

Davies, Gareth. *From Opportunity to Entitlement: The Transformation and Decline of Great Society Liberalism*. Lawrence: University Press of Kansas, 1996.

——. "The Great Society after Johnson: The Case of Bilingual Education." *Journal of American History* 88 (2002): 1405–29.

Davis, James W. *The President as Party Leader*. Westport, Conn.: Greenwood, 1992.

DeBenedetti, Charles, with Charles Chatfield. *An American Ordeal: The Antiwar Movement of the Vietnam Era*. Syracuse, N.Y.: Syracuse University Press, 1990.

Dent, Harry S. *The Prodigal South Returns to Power*. New York: Wiley, 1978.

Dougherty, Richard. *Goodbye, Mr. Christian: A Personal Account of McGovern's Rise and Fall*. Garden City, N.Y.: Doubleday, 1973.

Drucker, Peter. "Notes on the New Politics." *Public Interest* 4 (Summer 1966): 13–30.

Drury, Allen. *Courage and Hesitation: Inside the Nixon Administration*. 1971; London: Allen Joseph, 1972.

Durr, Kenneth D. *Behind the Backlash: White Working-Class Politics in Baltimore, 1940–1980*. Chapel Hill: University of North Carolina Press, 2003.

Dutton, Frederick G. *Changing Sources of Power: American Politics in the 1970s*. New York: McGraw-Hill, 1971.

Edsall, Thomas Byrne, with Mary D. Edsall. *Chain Reaction: The Impact of Race, Rights, and Taxes on American Politics*. New York: Norton, 1991.

Ehrlichman, John. *Witness to Power: The Nixon Years*. New York: Pocket Books, 1982.

English, David, and the Staff of the *Daily Express*. *Divided They Stand*. London: Allen Joseph, 1969.

Epstein, Edward Jay. "The Krogh Files—The Politics of 'Law and Order.'" *Public Interest* 39 (Spring 1975): 99–124.

Evans, Rowland, Jr., and Robert D. Novak. *Nixon in the White House: The Frustration of Power*. New York: Random House, 1971.

Faber, Harold, ed. *The Road to the White House: The Story of the 1964 Election by the Staff of the New York Times*. New York: McGraw-Hill, 1965.

Farber, David. "The Silent Majority and Talk about Revolution." In *The Sixties: From Memory to History*, edited by Farber, 291–316. Chapel Hill: University of North Carolina Press, 1994.

Flippen, J. Brooks. *Nixon and the Environment*. Albuquerque: University of New Mexico Press, 2000.

Ford, Gerald R. *A Time to Heal: The Autobiography of Gerald R. Ford*. New York: Harper and Row, 1979.

Formisano, Ronald P. *Boston against Busing: Race, Class, and Ethnicity in the 1960s and 1970s*. Chapel Hill: University of North Carolina Press, 1991.

Free, Lloyd A., and Hadley Cantril. *The Political Beliefs of Americans: A Study of Public Opinion*. New Brunswick: Rutgers University Press, 1967.

Freeman, Joshua B. "Hardhats: Construction Workers, Manliness, and the 1970 Pro-War Demonstrations." *Journal of Social History* 26 (1993): 725–44.

Friedman, Leon, and William F. Levantrosser, eds. *Watergate and Afterward: The Legacy of Richard M. Nixon.* Westport, Conn.: Greenwood, 1992.

Frymer, Paul, and John David Skrentny. "Coalition-Building and the Politics of Electoral Capture during the Nixon Administration: African Americans, Labor, Latinos." *Studies in American Political Development* 12 (1998): 131–61.

Garment, Leonard. *Crazy Rhythm: My Journey from Brooklyn, Jazz, and Wall Street to Nixon's White House, Watergate, and Beyond . . .* New York: Times Books, 1997.

Gellner, Irwin F. *The Contender: Richard Nixon—The Congress Years, 1946–1952.* New York: Free Press, 1999.

Genovese, Michael A. *The Nixon Presidency: Power and Politics in Turbulent Times.* Westport, Conn.: Greenwood, 1990.

Gillon, Steven M. *The Democrats' Dilemma: Walter F. Mondale and the Liberal Legacy.* New York: Columbia University Press, 1992.

Glad, Betty, and Michael W. Link. "President Nixon's Inner Circle of Advisers." *Presidential Studies Quarterly* 26 (1996): 13–40.

Goldberg, Robert Alan. *Barry Goldwater.* New Haven: Yale University Press, 1995.

Goldwater, Barry M. *The Conscience of a Conservative.* Shepherdsville, Ky.: Victor, 1960.

Goldwater, Barry M., with Jack Casserly. *Goldwater.* New York: St. Martin's, 1988.

Gottfried, Paul. *The Conservative Movement.* Rev. ed. New York: Twayne, 1993.

Gould, Lewis L. "Never a Deep Partisan: Lyndon Johnson and the Democratic Party, 1963–1969." In *The Johnson Years,* vol. 3, *LBJ at Home and Abroad,* edited by Robert A. Divine, 21–52. Lawrence: University Press of Kansas, 1994.

Graham, Fred P. "A Contemporary History of American Crime." In *Violence in America: Historical and Comparative Perspectives—A Report Submitted to the National Commission on the Causes and Prevention of Violence,* edited by Hugh Davis Graham and Ted Robert Gurr, 485–504. New York: Bantam, 1969.

Graham, Hugh Davis. *The Civil Rights Era: Origins and Development of National Policy, 1960–1972.* New York: Oxford University Press, 1990.

——. "Richard Nixon and Civil Rights: Explaining an Enigma." *Presidential Studies Quarterly* 26 (1996): 93–106.

Graham, Otis L., Jr. *Toward a Planned Society: From Roosevelt to Nixon.* 1976; New York: Oxford University Press, 1977.

Greenberg, Jack. *Crusaders in the Courts: How a Dedicated Band of Lawyers Fought for the Civil Rights Revolution.* New York: Basic Books, 1994.

Greene, Bob. *Running: A Nixon-McGovern Campaign Journal.* Chicago: Regnery, 1973.

Greene, John Robert. *The Limits of Power: The Nixon and Ford Administrations.* Bloomington: Indiana University Press, 1992.

——. *The Presidency of Gerald R. Ford.* Lawrence: University Press of Kansas, 1995.

Hainsworth, Brad E. "The 1970 Election in Montana." *Western Political Quarterly* 24 (1971): 301–7.

Haldeman, H. R., with Joseph DiMona. *The Ends of Power.* New York: Times Books, 1978.

Harper, Edwin L. "Domestic Policy Making in the Nixon Administration: An Evolving Process." *Presidential Studies Quarterly* 26 (1996): 41–56.

Hartmann, Robert T. *Palace Politics: An Inside Account of the Ford Years*. New York: McGraw-Hill, 1980.

Heineman, Kenneth J. *God Is a Conservative*. New York: New York University Press, 1998.

Hess, Stephen, and David S. Broder. *The Republican Establishment: The Present and Future of the G.O.P.* New York: Harper and Row, 1967.

Himmelstein, Jerome L. *To the Right: The Transformation of American Conservatism*. Berkeley: University of California Press, 1990.

Hixson, William B. *Search for the American Right Wing: An Analysis of the Social Science Record, 1955–1987*. Princeton: Princeton University Press, 1992.

Hodgson, Godfrey. *The Gentleman from New York: Daniel Patrick Moynihan—A Biography*. Boston: Houghton Mifflin, 2000.

——. *The World Turned Right Side Up: A History of the Conservative Ascendancy in America*. Boston: Houghton Mifflin, 1996.

Hoff, Joan. *Nixon Reconsidered*. New York: Basic Books, 1994.

Jacobs, Lawrence R., and Robert Y. Shapiro. "The Rise of Presidential Polling: The Nixon White House in Historical Perspective." *Public Opinion Quarterly* 59 (1995): 163–95.

Jamieson, Kathleen Hall. *Packaging the Presidency: A History and Criticism of Presidential Campaign Advertising*. 2d ed. New York: Oxford University Press, 1992.

Jeffreys-Jones, Rhodri. *Peace Now! American Society and the Ending of the Vietnam War*. New Haven: Yale University Press, 1999.

Jensen, Richard. "The Last Party System: Decay of Consensus, 1932–1980." In *The Evolution of American Electoral Systems*, by Paul Kleppner et al., 203–41. Westport, Conn.: Greenwood, 1981.

Jonas, Frank H., and Dan E. Jones. "The 1970 Election in Utah." *Western Political Quarterly* 24 (1971): 339–49.

Jones, Charles O. *The Presidency in a Separated System*. Washington, D.C.: Brookings Institution, 1994.

Kazin, Michael. *The Populist Persuasion: An American History*. New York: Basic Books, 1995.

Key, V. O., Jr. "Secular Realignment and the Party System." *Journal of Politics* 21 (1959): 198–210.

——. "A Theory of Critical Elections." *Journal of Politics* 17 (1955): 3–18.

Kimball, Jeffrey. *Nixon's Vietnam War*. Lawrence: University Press of Kansas, 1998.

Klein, Herbert G. *Making It Perfectly Clear*. Garden City, N.Y.: Doubleday, 1980.

Klinkner, Philip A. *The Losing Parties: Out-Party National Committees, 1956–1993*. New Haven: Yale University Press, 1994.

Kolodny, Robin. "The 1976 Republican Nomination: An Examination of the Organizational Dynamic." In *Gerald R. Ford and the Politics of Post-Watergate America*, edited by Bernard J. Firestone and Alexej Ugrinsky, 2:583–99. Westport, Conn.: Greenwood, 1993.

Kotlowski, Dean J. *Nixon's Civil Rights: Politics, Principle, and Policy*. Cambridge: Harvard University Press, 2001.

——. "Trial by Error: Nixon, the Senate, and the Haynsworth Nomination." *Presidential Studies Quarterly* 26 (1996): 71–91.

Krickus, Richard. *Pursuing the American Dream: White Ethnics and the New Populism*. Garden City, N.Y.: Anchor, 1976.

Kunz, Diane B. *Butter and Guns: America's Cold War Economic Diplomacy*. New York: Free Press, 1997.

Kutler, Stanley I. *The Wars of Watergate: The Last Crisis of Richard Nixon*. New York: Knopf, 1990.

Ladd, Everett Carll, Jr. "The Shifting Party Coalitions—1932–1976." In *Emerging Coalitions in American Politics*, edited by Seymour Martin Lipset, 81–102. San Francisco: Institute for Contemporary Studies, 1978.

Ladd, Everett Carll, Jr., with Charles D. Hadley. *Transformations of the American Party System: Political Coalitions from the New Deal to the 1970s*. 2d ed. New York: Norton, 1978.

Lamis, Alexander P. *The Two-Party South*. Expanded ed. New York: Oxford University Press, 1988.

Lesher, Stephan. *George Wallace: American Populist*. Reading, Mass.: Addison Wesley, 1994.

Leuchtenburg, William E. *Franklin D. Roosevelt and the New Deal*. New York: Harper and Row, 1963.

Levitan, Sar A., ed., *Blue-Collar Workers: A Symposium on Middle America*. New York: McGraw-Hill, 1971.

Levy, Mark R., and Michael S. Kramer. *The Ethnic Factor: How America's Minorities Decide Elections*. New York: Simon and Schuster, 1972.

Lipset, Seymour Martin, "George Wallace and the U.S. New Right." *New Society* 12 (October 3, 1968): 477–83.

Lubell, Samuel. *The Future of American Politics*. New York: Harper Colophon, 1951.

——. *The Future while It Happened*. New York: Norton, 1973.

——. *The Hidden Crisis in American Politics*. New York: Norton, 1970.

Lukas, J. Anthony. *Nightmare: The Underside of the Nixon Years*. New York: Viking, 1976.

Lunch, William L., and Peter W. Sperlich. "American Public Opinion and the War in Vietnam." *Western Political Quarterly* 32 (1979): 21–44.

MacDougall, Malcolm D. *We Almost Made It*. New York: Crown, 1977.

Magruder, Jeb Stuart. *An American Life: One Man's Road to Watergate*. 1974; New York: Pocket Books, 1975.

Manley, John F. "The Conservative Coalition in Congress." In *Congress Reconsidered*, edited by Lawrence C. Dodd and Bruce I. Oppenheimer, 75–95. New York: Praeger, 1977.

Martin, William C. *With God on Our Side: The Rise of the Religious Right in America*. New York: Broadway, 1996.

Massey, Donald S., and Nancy A. Denton. *American Apartheid: Segregation and the Making of the Underclass*. Cambridge: Harvard University Press, 1993.

Matusow, Allen J. *Nixon's Economy: Booms, Busts, Dollars, and Votes*. Lawrence: University Press of Kansas, 1998.

——. *The Unraveling of America: A History of Liberalism in the 1960s*. New York: Harper and Row, 1984.

May, Ernest R., and Janet Fraser, eds. *Campaign '72: The Managers Speak*. Cambridge: Harvard University Press, 1973.

Mayer, William G. *The Changing American Mind: How and Why American Public Opinion Changed between 1960 and 1988*. Ann Arbor: University of Michigan Press, 1992.

Mayhew, David R. *Divided We Govern: Party Control, Lawmaking, and Investigations, 1946–1990*. New Haven: Yale University Press, 1991.

——. *Electoral Realignments: A Critique of an American Genre*. New Haven: Yale University Press, 2002.

McAndrew, Lawrence J. "The Politics of Principle: Richard Nixon and School Desegregation." *Journal of Negro History* 83 (1998): 187–200.

McCloskey, Robert G. *The American Supreme Court*. 2d ed. Revised by Sanford Levinson. Chicago: University of Chicago Press, 1994.

McCracken, Paul W. "Economic Policy in the Nixon Years." *Presidential Studies Quarterly* 26 (1996): 165–77.

McGinniss, Joe. *The Selling of the President 1968*. New York: Pocket Books, 1969.

McGirr, Lisa. *Suburban Warriors: The Origins of the New American Right*. Princeton: Princeton University Press, 2001.

McGreevey, John T. *Parish Boundaries: The Catholic Encounter with Race in the Twentieth-Century Urban North*. Chicago: University of Chicago Press, 1996.

McWilliams, Wilson Carey. "The Meaning of the Election." In *The Election of 1976: Reports and Interpretations*, by Gerald Pomper et al., 147–62. New York: David McKay, 1977.

Milkis, Sidney M. *The President and the Parties: The Transformation of the American Party System since the New Deal*. New York: Oxford University Press, 1993.

Miller, Arthur H., Warren E. Miller, Alden S. Raine, and Thad A. Brown. "A Majority Party in Disarray: Policy Polarization in the 1972 Election." *American Political Science Review* 70 (1976): 753–78.

Miller, Warren E., and Santa A. Traugott. *American National Election Studies Data Sourcebook, 1952–1986*. Cambridge: Harvard University Press, 1989.

Morgan, Iwan. *Nixon*. London: Arnold, 2002.

Morris, Edmund. *Dutch: A Memoir of Ronald Reagan*. New York: HarperCollins, 1999.

Moynihan, Daniel P. *The Politics of a Guaranteed Income: The Nixon Administration and the Family Assistance Plan*. New York: Random House, 1973.

Murphy, Reg, and Hal Gulliver. *The Southern Strategy*. New York: Scribner's, 1971.

Musto, David F. *The American Disease: Origins of Narcotic Control*. Expanded ed. New York: Oxford University Press, 1987.

Nathan, Richard P. *The Plot That Failed: Nixon and the Administrative Presidency*. New York: Wiley, 1975.

——. "A Retrospective on Richard M. Nixon's Domestic Policies." *Presidential Studies Quarterly* 26 (1996): 155–64.

Nathan, Richard P., Allen D. Manvel, Susannah E. Calkins, and associates. *Monitoring Revenue Sharing*. Washington, D.C.: Brookings Institution, 1975.

Nessen, Ron. *It Sure Looks Different from the Inside*. Chicago: Playboy, 1978.

Nixon, Richard M. *RN: The Memoirs of Richard Nixon*. New York: Grosset and Dunlap, 1978.

——. *Six Crises*. 1962; New York: Touchstone, 1990.

Noble, Charles. *Liberalism at Work: The Rise and Fall of OSHA*. Philadelphia: Temple University Press, 1986.

Nofziger, Lyn. *Nofziger*. Washington, D.C.: Regnery Gateway, 1992.

O'Brien, Lawrence F. *No Final Victories: A Life in Politics—from John F. Kennedy to Watergate*. Garden City, N.Y.: Doubleday, 1974.

Orfield, Gary. *Congressional Power: Congress and Social Change*. New York: Harcourt Brace Jovanovich, 1975.

Orfield, Gary, Susan E. Eaton, and the Harvard Project on School Desegregation. *Dismantling Desegregation: The Quiet Reversal of* Brown v. Board of Education. New York: New Press, 1996.

Orren, Gary R. "Candidate Style and Voter Alignment in 1976." In *Emerging Coalitions in American Politics*, ed. Seymour Martin Lipset, 130–50. San Francisco: Institute for Contemporary Studies, 1978.

Osborne, John. *White House Watch: The Ford Years*. Washington, D.C.: New Republic Books, 1977.

Page, Benjamin I., and Richard A. Brody. "Policy Voting and the Electoral Process: The Vietnam War Issue." *American Political Science Review* 66 (1972): 979–95.

Panetta, Leon E., and Peter Gall. *Bring Us Together: The Nixon Team and the Civil Rights Retreat*. Philadelphia: Lippincott, 1971.

Parker, Richard. "The Myth of Middle America." In *New Perspectives on the American Past*, vol. 2, *1877 to the Present*, 2d ed., edited by Stanley N. Katz and Stanley I. Kutler, 408–22. Boston: Little, Brown, 1972.

Parmet, Herbert S. *The Democrats: The Years after FDR*. New York: Oxford University Press, 1976.

——. *Richard Nixon and His America*. Boston: Little, Brown, 1990.

Perlstein, Rick. *Before the Storm: Barry Goldwater and the Unmaking of the American Consensus*. New York: Hill and Wang, 2001.

Pettigrew, Thomas F., and Robert T. Riley. "The Social Psychology of the Wallace Phenomenon." In *Racially Separate or Together?*, by Pettigrew, 231–56. New York: McGraw-Hill, 1971.

Phillips, Kevin P. *The Emerging Republican Majority*. New Rochelle, N.Y.: Arlington House, 1969; Garden City, N.Y.: Anchor, 1970.

——. *Post-Conservative America: People, Politics, and Ideology in a Time of Crisis*. New York: Random House, 1982.

Polsby, Nelson W. "Strategic Considerations in 1964." In *Political Parties in American History*, vol. 3, *1890–Present*, edited by Paul L. Murphy, 1283–1306. New York: Putnam's, 1974.

Prendergast, William B. *The Catholic Voter in American Politics: The Passing of the Democratic Monolith*. Washington, D.C.: Georgetown University Press, 1999.

Price, Raymond. *With Nixon*. New York: Viking, 1977.

Quadagno, Jill. *The Color of Welfare: How Racism Undermined the War on Poverty*. New York: Oxford University Press, 1994.

Radosh, Ronald. *Divided They Fell: The Demise of the Democratic Party, 1964–1996*. New York: Free Press, 1996.

Rae, Nicol C. *The Decline and Fall of the Liberal Republicans: From 1952 to the Present*. New York: Oxford University Press, 1989.

Ransford, H. Edward. "Blue Collar Anger: Reactions to Student and Black Protest." *American Sociological Review* 37 (1972): 333–46.

Rather, Dan, and Gary Paul Gates. *The Palace Guard*. New York: Harper and Row, 1974.

Reeves, Richard. *President Nixon: Alone in the White House*. New York: Simon and Schuster, 2001.

Reichley, A. James. *Conservatives in an Age of Change: The Nixon and Ford Administrations*. Washington, D.C.: Brookings Institution, 1981.

Reinhard, David W. *The Republican Right since 1945*. Lexington: University Press of Kentucky, 1983.

Reston, James, Jr. *The Lone Star: The Life of John Connally*. New York: Harper and Row, 1989.

Richard, John B. "The 1970 Election in Wyoming." *Western Political Quarterly* 24 (1971): 362–68.

Rieder, Jonathan. *Canarsie: The Jews and Italians of Brooklyn against Liberalism*. Cambridge: Harvard University Press, 1985.

——. "The Rise of the 'Silent Majority.'" In *The Rise and Fall of the New Deal Order 1930–1980*, edited by Steve Fraser and Gary Gerstle, 243–68. Princeton: Princeton University Press, 1989.

The Ripon Society and Clifford W. Brown Jr. *Jaws of Victory: The Game-Plan Politics of 1972, the Crisis of the Republican Party, and the Future of the Constitution*. Boston: Little, Brown, 1974.

Rodgers, John. "The Seventh American Revolution." *Yale Review* 57 (1968): 528–44.

Roland, Charles P. *The Improbable Era: The South since World War II*. Lexington: University Press of Kentucky, 1975.

Rusher, William A. *The Making of the New Majority Party*. New York: Sheed and Ward, 1975.

——. *The Rise of the Right*. New York: Morrow, 1984.

Safire, William. *Before the Fall: An Inside View of the Pre-Watergate White House*. Garden City, N.Y.: Doubleday, 1975.

Scammon, Richard M., and Ben J. Wattenberg. *The Real Majority*. New York: Coward-McCann, 1970.

Schell, Jonathan. *The Time of Illusion*. New York: Random House, 1975.

Schlafly, Phyllis. *A Choice Not An Echo*. Alton, Ill.: Pere Marquette, 1964.

Schneider, Gregory L. *Cadres for Conservatism: Young Americans for Freedom and the Rise of the Contemporary Right*. New York: New York University Press, 1999.

Schoenwald, Jonathan M. *A Time for Choosing: The Rise of Modern American Conservatism*. New York: Oxford University Press, 2001.

Schram, Martin. *Running for President 1976: The Carter Campaign*. New York: Stein and Day, 1977.

Schulzinger, Robert D. *A Time for War: The United States and Vietnam, 1941–1975*. New York: Oxford University Press, 1997.

Shafer, Byron E. "The Notion of an Electoral Order: The Structure of Electoral Politics at the Accession of George Bush." In *The End of Realignment?: Interpreting American Electoral Eras*, edited by Shafer, 37–84. Madison: University of Wisconsin Press, 1991.

———. *Quiet Revolution: The Struggle for the Democratic Party and the Shaping of Post-Reform Politics*. New York: Sage, 1983.

———, ed. *The End of Realignment?: Interpreting American Electoral Eras*. Madison: University of Wisconsin Press, 1991

Sinclair, Barbara. *Congressional Realignment 1925–1978*. Austin: University of Texas Press, 1982.

Small, Melvin. *Johnson, Nixon, and the Doves*. New Brunswick: Rutgers University Press, 1988.

———. *The Presidency of Richard Nixon*. Lawrence: University Press of Kansas, 1999.

Solberg, Carl. *Hubert Humphrey: A Biography*. New York: Norton, 1984.

Stanley, Harold W., and Richard G. Niemi. *Vital Statistics on American Politics*. Washington, D.C.: CQ Press, 1988.

Steeper, Frederick T., and Robert M. Teeter. "Comment on 'A Majority Party in Disarray.'" *American Political Science Review* 70 (1976): 806–13.

Stein, Herbert. *Presidential Economics: The Making of Economic Policy from Roosevelt to Reagan and Beyond*. 2d rev. ed. Washington, D.C.: American Enterprise Institute, 1988.

Stewart, John G. *One Last Chance: The Democratic Party, 1974–76*. New York: Praeger, 1974.

Strober, Gerald S., and Deborah H. Strober. *Nixon: An Oral History of His Presidency*. New York: HarperCollins, 1994.

Sundquist, James L. *The Decline and Resurgence of Congress*. Washington, D.C.: Brookings Institution, 1981.

———. *Dynamics of the Party System: Alignment and Realignment of Political Parties in the United States*. Rev. ed. Washington, D.C.: Brookings Institution, 1983.

Sweeney, James R. "Southern Strategies: The 1970 Election for the United States Senate in Virginia." *Virginia Magazine of History and Biography* 106 (1998): 165–200.

Thompson, Kenneth W. *The Nixon Presidency: Twenty-Two Intimate Perspectives of Richard M. Nixon*. Lanham, Md.: University Press of America, 1987.

Thurber, Timothy N. *The Politics of Equality: Hubert H. Humphrey and the African American Freedom Struggle*. New York: Columbia University Press, 1999.

Train, Russell. "The Environmental Record of the Nixon Administration." *Presidential Studies Quarterly* 26 (1996): 185–96.

Walker, Samuel. *Popular Justice: A History of American Criminal Justice*. 2d ed. New York: Oxford University Press, 1998.

Weisbrot, Robert. *Freedom Bound: A History of America's Civil Rights Movement*. 1990; New York: Plume, 1991.

White, Theodore H. *The Making of the President 1968*. New York: Atheneum, 1969.

——. *The Making of the President 1972*. New York: Bantam, 1973.

Wicker, Tom. *One of Us: Richard Nixon and the American Dream*. New York: Random House, 1991.

——. "Richard M. Nixon 1969–1974." *Presidential Studies Quarterly* 26 (1996): 249–57.

Wilkinson, J. Harvie, III. *From Brown to Bakke: The Supreme Court and School Integration, 1954–1978*. New York: Oxford University Press, 1979.

Wills, Garry. *Nixon Agonistes: The Crisis of the Self-Made Man*. 1970; New York: Mentor, 1971.

Wilson, Graham K., and Philip M. Williams. "Mr. Nixon's Triumph." *Parliamentary Affairs* 26 (1972–73): 186–200.

Witcover, Jules. *Marathon: The Pursuit of the Presidency, 1972–1976*. New York: Signet, 1978.

——. *The Resurrection of Richard Nixon*. New York: Putnam's, 1970.

——. *The Year the Dream Died: Revisiting 1968 in America*. New York: Warner, 1997.

Woods, Randall Bennett. *J. William Fulbright, Vietnam, and the Search for a Cold War Foreign Policy*. Cambridge: Cambridge University Press, 1998.

Woodward, Bob, and Carl Bernstein. *All the President's Men*. London: Quartet, 1974.

Zelizer, Julian E. *Taxing America: Wilbur D. Mills, Congress, and the State*. Cambridge: Cambridge University Press, 1998.

★ INDEX ★

Abner, Alan, 102
Abortion, 94, 154–55, 182, 229–30
Affirmative action, 53–54, 181
Agnew, Spiro T., 75, 115, 159, 176, 202; as vice
  presidential candidate, 30, 52; and mobili-
  zation of "silent majority," 65–66; and
  1970 campaigns, 88, 99–100, 103, 106, 108;
  attempts to remove, 130–31, 138, 162; on
  McGovern, 164, 184; and ethnic groups, 168;
  resignation of, 208
Albert, Carl, 185, 203
*Alexander v. Holmes County Board of Educa-
  tion*, 52
Alinsky, Saul, 44
American Enterprise Institute, 116
American Federation of Labor and Congress
  of Industrial Organizations, 134–35, 177;
  Committee on Political Education of, 96–
  97, 135, 178. *See also* Meany, George; Orga-
  nized labor
American Independent Party, 102, 225–26. *See
  also* Wallace, George C.
Anderson, Patrick, 226
Andrews, T. Coleman, 225
Arends, Leslie C., 129
Armstrong, Anne, 146
Ash, Roy L., 126
Ashbrook, John M., 29, 138–39

Balzano, Michael, 168
Baroody, William J., Jr., 195
Barr, Joseph W., 61
Bauman, Robert E., 217
Beall, J. Glenn, 88–89, 110
Bentsen, Lloyd, 88, 129
Blackmun, Harry A., 55, 148
Bliss, Ray, 14
Blount, Winton M., 46

Boggs, Hale, 185
Borders, William H., 170
Brennan, Peter J., 144, 194
Brewer, Albert, 157
Brinegar, Claude S., 194
Brock, William E., 88–89, 102, 104, 110, 170
Broder, David S., 68
Brown, Clifford W., Jr., 200
Brown, Edmund G. "Pat," 105
Brown, Sam, 62
Buchanan, Patrick J., 26, 39, 63, 65, 140, 155,
  182; on public relations, 42; on *The Real
  Majority*, 84; on 1970 campaigns, 107; on
  domestic reform, 120, 158–59; on conserva-
  tives, 138; on Calley case, 144; on residential
  desegregation, 150; and Catholics, 152–54;
  on McGovern, 164; on disaffected Demo-
  crats, 172; on 1972 electoral strategy, 180; on
  Nixon's second-term goals, 193; on Republi-
  can Party, 197
Buckley, James L., 78, 95, 110, 129, 138, 150, 165,
  167, 217
Bull, Stephen, 71
Burch, Dean, 14
Burger, Warren E., 54, 148
Burnham, Walter Dean, 14, 111
Burton, Lawrence J., 88
Bush, George H. W., 88–89, 197, 200–201, 207,
  209
Busing, 104, 146–49, 187
Byrd, Harry F., Jr., 95, 165–66, 176
Byrne, Brendan T., 209
Byrnes, John W., 123–24

Caddell, Patrick, 233–34
Cahill, William T., 67, 209
Califano, Joseph A., Jr., 22
Callaway, Howard "Bo," 220

Calley, William L., Jr., 143–44

Cambodia, 69–71, 214

Campaigns. *See* Elections and campaigns

Cantril, Hadley, 10, 34, 205

Carswell, G. Harrold, 55, 89

Carter, Jimmy, 226–34, 238

Casey, Bob, 174

Catholics, 151–55

Changing Sources of Power (Dutton), 140–42, 164

Chanock, Foster, 223

Chapin, Dwight, 177

Chappell, Bill, Jr., 174

Cheney, Richard B., 216, 219

Chiles, Lawton, 103

China, People's Republic of, 137–39, 220

Chotiner, Murray, 98, 101, 108–9, 131, 133, 156

Christian, George E., 177, 185

Church, Frank, 71

Civil rights. *See* Race and civil rights

Clawson, Kenneth, 157

Cold War. *See* Foreign policy

Coles, Robert, 45, 130

Colmer, William S., 178

Colson, Charles W., 39, 55–56, 94, 166, 175, 188, 194, 236; and labor, 72, 97–98, 135–36, 144; and 1970 campaigns, 86, 103; on domestic reform, 121; on economy, 122–23; on revenue sharing, 124; and youth, 141; on busing, 146–48; and "parochaid," 154; on Republicans, 166; on McGovern and Democrats, 177; resignation of, 193, 208; on Nixon/Jackson parallel, 195; role in private sector of, 196

Committee for Freedom of Choice, 218

Committee for the New Majority, 218

Committee for the Re-election of the President, 131, 161–62, 166–68, 174, 200, 208; Black Vote Division of, 170; Youth Division of, 170–71; and Democrats for Nixon, 173

Committee on Conservative Alternatives, 218

Common situs picketing, 219–20

Connally, John B., 122, 125, 129–30, 154, 157, 166, 188; as potential vice president, 162, 208; and Democrats for Nixon, 172–73, 178, 184; on 1972 election results, 197; on new party, 198; as potential president, 198; as Republican, 201

Conservative movement and conservatives, 115–16; and Agnew, 130; criticisms of Nixon, 138–39; and foreign policy, 138–39; opposition to Rockfeller, 215, 217; criticisms of Ford, 215–26; and new party, 217–18; views of Republican Party, 217–18; support for Reagan, 218, 225

Conservative Party. *See* Buckley, James L.

Conservative Political Action Conference, 217–18

Conte, Silvio O., 174

Cooke, Terence, 152, 154, 182

Cooper, John Sherman, 71

Cox, Edward, 196

Cox, Tricia Nixon, 109, 125, 174

Cramer, William C., 89, 103

Crime, 12, 19–20, 31, 50–51, 82, 92–93, 101, 143

Cultural and social issues, 12, 83, 142–45, 186, 223, 229, 238; and race, 104, 145

Daley, Richard J., 150

Davis, Sammy, Jr., 171

Democratic Party, 79; and Roosevelt coalition, 1, 7, 43; and South, 9; and activism, 10; problems under Johnson, 14–23, 128; and "New Politics," 23–24, 191; and 1968 nomination, 30–31; and 1968 convention, 31; and coalition's 1968 strength, 33–34; and "middle America," 43; on affirmative action, 53; on Nixon's policies, 59–60, 132; 1969 problems of, 68–69; and *The Real Majority*, 83; and "radical liberalism," 90–92, 95; and 1972 presidential election, 114; southern Democrats, 129, 158, 173–74, 202, 229; on economy, 133–34; and support for Wallace, 147; and support for Nixon, 147, 177, 185; and 1972 presidential primaries, 148, 156–57, 163–64; and Catholics, 151–53; and social conservatism, 155; and party reform, 162–63, 226; and liberalism, 163–64; and defections to Republican Party, 165–66, 201–2; and defections from Republican Party, 167; and Jewish Americans, 170; Nixon's cultivation of Democrats, 171–78; in Pennsylvania, 175; in Louisiana, 176; in Virginia, 176; and 1972 election results, 189; and Carter, 228–29; 1976 strength of, 233, 238

Democrats for Nixon, 162, 172–73, 175, 177–78, 184–85. *See also* Committee for the Re-election of the President

Dent, Harry S., 52, 53, 74, 98, 120, 147, 157, 175–76, 196

Derge, David R., 106
Desegregation of housing, 149–50, 182–83
Desegregation of schools, 51–53, 104
Détente, 139, 214–15, 220–21, 224
Dewey, Thomas E., 151
Dickenson, James, 164–65
"Dirty tricks," 114, 156–57, 178–79, 236. *See also* Watergate scandal
Dodds, Bill, 97
Dole, Robert J., 2, 131, 200, 207
Domestic reform, 79–80
Dougherty, Richard, 183
Drew, Elizabeth, 42
Drugs, 21, 93, 143
Drury, Allen, 127
Dukakis, Michael, 238
Dunlop, John T., 220
Dutton, Frederick G., 164. See also *Changing Sources of Power*

Eagleton, Thomas F., 179
Eastland, James O., 173
Economy, 18, 44; and Nixon administration, 60–61, 75, 77, 81, 114, 118, 121–23, 132–34, 179–80, 183, 186–88, 204–7; and Ford administration, 211, 213, 223–24, 227–28
Ehrlichman, John D., 38, 74, 98, 204; on Congress, 41; and domestic reform, 100–101, 118, 124–25; and busing, 147; and "parochaid," 153–54; and Rizzo, 175; resignation of, 193, 208; on new party, 198
Eisenhower, David, 196
Eisenhower, Dwight D., 1
Elections and campaigns
—of 1960, 7–8
—of 1962, 105
—of 1964, 8–14; and nomination politics, 8; Republican strategy for, 8–9; issues of, 9–13; results of, 13–14
—of 1966, 22–23
—of 1968, 25–36; and nomination politics, 25–27, 29–31; Republican strategy for, 31–32; issues of, 31–34; results of, 34–36
—of 1969, 67–69
—of 1970, 77–113; Nixon's goals for, 77; Nixon's strategy for, 78–79, 82, 84–92, 100–102, 107; and Senate, 87; Nixon's candidate selection for, 88–89; and fundraising, 89; in New York, 94–95; in Virginia, 95; and Agnew's campaign activities, 99–100; in

Tennessee, 102, 170; in Ohio, 102–3, 106; and Nixon's activities, 107–9; results of, 109–11
—of 1972, 85–86, 161–91; and Republican nomination campaigns, 138–39; and Democratic nomination campaigns, 148, 156–57, 163–64; Nixon's strategy for, 161–62, 165–67, 168–73, 180–82; and Republican National Convention, 164–65; and Nixon's campaign activities, 169, 184, 186–89; and youth, 170–71; and television commercials, 184–85; results of, 189–90
—of 1973, 208–9
—of 1974, 208–9, 211–12
—of 1976, 219–33; and Republican nomination campaign, 219–24; and Republican National Convention, 224; and Democratic nomination campaign, 226–27; results of, 232–33
Emerging Republican Majority (Phillips), 27, 47–50, 82–83, 142. *See also* Phillips, Kevin P.
Energy crisis, 205, 213–14
Environment, 60, 117–18, 127–28
Environmental Protection Agency, 60
Equal Employment Opportunities Commission, 54
Equal Rights Amendment, 155
Ervin, Sam J., Jr., 92
Ethnic groups, 98–99, 168–69, 188
Evans, Thomas W., 131

Family Assistance Plan. *See* Welfare reform
Finch, Robert H., 26, 39, 141
Fisher, O. C., 174
Fitzsimmons, Frank, 136
Flanigan, Peter M., 50
Flemming, Harry S., 98
Fletcher, Arthur A., 89, 95
Ford, Gerald R., 129, 166, 208, 209; political characteristics of, 210–11; and 1974 campaigns, 211–12; on Republican prospects, 212–13; and economy, 213; and administration's agenda, 213–14; and congressional relations, 214; and foreign policy, 214–15, 220, 231; conservative criticism of, 215–26; and 1976 presidential nomination, 219–24; attacks on Reagan, 222–23; and Republican Party, 224; Carter's challenge to, 226–27; 1976 electoral strategy of, 227; public views of, 227, 232; 1976 campaign issues of, 228, 232; on abortion, 229; and South, 229

Foreign policy, 10–11, 105, 137–39; public views of, 17; and labor, 135; and 1972 presidential campaign, 188–89; and Ford, 214–15, 220
Fraser, Donald M., 162
Free, Lloyd, 10, 34, 205, 220
Friedman, Milton, 122
Fulbright, J. William, 16

Garland, Ray L., 95
Garment, Leonard, 26, 27, 56, 120
Gautreax v. Chicago, 150
Gavin, William F., 141
Gettys, Thomas S., 174
Gleason, Thomas W., 144
Godwin, Mills, 176, 202, 209
Goldwater, Barry, 7–14, 215; support for, 6–8, 10, 13; vision for Republican Party, 7–8; strategy for Republican Party, 8–9; and 1964 campaign, 9–14; and race, 10–11, 13; and foreign policy, 11–12; and social/moral issues, 12–13; and South, 13; reasons for 1964 defeat, 13–14
Goodell, Charles E., 62, 78, 91, 94–95, 110, 166, 231
Gore, Albert, 72, 97, 102, 110
Gore, Albert, Jr., 102
Government reorganization, 117–18, 126–27, 203–4
Government spending, 203–6
Graham, Billy, 151, 157
Great Society, 9–11, 17–19, 49
Green v. County School Board of New Kent County, 51
Griffin, Robert P., 168
Griswold, Erwin, 152
Griswold v. Connecticut, 21

Hacker, Andrew, 76
Haldeman, H. R., 38, 55, 74, 94, 135, 149, 175, 194, 236; on Congress, 40–41; on presidential popularity, 42, 106; on economic policy, 60, 122; on new party, 69, 78, 198; and 1970 campaigns, 77, 85–87, 89, 101, 103, 106–7, 110; on labor, 96–97; on domestic reform, 121; and Agnew, 130; on foreign policy, 139; on Committee for the Re-election of the President, 167; on 1972 strategy, 174, 185; on McGovern, 182; on Nixon's goals for second term, 193; resignation of, 193, 208; on 1972 election results, 197

Hallett, Douglas, 178, 196
Hamill, Pete, 45–46, 58
Harlow, Bryce N., 8, 40, 55, 74, 80, 91, 119, 130
Harris, Louis, 137, 139
Hartke, Vance, 88, 97
Hartmann, Robert, 207–8, 220
Hauser, Rita, 155
Haynsworth, Clement F., Jr., 54–55
Health care, 118, 125–26
Health, Education, and Welfare, Department of, 52, 202
Helms, Jesse A., 217–18
Henderson, David, 174
Hickel, Walter J., 165
Higby, Lawrence, 85
Hodgson, James D., 74–75, 118
Hoffa, James R., 136
Holton, Linwood, 67, 176, 209
Hoover, Herbert, 1
Housing and Urban Development, Department of, 149–50
Howard, W. Richard, 206
Hruska, Roman, 55
Humphrey, Hubert H., 31, 33–35, 78, 101, 133, 153, 162–63
Huston, Tom Charles, 47, 71, 74, 116–17

Jackson, Henry M., 60, 89, 95, 133
Jarman, John, 174
Javits, Jacob K., 94
Jewish Americans, 170
Johnson, Donald, 185
Johnson, Lyndon B., 9–19, 30–31, 34, 128, 177
Jones, Jerry, 220
Jungbauer, William, 171
Justice, Department of, 52

Kay, Richard B., 102
Kaye, Peter, 222
Keene, David, 138
Kennedy, David M., 122
Kennedy, Edward M., 96, 126, 153, 156
Kennedy, Robert F., 30, 78, 94, 136
Kent State University, 70
Keogh, James, 87
Key, V. O., Jr., 3
Khachigian, Kenneth, 158, 172
Kirk, Claude R., Jr., 89
Kissinger, Henry A., 115, 137, 204, 221, 231
Klein, Herbert G., 41, 98

Kleppe, Thomas S., 88
Kopkind, Andrew, 25
Kristol, Irving, 229–30
Krogh, Egil, Jr., 51
Krol, John, 154

Labor, Department of, 44, 46
Laird, Melvin R., 184
Laos, 113, 139
Laxalt, Paul, 22, 88
Lemon v. Kurtzman, 152
Liberalism, 5, 17–19
Lindsay, John V., 68, 150
Lipset, Seymour Martin, 8
Loeb, William, 138
Long, Russell B., 75, 158
Lott, Trent, 178
Lovestone, Jay, 72, 96, 135
Lowrey, Bette, 109–10
Lubell, Samuel, 187
Lyons, John H., 144

MacGregor, Clark, 40, 88–89, 101–2, 176, 184
Maddox, Lester G., 225–26
Magruder, Jeb Stuart, 79, 85, 109, 183, 194
Making of the New Majority Party, The (Rusher),
    216–17. *See also* Rusher, William A.
Malek, Frederic V., 166, 194
Manchester (N.H.) Union Leader, 157
Mango, Mike, 110
"Manhattan Twelve," 138, 216
Mansfield, Mike, 96, 199
Marsh, John, 212
Mathias, Charles McC., Jr., 167
Mayaguez incident, 214, 231
McCarthy, Eugene, 30, 75
McClellan, James, 173
McCloskey, Paul N. "Pete," Jr., 139
McClure, James A., 218
McElroy, Neil, 152
McGee, Gale W., 97
McGovern, George, 86, 91, 133–34, 155, 160,
    162–64, 181, 226, 238–39; and youth, 170–71;
    and Democratic opposition, 172; 1972 visit
    to Philadelphia, 175; on Democrats for
    Nixon, 178; and labor, 178; and Eagleton
    affair, 179; Nixon's view of, 180–81; response
    to attacks, 182–83; 1972 campaign activities
    of, 182–84; perceptions of, 183; and patrio-
    tism, 185–86; and Vietnam War, 187; sup-

port for, 187–88; and 1972 election results,
    189
McGovern-Fraser Commission, 162–63, 171
McLaughlin, William F., 49
McWhorter, Charles, 25, 130, 137
Meany, George, 53, 72, 96–97, 134–35, 173, 177,
    185. *See also* American Federation of Labor
    and Congress of Industrial Organizations
Mecklenburg, Marjory, 230
Metzenbaum, Howard, 102–3, 110
Meyner, Robert B., 67
"Middle America," 43–47, 55–56, 61, 63–65,
    67–68, 72–74, 81, 83, 96–101, 108, 118, 121,
    135, 151, 168–69, 189, 233, 235–38
Miller, Arjay, 58
Miller, Arthur, 172
Milliken v. Bradley, 149
Mills, Wilbur D., 75, 123–24, 133
Millspaugh, Peter, 131
Miranda v. Arizona, 21
Mitchell, John N., 26, 39, 47, 50, 51, 93, 149, 152
Mondale, Walter F., 228
Montgomery, G. V. "Sonny," 174
Moore, Richard, 228
Moorer, Thomas H., 144
Morey, Roy, 153
Morgan, Edward, 147
Morton, Rogers C. B., 49, 68, 88
Moss, Frank, 72
Mothers for a Moral America, 12
Moyers, Bill D., 45
Moynihan, Daniel Patrick, 22, 39–40, 57–59,
    74, 115–16, 236
Murphy, Michael, 21
Muskie, Edmund S., 60, 78, 109, 114, 137, 153,
    156–57

National Catholic Educators Association, 154
National Republican Congressional Commit-
    tee, 215
Native Americans, 128
"New American revolution," 118–20, 123, 125–
    27, 132, 138, 141–42, 158–60, 162, 191, 203–4,
    237
"New Federalism," 57, 60, 107, 125
New Republic, 28
New Right, 223, 230
Newsweek, 20, 43, 62
New York, 45
New York Times, 20, 57

Nixon, Edward, 196
Nixon, Richard:
—and electoral politics: and 1966 campaigns, 23; and conservatives, 25–26; and 1968 nomination, 25–30; and 1968 convention, 29–30; and 1968 strategy, 31–32; and 1968 campaigning, 32; 1968 success of, 34–36; as electoral strategist, 38, 235; interest in electoral politics and public relations, 41–43; and polls, 42, 147–48; and "middle America," 45–46, 98; on *Emerging Republican Majority*, 50; and use of symbolic politics, 55–56, 98; southern support of, 59–60; and coalition building, 62, 113; and patriotic appeals, 63–64, 70, 185; and "silent majority," 63–65; and support for Vietnam policy, 70, 140, 184, 187, 192; and 1970 electoral strategy, 77, 81–84, 88, 90–92, 99, 103, 105; and *The Real Majority*, 85–86, 144–45; and labor, 97–98, 134–36, 177–78; and ethnic voters, 98, 168–69; and 1970 campaigning, 99, 107–9; on 1970 campaigns, 106; on "new majority," 145, 181–82; and Wallace, 157; and 1972 Republican National Convention, 164–65; on African American vote, 169; 1972 campaign activities of, 169, 184, 186–89; and youth, 171, 185; and cultivation of Democrats, 171–78, 201–2; on Democrats for Nixon, 173; and Rizzo, 175; and Johnson, 177; on McGovern, 180; and 1972 electoral strategy, 180, 182, 188; on 1972 issues, 182, 185; and 1972 election results, 189; on 1974 campaigns, 209; and connection between strategy and issues, 235–36; and nature of quest for new majority, 237–38
—and party politics: vision for Republican Party of, 6–7, 27–28, 86–88, 119–20, 234; on new party, 69, 78–79, 162, 197–98; on Democratic Party, 78; on Republican Party, 78, 111, 161–62, 197; and Republican Party, 128–32, 164–65; Republican activities of, 131; on Republican National Committee, 131; and southern Democrats, 158, 173–74, 199, 206; on Connally, 198; plans for Republican Party of, 198–202, 208; on new congressional coalition, 199; on Agnew's replacement, 208
—political career and views of: political personality of, 2; early career of, 2–3; on conservatism, 8; on Agnew, 66, 130; on labor, 71–72, 135; on patriotism, 77, 182; on antiwar protest, 108; on pornography, 108; and "the establishment," 115, 204, 206, 210; and media, 115, 210; on youth, 141–42; on social conservatism, 144; and religion, 151, 154; Watergate's impact on, 192–93, 204, 208; resignation and pardon of, 210–11; on Reagan, 220–21
—and political issues: on Vietnam, 26–27, 50, 70, 140; and administration goals, 37; on affirmative action, 53, 181–82; on Supreme Court, 54–55, 148; and domestic reform, 56, 75, 114, 117–25, 132, 160, 181–82, 191, 236–37; on role of government, 56–57, 119, 124; as "American Disraeli," 58, 114, 181, 203, 236; lack of interest in domestic policy of, 58, 236–37; and congressional relations, 59, 78–80, 87, 119, 127, 129, 132, 199–200, 203–4; and economic policy, 60, 121–22, 132–33, 179–80; and domestic policy, 61–62, 85, 100–101, 127, 180–82, 203–4; on "permissiveness," 66, 90, 142; and congressional opposition, 71, 123, 132, 203–4; and foreign policy, 78, 105, 137–39, 184, 188; and "big spending," 80–81; and race, 104, 145–46, 149–50; and 1971 State of the Union address, 118–19; on aid to minorities, 128; and environmental policy, 128; on busing, 148; and "parochaid," 151–54; and abortion, 154–55; on women's issues, 155–56; second-term goals and plans of, 193–94, 195–96, 206; and appointments, 194–95; connection between issues and strategy for, 235–36
Nofziger, Lyn, 116, 174
Novak, Robert, 75

Obenshain, Richard, 176, 202
O'Brien, Lawrence F., 81, 97, 107, 131, 162
Occupational Safety and Health Act, 118
Office of Minority Business Enterprise, 54
Ogilvie, Richard B., 98
Organized labor, 71–72, 96–98, 134–36; and Calley case, 144; and Nixon, 177–78; and McGovern, 178; and common situs picketing, 219–20. *See also* American Federation of Labor and Congress of Industrial Organizations; Meany, George
Osborne, John, 37, 115, 212
Otten, Alan L., 111–12

Panama Canal Zone, 222, 224
Panetta, Leon, 52
Parochial schools, 151–54, 182
Pasztor, Laszlo, 98, 169
"Permissiveness," 20–21, 45, 65–66, 75, 77, 84, 90–92, 99, 116, 135, 142, 159, 186, 223
Perry, James M., 112
Philadelphia Plan. *See* Affirmative action
Phillips, Kevin P., 27, 47–50, 67, 75–76, 111, 117, 121, 190, 196, 236; and 1970 campaigns, 77, 100–101, 105. See also *Emerging Republican Majority*
Political Beliefs of Americans, The (Free and Cantril), 34
Pornography, 93–94, 108
Powell, Lewis F., Jr., 149
President Ford Committee, 223, 225, 227, 230
Price, Rayford, 201
Price, Raymond, 2, 113
Procaccino, Mario, 68
Prouty, Winston L., 95

Race and civil rights, 10–13, 15–16, 31, 44–45, 51–54, 104, 128, 145–50, 160; Civil Rights Act of 1964, 10–11, 13, 53; Agnew and assassination of Martin Luther King Jr., 30; and *Emerging Republican Majority*, 49–50; and electoral politics, 169–70. *See also* Affirmative action; Busing; Desegregation of housing; Desegregation of schools
Rafferty, Frank, 144
Raggio, William, 102
Raoul-Duval, Michael, 228
Rather, Dan, 75, 115
Reagan, Ronald, 7, 23, 29, 138, 165, 181, 210; and conservatives, 26, 218, 225; and 1976 Republican nomination, 219–24; attacks on Ford, 221–22; and conservative Democrats, 223; and Ford campaign, 231
Realignment, 1, 3–4, 28, 37, 48, 91, 111, 116–17, 212, 217, 233–34, 235–38
Real Majority, The (Scammon and Wattenberg), 68, 82–88, 91, 100, 103, 109–10, 142, 236
Rebozo, Bebe, 89
Rehnquist, William H., 149
Reichley, A. James, 23, 76, 158
Republican Coordinating Committee, 14, 207–8
Republican National Committee, 86, 98, 131–32, 162, 169, 171, 200–201, 207–8, 212, 225

Republican Party: and Roosevelt coalition, 1; and Great Depression, 4; Goldwater's vision for, 5; ideology of, 5; Nixon's vision for, 6–7, 86–88, 119–20, 128–32; support for Goldwater, 7–8; conservative strategy for, 7–8, 217–18; and race, 11, 13; and foreign policy, 11–12, 137–38; impact of 1964 defeat, 14; support for, 14; 1960s prospects of, 23, 27; and liberal Republicans, 24, 167; and 1968 national convention, 29–30; 1968 weakness of, 34; 1968 prospects of, 35–36; and Phillips, 47–50; in Virginia, 67–68, 95, 209; in New Jersey, 67–68, 209; 1970 optimism of, 69; "blue-collar" opportunity of, 73–75; elitist character of, 75–76; Nixon on, 78, 111, 161–62; and conservatism, 78–79, 120, 216, 225, 237; and "conservative coalition," 79; and southern Democrats, 79–80, 129, 202; and *The Real Majority*, 83; Nixon's 1970 strategy for, 86–88; and "radical liberalism," 94; in New York State, 94–95, 167; and plans for Senate control, 95, 165–66; and ethnic appeals, 98–99, 169; and domestic reform, 119–20, 126, 132, 158, 191; on Nixon, 131, 162, 207; and labor, 134; 1972 presidential primaries, 138–39; and youth, 141; and Committee for the Re-election of the President, 162, 167–68; and 1972 national convention, 164–65; and plans for House control, 165–66, 198–99; and defections from Democratic Party, 165–66, 201–2; and defections to Democratic Party, 167; and African American vote, 169–71; and Jewish Americans, 170; and party reform, 171; impact of Democrats' cultivation, 174, 178; in Pennsylvania, 175; in Virginia, 176–77, 202; and 1972 election results, 189–90, 197–98; and new party, 197–98, 217–18; Nixon's 1972–73 plans for, 198–202; 1973 prospects of, 209–10; and Watergate scandal, 209–10; and 1974 elections, 212–13; 1974 prospects of, 212–13; and 1976 presidential nomination, 219–24; and Reagan, 221; and economy, 223–24; and 1976 national convention, 224; and Ford, 224–25; and abortion, 230; 1976 weakness of, 233; outcome of Nixon's work for, 235
Reston, James, 32, 90, 100, 107
Revenue sharing, 57, 117–18, 123–25, 158
Rhatican, William F., 188

Ribicoff, Abraham A., 158
Rietz, Kenneth, 171
Right Report, 218, 225
Ripon Society, 24, 200
Rizzo, Frank L., 154, 174–75, 201
Rockfeller, Nelson A., 29, 94, 124, 165, 167, 181, 215, 217
Roe v. Wade, 229
Romney, George, 27, 29, 149–50
Roosevelt, Franklin D., 1, 7
Rosow, Jerome M., 40, 46, 73, 236–37
Rosow Report, 72–74, 97–98, 118, 142, 201, 236
Roth, Stephen J., 146
Roth, William V., Jr., 88
Roudebush, Richard L., 88
Rusher, William A., 29, 50, 138, 199, 216–18, 225–26

Safire, William L., 47, 50, 107, 164, 201
Sandman, Charles W., Jr., 209
Sawyer, Diane, 190
Saxbe, William, 50
Scammon, Richard M., 26, 51, 111, 117, 144–45, 173, 234, 236. See also *The Real Majority*
Schlafly, Phyllis, 9
Schram, Martin, 227
Scott, Hugh, 182, 192, 229
Scott, William Lloyd, 176
Scranton, William W., 8, 99
Sears, John P., 221
Semple, Robert, 62
Shafer, Raymond P., 143
Shriver, R. Sargent, Jr., 168, 179
Shultz, George P., 40, 46, 52–53, 74, 98, 115, 122, 177, 206, 236
Shuster, E. G. "Bud," 198
"Silent majority," 6, 37–38, 63–69, 71, 77–79, 81–83, 106, 109, 114–16, 129, 145, 164, 193, 195, 208, 235, 237
Sisco, Joseph J., 58
Slight, Fred, 218
Smathers, George A., 173
Smith, Howard K., 122
Smith, Ralph, 103
Social issues. *See* Cultural and social issues
Solzhenitsyn, Alexander, 215, 224
Soviet Union, 137–39, 214–15
Specter, Arlen, 175
Spencer, Stuart, 222
Spong, William, 176

Spottswood, Stephen G., 169–70
Steeper, Frederick T., 191
Stein, Herbert, 41, 74, 122, 133, 179, 206
Stennis, John, 129
Stenvig, Charles, 68
Stevenson, Adlai, III, 103, 110
Students, 99, 142, 171. *See also* Youth
Supreme Court, 12, 21, 146, 148–49, 152; nominations to, 54–55
Swann v. Charlotte-Mecklenburg Board of Education, 146

Taft, Robert, Jr., 88, 102–3, 106, 110
Tax reform, 61, 124
Teamsters, International Brotherhood of, 136
Teeter, Robert M., 191, 212; and Nixon polling, 146–47, 155, 170, 180, 184–85, 191, 205; and Ford polling, 223–24, 227–28, 232
Thomson, Meldrim, Jr., 218
Thurmond, Strom, 29, 52
Time, 43
Timmons, William E., 40, 198
Torrijos, Omar, 222
Train, Russell F., 128
Tunney, John, 110
Tydings, Joseph, 110

U.S. Postal Service, 117
University of Michigan, 3

Vietnam War, 11, 16–17, 26–27, 30–34, 50, 62–65, 69–72, 105–6, 113–14, 139–40, 159, 188, 192; and antiwar protest, 16–17, 62–63, 70, 159; and congressional opposition, 62–63, 71; and public views, 63; and pro-war demonstrations, 71; and 1972 presidential campaign, 183–85, 187; and amnesty proposals, 185, 230–31. *See also* Calley, William L., Jr.
Viguerie, Richard, 89, 215, 223, 225

Waggonner, Joe D., Jr., 174, 199, 229
Wallace, George C., 13, 24–25, 45, 47, 51, 147, 157, 225; and 1968 campaign, 31–33; on 1969 elections, 68; and 1972 primary elections, 148, 157
Wallace, Gerald, 157
Walton, Clarence, 152
Warren, Earl, 21, 54
Watergate scandal, 178–79, 190, 192–93, 204, 206–11, 226

Wattenberg, Ben J., 101, 103, 111, 117, 142, 191, 234, 236. See also *The Real Majority*
Wayne, John, 12
Weicker, Lowell P., Jr., 110
Welfare reform, 57–60, 75, 80, 117–18, 132, 157–59, 163, 180–81, 187
Whetmore, James, 70
White, F. Clifton, 209
White, Theodore H., 31, 161, 185–86
Wicker, Tom, 2
Williams, Harrison W., 97
Wills, Garry, 27–28
Wirthlin, Richard, 221

Witcover, Jules, 24
Wold, John S., 88
Women, 155–56
Wood, Robert C., 18
Woods, Rose Mary, 192
Worker rights, 118
Wydler, John W., 197

Yarborough, Ralph W., 88
Yorty, Sam, 68, 175
Young Americans for Freedom, 130
Youth, 66, 70, 140–42, 164, 170–71